LEADERS,

POLITICIANS, CITIZENS

Fifty Figures Who Influenced India's Politics

Rasheed Kidwai

hachette
INDIA

First published in India in 2022 by Hachette India
(Registered name: Hachette Book Publishing India Pvt. Ltd)
An Hachette UK company
www.hachetteindia.com

SRD

ISBN 978-93-91028-16-9

Hachette Book Publishing India Pvt. Ltd
4th & 5th Floors, Corporate Centre,
Plot No. 94, Sector 44, Gurugram – 122003, India

Typeset in Dante MT Std 10.5/14
by InoSoft Systems, Noida

Printed and bound in India
by Manipal Technologies Limited, Manipal

MIX
Paper from
responsible sources
FSC™ C043100

LEADERS, POLITICIANS, CITIZENS

Rasheed Kidwai is a journalist, author, columnist and a political analyst. He is a visiting fellow with the Observer Research Foundation (ORF). Formerly associate editor of the *Telegraph*, Kidwai tracks government, politics, community affairs and Hindi cinema. Kidwai is the author of *Sonia: A Biography*; *24, Akbar Road: A Short History of the People behind the Fall and Rise of the Congress*; *Ballot: Ten Episodes that have Shaped India's Democracy*; *Neta Abhineta: Bollywood Star Power in Indian Politics*; *Bharat ke Pradhanmantri: Desh, Dasha, Disha*; and *The House of Scindias: A Saga of Power, Politics and Intrigue*.

A graduate from St Stephen's College, New Delhi, Kidwai holds a Master's degree in mass communications from the University of Leicester, United Kingdom. He also contributes as a political analyst to numerous television channels, including CNN-News18, ABP News, NDTV, India Ahead News and India Today TV.

Praise for the Book

'An unusual anthology... Rasheed Kidwai, one of India's sharpest political commentators, brings together his assessments of several public figures originally written as obituaries. These luminous profiles both inform and educate, apart from evoking nostalgia.'

Jairam Ramesh, Member of Parliament and author

'Rasheed Kidwai's fascinating book provides a greatly readable and insightful window to understanding the lives of fifty Indians who have shaped the politics of India. As an insider to the tumultuous unfolding of events of modern India, he has the knack of effortlessly blending anecdote with history and fact with analysis. A must-read for anyone who wants to know India's past in order to understand its future.'

Pavan K. Varma, author, diplomat, politician

For my wife, Dr Farah Kidwai

CONTENTS

Author's Note

Before I humbly invite readers to pick up this book, I feel I owe them an explanation. I was never on a dead beat, if you can pardon the expression. As a political reporter, I have loved going beyond the quotes politicians dished out and the tea and biscuits that were served as they did so. For me, it was always the conversations that were had away from politics that revealed fascinating aspects of characters which would otherwise have remained buried. What drew me to explore the personalities behind the politicians were the stories of human ambition, emotions, insecurities and, invariably, the motivations behind individual quests for longevity in public life. Every life is unique and this volume attempts to showcase that uniqueness.

But how did I first hit upon the idea of writing obituaries of politicians and other key figures who had passed on? I am grateful to my friends Richa Sharma and Sobhana Nair for coming up with the suggestion. Both Richa and Sobhana insisted that I had a knack for storytelling and profiling the lives of some of the most influential and, often, whimsical individuals who brought colour to Indian politics.

Still, writing the obituaries was not easy. Penning down an idealized account was out of the question. Every time I sat down to write about someone whom I had met on numerous occasions, followed closely, or read and researched about extensively, a range of moral and ethical questions clogged my mind. What if the dead could speak or read? Would they be vexed, pleased or bemused by my accounts?

This, of course, gives rise to a counterargument. Surely, those who had been part of our national life and contributed to the making of the nation deserve a documentation of their journey, even if the exercise is conducted in a subjective manner. My attempt has been to describe what I knew the person to be, to be as candid as possible, to avoid euphemisms and remain sensitive. While these goals sound good, they are impossible to achieve fully.

Most personalities covered in the book deserve a full-length biographical account, but the idea was for this volume to simply give the reader a glimpse of their lesser-known sides. Discerning readers will notice that the work is not only packed with 'national figures' but also peppered with regional satraps. Leaders like N.D. Tiwari, Arjun Singh, Motilal Vora and A.R. Antulay dabbled in state politics as chief ministers. I must also concede that as a political journalist I have been more well-versed with Congress politicians as I mostly covered the activities of that party. Besides, the Congress played a pivotal role in India in the years after Independence, particularly up to the 1980s. To add to the flavour, a few lesser-known state-level politicians such as Babulal Gaur and Hazarilal Raghuvanshi have been included because their stories have a wide appeal.

My God-fearing wife, Dr Farah Kidwai, insisted that I be gentle with the deceased as they deserve the kind of remembrance that captures their essence rather than their follies or acts of indiscretion in a particular phase of their lives. She reminded me constantly that the dead were no more and could not speak for themselves. Thank you, Farah, for such sensitive and valuable advice.

Readers will notice the wide range of people represented in this compilation. Not all of them are politicians or elected representatives. Some are merely prominent personalities. While not all of them are well known, they all have, in their own way, left their mark in their chosen spheres. The idea was to tell their story in the most interesting way possible. It is up to my readers to decide if I have succeeded. All I can say is that I tried my best.

Since obituaries are not biographies, details such as important dates, affiliations, and the names of spouses and children have largely been excluded. Putting these profiles into some kind of order posed a challenge. My publisher suggested ordering them alphabetically by their surnames, keeping in mind the readers who may wish to easily locate profiles of interest to them. This is what has been followed.

I am grateful to the *Telegraph* (Calcutta), *Mumbai Mirror*, *The Print*, the News 18 blog, Observer Research Foundation (ORF), Rediff, the *India Today* web edition, the *ABP News* blog, *The Quint*, *The Wire* and other publications for having previously published parts of some of the profiles compiled here.

I cannot thank three people from Hachette India enough, for playing a key role in this endeavour – Poulomi Chatterjee, editor-in-chief and publisher, and editors Ansila Thomas and Anju Christine. They made significant and pertinent observations while discussing the final shape of the book. My thanks also to Sini Nair and others in the Hachette India team who make working with them truly memorable. This is my fourth book with Hachette India, after *24 Akbar Road: A Short History of the People Behind the Fall and Rise of the Congress*, *Ballot: Ten Episodes that have Shaped India's Democracy* and *Neta Abhineta: Bollywood Star Power in Indian Politics*. I am grateful to them for their faith in me.

I also take this opportunity to express my gratitude to Nirmal Pathak, Farhan Ansari, Priya Sahgal, Sunetra Choudhury, Nistula Hebbar, Naghma Sahar, Rama Lakshmi, Sheela Bhatt, Sudeep Mukhia, Faisal Mohammad Ali, Avinash Dutt, Marya Shakil, Krishna Kant Sharma, Deepal Trivedie, Atul K. Thakur, Ravi Dubey, Sumit Pande, Radhika Ramaseshan, Sandip Ghose, Shubhabrata Bhattacharya and advocate Leo for being part of the journey. Your suggestions, comments and critical inputs were of great help.

Friend, editor and blogger Ananda Sen deserves a special mention. Sen, a first-class editor from the *Telegraph*, took great pains to go through each profile and help identify weak spots. His sharp eye for detail, fact-checking and understanding of contemporary politics provided a lot of depth. We often talked and debated about the lives and times of the book's subjects and the concerns Farah had raised. These freewheeling conversations helped in capturing the nuances and also brought a degree of comfort as thoughts took shape in words.

I wish to express my gratitude to Dr Sunjoy Joshi and Samir Saran of the Observer Research Foundation (ORF) for their support and guidance.

Lastly, thank you, Falah, Abaan, Inaya, Farhan Saima, Saad Ghazia, Shahab Sadia, Saif Farah, Shams Shaista, Umar Maryam, Samad, Sabur, Umair and Ayesha Siddique for being an integral part of my life.

Rasheed Kidwai
New Delhi
December 2021

Foreword

India's finest asset is her democracy. The free and fair elections we hold, protecting that vital ability of each and every Indian to vote, are the very lifeblood of how India operates. Our political sphere can induce euphoria and rage, and if we were to be brutally honest, the practice of our politics disappoints as often as it inspires. Yet it is at the heart of what makes India great: the ability to express our opinions without fear or favour, and to continuously work to improve our country according to our own different lights.

Studying Indian politics is a captivating exercise, charting the rise and fall of parties and ideologies. But behind these abstractions are the individuals who shaped India's political history, and their engrossing lives. Rasheed Kidwai's *Leaders, Politicians, Citizens* compiles the stories of 50 figures who influenced India's political landscape over the past several decades, each in their own unique way. From a wide geographic and temporal scope, Kidwai, a highly respected political journalist and commentator, has selected a deeply interesting range of political figures. Regional mass politicians rub shoulders with prime ministers and religious leaders, with several parts of India being represented. Together, they represent a cohesive picture of the evolution of Indian politics and power. Serving the public through politics is a privilege and an honour; the complex figures in this book have sometimes used the power that their roles bestow to divide rather than unite, or for their own personal gain. Understanding the human behind the headlines helps us unravel the motivations behind the way each of these famous figures behaves.

Each profile combines well-researched analysis of the individual's contribution to Indian politics with revealing personal histories, from Phoolan Devi's hilarious Paris trip to Chandraswami's puzzling and surprising relationship with Margaret Thatcher. In this way, the author creates a portrait not just of each person as a politician, but, as the title suggests, an ordinary *citizen* too, with values and prejudices of their own. Kidwai acts both as political historian and storyteller; the reader gains a fuller understanding of our leading political figures when they are also described as human beings.

Of course, as an active politician, I cannot endorse each and every view expressed in this book. Nevertheless, I am confident that those interested in Indian politics will find *Leaders, Politicians, Citizens* an intriguing and indeed enjoyable introductory guide to the titans who have shaped India's raucous, frustrating and fascinating political history. My congratulations to Rasheed Kidwai on an unusual, and unusually readable, book.

Dr Shashi Tharoor, M.P.
Member of Parliament for
Thiruvananthapuram Lok Sabha constituency,
Chairman of the Parliamentary Standing
Committee on Information Technology, and
Chairman, All India Professionals' Congress

SHEIKH ABDULLAH

(1905–1982)

The national interest cannot be defined as a common interest of
the industrial, commercial, and financial companies of a country,
because there is no such common interest; nor can it be defined
as the life, liberty, and well-being of the citizens, because they are
continually being adjured to sacrifice their well-being, their liberty,
and their lives to the national interest.

– Simone Weil

THOUSANDS OF MILES AWAY FROM EUROPE – THE SOCIAL AND INTELLECTUAL
laboratory of French philosopher Weil – national interest was at the
centre of a conflict that would draw a charismatic Kashmiri deep
into its turbulent heart. Sheikh Mohammad Abdullah didn't merely
live through the tumultuous years that began in 1948; for most part
of his political life, he experienced it first-hand, as India's national
interest clashed with what he felt was in Kashmir's interest.

Abdullah would pay for his views with his liberty. From being
New Delhi's darling, who had thwarted Pakistan's designs, he would
fall out of favour and be subjected to long years of confinement,
only to be briefly rehabilitated towards the end of his life. By then,
however, secessionist sentiments had taken over and a mellowed
Abdullah was no more the leonine figure who had once gripped the
imagination of ordinary Kashmiris. From the zenith of adoration at
which he once found himself, he had become a subject of scorn of
Kashmiris, perceived as a 'collaborator' with the Indian government.

Forgotten in the turmoil were some of the people-oriented measures Abdullah had introduced during his reign as the *Wazir-e-Azam* (prime minister) of Jammu and Kashmir (J&K) from 1948 to 1953. Among the progressive steps he had taken were: the termination of the jagirdari/zamindari system; abolition of big, landed estates; fixing of the land ceiling; liquidation of debts; transfer of land to the landless; reorganization of educational institutions; and the establishment of Jammu and Kashmir University.

Abdullah died in September 1982, aged 76, during his second term as chief minister, leaving behind the indelible imprint of his personality on the history of the Indian subcontinent and a fascinating, if conflicted, legacy.

Early Life

Abdullah was born into a merchant family in Soura, a few miles outside the capital city of Srinagar, on 5 December 1905. Abdullah's father, Sheikh Mohammad Ibrahim, died two months before his son's birth, leaving behind his widow, five sons and a daughter. Abdullah was brought up by his mother and elder brothers, and went on to marry Akbar Jehan, whose father Michael Henry (Harry) Nedou (a.k.a. Sheikh Ahmed Hussain) was of Slovak and British descent.[1]

Abdullah came from a family of modest means whose main source of income was a business in shawls. After his schooling and early college education in Srinagar, Abdullah was sent to Lahore and later to Aligarh for higher studies. It was from Aligarh Muslim University (AMU) that he secured an MSc in 1930.

Destiny had many plans for the fatherless boy. From being a schoolteacher and peasant-rights activist, the physics postgraduate went on to become a freedom fighter against the British Raj and a voice of protest against Kashmir's whimsical and autocratic Dogra ruler, Maharaja Hari Singh. Abdullah's powerful oratory in his native tongue would also play a role; the 6-foot-4-inch-tall Abdullah's spell-binding recitations from the Quran fired the imagination of

Kashmir's Muslim majority. Not for nothing would they call him the *Sher-e-Kashmir* (Lion of Kashmir).

In 1931, Abdullah joined high priest Mirwaiz Maulvi Yusuf Shah in the struggle against the maharaja, but abandoned the *maulvi* in 1932 to form his own outfit, the All Jammu and Kashmir Muslim Conference.

Seven years later, under the influence of Mahatma Gandhi and fellow Kashmiri Jawaharlal Nehru, Abdullah would reject the communal politics of the Muslim Conference. Abdullah acknowledged that his action had been influenced by Nehru. 'Jawaharlal, a very sensitive man with a wide vision, advised me to broad-base the National Conference and to keep the doors of the organisation open to non-Muslims in spite of sharp opposition from landlords,' he would recall later.[2] Abdullah rechristened his outfit as the All India National Conference, a participatory coalition of Hindus, Muslims and Sikhs that sought home rule and democracy in Kashmir.

Those were heady years for Abdullah, but more success was to follow for this tall, imposing leader whom ordinary Kashmiris loved. The mass support that he enjoyed helped Abdullah thwart the Pakistan military's attempt to take control of Kashmir in August–October 1947, when India was in the throes of a testing period of a national partition on religious lines.

Pakistan had launched an attack on Kashmir on 22 October 1947, with its army regulars masquerading as tribals. New Delhi had initially refused to bail out Hari Singh, the maharaja of Jammu and Kashmir, because he was recultant to integrate with the newly formed Indian Union. Nehru eventually agreed to send troops on the advice of his home minister Sardar Vallabhbhai Patel, but before the Indian Army landed at Srinagar airport on 27 October, it was Abdullah and his local Kashmiri volunteers who defended the city for crucial hours and days. The volunteers, who called themselves the Dagan Brigade, patrolled Srinagar, while Hari Singh and his key lieutenants fled to Jammu. This group of volunteers later served as the nucleus for the formation of the Jammu Kashmir Light Infantry, a regular unit of the Indian Army.

The maharaja signed the Instrument of Accession, acceding the state to the Indian Union. However, the outgoing British governor-general Lord Mountbatten intervened, linking the accession of Kashmir to an offer of plebiscite. On 28 October, Nehru went public, promising a plebiscite on All India Radio. A formal complaint against Pakistan was made at the United Nations (UN), thereby globalizing the conflict. The prime minister (PM) was so confident of the valley's popular mood that he told the Constituent Assembly on 2 November 1947, 'We are, of course, vitally interested in the decision the state (of J&K) would take.'[3] In his telegram to the prime minister of Pakistan, Nehru had reiterated,

> I should like to make it clear that the question of aiding Kashmir in this emergency is not designed in any way to influence the state to accede to India. Our view which we have repeatedly made public is that the question of accession in any disputed territory or state must be decided in accordance with wishes of people and we adhere to this view.[4]

The idea of a plebiscite had first entered the conversation during efforts to resolve the Junagadh dispute with Pakistan. In 1947, the Muslim ruler of Junagadh in Gujarat had acceded to Pakistan. This had enraged Indian leaders and Sardar Patel had proposed a plebiscite. In the plebiscite held in 1948, the people of Junagadh chose to join India.

In November 1947, Mountbatten went to Lahore to propose a plebiscite to decide the fate of Kashmir. Mountbatten had even assured Pakistan's leader Muhammad Ali Jinnah that the UN would oversee the process. On 1 January 1948, the Government of India formally introduced the Kashmir issue at the UN under Article 35 of the UN Charter, which permits any member state to bring to the world body's attention any situation likely to endanger international peace and security. The UN subsequently passed a resolution and formed the United Nations Commission for India and Pakistan (UNCIP) to mediate between the two countries. A three-step process to end the dispute was recommended:

- Withdrawal of tribesmen, army and Pakistani nationals from the State of Jammu and Kashmir
- The Government of India was asked to reduce its force in Jammu and Kashmir
- The Government of India was also asked to appoint a plebiscite administration to hold a plebiscite

The idea of demilitarization of the India- and Pakistan-held regions of Kashmir was never implemented. Ahead of the first military conflict between India and Pakistan, Jinnah sent a three-member delegation to Kashmir to persuade Abdullah to cast his lot with Pakistan. When an aggressive member of the Pakistan delegation, Dr Mohammad Deen Taseer, kept insisting that Kashmir opt for Pakistan, an indignant Abdullah reportedly told him, 'It is none of your business to tell us what to do.' When Taseer warned that Pakistan would have to use 'other means', Abdullah retorted, 'Do whatever you like, but to enter Kashmir you will have to walk over our dead bodies.'[5]

Nehru acknowledged and valued Abdullah's ability to influence ordinary Kashmiris, who were opposed to siding with Pakistan in exchange for a secular autonomous state. Abdullah was appointed head of the 'Emergency administration' in Indian Administered Jammu and Kashmir. As a token of appreciation, the Nehru government was generous with economic safeguards, and promised to recognize Kashmir's unique status and protect its culture. Abdullah was, later crowned *Wazir-e-Azam* of the Indian state of Jammu and Kashmir.

On 2 November 1949, Nehru and Abdullah attended a massive rally at Lal Chowk in Srinagar, where they took a pledge of identity and the state's everlasting bond with the rest of the country. 'I want you to believe that Kashmir is yours,' Abdullah told Nehru at the meeting, adding, 'No power in the world can separate us. Every Kashmiri feels that he is an Indian and that India is his homeland.' Sheikh Abdullah, a bit overwhelmed with emotions, is said to have quoted a Persion couplet, *'Man tu shudi, Tu man shudi; Ta kas na goyed, Man degram tu degri* (I became you and you became I; so none can say we are separate)'.[6]

In 1948, Abdullah travelled to Paris as a member of the Indian delegation to attend a meeting of the UN Security Council, where the future of Kashmir was to be discussed. He defended the legality of his government. Addressing the Paris meeting, he said: 'We should prove before the Security Council that Kashmir and the people of Kashmir have lawfully and constitutionally acceded to the dominion of India, and that Pakistan has no right to question that accession.'[7] It must have been sweet music for India to hear Kashmir's prime minister and delegate to the UN stir citizens and outsiders alike with his patriotic oratory, especially his choice of words: the 'fountain-head of basic laws laying the foundation of a just social order and safeguarding the democratic rights of all the citizens of the state.'[8]

Abdullah championed free speech, a free press and a higher standard of living for the poor. At the core of his speech lay his belief in the 'equality of rights of all citizens irrespective of their religion, colour, caste, and class'.[9]

On his return from Paris, in March 1948, Abdullah was formally sworn in as the prime minister of Kashmir and soon launched a large-scale reform programme for the state. The zamindari system was abolished, and the estates of big landowners were taken over by the state to be distributed among the landless. People were also given debt relief.

Abdullah has summarized much of the passion and intrigue of this period in his autobiography, *Aatish-e-Chinar* (The Fire of Chinar

Trees), where he recounted the failed attempts of Pakistan to wrest Kashmir from India's grasp. He was, at that point of time, a darling of India, passionate about his Kashmiri identity and unabashed about Kashmir's integration with India. He relied heavily on his friend Nehru, and the two stood together like a rock against several overt and covert machinations by colonial powers and other vested interests.

Till early 1953, Abdullah's sincerity towards the Indian Union seemed unconditional. His pronouncements, too, vouched as much. At a press conference in Bombay (now Mumbai) on 25 January 1951, Abdullah explained why his state had opted to accede to India. 'The people of Kashmir know that they cannot develop unless they are under a secular democracy. They have, moreover, always received nothing but affection, sympathy and active help from the people of India,' he said. Days later, speaking in Madras (now Chennai) on 11 February, he remarked, 'There has been community of suffering and ideals between the people of India and the people of Kashmir in the past and today we tie our destiny with the rest of India because of her belief in secularism, democracy and progress.'[10]

Later that year, Assembly elections were held in Jammu and Kashmir, with 75 seats allocated to the India-administered part of Kashmir and 25 seats reserved for the part administered by Pakistan. Abdullah's National Conference won all the 75 seats.

Change in Attitude

The Nehru–Abdullah bonhomie, however, would be short-lived, as the central government began asserting Kashmir's 'intimate connection' with the rest of India. India's national interest clashed with Abdullah's ideas and by early 1953, political commentators in New Delhi could discern visible changes in his perception of Kashmir's accession to India and its position within the Indian Union. Among other things, Abdullah's critics argued that his speeches and pronouncements were increasingly laced with calls for an independent or autonomous Kashmir, on the lines of Switzerland, referring frequently to a guarantee to that effect by the UN. It upset the Indian political leadership, including Nehru.[11]

For Abdullah, the preservation of Kashmir valley's linguistic, cultural and religious identity was paramount. In more substantive terms, the Indian state was asked to give autonomy in all matters except for defence, communication and currency. He also accused New Delhi of reneging on its promise to hold a plebiscite on the state's future. Nehru would often invite Abdullah to sort out their differences but the issues remained unresolved.

On 8 August 1953, days after slogans like 'Indian Army must get out of Kashmir' were heard in the Valley, guided by national interest Nehru dismissed the Abdullah government. Subsequently, Abdullah was arrested. The trigger for the arrest was an intelligence report sent by Nehru's hand-picked head of the Intelligence Bureau (IB), Bhola Nath Mallick, which stated that Abdullah had left on 8 August for Gulmarg to meet a representative of Pakistan. In the fifth volume of *The Papers of Adlai Stevenson*, it is mentioned that some Indian leaders believed that some CIA agents and Mrs Loy Henderson, the wife of the US ambassador stationed in New Delhi, had encouraged Abdullah to toy with the idea of an independent state.[12] Abdullah's arrest drew sharp reactions not only from Pakistan but also from the United Kingdom and the United States. The then prime minister of Pakistan, Mohammad Ali Bogra, pressed for a meeting with Nehru to finalize the appointment of a plebiscite administrator for Kashmir.

In the subsequent Kashmir conspiracy case, the Union home ministry, police and intelligence agencies worked assiduously to establish that Abdullah was collaborating with external forces – namely Pakistan, UK and the US – to get Kashmir to secede from India. Abdullah was jailed, accused of conspiring against the state. Despite being Nehru's close friend for eleven years, Abdullah languished in jail because the prime minister, Nehru, felt that India's national interest subsumed that of Kashmir or his friendship.

Bakshi Ghulam Mohammad, who succeeded Abdullah as prime minister of Jammu and Kashmir, ruled till early 1964. While some consider Ghulam Mohammad the architect of modern Kashmir, he faced a stiff challenge on the political front from those seeking the right to self-determination.

Discontent had also set in among the people in the post-Sheikh Abdullah era, as they felt that successive state governments ruled only at the mercy of the Government of India. That perception was strengthened when the Kamraj Plan, mooted in the Indian National Congress in May 1963, led to the resignation of senior Union ministers and chief ministers of party-ruled states. Ghulam Mohammed was not part of the Congress – he belonged to the National Conference – but was still persuaded to offer 'a token resignation' to strengthen Nehru's hand. In a move that typified the strange relationship between Kashmir and New Delhi, Ghulam Mohammad's resignation was accepted along with those of five state chief ministers and six Union ministers.

Plebiscite Puzzle

Ironic as it might sound, Nehru was reiterating India's and Pakistan's desire for a plebiscite when Abdullah was jailed in the Kashmir Conspiracy case. In the later part of 1953, when Pakistan's prime minister, Mohammad Ali Bogra, arrived in New Delhi, Nehru, moved by idealism, agreed to issue a joint communique reaffirming the two countries' commitment to a plebiscite. The communique read, 'Both the prime ministers were actuated by a firm resolve to settle these problems as early as possible peacefully and cooperatively to the mutual advantage of both countries.'[13]

However, in 1957, Nehru's friend and India's defence minister, V.K. Krishna Menon, told the UN Security Council that 'self-determination was a principle which could be applied to dependent territories governed by a colonial power; it could not be used in regard to a constituent unit like Minnesota which forms part of the federal union'. What he implied was that after 1947, the entire territory of Jammu and Kashmir had become a part of India.[14]

Govind Ballabh Pant, who was the Union home minister in Nehru's cabinet, had articulated similar sentiments in 1955. 'The Constituent Assembly of Kashmir, which was elected on the basis of adult franchise, has taken a definite decision. While I am not oblivious of the initial declaration made by the Government of India (about plebiscite), I cannot ignore the important series of facts.' Pant had said.[15]

In 1962, Krishna Menon again reminded the Security Council that Pakistan had failed to honour its commitment and the conditions for a plebiscite, and also that the UN resolution had become obsolete after Kashmiris had participated and expressed their democratic will in Assembly and Lok Sabha elections. 'On no condition shall we sell our heritage. On no condition shall we open the door for the disruption and disintegration of India.' the defence minister said.[16]

It had taken India nearly fifteen years since Independence to arrive at a firm position on Kashmir. While the Nehru government handled Kashmir with sophistication, the prime minister and Sardar Patel seemed unable to decide whether to hold on to Kashmir or not.

In his book, *Pakistan: The India Factor*, author Rajendra Sareen has documented a conversation between Sardar Patel and Sardar Abdul Rab Nishtar, a minister in the Pakistan cabinet. Sareen has quoted Patel as saying, 'Bhai, give up this talk of Hyderabad and Junagarh, and talk of Kashmir: Take Kashmir and settle the issue.'[17]

Sareen offers another gem later in his book, where he quotes Sirdar Shaukat Hayat, a member of Pakistan's Constituent Assembly, who was present at a meeting between Lord Mountbatten and Prime Minister Liyaqat Ali. Mountbatten had conveyed Patel's message to Liyaqat Ali that if Pakistan kept out of Hyderabad, India would exit Kashmir. Hayat had commended the proposal, prompting a sharp retort from Liyaqat Ali: 'Sirdar Saheb, have you gone out of your mind? Why should we leave a province [Hyderabad] larger than Punjab and settle for some mountain rocks?'[18]

Patel's trusted aide V.P. Menon, who was Secretary of the Ministry of States, corroborates Sareen's account. Menon, who reported directly to Patel, chronicles a meeting between Hari Singh and Mountbatten in June 1947. The governor-general had told the maharaja that 'if he [Hari Singh] acceded to Pakistan, India would not take it amiss and he had firm assurance on this from Sardar Patel himself.'[19] V. Shankar, political secretary to Patel, has also observed in his memoirs that Patel was willing to back the maharaja. 'If the ruler (of J&K) felt that his and his state's interest lay in accession to Pakistan, he would not stand in his way,' Shankar has quoted Patel as saying.[20]

Nehru was instinctively opposed to the idea of giving away Kashmir. For him, such a move would have amounted to an endorsement of the two-nation theory. Nehru also remained extremely conscious of international opinion. Nehru's biographer, S. Gopal, mentions a letter the prime minister had written to Patel from Paris, wherein he mentioned that France and Britain were not finding India's Kashmir policy as impeccable as he would have liked them to.[21]

The UN resolution, adopted by the Security Council at its 286th meeting held on 21 April 1948, had laid down several conditions for India and Pakistan to facilitate a plebiscite. While the US, UK, France, Canada and China were among those who had voted in favour of the resolution, Belgium, the Ukrainian Soviet Socialist Republic and erstwhile USSR had voted against it, considering the language and some of the contents a bit hostile to India.

In and Out of Jail

Towards the end of his life, Nehru ordered Abdullah's release. In early 1964, Abdullah met Nehru and other leaders in Delhi. The Government of India authorized him to hold a dialogue with Pakistani leaders to resolve the Kashmir problem and arranged his visit to Pakistan. Abdullah was able to convince Pakistan President

Ayub Khan to meet Nehru on 16 June 1964. But before the meeting could take place, Nehru died on 27 May. Abdullah was still in Pakistan when he heard the news and is said to have wept bitterly over the loss of his friend, sobbing like a child for hours.[22]

In 1965, Abdullah went on a pilgrimage to Mecca and Medina. On his way back, he stopped over at Jeddah, Baghdad, Cairo, London and Algiers; his utterances at all these places were marked by a perceptible anti-India tinge. At Algiers he had a long meeting with the Chinese leader Chou En-lai. Back home, Indian leaders were outraged that Abdullah had met the leader of a country that had attacked India a few years earlier. When Abdullah returned to Delhi, the government impounded his passport. Abdullah was arrested again and detained at Kohinoor Palace in Kodaikanal, Tamil Nadu. He was released in January 1968.

That, however, wouldn't be his last stay in jail as Abdullah would be arrested again on the suspicion of hobnobbing with foreign powers. His prison stints at various Indian jails, with brief intermissions, would finally end only in 1973, two decades after the Nehru government had first put him behind bars on the charge of treason.

Abdullah, however, remained popular in his state. Upon one release from jail in 1968, Abdullah was received by a surging, ecstatic crowd of thousands. Local media compared the welcome Prime Minister Indira Gandhi got when she flew to Srinagar with the reception Abdullah received. While Gandhi had travelled the six miles from the airport to Srinagar town in 15 minutes, it took Abdullah's car five hours to inch through the crowd to cover nearly the same distance that year.

In 1973, after his final release from detention, Abdullah told an interviewer his views had moderated over the years. 'Age has mellowed us,' he said. 'The situation is difficult and I don't see any signs of change. But you don't lose hope. You can't.'[23]

At this time, Indira Gandhi also signed an accord and made a Congress ministry in Jammu and Kashmir, headed by Syed Mir

Qasim, who step down in favour of Abdullah. It was an act of statecraft and wisdom. By sacrificing a Congress government in Kashmir for the return of a more popular and representative ministry, Indira Gandhi set a precedent that her son Rajiv Gandhi would follow while pursuing the Mizo peace accord in 1986. In 1975, Abdullah returned to political office as chief minister of Kashmir, a post he held until his death.

According to noted editor M.L. Kotru, who hailed from Kashmir, no other Kashmiri leader had so completely dominated the political scene in the state, and for so long, as Sheikh Abdullah did. Kotru felt it was one of the most remarkable ironies of history that the man who was instrumental in mobilizing Muslim opinion in the Valley in favour of India after Partition was later accused of being anti-national and jailed, first by Nehru and then by Indira.[24]

In *Aatish-e-Chinar*, his autobiography in Urdu published posthumously in 1982, Abdullah seems to write more in anguish than anger. He said that he had strongly advocated that the people of Kashmir should cast their lot with India in 1951, yet he was subsequently accused of anti-national activities. 'Thirty years have passed since then and we have gone through hell. We have been subjected to all kinds of sufferings and humiliation, and yet I stand by what I said then: The solution that I offered then (union with India) is still valid.'[25] Abdullah gave his side of the story on the charges that the Nehru and Indira regimes levelled against him—being in collusion with Pakistan and the US. Abdullah has also noted that he was often detained without a formal charge-sheet.

According to Abdullah, there were three options for Kashmiris: Go over to Pakistan, remain an independent state or become part of the Indian Union. 'I told them that they can choose any of the three options, but they must remember that the need of the moment was to get liberation from the oppressive Dogra rule and that could be more effectively achieved while maintaining the status quo... [T]hat is, remain with India.'[26]

Image Tarnished

By the time Abdullah returned to power, much had changed in Kashmir's politics. Successive state governments were seen as Delhi's puppets while maladministration – including lack of electricity in winter, inadequate supply of rations, and congestion and lack of even basic civic services in Srinagar – had led to mass discontent. Sectarian violence too had marred the landscape. This was also a time when the subcontinent was fraught with tensions, after yet another war between India and Pakistan that had led to the creation of Bangladesh.

Abdullah was left with no choice but to compromise with Indira Gandhi. Many Kashmiris who harboured secessionist sentiments viewed it as a sign of weakness and betrayal. Some even felt that a politically ambitious Abdullah had sold out to the Centre as part of quid pro quo.

The Sher-e-Kashmir's popularity plummeted so much that his mortal remains at Naseem Bagh on the banks of the river Jhelum in Srinagar now have to be guarded round the clock by police and paramilitary personnel. There have been several attempts to desecrate his grave. Many local Kashmiris today blame Abdullah for the present-day fate that has befallen them. When Article 370, which gave Kashmir its special status, was abrogated in 2019, the mausoleum of the National Conference founder bore a deserted look. In a report published in the *Telegraph*, its Srinagar correspondent Muzaffar Raina quoted a policeman as saying, 'Sheikh Mohammad Abdullah, who got Article 370 incorporated in the Indian Constitution, usually attracts a few visitors and more abuses. These days, there are no visitors and only abuses.' The policeman had added:

> There has been no visitor in the past 10 days (after the scrapping of Jammu and Kahmir's special status). [...] More than visitors, you get to see people on motorcycles or in cars hurling abuses. They say things like *'Baba aaya jahannum*

(father be in hell)'. This happened always, but is happening more often now.[27]

Despite the infamy he acquired in subsequent years, three great Urdu poets of the Indian subcontinent have written poems in Abdullah's praise. Hafeez Jalandhari, Josh Malihabadi and Faiz Ahmad Faiz – all Pakistani nationals – have written about Abdullah's lifelong struggle against injustice and for the democratic rights of the common man. Faiz, in his tribute to Abdullah, writes:

> *Bol ke lab azaad hain teray,*
> *Bol ke jaan ab tak teri hai,*
> *Tera sutwan jism hai tera,*
> *Bol, ke jaan ab tak teri hai.*

('Speak, for your lips are free; Speak, your tongue is still yours; Your upright body is yours; Speak, your life is still yours.')

———

DEV ANAND
(1923–2011)

DASHING. ROMANTIC. EVERGREEN. DEV ANAND, ONE OF BOLLYWOOD'S most enduring legends, had a more than healthy interest in politics. He could be cheeky as well. In 1962, the actor, then 39, had asked Jawaharlal Nehru: 'Is it true, Sir, that your devastating smile stole the heart of Lady Mountbatten?'[28]

Dev Anand himself had a smile that left millions of hearts aflutter, but the actor could present a grim visage too when provoked – as he did one day during the Emergency. Asked to say a few words in appreciation of Sanjay Gandhi and the Youth Congress, Anand had refused, responding to what he described as a 'call of conscience'. The actor's films were subsequently banned from being screened on television, while All India Radio too forbade any reference to his name.

When the 1977 parliamentary elections were announced, lawyer Ram Jethmalani urged Dev Anand to join the Janata Party, and its campaign against Indira Gandhi and her son, Sanjay. Caught in a dilemma, Anand had apparently paced up and down the garden behind his residence, all night, lost in thought, before he finally went to bed. By the time he woke up, he had made up his mind. He agreed to share the dais with Morarji Desai and Jayaprakash Narayan, whom he admired deeply, and make a short speech condemning Indira Gandhi. The Janata Party experiment would, however, disillusion him soon.

Desai resigned from the prime ministerial post in July 1979 following internal differences. Indira Gandhi withdrew her support for the subsequent Charan Singh government, paving the way for the 1980 general election. It was at this point that Dev Anand decided to 'teach the politicians a lesson' and formed his own party – the National Party of India (NPI). He envisaged a party that would include the country's luminaries. 'If MGR could spell magic in Tamil Nadu, why not me in the whole country?' he had told his supporters, one of whom was Jawaharlal Nehru's sister, Vijaya Lakshmi Pandit.[29] 'We felt it was time for intelligent, well-informed, well-meaning figures to represent India's electorate in Parliament,' the actor would say later.[30]

A rally was held at Shivaji Park, the historic ground in Mumbai (then Bombay). It is Dev Anand's belief that a packed house prompted Indira Gandhi to send him feelers, asking if he would join hands with her. The actor snubbed her again. 'Joining hands with an autocrat was absolutely out of question.'[31]

On the eve of the 1980 general election, Dev Anand was dreaming big. Ideas kept surging in his mind. He would later describe the time in his autobiography, which would be released by Prime Minister Dr Manmohan Singh on 26 September 2007 – on the occasion of the actor's 84th birthday and, coincidentally, Singh's 75th. In his words:

> A giant forward leap was required to link the ancient civilization with modern India. What if all villages are transformed into neat small towns flashing with electricity and gushing merrily with water facilities... What if English is taught to all and farmers, labourers, coolies and aristocrats mov[ing] around in cars, waving at each other in a spirit of bonhomie. It was the utopic vision of [a] visionary, and I wanted to make it happen if I joined politics.[32]

Congress president and United Progressive Alliance (UPA) chairperson, Sonia Gandhi, was also present at the event where the actor hailed her, along with Singh, for 'their capacity to take the country skywards so that it becomes an envy of the world'.[33]

The National Party of India, with Dev Anand as its president, would, however, close shop within months when Nani Palkhivala and then Vijaya Lakshmi Pandit declined to contest the Lok Sabha elections. Palkhivala, a noted jurist and economist who had attended the actor's Shivaji Park meet, reportedly sent a message saying that while he was open to the idea of joining the Rajya Sabha, he was reluctant to contest for a seat in the Lower House.

Dev Anand had prepared his party manifesto but learnt subsequently that his party colleagues had modified some of his radical suggestions. Moreover, there was no sign of the funds that certain affluent individuals had promised him. Even finding candidates for over 500 Lok Sabha seats proved a Herculean task.

In Dev Anand's own words, 'The inertia already visible amongst the early enthusiasts dampened my spirits... And that was the end of (the) National Party. It was a great idea that was nipped in the bud.'[34]

According to Rajkumar Keswani, a Bhopal-based journalist and film historian, the Dev Anand-led party was a well-intentioned flop. Keswani has written about it quite candidly in his article 'One Reel for Politics', published in the *Outlook* magazine in April 2014. Keswani's account reads as follows:

> It was a strange but real event in the political history of India. Dev and his colleagues in the enterprise called their party a 'crusade' against the corrupt politicians of the country. And the crusaders were none other than our own film folks who wanted to 'teach a lesson' to politicians, who they thought were a pack of greedy fools, a motley crowd of self-seeking opportunists.[35]

Keswani was present at a press conference held on 14 September 1979 at the Taj in Mumbai – the same venue where the actor had previously launched the National Party of India and released its manifesto. Keswani reports having seen a huge assembly of film personalities – such as V. Shantaram, Ramanand Sagar, G.P. Sippy, Shriram Bohra, Atma Ram and I.S. Johar – and stars like Hema Malini, Shatrughan Sinha, Sanjeev Kumar and others, all backing Dev Anand's party to the hilt. 'Several teams were formed by Dev and his colleagues, including his brother Vijay Anand, to draft the constitution of the party, launch a membership drive and create a manifesto for elections,' Keswani's article says.[36]

Dev Anand himself brimmed with hope and confidence. 'Why not, for a change, and for the sake of the country we love, form a political party that would transform the ugly[,] slushy shape of things[,] and give it a new shape as magnificent and glittering as a grand film?' were the words the actor would use in his autobiography to describe his feelings then.[37]

Membership was not a problem. Keswani says the membership drive evoked a positive response across the country:

> Everyone thought they will be in the company of stars by paying a rupee as membership fees. While releasing the party manifesto, Dev, who looked every inch an angry young man, told the media that they were launching a crusade...a crusade against poverty, unemployment, illiteracy and corruption. A party to promote a prosperous and growth-oriented society.[38]

The speech, in retrospect, sounded part Narendra Modi, part Arvind Kejriwal. But it did not get much media attention at that time; it was dismissed as just another film promotion.

Dev Anand died in London on 3 December 2011, following a heart attack. He was 88.

———

A.R. ANTULAY
(1929–2014)

ABDUL RAHMAN ANTULAY WAS THE FIRST SERVING CHIEF MINISTER who had to step down from office after allegations of a scam. The Congress leader was accused of favouring donors to a trust – the Indira Gandhi Pratibha Prathisthan – in the grant of cement quotas.

Antulay fought a protracted legal battle from 1982 – when he was convicted, finally clearing his name only in 2013. But the final judgment, while giving him a clean chit, also noted that the former Maharashtra chief minister's use of Prime Minister Indira Gandhi's name amounted to misuse of office.

The allegation of a cement scam had come from a lobby of Congress leaders who were reportedly uncomfortable with the balance of power shifting from Marathas to a Muslim. Shalini Patil, who was the revenue minister in Antulay's cabinet, was the most vocal and also a prosecution witness. Her husband, Vasantdada Patil, had accused Antulay of helping Muslims build mosques in Mumbai. The charge had evoked a trenchant response from Antulay: 'If Dada thinks I am as communal as he is himself, it is unfortunate for the Congress.' He had further told the interviewer,

> Let him mention even two mosques for which I arranged monetary help, either directly or indirectly. On the other hand, I can give at least two illustrations among many in which I raised monetary assistance for a Hindu and a neo-Buddhist temple. I am proud to be a Muslim but I have never claimed to be a Muslim leader.[39]

Antulay, who ruled Maharashtra for a year and a half till January 1982, was famous for stepping out after midnight to keep an eye on the law and order situation.

A barrister from Lincoln's Inn, Antulay was a staunch supporter of Indira Gandhi and Sanjay Gandhi, and remained so through the Emergency, surpassing even D.K. Barooah's 'India is Indira, Indira is India' brand of loyalty. At one point during the Emergency, Antulay had created a flutter by asking for a 'fresh look' at existing constitutional provisions, suggesting that the parliamentary elections held every five years be done away with. One of his famous comments in this context was: 'It has been left to Nehru's proud daughter, the daughter of the Indian nation, the daughter of India, ancient, present and future, to bring into effect what Nehru had visualized.'[40]

But neither allegations of corruption nor his well-known loyalty to Indira Gandhi had stopped the then prime minister, Atal Bihari Vajpayee, and Shiv Sena chief, Balasaheb Thackeray, from trying to get Antulay on their side. When Vajpayee returned as prime minister in 1998, he had reportedly sent feelers to Antulay inviting him to be the 'Muslim face' of the National Democratic Alliance (NDA). Antulay did not reject the offer outright. He had turned to former prime minister P.V. Narasimha Rao for advice. Rao reportedly told him to switch sides but Antulay decided to consult Sonia Gandhi, who had by then taken over as Congress chief. Sonia Gandhi is said to have pleaded with him not to compromise on 'secularism'. Towards the end of his life, Antulay regretted having missed the chance of joining hands with Vajpayee.[41]

As a minister in Rao's cabinet, he had stunned Congressmen by declaring himself a 'Shiv Sainik' and had urged an interviewer not to address him as 'Abdul Rahman', saying he preferred to be called A.R. Antulay.[42]

In 1982, as the chief minister of Maharashtra, he had sought an appointment with the Queen of England, requesting her to return the sword 'Bhawani' which had belonged to Chhatrapati Shivaji. The request, moved through the Indian mission in London, had resulted in Antulay getting an appointment, but he was unseated before his London visit.

After the November 2008 terror attack in Mumbai, Antulay had kicked up a storm by alluding to the alleged role of Hindu fundamentalists in the death of Anti-Terrorist Squad chief Hemant Karkare in the 26/11 siege. Both Sonia Gandhi and Dr Manmohan Singh had distanced themselves from the remark. Antulay later sought to clarify his comment, saying he was not talking about who had killed Karkare but that the officer might have been sent in the wrong direction.

Antulay died on 2 December 2014 after a long illness. He was 85.

TEJI BACHCHAN
(1914–2007)

TEJI BACHCHAN, OFTEN BETTER KNOWN AS AMITABH BACHCHAN'S mother, died in Mumbai's Lilavati Hospital at the age of 93, leaving her family and the Nehru–Gandhis bereft of their strongest link over three generations. Amitabh and Jaya Bachchan were at the hospital when the end came at 1.15 p.m. on 21 December 2007. Their daughter-in-law Aishwarya Rai Bachchan too cancelled a trip to reach Lilavati and her husband, Abhishek, flew in from Rajasthan. Ajitabh Bachchan and his family arrived a few minutes after Teji Bachchan's death.

When Teji Bachchan died the next day, the Congress paid its respects, with spokesperson Shakeel Ahmed saying that the 'mother of the famous actor, Amitabh…[had] contributed a lot to society when she was active'.[43] Nearly five years earlier, Sonia Gandhi had made it a point to send Rahul Gandhi to the funeral of Amitabh Bachchan's father, poet Harivansh Rai Bachchan, in January 2003. Remembering the actor's mother now, Sonia Gandhi said she had been her 'third mother'.[44] In many ways, Teji had indeed acted as Sonia Gandhi's 'third mother'.

The Bachchans' tale of friendship with the Nehru–Gandhis dates back to Anand Bhavan, Allahabad (now renamed Prayagraj). Indira Gandhi was still unmarried at the time. Sarojini Naidu had introduced poet Harivansh Rai Bachchan and his Sikh wife, Teji, to Jawaharlal Nehru and his daughter as 'the poet and the poem'.[45]

Amitabh Bachchan was barely four when he was introduced to Rajiv Gandhi, who was two then. There was a fancy dress party at the Bachchans' Bank Road residence in Allahabad, at which Rajiv Gandhi had shown up dressed as a freedom fighter. In an interview, Amitabh Bachchan had recalled: 'Ma (Teji) says he messed up his pants. We were all such tiny kids then, absorbed in our little games that it did not seem a big deal that Pandit Nehru's grandson was in our midst.'[46]

When Nehru moved to New Delhi's Teen Murti Bhavan as India's first prime minister, Rajiv Gandhi and his brother Sanjay were often spotted playing with the Bachchan siblings – Amitabh and Ajitabh, Adil Shaharyar (the son of Indira Gandhi's aide Mohammed Yunus) and Kabir Bedi. While Rajiv and Sanjay Gandhi were studying at Doon School, Amitabh and Ajitabh Bachchan were at Nainital's Sherwood. But during the holidays in New Delhi, which fell around the same time, the boys met and swam together every day at the pool of Rashtrapati Bhavan.

Rajiv and Sanjay Gandhi exposed Amitabh Bachchan to avant-garde cinema. European films were specially screened at Rashtrapati Bhavan for the Nehru–Gandhi family then. Amitabh Bachchan recalls attending with Rajiv and Sanjay Gandhi the screening of films like *Cranes are Flying,* and other Czech, Polish and Russian movies rich in anti-war messages.

Indira Gandhi's close aide Yashpal Kapoor, more famous now for toppling Opposition governments in states, was extremely fond of Amitabh Bachchan. Kapoor is said to have tried getting Amitabh Bachchan into Delhi's prestigious St Stephen's College. For some reason (perhaps due to a better course option), Amitabh Bachchan did not join, preferring to move to Kirorimal College instead. But his younger brother Ajitabh studied economics at Stephen's.

Amitabh Bachchan's first break in Bollywood was in K.A. Abbas's *Saat Hindustani,* based on the liberation of Goa. Abbas was considered close to Indira Gandhi, the then prime minister, and there were whispers that she had put in a word for the struggling actor. But Abbas stoutly denied having acted at her behest.

Harivansh Rai Bachchan – later to become a Rajya Sabha member – was requisitioned in the foreign office by Nehru's government while Teji was made director of the Film Finance Corporation in

1973. This was the time when Amitabh Bachchan married Jaya. The guest list was extremely short but Sanjay Gandhi was present, representing the Gandhis.

When Amitabh Bachchan emerged as a successful actor, Rajiv Gandhi would often visit him on the sets, extremely unobtrusive, waiting patiently till he completed a shot. Amitabh Bachchan recalled: 'His nature was that he would never misuse his family name. More often than not, Rajiv would not disclose his surname, fearing the distance it would create between him and the common man.'[47]

Then came the Emergency. Amitabh Bachchan, who was frequently seen in Sanjay Gandhi's company, faced the media's wrath for supporting it. On 11 April 1976, Delhi hosted a music function called 'Geeton Bhari Sham', ostensibly to raise money for Sanjay Gandhi and Rukhsana Sultana's (actress Amrita Singh's mother) controversial family planning programme. Both Amitabh and Jaya Bachchan were present in the company of Sanjay Gandhi. Around this time, when Indira Gandhi's Emergency information and broadcasting minister Vidya Charan Shukla was busy clamping down on violence in Hindi films, came Ramesh Sippy's Sholay.[48] Writers Salim–Javed and the rest of the crew were concerned about whether the film would pass the censor board. Amitabh Bachchan's association came in handy as the otherwise intimidating Shukla cleared it with minor cuts, including a change in the climax.

Throughout the 19-month Emergency, Amitabh Bachchan remained silent on the ban imposed on Kishore Kumar by All India Radio and Doordarshan, and the ostracism of the likes of Pran and Dev Anand – both outspoken critics of the government. Film journalism faced stiff censorship where even a gossip item about a young Amitabh Bachchan and the sensational Zeenat Aman was not tolerated.

There were minor differences between Gandhis and Bachchans though. For instance, when Indira Gandhi, whose proximity to Teji Bachchan was well established, chose Nargis as a Rajya Sabha member in 1980, the move had reportedly upset Teji Bachchan because she fancied herself as a contender. But Indira Gandhi had stoutly defended her decision, insisting that Nargis had deserved the recognition much more than anyone else. The incident was reported in a snippet column of a magazine that was edited by Indira Gandhi's younger daughter-in-law, Maneka.

The post-Emergency era had seen the Bachchans distancing themselves from the Gandhis when the Janata Party, under Morarji Desai, went out of its way to target Indira Gandhi and her son Sanjay. Sanjay's side of the family claims that when Indira Gandhi was out of power, there was a proposal to invite the Bachchan clan to a public rally, but Teji Bachchan reportedly declined, citing potential implications for her son's career as the reason. Sanjay Gandhi was reportedly livid and relations between the two families snapped for the time being. Sanjay was also upset when, out of power, he arrived in Mumbai, his friend Amitabh Bachchan did not come to receive him – a task that the actor had greatly relished in happier times, it seems. Sanjay Gandhi's son, Feroze Varun, had once told this writer that the Bachchans made their return to the Gandhi household only after Rajiv Gandhi entered politics – months after Sanjay's death.

When Amitabh Bachchan met with a near-fatal accident in 1982 though, one of the first people to support him and the Bachchans was family mentor Indira Gandhi who travelled to Mumbai, Rajiv in tow. She had just returned from her official visit to the US. Sanjay Gandhi had died some months previously and the tragic parallels in the lives of the two families further strengthened the friendship.

When Indira Gandhi headed to see the actor, she wrote a letter to her friend Dorothy Norman:

In Los Angeles, a message came that his [Amitabh Bachchan's] condition was critical. Had I been in India[,] our entire family would have gone to Bombay to be with them all. As it was, we decided that Rajiv should fly back and on my return to Delhi, Sonia and I also went down to Bombay for a few hours. When one is battling for one's life

or indeed for anything else, it makes an enormous difference
if close friends are there to help build morale.[49]

As Rajiv Gandhi emerged as Indira's heir apparent after Sanjay's
death, a newly rehabilitated Amitabh Bachchan was now once again
very much a part of the Gandhi inner circle. Amitabh Bachchan
was chosen to offer his signature baritone voice to the 1982 Asian
Games' opening ceremony in Delhi's Jawaharlal Nehru Stadium.
Rajiv Gandhi, the chief organizer, sat in the front row as Amitabh
Bachchan anchored the show reading hymns.

However, following the Bofors uproar, Amitabh Bachchan, a
Member of Parliament (MP) from Allahabad then, left politics,
disillusioned. The cinematic superman was accused of being a
middleman. Amitabh Bachchan fought for his honour and won a
protracted legal battle, but he could not sever his links with politics.
Bachchan's parting with Gandhis singularly contributed for Rajiv
Gandhi's downfall as the Allahabad Lok Sabha by-elections in 1987
gave the fragmented opposition the sense that together they could
humble the Congress, which was holding 413 MPs in the 542-member
Lok Sabha.

Several years later, Amitabh Bachchan spoke about the Emergency
to Arnab Goswami on Times Now, saying that he didn't feel angry
with its imposition but quickly added, that it was 'perhaps the
wrong decision'. 'Democracy was being curtailed', including in the
film industry, he conceded. He agreed with Arnab Goswami that
Bollywood in general (and Bachchan himself) does not want to upset
the 'powers that be'.[50]

Despite all that had transpired, Sonia Gandhi always retained her
affection for Teji, who acted as her godmother and schooled her in
Indian customs when she first arrived in Delhi as Rajiv Gandhi's
fiancée in 1968 and was put up at the Bachchans'. 'I came to learn a
lot from them. Teji aunty is my second... no, my third mother (after
her own mother and mother-in-law, Indira Gandhi),' she had said
in a 1985 interview in the Hindi magazine *Dharmayug*. 'Amit and

Bunty (Ajitabh) are my brothers.'[51] Several wedding rituals, like Sonia Gandhi's *mehendi* ceremony, too were held in the Bachchan home.

In October 1984, when Indira Gandhi was assassinated by her security guards, there was absolute panic at the residence of the then prime minister. At one point, Sonia Gandhi, who was attending to her mother-in-law (yet to be officially declared dead), became hysterical fearing for the lives of Rahul and Priyanka who were in school just then. She told Arun Nehru that Indira had feared a repetition of Mujib-ur-Rahman – the towering Bangaldeshi leader whose entire family, except for daughter Hasina, up to three generations was wiped out. Arun Nehru took charge and transported the children from school to Teji Bachchan's Gulmohar Park residence in Delhi for safety.

Years later, in October 2004, sources close to the Bachchan family said that Teji Bachchan had got her son Amitabh to quickly smother the fire when Rahul Gandhi and Amitabh's wife Jaya Bachchan, who had joined the Samajwadi Party by then, traded charges over which family had let down whom. A Samajwadi Party source said that had Teji Bachchan not been so ill (she had been bedridden for months), she would have worked towards a rapprochement and perhaps dissuaded Jaya Bachchan from joining the Uttar Pradesh-based party.

The tirade that Jaya Bachchan let loose against Sonia Gandhi and her family must have been abhorrent to the dignified Teji Bachchan. The special relationship she shared with the Nehru–Gandhi dynasty was one that she valued greatly. Teji Bachchan prided herself on being a good friend, as did Indira Gandhi, and both the families had proved that their relationship could weather the highs and lows of life.

Born in a family of army officers, Teji 'Suri' had shared Harivansh Rai Bachchan's keen interest in poetry, literature and theatre. In his autobiography, Harivansh Rai Bachchan had admitted that he was 'enamoured by Teji's charms and spirited commitment to society'.[52]

The couple married in 1941. Teji Bachchan was his second wife.

In a blog written to mark his mother's birthday in 2014, Amitabh Bachchan gave a graphic account of his parents' love:

> My Mother, unknown to my Father till they accidentally met, My Mother, who had never heard of who my Father was. My Mother who left her all – her luxuries of her opulent home in Lahore and Rawalpindi and Lyalpur and Karachi, her English Governesses and a fleet of my Grandfather's Lancers and Rolls Royces, to marry my Father, an unknown of meagre means.[53]

Amitabh chronicled that Teji Bachchan was just three months old when her mother passed away. He described the experience as follows:

> She never did ever experience the joy and care and the most important company of a Mother. She never knew what a Mother was! Is that in some way indicative of how dear a Mother she herself became, when we were born? I often wonder, as does my Father in his autobiography. I touch their faces through the enlarged miracles of photography, stand silently before them [at the] beginning of the day, and wish and pray that they extend their love and care to me and the family.[54]

Author and journalist Promilla Kalhan was well known to the Bachchans. In her book, she describes Teji Bachchan as an accomplished singer and a theatre artist. Teji Bachchan performed with several troupes in Delhi and Allahabad. After her marriage, she acted in Shakespeare's plays translated by her husband. It may sound incredible, but Prime Minister Nehru once snuck in to attend when a Hindi version of Shakespeare's Othello was being performed by her:

> When the play was halfway through at a New Delhi theatre hall, Jawaharlal Nehru, accompanied by his secretary,

walked into the hall and quietly took a back seat. But his entry did not go unnoticed. From the stage, Teji Bachchan called out to the prime minister and requested him to take a front seat.[55]

~

JYOTI BASU
(1914–2010)

THE THRONE WAS ON OFFER. HE HIMSELF WAS WILLING. BUT HIS party colleagues wouldn't let him occupy it. The year was 1996. Jyoti Basu had come within a whisker of becoming India's first communist prime minister, only to be denied the opportunity by the party he had founded. The Communist Party of India (Marxist) (CPI[M]) politburo nixed the proposal, believing that his continuation as the chief minister of Bengal was more important than leading a rainbow coalition of centrist and Left-leaning parties at the Centre. A dejected Basu had gone public, terming the politburo's decision a 'historic' blunder. That was, perhaps, the only time Basu broke his party's code of discipline. A lesser man might have invited censure but Basu was too tall a leader to be hauled up by the party. In any case, subsequent events would prove him right.

Over the next 18 months, the country saw two prime ministers flunking the coalition test and paving the way for the Right-wing Bharatiya Janata Party (BJP) to come to power. Virtually everyone, except for the no-changers in the CPI(M), would later concur with Basu's assessment.

Several political leaders cutting across party lines were disappointed by CPI(M)'s veto. Years later, Sitaram Yechury, who had voted against Basu's candidature in the central committee meeting, admitted that senior Congress leader Arjun Singh did not forgive him for it. Speaking at a function to mark the release of a souvenir in memory of Arjun Singh in 2016, Yechury said, 'Arjun Singh ji never forgave me for the decision taken by the CPI(M) central committee in not allowing Jyoti Basu to become (the) prime minister of India.'[56]

Some political observers believe that Basu was in the same league as Sardar Vallabhbhai Patel and Pranab Mukherjee – great prime ministers India never had. There are also many who would disagree with such an assessment, including those from Bengal, who even today, two decades after Basu withdrew from public life, cite the eastern state's lack of development under his rule. But despite such polarized viewpoints, the fact remains that Basu was a legend in his lifetime, a Marxist who was equally at home with bourgeois democracy and remained the longest serving chief minister of any Indian state till Pawan Kumar Chamling of the tiny hill state of Sikkim broke his 23-year record at the helm.

Basu died on 17 January 2010, aged 95, leaving behind a political and economic legacy that is still debated. What is beyond dispute is that he was among the last of a disappearing breed of politicians whose acceptance went beyond party barriers.

Early Life and Education

Basu was born as Jyotirindra at 43/1 Harrison Road (now Mahatma Gandhi Road) in Kolkata (Calcutta then) on 8 July 1914. He was the third child of Nishikanta and Hemlata Basu. After graduating from Presidency College (Hindu College then) in 1935, Basu had travelled to London, where he studied for the Bar. According to records at the Middle Temple, documented by the *Telegraph*'s Amit Roy, Basu was a student at University College London where he was admitted on 27 October 1935. 'He registered as the son of Nishi K. Basu of

55 Hindustan Road, Calcutta. He was called to the Bar on January 26, 1940, in absence – which means he could not come in person but he had qualified as a barrister,' Roy wrote shortly after Basu's death in January 2010.[57]

Basu, however, did not practice law at the Middle Temple, one of the four Inns of Court exclusively entitled to call their members to the English Bar as barristers. The political mood in London after the Great Depression was such that many young minds were attracted towards Marxism. Basu too would embrace Marxism, which provided a vision of an alternative social order. This was also a time when the Soviet Union was the most uncompromising opponent of Adolf Hitler's Germany, seeking alliances with Great Britain, France and the United States to promote a popular front of sorts that would consist of both liberals and socialists across the world to halt the spread of fascism. Committed to the core, Basu often himself identified as a proud 'Stalinist' till his last breath although, paradoxically, he worked for free speech, liberal values and the cause of peasants and workers for most of his public life.

Basu returned to India in 1940. He had no desire to settle in the UK but would keep going back to London almost every year, frequently spending two to four weeks in the British capital. That would remain a habit throughout his active public life; his trips were made always on some pretext – never as a holiday. It was obvious that Basu felt at home in London.

Gopalkrishna Gandhi, a former diplomat who later served as Bengal's governor, recalls an incident when the otherwise reticent Basu opened up while delivering a lecture in 1993. Gandhi was then serving as director of the Nehru Centre in London, which had organized a commemoration of the 200th year of Charles Cornwallis's Permanent Settlement. Basu was the chief speaker. 'His head buried in the text, he read in an unfluctuating timbre and tone from a prepared script. And as he progressed from page to page of the closely typed document I could see many in the audience "switching off",' Gandhi recalls.

Basu too had sensed the disconnect and stopped midway. Gandhi says:

> [L]ooking up through his spectacles, Basu said, 'You can see I am reading this out. It has been written for me by an expert who knows all these things. I do not know all this myself. I am also learning as I read this. You see, for most of my life I have been among the people, with little time to read or study.' The audience burst into applause in appreciation of the candour of this man who had shaped history, while most of the listeners had only read history and some had written on aspects of it.[58]

It was a comment typical of the man who had learnt through nearly half a century of experience. Basu was adept at reading the public's pulse, hardly surprising for someone who had begun his political career as a 30-something trade union leader and reached a position where few, if any, could challenge his authority.

Early Political Activism

By early 1944, Basu was actively involved with the trade and railway unions of Bengal and had become general secretary of the Bengal Nagpur Railway Workers' Union. This was a period that coincided with his involvement with the then banned Communist Party of India (CPI), despite strong resistance from his parents. The British had declared the CPI 'illegal' after the Meerut Conspiracy case of 1929. Leading communists such as Muzaffar Ahmad, S.A. Dange, S.V. Ghate, Dr G. Adhikari, P.C. Joshi, S.S. Mirajkar, Shaukat Usmani and Philip Spratt had been arrested on charges of conspiracy to overthrow the British Government of India through strikes and other militant methods. Basu's main task was to maintain links with leaders who had gone underground, and provide them with shelter and collect subscriptions at secret meetings.

The transition from secret grassroots activism to electoral politics would take only two years. By 1946, Basu had been elected to the Bengal Legislative Council in an electoral college vote from the railway employees' constituency. It would be the beginning of an extended journey.

By the time he stepped back from power politics and the hurly-burly of the electoral arena and into retirement over half a century later, Basu had earned a host of labels, some of them seemingly contradictory: 'Sahib in a dhoti', 'bhadralok', 'pragmatic patriarch', 'Marxist by conviction, liberal democrat in practice', 'mass leader and recluse'. Basu remained a bit of all this throughout his life. He was an unconventional politician and the Left did not always approve of his decisions, but that hardly deterred him from charting his own course.

By the 1960s, it became evident that the party needed him more than he needed the party. Basu was a key player in 1964 when the breakaway CPI(M) was formed, carved out of the 31 national council members from the CPI. Basu was one of the nine members of the CPI(M)'s politburo, the party's highest decision-making body between two party congresses. The shift from the CPI to the CPI(M) was path-breaking on many counts.

Ironically, it would be the politburo that would in 1996 shoot down a suggestion that Basu be made the consensus candidate for prime minister at the helm of a United Front coalition government at the Centre. This is what happened in a nutshell: the exit of the Congress-led P.V. Narasimha Rao government in May 1996 had led to dramatic developments. The Congress had won just 140 seats in the Lok Sabha and the BJP – the largest single party with 161 MPs – hurriedly staked its claim to form the government, although it was way short of the majority mark of 273. BJP leader Atal Bihari Vajpayee became prime minister but had to make an exit within 13 days as he failed to prove his majority.

Many non-Congress and non-BJP players then swung into action and formed the United Front. The rainbow coalition of 13 parties, including the Janata Dal, Telugu Desam Party, Dravida Munnetra Kazhagam (DMK), Samajwadi Party, the CPI and a range of regional players, sought the Congress's support from outside to cross the magic figure.

But more than the numbers, the United Front struggled to find its prime ministerial nominee. The Front, stitched together carefully by former prime minister V.P. Singh and, CPI(M) general secretary Harkishan Singh Surjeet, first offered the post to Basu, who was then Bengal's chief minister. It all looked fine with Bengal newspapers running headlines like 'Red Flag Over Delhi'. The Basu–Surjeet duopoly was considered invincible. If Basu was credited with holding the Left Front together in power in Bengal, Surjeet towered in Delhi's milieu of intrigues.

However, following a formal resolution by the United Front constituents, the CPI(M) central committee held an emergency meeting in Delhi and decided against Basu leading the cabinet at the Centre. The insistence of Samajwadi Party leader Mulayam Singh Yadav and rumblings within the CPI(M) forced the party to convene another meeting of the central committee to revisit the issue, but Basu's candidature was vetoed again.

Surjeet and Buddhadeb Bhattacharjee (who would succeed Basu as chief minister of Bengal in the year 2000) were among those who were in favour of Basu taking up the country's top executive job. But led by Prakash Karat, a hawk, who later became CPI(M) general secretary, the no-changers opposed the move, saying that the CPI(M) – with just 32 MPs – would be in no position to influence the government's policies.

So sharp were the differences in the party that at one point, it was reported, Surjeet offered to resign after he was attacked by the no-changers for pushing the proposal to elevate Basu. Matters came to such a pass that the central committee, at its second meeting on 14 May 1996, had to take recourse to a vote – something rare in the CPI(M). Twenty-seven no-changers prevailed over 22 pragmatics.

Towards the end of 1996, Basu would utter the now-immortal phrase, 'historic blunder', during an interview. He would later recount the 'strong debate' within the party when he was chosen as a prime ministerial candidate.

In May 2004, Basu would explain why he had called his party's decision a historic blunder. 'Yes, I still think it was a historic blunder,' he said while speaking to Shekhar Gupta, then editor of the *Indian Express*, on NDTV's *Walk the Talk* show. He then added:

> Why historic? Because such an opportunity does not come. History does not give such opportunity. Knowing who I am – a Marxist, a communist, in the party here, for so many years I have been in politics, they invited me because they had no other prime minister in view. So we thought that even if we last for one year in that coalition with myself as the prime minister and our party joining it, then people would understand backward sections. In many places, they don't even know what we are all about.[59]

That was a confession Basu had made without securing the party's nod. The CPI(M), however, sought to credit him with declining the post. Three years after his death in January 2010, a letter seeking a commemorative postal stamp on Basu's upcoming 100th birth anniversary, a CPI(M) central committee member claimed that the former chief minister had 'refused' the prime minister's post in 1996.

The letter written by Shyamal Chakraborty and addressed to then prime minister Manmohan Singh said:

> Sri Jyoti Basu entered into arena of Parliamentary Democracy by the end of British Rule in India and remained in the pivot for a longest period. His name was proposed as the prime minister of India by the National Leaders, with whom he had wide ideological differences. But he refused the offer.

The letter added: 'This has been an unprecedented phenomenon in the post-Independence political history of India.'[60]

The post went to H.D. Deve Gowda instead, whose government flunked out in less than a year. Gowda's successor, Inder Kumar Gujral, too fell by November 1997, paving the way for the return of the Vajpayee-led BJP to power. Had Basu been given a chance, he may have worked out a broad anti-BJP front that would eventually come into existence between 2004 and 2014. But the CPI(M) politburo put the party's interest before national interest.

Counterfactual Assessment

Did Basu's party deny India an opportunity to be ruled by a stalwart leader at a crucial point in its post-Independence history? Someone who might have changed the nation's political destiny? Journalist Sumit Mitra doesn't agree. Mitra believes there was nothing outstanding about Basu:

> He [Basu] had neither Jawaharlal Nehru's eloquence nor the moral authority of Jayaprakash Narayan. By the standards of communist stalwarts of the day, SA Dange or EMS Namboodiripad, the [then] longest-serving chief minister (1977–2000) in India was no intellectual giant. He spoke with the drabness of an apparatchik, and wrote his memoirs in Bengali, *Jotodur Mone Pore* (As Far As I Remember), with the legal twist in the title that absolves him of accountability for being economical with the truth. Nor was he a model of financial saintliness. [...] But Basu's role in shaping modern India is better seen in counterfactual terms, as what could have happened if he had played a determined reformer back in the 1980s by becoming a champion of development through industrialisation, like Deng Xiaoping in China.[61]

To be fair, throughout his tenure as chief minister at the helm of a Left Front coalition government, Basu tried restoring political stability through consensus and dialogue, and bringing in land reforms to give poor farmers an opportunity to own land. He believed in equity and empowerment, and successfully piloted radical agrarian reform. Basu launched Operation Barga in 1978 to secure rural income guarantees and introduced local self-government much before Rajiv Gandhi's much-touted *panchayati raj* system. Among his many achievements, Basu will be remembered for making communism look respectable. However, he was also accused of failing to stand up to powerful trade unions which resisted his attempts to bring in foreign investment and rejuvenate local industry.

Basu retired from active politics in 2000, leaving the Left Front government in the hands of Buddhadeb Bhattacharjee, who then ruled for eleven years. Basu remained a member of the CPI(M) politburo till 2008, and a special invitee to the party's central committee till his death.

Former director of the Central Bureau of Investigation (CBI) and Bengal police chief, Arun Prosad Mukherjee, makes an interesting claim regarding Basu in his book *Unknown Facets of Rajiv Gandhi, Jyoti Basu, Inderjit Gupta*: Rajiv Gandhi had wanted Basu to be the prime minister during the politically tumultuous times of 1990–91. Mukherjee was Special Secretary in the Union home ministry when Rajiv Gandhi, leader of the opposition in October 1990, was said to have asked him to arrange a meeting with Basu. They met at CPI(M) MP Biplap Dasgupta's house. In his memoirs, Mukherjee wrote, 'But my worst conjecture proved right...and thus ended an opportunity of putting up Left Front's best foot forward in the larger interests of Bengal.'[62]

Mukherjee, who later served as Union Home Minister Inderjit Gupta's principal secretary and governor of Mizoram, insists that twice, before Chandra Shekhar was sworn in as prime minister and after his exit between November 1990 and March 1991, Rajiv

Gandhi wanted Basu to head a coalition government at the Centre. Mukherjee's assertions could not be independently verified.

Not everyone is happy with Basu and his political legacy. Soon after his death, Ramdas Menon wrote a piece in the *New Indian Express* recalling his days in Kolkata when Basu was Bengal's chief minister and the name they had given him – 'Jyoti "The Candlelight" Basu' – an allusion to the frequent power cuts then. 'We do not remember using electric lights during the endless night which lasted 23 years. I say this because I lived there from my birth in 1965 to middle age in 1995, and endured 18 years of his misrule,' Menon writes.[63]

Menon claims there was not a single day when the people could sit or study or sleep in peace:

> I remember sleepless mornings and nights in the hot summers, day after day, week after week, month after month, year after year – he merely sipped his Scotch on the rocks in air-conditioned comfort when we had 14-hour power cuts. Yes sir, he was a pucca sahib. When he was asked in the late Sixties why West Bengal was not investing more in the power sector, he famously replied, 'What shall we do with more power, eat it?' The great man thought that the hungry and the dispossessed whom he ruled would eat it. He went on to eat crow, but let's move on.[64]

Writer and BJP MP Swapan Dasgupta remembers Basu in a more measured manner. He says:

> When it came to the revival of manufacturing and the creation of a new services sector, the chief minister found himself outvoted inside the party. His government adopted measures such as the abolition of English teaching till Class 5 and the politicisation of institutions which set West Bengal behind by decades. Trade union militancy and crippling

power cuts led to the decimation of small and medium industry. To the investing classes, Bengal became a big no-no. Its efficiency was limited to the organisation of bandhs... He inherited a crumbling edifice and bequeathed a similar structure to his predecessor. He merely prevented the roof from caving in.[65]

To Aditya Nigam, author of books on the Indian Left, Basu was neither Bonaparte nor Caesar:

He was certainly not a 'heroic' personality, and not by any means a demagogue. His political appeal came from his 'ordinariness'. His political speeches in rallies at the Brigade Parade ground were delivered in simple conversational style, almost sounding like one-to-one conversations. No fire-spouting rhetoric; no big words whose meaning only the converted can understand.[66]

According to Nigam, Basu's politics was certainly uncluttered by ideology: there was nothing predetermined about his responses. It was as if one had been 'thrown' into a political context where all that one could fall back upon was political instincts.[67]

The *Telegraph*'s Monobina Gupta, who covered the Left parties in New Delhi, recalled Basu's 'exasperatingly short, brusque replies, sometimes even with outright sarcasm or rudeness'.[68]

Veteran journalist Barun Ghosh, however, has a different view. Writing a piece for the *Telegraph* after Basu's death, Ghosh gave a vivid account of how Basu had once saved his job. This was in July 1984 when Ghosh, the newspaper's reporter covering Writers' Buildings (the chief minister's office), had reached late and missed an important press conference. Ghosh decided to do the unthinkable: barge into Basu's office. 'There wasn't much security those days in the secretariat and I barged into Basu's chamber. His private secretary tried to stop me, but [he] didn't seem to mind the intrusion all that much as mine was a familiar face at Writers,' he recalled.[69]

When Ghosh entered the chief minister's office, Basu looked at him wondering what he was doing there since the news conference was over. Ghosh recounts:

> I stammered something and then almost broke down at his feet. I would be pulled up, I pleaded, if I didn't get the details of the news conference. Basu looked at me, paused for a moment, then asked me to take a seat. Basu then told his personal staff to get a cup of tea and cashew nuts for Ghosh. 'I know your editor,' he smiled at me. '*Aage ek cup garam cha khao, tarpor tomake shob bole debo* (First have a cup of hot tea, then I'll tell you everything).'[70]

Next, the chief minister dictated everything that he had spoken at the press conference. 'After I had jotted them down, he asked me to read out what I had written. I was allowed to leave after he was satisfied that there had been no distortion of facts,' Ghosh wrote in his article.[71]

Ghosh had several other nuggets to narrate. A senior minister, Ram Chatterjee, had one day taken out a revolver and pointed it at Ghosh, threatening to shoot him if he didn't leave. The next morning Ghosh had gone to Writers' and narrated the incident to Basu. 'When I told Basu about my experience, he summoned Chatterjee to his chamber,' Ghosh says. 'Right in front of me he rebuked the minister. Chatterjee later shook hands with me as Basu looked on.'[72]

Basu's death was condoled all over the world. The Cuban ambassador to India recalled how Basu had welcomed President Fidel Castro in Kolkata in September 1973. Basu had lost the elections held the previous year, allegedly because of large-scale rigging, and did not hold any formal position, but his picture with fellow communist Castro had become famous.

NRI industrialist Lord Swraj Paul dubbed Basu as the 'great prime minister India never had.' Paul, who had business interests in Bengal, said, 'In Basu we have lost a great son of Bengal, a great Indian and for me a great friend and a great prime minister India never had.' He added, 'A very committed and disciplined party worker, he always sacrificed his personal gain for party discipline.'[73]

Bangladesh's prime minister Sheikh Hasina expressed her deep shock at the death of veteran Marxist leader and described his death as an immense loss for Bangladesh. 'It is also an immense loss for Bangladesh as well as myself... we have lost a tested friend and well wisher of ours,' she said adding, '[W]e recall with deep gratitude Mr Basu's enormous support. I also remember his role and personal initiative in strengthening the bilateral relations between Bangladesh and India, particularly the efforts he made for the conclusion of the Ganges water sharing treaty.'[74]

'Commoner Like Us'

The two-storey house on the Meghna's banks in Bangladesh, where Basu spent a part of his childhood and kept returning to in his later life, has been turned into a library and a museum, in keeping with his wishes. Basu's family had lived in the house, situated on a 2.04-acre plot in Chowdhury Para in Barudi village, about 20 km from Dhaka, till the early 1940s before moving to Kolkata. Basu had visited the house during his last trip to Bangladesh in 1999 and expressed a desire to have it converted into a library.

When the *Telegraph*'s Ananya Sengupta visited the house in August 2010, she found that no blood relatives of Basu were around. But the house caretaker Shahidullah's mother, a nonagenarian Ayatunnessa (now dead) remembered seeing Basu, the youngest of three siblings after Surendra Kumar Basu and Sudha Datta Basu.

Sengupta also interviewed Mohammad Rafiq, a farmer who told her how Basu had charmed Barudi during his trips when he was Bengal's chief minister. 'He spoke to ordinary villagers like us and asked about our welfare as though we were very close to him,' Rafiq had said after Basu's death. 'He behaved as if he was a commoner like us; that's how sincere he was.'[75]

The house has two bedrooms and a drawing room on the top floor and two rooms and a meeting space on the ground floor. It has been taken over by Bangladesh's cultural affairs ministry and put under the care of the archaeology department.[76]

When Basu died on 17 January 2010, aged 95, his eyes – which had seen two world wars, the freedom movement, the Partition and the communist movement's rise to prominence in India – continued to see. Basu had pledged to donate his body for medical research on 4 April 2003 at an event organized by Ganadarpan and the Susrut Eye Foundation in Kolkata. Basu's corneas, which were removed by a team of doctors from the Susrut Eye Foundation, were transplanted to a patient suffering from corneal blindness. The operation had taken place after the mandatory blood and micro-biological tests were carried out on the beneficiary whose identity was kept a secret. His body was donated to the government-run SSKM Hospital for scientific research.

'We communists say that one should serve the people till one dies,' the former chief minister had said. 'Now I find that one can still serve the people even after he is no more. This is a rare opportunity and no one should let it go by.'[77]

CHANDRASWAMI
(1948–2017)

'WHAT DID YOU WANT TO SEE ME FOR?' SHE ASKED. 'TELL HER SHE will soon find out,' he replied. Margaret Thatcher did – and fell under Chandraswami's spell.[78]

The former British prime minister was not the only public figure to have become a devotee of the controversial godman. Among others on the list of those charmed by the self-styled guru were people like Jayaprakash Narayan (JP), Elizabeth Taylor, Adnan Khashoggi and P.V. Narasimha Rao.

By the time he died on 23 May 2017, at the age of 69, Nemi Chand Jain (alias Chandraswami) had traversed the entire gamut of fame and notoriety. The much sought after mystic, a modern-day Rasputin, represented the seamy side of spiritualism and often found himself on the wrong side of the law. He was a suspect in the assassination of Rajiv Gandhi and was an active player in one of the most controversial arms deals ever, the Iran–Contra affair. In June 2011, the Enforcement Directorate even imposed a fine of ₹9 crore on Chandraswami for Foreign Exchange Regulation Act violations.

But to those who came under his influence, he was a man who could work miracles. Till the last days of her life in 2011, for instance, Elizabeth Taylor remained a Chandraswami devotee. She had reportedly met him in the US in 2001 when she was diagnosed with cancer, and firmly believed that Chandraswami's healing touch had brought her breast cancer under control. Taylor would call Chandraswami every year on his birthday.[79]

Chandraswami, the son of a Rajasthani moneylender, was still in his twenties in 1975 when JP, the patriarch whose call for 'total revolution' had galvanized a whole generation of leaders, wrote a personal letter to his friends to introduce the young astrologer-godman. Bhavdeep Kang, author of *Gurus: Stories of India's Leading Babas*, has devoted an entire chapter of his book to the godman, titled 'The Shaman–Shyster: Chandraswami'. Kang recalls how the Gandhian JP had first met the young sadhu in white with bushy hair, a frizzy beard and a heavy gold amulet around his neck, at New Delhi's Gandhi Peace Foundation.[80]

For the next four decades, Kang says, Chandraswami would remain associated with arms, drugs, money, crime and power-broking.[81] His ashram in Delhi's Qutub Institutional Area saw several prime ministers, from Chandra Shekhar to Rao, come and go. When Chandraswami turned 46 in 1994, the entire ashram was lit up with the likes of Balram Jakhar, Buta Singh, N.D. Tiwari, Imam Syed Ahmad Bukhari of Delhi's Jama Masjid, Rajmata Vijayaraje Scindia and T.N. Seshan.[82]

Chandraswami's influence reached its peak during Rao's five-year rule from 1991 when the godman acted as the prime minister's troubleshooter, astrologer and Congress fund manager.

Interestingly, it was S. Jaipal Reddy, who always insisted upon being a rationalist and an agnostic, that had introduced Chandraswami to Rao. Kang says that sometime in 1972, Reddy had realized that Chandraswami knew everything he (Reddy) wanted to ask.[83] The next step was to meet Rao, who was then the chief minister of Andhra Pradesh.

Chandraswami had told Kang that he learnt tantric practices from Mahaupadhyay Amar Muni, a Jain saint, and Kaviraj Mahaupadhyay Gopinath of Varanasi.[84] Diplomat-turned-politician K. Natwar Singh was witness to Chandraswami's allegedly extraordinary powers as an astrologer and mind reader.

In his book, *Walking with Lions: Tales from a Diplomatic Past*, Natwar Singh gave a vivid description of how Chandraswami impressed Thatcher, then the leader of the Opposition in the House of Commons in the summer of 1975.[85] Chandraswami had approached Natwar Singh with a reference from Yashpal Kapoor – a key Indira Gandhi aide. He asked the diplomat to introduce him to Lord Mountbatten and Thatcher. Singh writes:

> She (Thatcher) had been elected leader of the Conservative Party six months earlier. Doubts still assailed me about Chandraswami meeting Margaret Thatcher, not yet the iron lady. Suppose Chandraswami made an ass of himself. I would look a bigger ass. I sought an appointment with the Leader of the Opposition. She promptly obliged. I met her in her tiny office in the House of Commons.

When Singh cautioned Chandraswami not to do or say anything silly, he told the diplomat, '*Chinta mut kareay* (Don't worry).'[86]

'Chandraswami was dressed in his "sadhu" kit, with a huge tilak on his forehead and a staff in his right hand. Rudraksha malas round his neck. He banged the staff on the road till I told him to stop doing so. I confess, I was feeling self conscious,' Singh recalls in his book. When the introductions were over, Thatcher supposedly asked: 'What did you want to see me for?' Chandraswami spoke in Hindi while Singh acted as a translator. 'Tell her she will soon find out,' he had said.[87]

When Thatcher said she was waiting, Chandraswami asked for a large piece of paper. Singh described what happened after this as follows:

> He gave Mrs Thatcher five strips of paper and requested her to write a question on each. She obliged, but with scarcely camouflaged irritation. Chandraswami asked her to open the first paper ball. She did. He gave the text of the question in Hindi. I translated. Correct. I watched Mrs Thatcher. The irritation gave way to curiosity. Next question. Again bull's eye. Curiosity replaced by interest. By the fourth question the future iron lady's demeanour changed. She began to look at Chandraswami not as a fraud, but as a holy man indeed. My body language too altered. Last question. No problem. I heaved a sigh of relief. Mrs Thatcher was now perched on the edge of the sofa. Like Oliver Twist, she asked for more.[88]

Natwar Singh says Chandraswami was like a triumphant guru, and he adds:

> He took off his chappals and sat on the sofa in the lotus pose. I was appalled. Mrs Thatcher seemed to approve. She asked supplementary questions. In each case Chandraswami's

response almost overwhelmed the future prime minister. She was on the verge of another supplementary, when Chandraswami regally announced that the sun had set. No more questions. Mrs Thatcher was not put out. She enquired if she could meet him again. I was entirely unprepared for this. Very coolly, almost condescendingly, he said, 'On Tuesday at 2.30 p.m. at the house of Shri Natwar Singh.'[89]

Singh told Chandraswami he was overreaching himself by dictating the day and time without taking into account her convenience. This was not India, but the godman remained unmoved. '*Kunwar sahib, anuvad kar dijiye aur phir dekhiye* (Please translate and then see),' he said. Singh recalls being astounded when Thatcher asked him, 'Deputy High Commissioner, where do you live?'[90] He says:

This was not all. What followed was something out of a weird novel. Just as we were about to leave, Mr Holy Man produced a talisman tied to a not-so-tidy piece of string. He then pronounced that Mrs Thatcher should tie it on her left arm when she came to my house on Tuesday. I was now on the verge of losing my temper. I said I would not translate this *dehati* (rustic) rubbish. Mrs Thatcher intervened to know what the holy man was saying. 'Mrs Thatcher, please forgive me, but Chandraswami would like you to wear this talisman on your left arm.' She took the talisman. We were saying our goodbyes, when Chandraswami produced his sartorial bomb. Turning to me he said 'Kunwar Sahib, kindly tell Mrs Thatcher that on Tuesday she should wear a red *poshak* (outfit).' I felt like hitting him. He was overdoing this. I firmly told him it was the height of bad manners to tell a lady what she should or should not wear. Mrs Thatcher looked a bit apprehensive at this not-so-mild altercation between a distraught Deputy High Commissioner and a

somewhat ill-mannered holy man. Very reluctantly I said
to her that the holy man would be obliged if she wore a
red dress on Tuesday. I was looking down at the floor as
I said this.[91]

When Thatcher turned up at Natwar Singh's residence at Sun
House, Frognal Way, Hampstead, she was wearing a red dress
and the talisman given by Chandraswami was in its proper place.
Natwar recalls Thatcher asking Chandraswami about her chances
of becoming British prime minister. Singh writes:

> Chandraswami did not disappoint Mrs Thatcher. He
> prophesied that she would be prime minister for nine,
> eleven or thirteen years. Mrs Thatcher no doubt believed
> that she would be prime minister one day. Nine, eleven,
> thirteen years was a bit much. Mrs Thatcher put one final
> question. When would she become a prime minister?
> Chandraswami announced – in three or four years. He was
> proved right. She was PM for eleven years.[92]

The diplomat met Thatcher again in Lusaka, Zambia, in 1979,
when she had become the British prime minister. At the airport,
Singh said he had gently whispered to Thatcher, 'Our man proved
right.' For a moment, he says, Thatcher looked flustered. 'She took
me aside, "High Commissioner, we don't talk about these matters."'
'Of course not, prime minister, of course not,' Natwar Singh seems
to have replied.[93]

Another of Chandraswami's devotees was Khashoggi, the arms
dealer who was allegedly involved in the 'Iran–Contra affair', a
political scandal in the US during the second term of Ronald Reagan
as President. Senior Reagan administration officials had secretly
facilitated the sale of arms to Iran, which was the subject of an
arms embargo.

Chandraswami was also named in the Jain Commission of inquiry which had probed the conspiracy angle in Rajiv Gandhi's assassination in May 1991. Justice M.C. Jain had alleged that Chandraswami was involved in the assassination as a financier. The godman had come under the scanner of the Enforcement Directorate and was banned by the Supreme Court from travelling abroad. It was only in 2009 that the Supreme Court lifted his travel ban.

PHOOLAN DEVI
(1963–2001)

IN THE MURKY SAGA OF CHAMBAL DACOITS, PHOOLAN DEVI'S STORY IS possibly the most poignant. Not merely owing to her violent end, but also because of the way fate had crammed so much into her short 37 years – a dizzying roller coaster of struggle, notoriety and fame – that it seemed as if she had been born to be a template for life's unpredictability. But the durability she was denied by life, death has restored to an extent. The dacoit-turned-parliamentarian is remembered even today as someone with an extraordinary crowd-pulling ability and an appeal that still endures, especially among the socially weaker sections of society.

'Phoolan's inimitable and unmatched spirit endures. She continues to be a Bahujan feminist icon and an inspiration to countless young people,' Anusha Chaitanya, a Dalit author, writes about her.[94]

No wonder then, two decades after her murder, Phoolan Devi's political legacy continues to be an electoral issue in Uttar Pradesh, where Assembly polls are due in 2022.

Phoolan Devi's continuing appeal was evident when idols of the outlaw-turned-lawmaker were desecrated in July 2021 in the eastern Uttar Pradesh. In some of these cases, police and officials in the BJP-ruled heartland state confiscated the idols before they could be installed. The Vikassheel Insaan Party, an influential caste-based party in Uttar Pradesh and Bihar, had announced that it would distribute 50,000 statues of Phoolan Devi all over eastern UP. Mukesh Sahani, who heads the Vikassheel Insaan Party, had said the statues would keep the 'ideology of Phoolan' alive among the masses. Sahani also promised to distribute five lakh lockets with Phoolan Devi's picture among women from her oppressed Mallah community (of boatmen), made up largely of people belonging to the Bind caste and Nishads (a group whose name is often considered to be synonymous with the Mallah community).

But before we go into Phoolan Devi's legacy, it is important to rewind to her early days in order to fully appreciate it. She was born on 10 August 1963, into a poor boatman's family in Gurha ka Purwa, a small village in Bhognipur tehsil, Kanpur Dehat district, Uttar Pradesh, on the banks of the Yamuna river. The family, socially underprivileged and with no land they could call their own, lived in a mud house.

Phoolan Devi's story traces the similar trajectory as many other women dacoits – Putli, Bijli, Kuntala, Sheela, Kamla, Maya, Ketaki, Haseena Begum, Kapoori, Bachchi and Kusuma Nain, to name a few; at least the initial years of her life fall into that pattern: a broken home, kidnapped when still a teen, and sexually abused and exploited, which then leads to a wayward existence. Eventually, Phoolan Devi too would become the leader of a gang of bandits. Where her story deviates from the others', the storyline still remains predictable – jail, encounter and ignominious end. But Phoolan Devi would have a fling with stardom. This spunky, real-life heroine and her story were fascinating enough for a film to be made on her, the Shekhar Kapur-directed *Bandit Queen*.

But even her most optimistic supporter would've balked at the idea that such a turn, however transient it may have been, was possible when her father, Devidin Mallah, married her off at the tender age of 13 – reportedly exchanging her for a bicycle and a cow. In academic John Arquilla's seminal work, *Insurgents, Raiders and Bandits*, where Phoolan Devi features as the only woman in it, the author records that she was married off to a man thrice her age, Puttilal Mallah, who sexually and physically assaulted her.[95] Phoolan Devi would eventually escape the abusive marriage and join a gang of dacoits, rising to popularity as someone who fought for the interests of the oppressed castes, as a vigilante justice-giver.[96]

Phoolan Devi herself had a simple explanation as to why she chose to become a dacoit. '*Kismet ko yehi manzoor tha* (It was the dictate of fate),' she wrote in her autobiography.[97] Years later, she would also repeat the words on several occassions in the corridors of the Parliament during her first stint as an MP between 1996 and 1998.

The escape from marriage would not end her ordeal, though. After allegations of theft by a relative, she was taken into police custody – where once again she was subjected to physical abuse. In her autobiography, published in 2006 after her death, Phoolan Devi has alleged that some time after this, a dacoit, from a gang she had befriended, called Babu Gujjar raped and brutalized her. Gujjar was reportedly killed by his second-in-command, Vikram Mallah, who belonged to Phoolan's caste. She then switched loyalties and became Mallah's mistress. For the next twelve months or so, the gang carried out a series of robberies, kidnappings and murders in the Chambal region spread over 8,000 square kilometres across Uttar Pradesh and Madhya Pradesh. Perhaps, for the first time in her life, she felt happy and liberated.[98]

The bliss, unfortunately, did not last long.

Vikram was shot dead by two dreaded dacoit brothers, Lalaram and Sriram; they were upper-caste members of her gang who had been away in jail when Gujjar was killed. What followed was weeks of terrible torture for Phoolan Devi. Journalist Tarun Kumar Bhaduri – actress Jaya Bachchan's father, and author of *Abhishapta Chambal* (The Cursed Chambal) and *Off the Record* – has claimed that Lalaram and Sriram, both Rajputs, had been planted in Vikram Mallah's gang by Uttar Pradesh police. 'When Vikram was dozing off after a rather heavy lunch, Sriram killed him at a point-blank range. Not only this, they dragged Phoolan to Behmai village and made her to draw water from a well for three days continuously and at the night, she was raped repeatedly,' Bhaduri says in *Off the Record*.[99] In a final indignity, they paraded her naked around the upper caste-dominated village in Kanpur.

Phoolan Devi escaped after three weeks of captivity and formed a new gang. On 14 February 1981, she returned to Behmai to avenge Vikram's death and her own humiliation. She was informed that Lalaram and Sriram were in the village, but the brothers had been tipped off and escaped before she could reach the village. Phoolan Devi's wrath was now directed at the Thakur community in the village that had silently witnessed her humiliation. She shot dead 22 men, all Rajputs, in a murderous frenzy that the western media dubbed the St Valentine's Day Massacre.

Luke Harding of *The Guardian* would write a graphic account of the episode:

> Several months later, she came back to Behmai. Dressed this time in a khaki coat, blue jeans and wearing bright lipstick. A Sten gun hung from her shoulder, and in her hand she carried a battery-powered megaphone. Devi called all the villagers out and asked them to hand over Sri Ram and Lala Ram. 'If you don't hand them over to me, I will stick my gun into your butts and tear them apart. This is Phoolan Devi speaking. Jai Durga Mata [Victory to Durga, the Mother Goddess],' she is alleged to have said. The two men could not be found. And so Devi rounded up all the

young men in the village and stood them in a line before
a well. They were then marched in single file to the river.
At a green embankment they were ordered to kneel. There
was a burst of gunfire and 22 men lay dead.[100]

The massacre would have huge repercussions. Uttar Pradesh chief
minister (and future prime minister), Vishwanath Pratap Singh, who
had promised to eliminate criminal gangs from the state, resigned
after declaring himself a failure.

Tool of Oppression

The indignities Phoolan Devi was subjected to was merely the
continuation of a form of tyranny that has existed down the ages.
Rape has been, and continues to be, a tool to oppress and exploit
the power skew between genders and communities. For centuries,
caste and gender have been two major forms of discrimination. In
her 2004 study, academic T. Orchard has observed how women
from lower castes, especially Dalit castes, are regularly raped by men
belonging to higher castes to reinforce their power and authority.
She describes how in many Indian villages, women from the socially
weaker castes are often forced to have intercourse with high-caste
men to settle debts and disputes.[101]

Earlier, in their 1987 study, researchers J. Hanmer and M.
Maynard too had said something similar: 'Violence has always been
a commonly used tool to keep an oppressed group under terror and
rape is perhaps the ultimate form of violent expression of both class
and patriarchal oppression.'[102]

It is a great injustice that Phoolan Devi's life and image have
been highly sexualized. In a report in the *Atlantic* magazine, Mary
Anne Weaver, for instance, quoted a police inspector as saying,
'For every man this girl [Phoolan Devi] has killed, she has slept
with two. Sometimes she sleeps with them first, before she bumps

them off.'[103] This story appeared in November 1996 when Phoolan Devi had become the Lok Sabha MP of the Samajwadi Party from Bhadohi, Uttar Pradesh.

Although the torture and indignities are condemnable, they made her mentally strong. She became scheming, too, and would wait before exacting revenge. For about five years, between 1978 and 1983, Phoolan Devi's reign of terror was marked by bloodshed, cruelty and even a streak of perversity. After the Behmai massacre she became a well-known dacoit and was wanted by the police of Uttar Pradesh and Madhya Pradesh. But hot on her heels, she managed to escape the dragnet every time.

Bhaduri says that during this period, Phoolan Devi wanted to attain motherhood. He writes, 'She took one paramour after another for this. Phoolan was totally dejected when finally she was told that she could not have one.'[104]

The journalist, who later witnessed Phoolan Devi's surrender in 1983, makes many telling observations about her in his writing. He says:

> Fleeing from the law, women dacoits are sometimes as deeply scarred by events as the wounds they inflict on their victims. V.P. Singh's counterpart in Madhya Pradesh was chief minister Arjun Singh, a politician among politicians. Arjun, who had made a strong bid to become the Prime Minister in the mid-1990s, was always keen to project himself as a messiah of the downtrodden. As chief minister of Madhya Pradesh thrice, he had tried changing the fate of lakhs of slum-dwellers in Bhopal and other parts of the state, giving them a 'patta', or ownership right, to the land they had encroached upon. He was a champion of the cause of the minorities, Dalits and backward castes, just to gloss over his upper caste, feudal background.[105]

Public Surrender

By the latter half of 1982, Phoolan Devi had 48 criminal cases against her, including countless murders, plunder and arson as well as kidnapping for ransom. Arjun Singh is said to have summoned Rajendra Chaturvedi, superintendent of police, Bhind, and given the officer a mission – to ensure Phoolan Devi's surrender in exchange for amnesty. Chaturvedi embarked on his assignment by trying to reach out to her through a slew of informers, and religious and community leaders. Finally, he had a breakthrough on 6 September 1982, when Phoolan Devi met Chaturvedi. The officer kept the meeting a secret and, bypassing the police hierarchy, directly informed the chief minister.

Many years later, in 2001, Ambreen Ali Shah of the *Telegraph* interviewed Chaturvedi where they spoke about his secret mission. Chaturvedi's memory of meeting Phoolan Devi was still vivid. 'I started getting feelers through the villagers sometime in July that she wanted to surrender. It took Phoolan and her men two months to decide,' he recalled. 'I was stopped at three different points by Phoolan's men and had to give the code word "Teetar" [The grey francolin].'[106]

Phoolan Devi had appeared before Chaturvedi, her face wrapped in a scarf. She placed ₹501 at Chaturvedi's feet as a sign of goodwill. She then offered him food and made rotis for him. In the conversation that followed, Phoolan Devi would betray a range of emotions, often turning belligerent, rude, defiant and weary. 'She was worried about her surrender and kept asking me *"Kya hone wala hai* (What's going to happen)"?' Chaturvedi told Ambreen. He said he had carried with him a Polaroid camera and a tape recorder. 'I took pictures of Phoolan... I showed them the Polaroid photograph because I was worried that they might think I was carrying some weapon. These were the first-ever pictures taken of her.'

The pictures would later find their way to the prime minister's residence, as Arjun Singh had asked Chaturvedi to fly to Delhi and meet Indira Gandhi. When Phoolan Devi's photographs were reportedly shown to Indira Gandhi, the prime minister had remarked: 'She is not very nice looking.'[107]

On 12 February 1983, Phoolan Devi surrendered. She was dressed in khaki trousers and shirt and had wrapped a bright red shawl around her, with a red bandanna on her head. She wore jungle boots. A .315 hung from her shoulder. Phoolan Devi then climbed the steps on to a stage and surrendered. Seven other members of her gang also laid down their arms.

In his brief speech, Arjun Singh claimed that Phoolan Devi's surrender was a result of continuous police pressure on Chambal dacoits. He gave her a solemn assurance that none would be killed in any police encounter or deceitfully.

'It is hard to believe looking at her slight short figure – she is under five feet in height – and her ravaged face that this is the woman who terrorised large sections of the population in two states,' columnist Sunil Sethi, who was present at the surrender at Bhind, would write for the *India Today* magazine. 'It is hard to imagine this scruffy, edgy, nervous girl as someone who toted a gun – her wrists seem too painfully thin to even carry one around.'[108]

Phoolan was later taken to the Gwalior jail where she would remain in custody for the next nine years. In 1992, she was shifted to Delhi's Tihar Jail. But destiny was not yet done with Phoolan; an unexpected turn of events would catapult her back into the national consciousness – this time, as a politician.

Political Career

If one politician had orchestrated Phoolan Devi's surrender, another politician and chief minister – Mulayam Singh Yadav of Uttar Pradesh – would hand her a ticket to Parliament, following her release on parole in 1994. Mulayam, who ordered the withdrawal of all criminal cases against Phoolan Devi, inducted her into his Samajwadi Party.

She was declared the party candidate for the Bhadohi parliamentary seat (near Mirzapur) in the 1996 general election. As a correspondent then, this author remembers large numbers of people, mostly women, walking miles on foot, just to get a glimpse of her or hear her speak. At these gatherings, Phoolan Devi had the courage and strength to narrate her ordeal for the masses. It was a common sight to see many in the crowd weeping as she recounted those moments of trauma.

As a politician, Phoolan Devi tasted both success and defeat. She won in 1996, but lost in 1998 when the fall of the United Front government forced early elections on the country. The former bandit queen was, however, back in action in 1999 when she got elected to the 13th Lok Sabha.

Her political life seemed well settled during these years; every morning, she could be spotted at her 44 Ashoka Road residence in New Delhi meeting hordes of political workers, calling up ministers requesting them to expedite work and making requests to get things in order – seeking confirmation of a railway reservation, allotment of a telephone or a domestic cooking gas connection.

On 25 July 2001, the monsoon session of Parliament was in progress when Phoolan Devi returned home for lunch and siesta. It all happened in a flash; around 1.30 p.m., three assailants pumped nine bullets into her the moment she got off her car and started walking towards her residential quarter. The killers were masked, carrying two revolvers and a Webley Scott pistol. She died on the spot, even though her body was rushed to the nearby Dr Ram Manohar Lohia hospital where she was officially declared 'brought dead.'

Destiny had intervened again, in a manner as violent and unpredictable as her life had been when she roamed through the ravines with her gang of bandits. Newspaper reports wrote that the three assailants fled in a green Maruti 800 (CIM 907), which had been kept revving nearby with the help of an accomplice.

Her body was cremated at the Chaube Ghat on the banks of the Ganga in Mirzapur, her parliamentary constituency. She was a few weeks short of her 38th birthday when she died.

Two days after her assassination, Sher Singh Rana surrendered to police and confessed to the killing; he said that he had wanted to avenge the 1981 Behmai massacre in which the then bandit queen killed 22 persons belonging to Thakur community. The progress of the investigation of the murder was so tardy that the accused was convicted for life only in 2014. In 2004, Rana had even escaped from Tihar Jail, but he was re-arrested at Calcutta in 2006.

Muskmelon in a Limousine

Any account of Phoolan Devi's life will be incomplete without a mention of her trip to Paris; in hindsight one recognizes this was yet another beguiling episode in her journey from a village mud house to Parliament – before the bloody epilogue of her untimely death. Vijay Kranti, a senior journalist and chairman of the Centre for Himalayan Asia Studies and Engagement (CHASE), accompanied her on that trip to the French capital. Kranti had plenty of opportunities to interact with Phoolan Devi after a French publisher M/S FIXOT, which brought out her autobiography, hired him as an interpreter. More than the money, he says, it was the opportunity of meeting Phoolan Devi that made him accept the assignment, which involved interviewing her and translating the interview into English for the team of French writers in Paris. The project continued for two years. 'The journey was punctuated with some of the most tense, hilarious, educative and challenging events that I've ever witnessed as a journalist over the past half a century,' Kranti would write later, adding that his 'most interesting memories and peeps into the mindscape of Phoolan relate to her Paris trip. The publisher wanted me to accompany her to Paris as he could not afford any surprises.'[109]

Kranti recalls that he got a glimpse of Phoolan Devi's 'influence and international popularity' in Chanakyapuri, Delhi, itself. He says:

After collecting our passports and Schengen visas from
the German embassy, I arrived at the gates of the Swedish
embassy to submit our applications. We had plans to fly
the next morning but it was already far beyond the closing
time and the guard initially tried to dispose me of (sic) with
the contempt that is [a] signature of the embassies in the
diplomatic enclave. But the moment I told him that it was
Phoolan Devi's visa application, he called up the visa officer
who showed more enthusiasm and alacrity than the guard
and instructed him to invite me inside. The visas were
stamped within an hour.[110]

For Kranti, 'the real fun' began in Paris, though, when a shiny,
black six-door Mercedes limousine with a handsome young French
chauffeur showed up to take Phoolan Devi and him around the
city. He recollects:

Phoolan tried her hands on everything that was different
from my Maruti 800 back in India. The most exciting
object was the satellite phone. She persuaded the chauffeur
to connect her to Munni, her darling youngest sister in
Delhi. For most of the time the two sisters discussed the
limousine.[111]

Phoolan then discovered a roadside fruit shop with muskmelons
on display. 'Excited like a child, she commanded the chauffeur to
stop the car and bring a muskmelon to her...,' Kranti says.[112]

The young Frenchman must have thought his quota of surprises
was over for the day by this point. But what followed next would
leave him speechless. 'Perhaps for the first time ever in his career,
he was watching his guest squatting on the leather upholstery of his
delicate limousine. She was chopping off pieces of the melon with
his Swiss knife, while drops of the juice were oozing out on the seat
and the floor,' Kranti would write.[113] But Phoolan Devi persisted:

With the speed of a commando, he took out a nice looking towel from somewhere in the dashboard and spread it out in front of her to put it under the melon. But like an affectionate Indian housewife, Phoolan started resisting by saying, *'Arey Bhaiya, iski zaroorat nahin hai. Hum kharbooza aise hi khaate hain apne des mein* (Brother, I don't need a towel. In India this is how we eat muskmelon, barehanded).'[114]

The French chauffeur wouldn't be the only one to be surprised by Phoolan Devi's unconventional manner. By the time she wrapped up her visit to the city, Phoolan had left many others reeling in shock.

One of the places Phoolan Devi was taken to during the tour of the city was the Sacré-Coeur Basilica, a minor Roman Catholic basilica. Kranti describes her visit as follows:

It's a beautiful white cathedral on a hilltop and is visible from many parts of the city. Inside the cathedral, one of our hosts bought wax candles for Phoolan and all of us to light and offer on a stand near the altar. Dozens of candles, offered by other devotees, were already presenting a beautiful and soothing image of a pyramid of flickering lights. While all of us found a vacant place for our respective candles, Phoolan had her sight at the pinnacle where a solitary candle stood lighted already. Quietly she raised her right hand, picked up the candle, threw it to the ground and planted her own candle in its place. It was a sight to behold, with dozens of eyes popping up in shock.[115]

To Kranti, it was yet another reflection of a bandit leader who would never tolerate anyone occupying the centre of power in her presence.

NAMDEO DHASAL
(1949–2014)

I've often said that all poetry is political. This is because real
poems deal with a human response to reality and politics is part of
reality, history in the making. Even if a poet writes about sitting in
a glass house drinking tea, it reflects politics.

—Yehuda Amichai

NAMDEO DHASAL'S MEDIUM OF EXPRESSION TOO WAS POETRY: RAGING,
unconventional and hard-hitting. He was also a scholar, reformist
and political activist, and believed in the power of the written word
in bringing about social change. He tried to bring change through
his poetry, writings and street activism as he drew youth to the Dalit
movement he spearheaded in the seventies.

His life was a story of struggle against odds – a challenging cocktail
of a rough childhood, grinding poverty, alcoholism and debilitating
diseases, including myasthenia gravis, a neuromuscular disorder,
and cancer. Yet in the few decades after the country's Independence,
he remained focused on lofty issues of freedom, democracy and
modernity's meaning for ordinary Indians, particularly socially
downtrodden Dalits.

Dhasal was not a success as a politician, in the sense of becoming
an elected representative. He never won an election. He would
also lay himself open to criticism with some of his experiments and
compromises. They were driven by his lack of political tact, his
ideology and sense of idealism more than anything else. Take for
instance, his decision to split the group he had founded, his praise of
Indira Gandhi – both in his poetry and actions, and his later attempts
to forge an alliance with Balasaheb Thackeray's Shiv Sena, an outfit
he had detested and resisted all along. But no one can take away

from him his lasting legacy: the voice he succeeded in providing to the problems of the poor and the oppressed.

Many critics and observers have sought to interpret Dhasal's artistic and political vision, including the contradictions and complexities they sometimes threw up. But perhaps the most accurate assessment would come from the man himself. Dhasal said he was committed to expressing 'whatever contradictions are there in my political act and in my literary act with all their complexities and agonies'.[116]

Political Influences

Dhasal was deeply influenced by the Black Panther Party in the United States, whose charter ranged from patrolling African American neighbourhoods and protecting black residents from acts of police brutality and discrimination to seeking compensation for centuries of exploitation by white Americans. Just as the Black Panther Party developed into a Marxist revolutionary group, Dhasal's Dalit Panther Movement, launched in June 1972 in the slums of Mumbai, was inspired by Karl Marx and Dr Bhimrao Ambedkar. Poet-activists J.V. Pawar, Raja Dhale and Arjun Dangle were some of the other founder members of the Dalit Panthers Movement. Pawar had even named his daughter Angela after Angela Davis, a notable Black Panther activist.

The Black Panther Party, in turn, acknowledged and supported the Dalit Panthers through the Black Panther newspaper, which was circulated worldwide on a weekly basis from 1967 to 1980.

The Dalit Panther Movement also owed its rise to the circumstances arising after the death of Dr B.R. Ambedkar, a prominent Dalit icon, Union minister and chairman of the committee for drafting the Indian Constitution. Ambedkar, who had converted to Buddhism shortly before his death, was successful in getting a quota of parliamentary and Assembly seats for Dalits, but the social condition of Dalits continued to be poor, relegated to performing menial or degrading jobs such as removing human waste and dead animals or sweeping streets – jobs that the so-called upper castes wouldn't do.[117]

After Ambedkar's death in 1956, his Republican Party of India was in a shambles. Several self-proclaimed Dalit leaders had joined hands with forces Ambedkar had opposed in a bid to stay politically relevant. By 1966, a new outfit, the Shiv Sena, known then for its aggression, unruly behaviour and violent campaigns against south Indians, communists, Muslims, Biharis and north Indian residents, had emerged in Maharashtra.

Ambedkarites, uncomfortable with the hawkish Hindu cultural and political rhetoric, desperately looked for a platform to raise their voices for equality and freedom. Between 1959 and 1964, a large land-rights movement led by Dadasaheb Gaikwad, who was associated with the Left in Maharashtra, conducted agitations in Marathwada and Khandesh. Over one lakh people were reportedly sent to jail. In the late sixties, Maharashtra chief minister Y.B. Chavan was forced to extend reservation benefits to converted Buddhists too.

Between 1972 and 1977, the Dalit Panthers carved out a niche for themselves, imparting self-defence skills to physically counter atrocities against the community. They organized boycotts of civic and Assembly elections, held demonstrations against the ruling Congress and even attacked some temples to protest against caste-based oppression.

There was a huge furore in 1972 when the Dalit Panthers called for a boycott of that year's Independence Day celebrations. Dhasal dubbed it a 'Black Independence Day' in protest against two incidents. In the first incident, a Dalit woman had been paraded naked in Pune district and, in the second, the eyes of two Dalit men were gouged out in Dhakali village in Akola district.

Dhasal's comrade-in-arms Dhale wrote an essay in *Sadhana*, the Dalit Panthers' official mouthpiece published from Pune, titled 'Tirangaa' (The tricolour, Indian national flag), provocatively asserting, 'If it [the flag] couldn't protect a Dalit woman's dignity, it was only a rag,'[118] Dhale faced a defamation case while the Dalit Panthers gained wide publicity.

The Panthers would go to villages where incidents of atrocities had been reported and hold protests, developing pockets of influence in Mumbai's Matunga Labour Camp, Naigaon-Dadar, Chembur, Ghatkopar, Sewri, Parel and Worli. In 1973, the Dalit Panthers came up with a charter fraternizing Marxist thinking with Buddhism, identifying landlords, capitalists, moneylenders and the government as the enemies of Dalits. It was named *Zahirnama* (evidence of facts). The scope of the term Dalit was widened to include other oppressed peoples such as the so-called Scheduled Castes, neo-Buddhists, landless and poor peasants, and exploited women. Poetry was a powerful tool of the Dalit Panther campaign. Dhasal and fellow poet-activist Pawar's poems were recited at every Dalit Panther gathering, highlighting their struggle, agonies and hopes. Within months, over 30 units of the organization had sprung up in various parts of the city. When street protests were held, these units would hold sessions to recite poetry and read short stories.

Ideological Differences

While the movement was picking up pace, Dhasal and Dhale began having differences. The conflict was over ideology: the fusion of Marxism and Buddhism versus a strictly Buddhist identity. There were external pressures too on account of intense police surveillance and Indira Gandhi's dreaded Emergency, which came into force in June 1975. On 7 March 1977, Dhasal and Pawar announced the dissolution of the Dalit Panthers as a result of the infighting and political repression. For Dhasal, Ambedkarism and Marxism were ideologically compatible. He believed that a combination of Ambedkarite ideology and Marxism would help the Dalit cause and give the movement a cultural identity. But some of his colleagues felt that the category of caste could not be reduced to class. Some Ambedkarites of that era also did not accept the contention that

Buddhism could serve as the proverbial 'opium of the masses'. It was around this time that Dhasal wrote his poem 'Priyadarshini', praising Indira.

Shortly after the dissolution of the Dalit Panthers, around the time the Emergency ended in March 1977, some leaders formed the Bharatiya Dalit Panthers (BDP); Dhasal was not part of this group. BDP spread across India to nearly 20 states and was most active near the India–Nepal border and in Tamil Nadu. In Tamil Nadu, the party came to be known as the DPI (Dalit Panthers of India or the Dalit Panthers Iyyakkam), now the major Dalit political outfit in the southern state is known as Viduthalai Chiruthaigal Katchi (translation: Liberation Panther Party; abbr. VCK). The name Dalit Panther was taken up by others in many parts of Maharashtra and Karnataka too.

Those sympathetic to Dhasal say that his decision to lend support to Indira Gandhi during the Emergency stemmed from his need to get court cases against his party workers annulled. When the Emergency was imposed in June 1975, the Dhasal-led Dalit Panthers had vehemently opposed it but their method of protest, which often turned violent, proved costly. Close to 200 cases had piled up against Dalit Panthers leaders, including Dhasal. Incidentally, Shiv Sena boss, Balasaheb Thackeray, too had supported the Emergency. It was said that Thackeray had backed Indira Gandhi's dictatorship just to avoid arrest and jail.

Later Dhasal also drew flak for his attempts to forge an alliance with the Sena. In Dhasal's scheme of things, an alliance with the Sena could help Dalits enter mainstream politics. But the move backfired and the Sena too went back on its promise to give him an election ticket in the state polls.

Life and Art

The young Dhasal's days were spent in the company of petty thieves, gangsters, pimps, sex workers, drug peddlers and addicts, and *hafta-*

fleecing cops. In the process, Dhasal had begun to see life through these prisms; that familiarity was reflected in his writings. 'I was born/on footpath/when the Sun was leaked/and being dimmed/ into the bosom of night,' he would write while giving an account of his life.

Dhasal grew up in grinding poverty and never finished school, but his self-education was impressive. He could not go to college but enthusiastically read everything he could get hold of, even while trying to make a living as a taxi driver – he would often read between long waits and halts. He once described a part of his life in these words:

> I boozed. I visited brothels. I went to mujra dancing women's establishments and to houses of ordinary prostitutes. The whole ambience and the ethos of it was the revelation of a tremendous form of life. It was life! Then I threw all rule books out. No longer the rules of prosody for me. My poetry was as free as I was. I wrote what I felt like writing and how I felt like writing.[119]

Dhasal's father, Lakshman Dhasal, had come to Mumbai from his native Pur-Kanersar village in Khed *taluk*. Like many migrants, the Dhasals' first place of rest was in the metropolis's Golpitha, on the periphery of the Kamatipura red light district where his father worked with a butcher. Dhasal would later name his first, and perhaps his most celebrated, poetry collection *Golpitha*.

The influence of his younger days' surroundings is most visible in *Golpitha*, which was published in 1971, earning him the prestigious Soviet Land Nehru Award. *Golpitha* belongs to the tradition of modern urban poetry and brings a flair reminiscent of '*Les Fleurs du Mal*' (The Flowers of Evil), Charles Baudelaire's masterpiece where the French poet discards conventional distinctions to represent the modern man's moral complexity. Much like Baudelaire's poems in the volume had dealt with decadence as he sought beauty in the perverse, Dhasal too would use a different kind of expression – raw, wrenching and compelling, an idiom that would hold up before the downtrodden the language of their struggle.

According to poet Dilip Chitre, Dhasal's biographer, the poet-activist embraced people supposedly discarded by society as useless. In *Namdeo Dhasal: Poet of the Underworld*, Chitre repeatedly notes that Dhasal's poetry talks about pimps, criminals, prostitutes, street urchins, gangsters, mujra dancers and labourers, based upon his personal observations.[120]

Sachin Ketkar, a bilingual writer, translator, editor, critic and professor of English at M.S. University of Baroda, says that what differentiated Dhasal from other Dalit writers was his radically innovative use of language. At times, though, such was the complex use of what Chitre called *bibhatsa rasa*, or 'bastard language', that Dhasal's poetry was barely accessible to either an average Dalit listener or a highly literate reader. 'The surrealistic imagery and flow of his poems and his sudden but deliberate evocation of extension or orchestration of different contexts of experience baffled both the uninitiated and the literate among his audience,' Ketkar says.[121]

Take, for instance, Dhasal's poem 'Approaching the Organised Harem of the Octopus', which dwells upon the dominance of Brahmanism, Buddhism and the emergence of the Dalit Panthers:

> We are approaching the organised harem of the octopus
> I am the seal bearing the image of the bull dated March '65
> My properties are Mohenjodaro
> I am the one who drew the head on the lion pillar
> My ornamental daily weather
> Radiates from the feet
> From hand-to-hand, I release my catacombs
> Go scatter curds milk butter in the courtyard
> Organised harems of the octopus are approaching us...[122]

While the poem evokes powerful disturbing images, it can baffle too.

When Marathi poets Satish Kalsekar and Pradnya Lokhande interviewed Dhasal for the Marathi literary journal *Anushtubh* in 1997, the poet-activist insisted that he did not differentiate between political poetry and non-political poetry. Citing the example of his poem *'Moorkha Mhataryane Dinga Halavile'* ('The Stupid Old Man Moved Mountains'), he said:

I have been criticised by many. Whenever I find the time I read what my critics write. However, it does not affect me, I understand from the criticism that the literary establishment, such as this, finds unacceptable only poetry that deals with the political and social processes of our life. Our times are such that we have to move on, leaving the establishment in its own fix. [...] I have been criticised and the critics say Namdeo Dhasal is a political propagandist poet. I do not think so. That collection has poems on one's beloved own wife, one's aunt, anyone's mother. They capture the spirit of a period and I am happy I could write poems of this kind as well.[123]

Asked about the poem he wrote praising Indira Gandhi, he said,

Every word in that poem bears the weight of responsibility. I am a committed person and I am constantly involved in political activity. However, during these activities, I write poems too. On the other hand, if I read a book like [on] Dialectic[al] Materialism, I enjoy it as though it were a poem. Others become serious when they read such a book. They are stunned I am inspired to write a poem.[124]

In the early 1960s and 1970s, a section of Marathi literature saw non-conformist, urban, sexually explicit and politically charged writing practices. B.S. Mardhekar, for instance, did something similar to what Baudelaire had over a century ago, highlighting a decadent urban ethos in Marathi poetry. Dhasal's poems embodied this asymmetry of the core and the periphery – the 'us' and 'them', the 'ours' and 'theirs' – and questioned the nature of the Marathi world to which Dalits had been relegated. His poems questioned the givenness of this cultural memory and attacked the oppressiveness, exclusivity and cruelty of the *savarna* (upper caste) structure, or what Dhasal used to call the culture of 'three and half percent of the population'.[125]

'My commitment is that I will express whatever contradictions are there in my political act and in my literary act with all their complexities and agonies. Earlier, the structure of poetry was equal to feelings plus imagination and composition. Academic people used to think like that,' Dhasal would say while discussing his artistic and political vision in 1998.[126] But poetry, he added, is also about contradictions.

> Poetry is reaching out into the 10,000 contradictions in the story of what is called the 10,000-year-old human civilisation and the life of a person who carries it. That is how I define poetry. Hence I am extremely free, with no burden, no conventions. From this point of view I let others say whatever they like about my 'isms' and traditions, but I have this honest opinion about Dalit literature. You should go beyond the narrow concept. The term 'Dalit' is a synonym for proletarian. What a vast world you can access with this kind of vision![127]

Marathi playwright and critic Vijay Tendulkar compared Dhasal with Tukaram, the famous Bhakti saint-poet of Maharashtra.[128]

According to author Sudhir Arora, Dhasal's poetry waged a war against all kinds of exploitation. In an article titled 'Voicing Dalits: The Poetry of Namdeo Dhasal', Arora wrote that through his poetry

Dhasal had launched 'from the very start – single-handedly – a guerrilla war against the effete middle-class and sanitized world of his literary readers'.[129]

In one of his poems, Dhasal describes how a caste-ridden and male dominated society had impacted his mother, turning her into 'machinery for the production of worms'. The poet in him sought to dub it as some sort of 'spiritual butchery' at the hands of a bigoted society and addressed her saying, 'Just as I have been stripped bare, so have you.'[130]

To some, this form of identification with his mother gave his misery an erratic edge. In the poem, he went on to ask her, 'On the day you cut my umbilical cord, why didn't you slash my throat with your fingernail?' He then proceeded to rail at her further: 'You didn't even moo once from the depths/You didn't stir the sky with a shrill cry/The earth didn't crack/How easily you lived, wrapped in rhinoceros hide.'[131]

Personal Life

Dhasal's life was a bundle of contradictions. In her autobiography titled *I Want to Destroy Myself: A Memoir*, Dhasal's wife Malika Amar Sheikh added another chapter to the poet's sufferings. She documented both her love and loathing for Dhasal, who was an alcoholic and cheated on her. Ably translated from Marathi into English by Jerry Pinto, Sheikh's story is a powerful account of a woman torn between the personal and the political, one who was abused and beaten by a man who claimed to be a revolutionary and a champion of the downtrodden. Sheikh, however, never left or abandoned Dhasal.

Theirs was a love marriage that defied the barriers of religion. Her father, Shahir Amar Sheikh, was one of Maharashtra's leading Left intellectuals and revolutionaries, a full-timer with the Communist Party of India and the founder of its art wing, Laalbavta Kalapathak.

Unlike Dhasal, Malika Sheikh grew up in the better surroundings of south Mumbai at their Saat Rasta residence.

Sheikh met Dhasal when she was 19. By her own admission, she found the poet to be handsome and charismatic. She recorded her fascination with him in her memoirs, adding how, after a brief courtship, the two got married:

> His worldview appealed to me. He was also a Marxist and, at that time, I had a notion, probably inherited from my father, that Marxist poets are good human beings. Breaking the norms set by convention, his poetry tore into and shattered you. It spoke of and for the downtrodden, the outcast living on the fringes of the society. There was idealism and hope in his writings as well as his politics.[132]

The newly-weds would often spend the night reading Walt Whitman and Sadanand Rege to each other. She wrote about this period:

> 'We shared our poetry with each other. We were each other's first audience,' Sheikh told an interviewer, recalling that even when Dhasal was hospitalized, be it at 2 at night or 6 in the morning, she would read some poetry to him. And then he would, sometimes, break into a laugh and sometimes just nod in approval.[133]

Dhasal's political life and responsibilities meant an endless stream of visitors and party workers to their house, which left her very little time with her husband. The constant pressure of playing host and cooking left her exhausted. They were also broke. As Dhasal's drinking went out of hand, their arguments and fights took a violent turn. They grew apart after their son Ashutosh was born. In the book she admits with a hint of regret that motherhood was a role she took on reluctantly, and that she felt that it only held her back as she attempted to leave Dhasal to focus on films, theatre, dance and music.

Accepting infidelity in their married life was tough on Sheikh. She was ashamed and disappointed to have 'lost my Namdeo'. She was also pained to note that Dhasal was oblivious of her feelings. 'He was changing, drifting away and there was nothing I could do to stop it. I had loved his companionship but he felt no need for me now,' she wrote.[134]

In Sheikh's assessment, Dhasal was not a politician by nature. Sheikh told an interviewer:

He was an honest social worker. He really wanted to better society. He was extremely passionate and bright but he wasn't vulpine. Politics is not for the gullible. I don't like politics. In fact, I resent politicians – they don't let social workers be. Probably, that's why the revolution isn't alive any more. All that is alive are questions, several unanswered questions.[135]

Sheikh did not leave Dhasal; instead, she chose to stay with him right till the end, taking care of him as diseases took over his body. He was diagnosed with myasthenia gravis in 1981. 'Which woman wants her family to disintegrate?' she asks. 'I was committed to him. How could I have left him in his days of sickness? And then there was Ashu. When a woman is faced with a mother, the latter always stands taller.'

The last six months of the poet's life were spent in hospitals. After a long and debilitating battle with colon cancer, Dhasal died in Mumbai at the age of 64 on 15 January 2014.

Awards and Recognition

Dhasal was awarded the Padma Shri in 1999 for his achievements in Marathi literature. He was conferred with the Maharashtra State

Award for literature four times – in 1973, 1974, 1982 and 1983. The Sahitya Akademi presented him with the Golden Lifetime Achievement Award in 2004.

R.K. DHAWAN
(1937–2018)

Parastish ki yahan tak ki ae but tujhe,
Nazar mein sabhon ki khuda kar chale.

(I have venerated you so much so
I have you in men's eyes, God!)

—Meer Taqi Meer

A FEW YEARS AGO, CONGRESS PRESIDENT SONIA GANDHI WAS AT A meeting with senior party leader at 10 Janpath when she suddenly turned to R.K. Dhawan. 'So you are also writing a book?' she asked. Dhawan was speechless, and his book, an autobiographical account, was subsequently shelved.[136]

This was around the time when M.L. Fotedar, Natwar Singh, Salman Khurshid, Pranab Mukherjee, Margaret Alva and a host of other Congress leaders had written books and memoirs that had caused embarrassment to Sonia Gandhi and the party.

In October 2014, Dhawan had gone public saying he was 'inclined' to write a book that would 'reveal a lot' about former prime minister

Indira Gandhi and her son Rajiv Gandhi. Dhawan had told Ritu Sarin of the *Indian Express*:

> My book will not be like that of Natwar Singh, which says
> nothing. It will reveal a lot. This is because I strongly feel
> a leader should not appoint any friends or relatives to posts
> like that of a minister. This is the mistake Rajiv Gandhi
> made with the likes of Arun Nehru, Arun Singh and M.L.
> Fotedar, all of whom poisoned him against me.[137]

Dhawan, addressed as R.K.D. in party circles, was a curious mix of a die-hard Nehru–Gandhi family loyalist, gatekeeper and an executioner who installed and removed duly elected chief ministers of Congress-ruled states, almost at will. Such was his influence that he was referred to as 'Dhawan Saab' by even the rich and the powerful who wanted an audience with Indira Gandhi.

In the early 1970s, Dhawan, who was Indira Gandhi's stenotypist then, had shot to fame for being the prime minister's messenger. Gandhi used to avoid direct instructions to her ministers, chief ministers and state party heads; Dhawan was her conduit who conveyed unpleasant and often awkward decisions. The game plan was that if things went wrong, Dhawan would get the blame – an arrangement that placed great powers in his hands.

Dhawan is credited with spotting Sanjay Gandhi's political ambitions. The young man had just returned from Crewe after an internship at Rolls Royce when Dhawan, as Indira Gandhi's personal assistant, started introducing him to Congress bigwigs. He also advised some Congress leaders to praise him in Indira Gandhi's presence. Within months, Indira Gandhi was somewhat convinced of her son's political acumen and by the time the Emergency was imposed, Dhawan enjoyed the confidence of both mother and son.

Dhawan was responsible for setting up a special telephone line in Sanjay Gandhi's room at the prime minister's residence. Calls and instructions were issued for and on behalf of Sanjay Gandhi to many chief ministers of party-ruled states and, on most occasions, Indira Gandhi was not even aware of her son's growing unconstitutional clout.

Three days before the Emergency was imposed, Dhawan and Sanjay had managed to shunt out Union Home Secretary N.K. Mukherjee and replace him with S.L. Khurana, the chief secretary of Rajasthan then. A core team consisting of a junior home minister Om Mehta and Bansi Lal was in place to ensure that electricity supply to newspaper offices was cut off on the night of 25 June 1975 when the Emergency was declared.

Post-Emergency, however, Dhawan tried to distance himself from the excesses committed during the period. He told author Coomi Kapoor: 'The real culprit of the whole Emergency was S.S. Ray. Afterwards, he (Ray) tried to disown responsibility, and put the blame for everything on Indira in the Shah Commission.'[138]

Dhawan has been quoted by Kapoor in her book *The Emergency: A Personal History* as saying the following about the time of the Shah Commission hearings:

> Ray once went up to Indira and remarked, 'You are looking fit.' She replied coldly, 'You are doing your best to keep me fit.' She never spoke to him again. [...] Ray, like so many of those who were party to the Emergency excesses had, post-March 1977, tried to deny his involvement and pin the blame entirely on Sanjay and Mrs Gandhi.[139]

With the exception of Ambika Soni and Jagmohan, Dhawan was one of the last important players of the Emergency era. He always defended Indira Gandhi and blamed the likes of Siddhartha Shankar Ray and law minister H.R. Gokhale for 'misleading' Gandhi on the constitutional provisions of the Emergency to deal with internal disturbances.

Dhawan's influence on Indira Gandhi can be gauged from one episode when he made her offer *namaz*. Before the January 1980 general election, when Indira Gandhi was out of power, Dhawan would bring in a range of gurus, *maulvis*, *babas* and *munis* to provide some kind of solace to her. One such visitor was Maulana Jameel Ilyasi, a Mewati, who ran a mosque at New Delhi's Kasturba Gandhi Marg. Ilyasi, a glib talker, predicted a landslide victory for Indira Gandhi in the seventh Lok Sabha elections provided she allowed him access to her bedroom. The unusual demand was met with Dhawan's approval and Ilyasi tied a *ganda* (charm) to the ceiling, instructing her to summon him immediately after securing 350-plus parliamentary seats. The Indira Gandhi-led Congress won 353 seats in the elections.

After the victory, Indira Gandhi forgot about Ilyasi and his charm. On 23 June, her son Sanjay Gandhi died in a plane crash. Indira Gandhi was devastated. Ilyasi was soon back in Indira's court lamenting why he had not been allowed to remove the powerful charm that he claimed had produced an adverse impact on her life. The 'wrong', Ilyasi declared, had to be rectified immediately. Indira Gandhi, shaken and emotionally weak after the tragedy, conceded.

Ilyasi told her to pray to God and the physical drill he instructed her to follow was almost like offering *namaz*. When Indira Gandhi said she did not know how to offer *namaz*, Ilyasi told her to follow what he was doing; she obliged under the watchful eyes of Dhawan.[140]

Dhawan himself turned extremely religious when he was implicated by the Thakkar Commission of Inquiry in Indira Gandhi's assassination. Dhawan was a step behind her when two of her security guards – Beant Singh and Satwant Singh – sprayed her with bullets. One unauthorized version claimed that Beant, at the time of the shooting, had instructed Satwant, his junior, to ensure that Dhawan was not hurt. The report that was selectively leaked in the *Indian Express* pointed the needle of suspicion at Dhawan. Rajiv Gandhi, who was prime minister and the Congress president then, did not waste any time in removing Dhawan from all key posts and positions.

For about a couple of years when Dhawan was in the doghouse after this, he would visit the Hanuman temple at Baba Kharak Singh Marg, praying for divine blessings to help him establish his innocence. Then, one day, in 1988, Rajiv Gandhi summoned him. That was a time when the Bofors controversy and V.P Singh's rebellion had started to hit the prime minister hard. The exit of Arun Nehru had shattered Rajiv Gandhi politically, and Dhawan was back in favour and action. The gatekeeper's court was full again – with chief ministers of Congress-ruled states, Union ministers and state party heads.

Sonia Gandhi, who had seen Dhawan serve the family from close quarters, had reasons to be indebted to him. On 15 May 1999, when virtually everyone was getting restless to watch India's World Cup cricket open against South Africa in England, a CWC meeting was convened. The meeting was supposed to be brief because everyone was in a hurry to finalize the list of candidates for the Goa Assembly elections and then return to their television sets to watch the match. As the meeting started, Sharad Pawar smiled and P.A. Sangma stood up. The rebellion in the Congress had begun, signalled by Pawar and executed by Sangma with a swish of his razor-sharp tongue. Sonia Gandhi and the rest of her council were stunned.

As recounted by those present at the meeting, Sangma slowly built a case for how the BJP campaign against Sonia Gandhi's foreign origins was seeping down to even remote villages. Then came the unkindest cut. 'We know very little about you, about your parents,' Sangma had told her.[141] Those present at the meeting claim that Sonia Gandhi was shocked by Sangma's bluntness; Sangma had been drafted into the CWC as her nominee. 'When people ask us why the Congress has failed to get a qualified Indian among (India's) 980 million citizens as its prime ministerial candidate, we have no answer. I think they are right,' Sangma said.[142]

Pranab Mukherjee, Manmohan Singh, Jitendra Prasada, Madhavrao Scindia, Rajesh Pilot, Ahmed Patel, Ghulam Nabi Azad,

Arjun Singh, Ambika Soni and other 'loyalists' kept hearing Sangma out until Dhawan lost his cool. He rubbished Sangma's theory and said, '*Bhai*, you seem to be taking up the BJP–RSS agenda.' Seated next to the kingpin of the rebellion, Pawar, Dhawan told Sonia Gandhi: 'Madam, you are not alone in this battle. We are all with you.'[143] Congress insiders told this writer then that Dhawan's act of loyalty left a deep mark on Gandhi. She had kept wondering why the likes of Scindia, Mukherjee and Soni could not do what Dhawan had done – counter Sangma and ask him to shut up.

In his personal life, too, Dhawan was known for his loyalty. A confirmed bachelor till the age of 74, Dhawan married his long-term companion, 59-year-old Achla Mohan, in 2011. He and Achla had known each other since the 1970s. Achla had been previously married to a pilot and had moved to Canada but they divorced in 1990. To many in Congress circles, after her divorce, much before they got married, Dhawan and Achla were seen as a couple – always together at wedding receptions and social dos they attended.

Dhawan had revealed to journalist Sarin why he married Achla. Dhawan described how he arrived at the decision once when he had come down with a particularly severe bout of viral fever. Achla had been taking care of him but he had to be admitted to hospital. The hospital authorities insisted that a blood relative sign the necessary consent form. 'I felt very bad that she has taken so much care of me but could not sign the form,' Dhawan told the journalist.[144]

Like M.O. (Mac) Mathai, Yashpal Kapoor, M.L. Fotedar and Vincent George – all of whom rose from modest beginnings to a position of trust and influence, as retainers or personal assistants to the Nehru–Gandhi family – Dhawan too came to enjoy disproportionate power and prominence. There was nothing he could not do. In the Indira Gandhi era, he was the ultimate gatekeeper with powers to screen visitors and telephone calls, and often made decisions on the prime minister's behalf.

Extremely hardworking, Dhawan is said to have not taken a single day off from 1963 onwards when he was introduced, courtesy his uncle Kapoor, to the prime minister's residence where Indira Gandhi was the official hostess for her widower prime minister father, Jawaharlal Nehru. Veteran political journalist Janardhan Thakur quoted him as saying: 'I am with the prime minister (Indira Gandhi) since eight in the morning every single day to the time she retires (to bed), all the 365 days of the year... No casual leave, no earned leave, no holidays...'[145] This was perhaps also why Dhawan chose to marry at the age of 74 in October 2011. By then he had virtually retired from active politics, though he was still a permanent invitee to the CWC.

When many Opposition leaders were jailed during the 21 months the Emergency was in force, Dhawan was instrumental in getting some concessions for old and ailing leaders. No humanitarian consideration was, however, involved; those granted relief had to sign a paper that had a line written on it: *Hamein bees sutri karyakarmon par vishwas hai* (I/We have faith in the twenty-point programme). The twenty-point programme was Indira Gandhi's pet theme, ostensibly to accelerate the country's agricultural and industrial productivity. In political terms, accepting the programme was a euphemism for surrender before Indira Gandhi. Inside and outside Parliament, Dhawan would often threaten to make the list of such 'compromised' persons public. He had promised to share the list with this writer but destiny willed otherwise.

Dhawan died on 6 August 2018. He was 81.

SHEILA DIKSHIT
(1938–2019)

Kahein kya jo poochhe koi ham se ki Meer:
Jahan mein tum aaye they, kya kar chale.

(What will I say, O Meer, when they ask:
You came into this world, what did you do here?)

—Meer Taqi Meer

THE UNEXPECTED OFFER CAME SOMETIME IN 2012. HER BOSS HAD recommended her for the promotion that many would have given their right hand for. All she had to do was relocate by a few kilometres to a new office. No change of city required. Sheila Dikshit turned down the offer. She preferred Delhi's narrow lanes to North Block; she would rather be chief minister than the country's police boss.

Her decision did upset a few calculations for the Congress – perhaps even more in the long run – but Dikshit was like that. Unconventional and, needless to say, someone with a mind of her own.

Dikshit was a good organizer too. Not many would be aware that she was instrumental in setting up the Delhi chapter of the National Union of Students (NUS) in 1972. The NUS later emerged as the National Students' Union of India (NSUI), the student wing of the Indian National Congress. This was when Priya Ranjan Dasmunsi headed the Indian Youth Congress and Rangarajan Kumaramangalam was its general secretary. Young, able leaders were coming up across the country, powered by the party's history of struggle and freedom, and inspired by those who had helped shape a modern India. It was in this period of hope and change that Dikshit emerged – a spunky, convent-educated young woman impatient to make her mark.

Her critics might say she got a head start in politics because her father-in-law, Pandit Uma Shankar Dikshit, was a towering Congress leader who was close to Jawaharlal Nehru, Indira Gandhi and, later, Sanjay Gandhi. But nobody can deny that Dikshit converted that head start into marathon mileage: She went on to become the three-time chief minister of Delhi, re-elected each time without a break – the longest to have ruled the capital till now.

It was Rajiv Gandhi who gave Dikshit her break in parliamentary politics when in 1985 he chose her as minister of state in the Prime Minister's Office. Dikshit's victory from Kannauj, Uttar Pradesh, and her elevation as a minister did not go down well with a section of Congress leaders, but Rajiv Gandhi had faith in her.

After Rajiv Gandhi's assassination, P.V. Narasimha Rao became the Congress president and prime minister. But differences soon emerged between a section of the party and Rao. Dikshit was among the first to revolt against Rao, along with N.D. Tiwari, M.L. Fotedar, Arjun Singh, Natwar Singh, P. Shiv Shankar, Mohsina Kidwai, Kumaramangalam, Shiv Charan Mathur and others who formed the breakaway All India Indira Congress (Tiwari). Dikshit would often be seen rushing in and out of 10 Janpath in her second-hand blue Fiat with Natwar and Fotedar.

Revolt also brought with it a taste of something else not uncommon to the country's politics or that of the Congress: insults and whisper campaigns. In his column in a news magazine, Mani Shankar Aiyar had described Dikshit as a 'gangster's moll'.[146] It created a flutter.

Sheila suffered a setback in the 1996 general election when she lost to B.L. Sharma, 'Prem', of the BJP from Delhi (East). But her grit and determination had caught the eye of Sonia Gandhi, who had by then started taking a keen interest in Congress politics. When the latter took over as AICC chief, dethroning Sitaram Kesri, she pitched Sheila Dikshit as the Congress's chief ministerial face for the November 1998 Assembly elections in Delhi. The move faced strong resistance from Delhi Congress stalwarts such as H.K.L. Bhagat, Sajjan Kumar,

Jagdish Tytler, J.P. Aggarwal and others. But the 'outsider' Sheila Dikshit turned the tables on both the BJP and her Congress rivals. She went on to rule Delhi for the next fifteen years.

Dikshit's zeal for Delhi and state politics, however, prevented her from moving higher. In 2012, when Pranab Mukherjee became President, a big rejig was planned in the Union cabinet. Dikshit was reportedly Sonia Gandhi's choice to be home minister while the post of Delhi chief minister was offered to her arch-rival Ajay Maken. Dikshit refused. '*Kaun jaye Dilli ki galiayan chhor kar*? (Who can ever leave the narrow lanes of Delhi?)' she is purported to have said.[147]

Meanwhile, a powerful lobby within the Congress worked overtime to scupper her chances. Sushil Kumar Shinde was eventually brought in as home minister.

Even today, some Congress leaders rue her decision to stick to Delhi, where the party has been out of power for the past eight years. In their assessment, a change of guard in Delhi then would have helped the Congress stay in the hunt while Dikshit's elevation would have given the country a capable home minister.

The Congress lost the December 2013 elections in Delhi, Sheila Dikshit herself biting the dust, defeated by Aam Aadmi Party chief Arvind Kejriwal.

In March 2014, Dikshit moved to Kerala as governor, a few weeks short of her 76th birthday. She later expressed her desire to lead a life of retirement but her sense of loyalty to the party brought her back to Delhi and Uttar Pradesh politics where her career continued to slide.

A movie buff, Sheila Dikshit disliked being compared to Dev Anand, who tried to reinvent but failed. Like the late actor, her last few years too did not cover her in glory. She remained popular in the public imagination but, as a politician, her days were over.

MAKHAN LAL FOTEDAR

(1932–2017)

MAKHAN LAL FOTEDAR WILL GO DOWN IN HISTORY AS A STAUNCH Nehru–Gandhi loyalist who died a dissident. Moving from total allegiance to utter disillusionment, what changed in between? Fotedar would have us believe that the answer is the quality of leadership since that fateful October day, nearly 36 years ago, when a prime minister was shot dead by her own bodyguards.

Fotedar's loyalty towards Indira Gandhi was absolute. It was evident from the manner he would bow each time he passed through the Safdarjung Road–Akbar Road roundabout in Lutyen's Delhi where she had last lived in 1984. Fotedar died nearly 33 years later, on 28 September 2017, impatient with the grandson of the leader he adored.

His book, *The Chinar Leaves: A Political Memoir*, chronicles that impatience: 'Rahul Gandhi's leadership is unacceptable to this country and Sonia Gandhi has her best years behind her. The party has no one to provide direction. It refuses to learn.'[148] It was 2015, a year after the Congress had been voted out of power at the Centre, the Grand Old Party suffering its worst electoral defeat under Rahul Gandhi's leadership. Fotedar goes on to express his sense of dismay: 'Rahul needed more exposure and grinding to become ripe for the top job. Also, there was nobody to tutor or mentor Rahul. Sonia Gandhi is not Indira Gandhi and was herself dependent on so many people for what she should do.'[149] It was clear that Fotedar was deeply disappointed with Sonia Gandhi and the team that surrounded her too.

Party leaders close to Fotedar attributed his disillusionment to the veteran's removal from the CWC, of which he had been a full-time member, and as informal adviser to Sonia and Rahul Gandhi.[150]

Fotedar had long been part of the inner circle. The removal was a public manifestation of his disconnect with the family. In his memoir, Fotedar has observed:

> Rahul had a certain stubbornness and his motivation to become a leader was not very strong. People around Soniaji secretly did not wish him to succeed because they realised that if Rahul grew as a leader they would themselves become irrelevant. The dilemma before Soniaji was that, on the one hand, she could not do without her coterie, while, on the other, she had an overriding desire to see her son succeed in politics.[151]

Several senior Congress leaders had privately said they saw some merit in Fotedar's criticism. They also confirmed that Fotedar had of late seldom been given an audience at 10 Janpath – something he found disturbing. Both Sonia Gandhi and her daughter Priyanka Gandhi Vadra had, however, visited Fotedar when he was ailing in a Delhi hospital.

While Fotedar was sceptical about Rahul Gandhi's leadership, he had high hopes from Priyanka. He has even claimed that Indira Gandhi had a premonition about her death just days before she was assassinated and wanted her granddaughter to carry forward her political legacy.[152]

In his tell-all book, Fotedar has also revealed that Indira Gandhi had warned son Rajiv Gandhi against involving actor Amitabh Bachchan in politics and including Madhavrao Scindia in his cabinet. A few days before her assassination, Fotedar recalls, Indira Gandhi had summoned Rajiv, the AICC general secretary then, and Arun Nehru. 'During the course of the conversation regarding parliamentary elections, she categorically told her son two things he should never do in future,' Fotedar, who was present at the meeting, says. 'She said: Do not ever bring Teji's son – Amitabh Bachchan – into electoral politics and do not induct Madhavrao Scindia in your cabinet if you ever become the prime minister.'[153] Teji Bachchan, the actor's mother, was known to be a friend of Indira. Fotedar says Rajiv Gandhi heard his mother out in 'disbelief' without uttering a word.

Bachchan was, however, given a Congress ticket in the 1984 Lok Sabha elections that followed Indira's death and Scindia was made a minister subsequently. '[S]ince Rajivji was adamant I left it at that,' Fotedar says in his autobiography dedicated to 'the memory of my leader Smt. Indira Gandhi'.[154]

Fotedar says Bachchan, elected MP from Allahabad, wielded enormous power between 1985 and July 1987 at the time of his resignation. 'I was also getting reports about Amitabh's interference in the appointment and transfer of officers in the ministries,' he writes, claiming that many senior party leaders would complain against what he described as 'Amitabh's interference in administrative matters'. Bachchan, he alleged, interfered in matters not only related to Uttar Pradesh, which was ruled by the Congress then, but also beyond – 'in matters concerning Madhya Pradesh, Rajasthan and Maharashtra.'[155] Fotedar further writes:

> Amitabh came to see the prime minister. They had discussions. That day around 2.45 p.m. or so when I was about to leave for lunch, the prime minister called me. He was accompanied by Amitabh, looking charismatic as usual in a white kurta pyjama. They were walking towards 7 Race Course Road (the prime minister's residence). We went inside. The PM took a chair. On his right was Amitabh and I was asked to sit on his left. [...] Rajivji said: 'Fotedarji wants you to resign.' That was a surprise to me – and it must have been to Amitabh also. [...] The truth is that I had never discussed this matter with the PM nor had Rajivji ever discussed it with me.[156]

Fotedar records Bachchan as saying: 'If Fotedarji wants me to resign, I am ready to resign. Come on, give me the papers. What do I have to write?' Fotedar then asked Vincent George, personal assistant to Rajiv Gandhi, to get a Lok Sabha member's letterhead pad. 'I told Amitabh: "Write in your hand to the Speaker, I resign from the Lok Sabha." [...] In response, Amitabh said: "That is it?"' The note was sent to the Speaker and the actor's resignation was accepted.[157]

Chinar Leaves also dwells on how Sonia Gandhi had been deeply upset by Manmohan Singh's defeat in the 1999 general election from the South Delhi seat because of Arjun Singh and Sheila Dikshit's alleged manipulations. Fotedar claims Sonia Gandhi had asked her political aides Ambika Soni and Ahmed Patel to remove Dikshit as Delhi's chief minister but he (Fotedar) had intervened to save Dikshits's chair.[158]

At the height of his political power, Fotedar could decide the fate of any chief minister in Congress ruled states and many high and mighty. But towards the end of his life, he had become totally disillusioned with Sonia and Rahul Gandhi. Some party leaders who had seen Fotedar's clout, started narrating a story from the legend of Laila–Majnu to accuse Sonia Gandhi of being a 'fair-weather friend'. The story went like this: Laila, having heard that her beloved was wandering the streets of Baghdad hungry, sent her chambermaid with milk for him. A greedy beggar cornered the milk by pretending to be Majnu and chanting: 'Hai Laila.'

Hearing from other sources that Majnu's condition had worsened further, Laila sent out her maid again with milk and the instruction to bring back a bowl of Majnu's blood. This time, the beggar pointed to the real Majnu and said: '*Hum to doodh wale Majnu hain, khoon wala woh raha* (I'm the Milk Majnu, that one's the Blood one).'

INDIRA GANDHI

(1917–1984)

ON THE MORNING OF 31 OCTOBER 1984, INDIRA GANDHI HAD KISSED her grandchildren Priyanka and Rahul goodbye before they left for school. Priyanka Gandhi, who was twelve then, would later recall that her grandmother held her longer than usual. Indira Gandhi had then moved to Rahul.

Death was very much on Indira Gandhi's mind. Turning to Rahul, she had asked him to 'take charge' and not cry in the event of her death. This was not the first time she had spoken about death to her grandson. A few days previously too, she had told him about funeral arrangements and that she had lived her life. Indira Gandhi, considered an astute judge of personality, used to value Rahul Gandhi's grit and determination, and despite him being barely fourteen at the time, she often considered him mature enough to be taken into confidence on subjects she avoided discussing with his parents, Rajiv and Sonia Gandhi. Earlier that month as well she had written that if she died a violent death, the violence would be in the thought of the assassin, not in her death, 'For no hate is dark enough to overshadow the extent of my love for the people and my country, no force is strong enough to divert me from that purpose and my endeavor to take this country forward.'[159]

That fateful morning, Indira Gandhi was to begin her official engagements with an interview with Peter Ustinov. The cameras were in place when Gandhi, in a bright saffron sari, crossed the wicket gate between her home 1 Safdargunj Road and her 1 Akbar Road office. It was 9.12 a.m. As she crossed the gate, she acknowledged the greetings of a turbaned security guard. When she smiled back, she saw him pointing a gun at her. Constable Narain Singh, who was holding an umbrella over her, screamed for help. But before other guards of the Indo–Tibetan Border Police could reach the spot, the assassins – Beant Singh and Satwant Singh – had pumped 36 bullets into her.

Gandhi had been advised to wear a bulletproof vest and remove her Sikh security guards after Operation Blue Star, but she had refused to do either. She felt it was unnecessary to wear a heavy bulletproof jacket at home and hated the idea of 'discriminating' among her security guards. In fact, a few weeks ago, she had proudly pointed at Beant Singh and said: 'When I have Sikhs like him around me, then I do not have to fear anything.'[160]

Before turning an assassin, Singh had been a household figure at 1 Safdargunj Road. As Rahul Gandhi later revealed, Singh had taught him to play badminton.

After her assassination, many had wondered why the matter of keeping Sikh security guards had been referred to Indira Gandhi. After all, a VVIP (Very Very Important Person) is never usually involved in the arrangements concerning his or her security.

Indira Gandhi had an obsessive fear of her family being harmed, according to P.C. Alexander, who served as secretary to her. 'From June 1984 she lived with a dreadful thought. She kept repeating that there was a plot to kidnap the children. Nothing I said could allay her fears,' Alexander recalls.[161]

When Arun Nehru, a member of the Nehru–Gandhi family, arrived at the All India Institute of Medical Sciences (AIIMS), he saw a hysterical Sonia Gandhi fearful for the lives of Rahul and Priyanka. She kept telling him that Indira Gandhi had always feared a repeat of the assassination of Mujib-ur-Rahman, the towering Bangladeshi leader up to three generations of whose had been wiped out, with the exception of his daughter Hasina. When Arun Nehru reached the Safdarjung Road residence of Indira, Rajiv and Sonia Gandhi, he was stunned to see there was not a single security guard around to protect Rahul and Priyanka, both of whom had been brought back from school. Arun Nehru then took them to the Gulmohar Park residence of Teji Bachchan, actor Amitabh Bachchan's mother.

As Indira Gandhi's body lay in state at Teen Murti House, the crowd waiting outside for a last glimpse of her mortal remains chanted 'Khoon ka badla khoon' (blood for blood). Delhi, which had last witnessed a massacre during Nadir Shah's invasion over 200 years ago, now saw blood everywhere. Within three days, over 2,500 people were killed – many of them burnt alive.

In the Indira Gandhi assassination case, her close aide R.K. Dhawan's name had come under a cloud. A commission of inquiry headed by a retired Supreme Court judge, M.P. Thakkar, had recommended that 'the Central government should seriously consider the question of appropriate agencies to investigate the matter as regards the involvement of R.K. Dhawan, the then special assistant to the former prime minister.'[162] Rajiv Gandhi and the Congress, however, decided to relegate the Thakkar report to the archives and Dhawan was given a clean chit.

Dhawan had joined Indira Gandhi's staff in 1962. Many people had come and gone, including the likes of P.N. Haksar, P.N. Dhar and R.N. Kao, but Dhawan had stayed with her till the end. On his part, Dhawan, who died in August 2018, vehemently denied the allegation of involvement, insisting that his shirt had been dyed with her blood post facto.

Several years after Indira Gandhi's assassination, Dhawan spoke to the Rediff news portal to narrate the entire sequence of the events of 31 October 1984. Since Gandhi had returned from a trip to Bhubaneswar the previous night, Dhawan had suggested that the morning's durbar be cancelled and that she rest. But she had insisted on the appointment with Ustinov, as he had already recorded a part of the film during her tour of Orissa (now Odisha). When Dhawan reached Safdarjung Road at 8 a.m. on 31 October, Gandhi had demanded a good hairdresser, and Nathu Ram, her attendant, had found someone.

When Dhawan approached her, Gandhi was getting her hair styled. Apparently she was very particular about personal aesthetics.

So much so that if even a single strand of hair was out of place, Dhawan would often indicate it to her by placing his hand on his hair. Indira Gandhi had planned a dinner for Princess Anne that evening at her residence and had instructed Dhawan on a few specifics about the guest list. 'I still have the page on which I took her last orders,' Dhawan recalled.[163]

By 9 a.m. she was ready for the cameras and had started walking towards the wicket gate connecting 1 Safdargunj Road with her Akbar road office. As usual, Dhawan was a few steps behind her. She was such a brisk walker that it was sometimes tough to keep pace with her. A waiter passed by, with cups and saucers on a tray. She stopped, asked the waiter to show her the cups and enquired about where he was taking them. The waiter said Ustinov had requested for a full tea set to be placed before her during the interview. She immediately dismissed the tea set and instructed him to go back and get the special ones.

As soon as she reached the wicket gate, Dhawan said, Gandhi had folded her hands in a 'namaste' for the guards. Dhawan said he saw Beant raise his pistol and shoot. She spun around and fell to the ground. Satwant then started firing his Sten gun. She was not even standing when Satwant opened fire.[164]

Sonia Gandhi had just finished washing her hair when she heard the gunshots, which sounded a little like Diwali crackers going off somewhere close by. Then she realized what had happened and ran to where Indira Gandhi lay, crying out, 'Mummy, Mummy!' There was no ambulance to take Indira Gandhi to a hospital, so Sonia put her in an Ambassador. Still wearing a gown, she cradled her mother-in-law's head on her lap as the car raced the 3 km distance to AIIMS, where doctors laboured for hours to revive her with uninterrupted blood transfusions. Indira Gandhi was later officially declared dead by doctors at the hospital, but it is possible she had passed away in Sonia Gandhi's lap.

The Punjab Issue

Indira Gandhi had been bitterly opposed to the creation of the state of Punjab on linguistic lines as she closely identified with her minority Hindu supporters in the state. Barely six months before her assassination, the prime minister had sought to assure the majority community that, 'if there is injustice to them or if they did not get their rights, then it would be dangerous to the integrity of the country'.[165]

Indira Gandhi had just taken over as prime minister for the first time in 1966 when the demand for the creation of a Punjabi suba (state) was conceded. In her book, *My Truth*, published in 1980, she had recalled her concerns of 1965 when she was minister for information and broadcasting in Lal Bahadur Shastri's cabinet and a committee under the then Lok Sabha Speaker Sardar Hukum Singh had favoured the creation of a Punjabi suba. She wrote that she was opposed to the formation of Punjab on the basis of language as it let down the Congress's Hindu supporters. 'To concede the Akali demand would mean abandoning the position to which it (the Congress) was firmly committed and letting down its Hindu supporters in the projected Punjabi Suba... [T]his startling reversal of Congress policy was totally unexpected.'[166]

After the 1947 Partition of Punjab, Sikhs had demanded the formation of a Punjabi-speaking state but the first States Reorganization Commission of 1955 under Justice Fazal Ali had failed to address their concerns. Influential Akali leaders Fateh Singh and Tara Singh spearheaded a movement for a separate state in which Sikh religious, cultural and linguistic integrity could be preserved.

When the 1961 census was conducted, the Akali leadership had alleged that an overwhelming number of Hindus had listed Hindi as their mother tongue just to stall the formation of a Punjabi-speaking state or to prevent Sikhs, who formed 58 per cent of the population, from running the state. In 1966, Punjab was split into three states – Punjab, Haryana and Himachal Pradesh.

In this context, Indira Gandhi's solicitude for Hindu sensitivity was significant. Even in 1980, when she was prime minister, her recollection of the 'startling reversal of Congress policy' in letting down the party's Hindu supporters during the formation of a Punjabi suba reflected her deep concern for the Hindu community. Some of Indira Gandhi's biographers like Katherine Frank, S.S. Gill and Pupul Jayakar noticed that when she had returned to power in 1980, she had turned a lot more sensitive towards the Hindu community than towards Muslims or Sikhs.[167]

The Jana Sangh's dominance over the Janata Party, the formation of the BJP and a mass conversion of 1,300 Harijans to Islam in Meenakshipuram, Tamil Nadu, in February 1981, had made the prime minister worried that communal issues would dominate the political narrative.

The RSS had recognized Indira Gandhi's concern for Hindus living in Punjab. Soon after her assassination, veteran RSS ideologue, Nanaji Deshmukh, wrote a piece titled 'Moments of Soul Searching' (published in the Hindi magazine, *Pratipaksh*), where he described Gandhi as a 'great martyr'. 'Indira Gandhi ultimately did secure a permanent place at the doorstep of history as a great martyr. With her dynamism born out of her fearlessness and dexterity, she was able to take the country forward like a colossus for over a decade... She alone had the ability to run the decadent political system of our corrupt and divided society,' Deshmukh wrote in the Hindi journal.[168]

The creation of a Punjabi *suba*, however, did not fulfil the Sikh community's political aspirations. Punjab was not given Chandigarh as its capital in spite of Indira Gandhi herself promising it in January 1970. Several rounds of talks at both formal and informal levels were held throughout the 1970s and the early 1980s, but the Chandigarh issue remained unresolved.

Harkishan Singh Surjeet, the late CPI(M) leader, told the British Broadcasting Corporation's (BBC's) Mark Tully and Satish Jacob in 1982: 'Three times in six months an agreement was reached and three times the prime minister backed out. Each time the interests of the Hindus of Haryana were weighed more heavily with her than a settlement with the Sikhs.'[169]

According to the arrangements made, the two tehsils of Fazilka and Abohar were not transferred from Punjab to Haryana as these tehsils were not contiguous with Haryana. A 10 km corridor was required to link them to Haryana.

Indira Gandhi's favourite, Bhajan Lal, who created a dubious history of sorts in defecting the entire council of ministers to the Congress in Haryana, contributed to spoiling the delicate Hindu–Sikh ties. When the Akalis threatened to disrupt the 1982 Asian Games held in New Delhi, Bhajan Lal made extraordinary arrangements to thwart Akali protests. Every Sikh coming from Punjab to Delhi by train or road was frisked. There were instances of Sikhs being forced to remove their turbans. By early 1984, anti-Sikh riots had erupted in Haryana in retaliation for the killings of Hindus in Punjab, where militancy and separatism was peaking.

In their book, *Amritsar*, Tully and Jacob recorded how Hindu mobs burnt down a gurudwara in Panipat and Sikhs were pulled out of buses, shaved and killed.[170] Indira Gandhi remained a mute spectator, just as she had watched separatists in Punjab kill Hindus almost at will.

Troubled Beginning

Sikh militancy may have significantly marked Indira Gandhi's final days, but violence had erupted as early as her very first year as prime minister. On 7 November 1966, thousands of *gau rakshaks*, with sadhus and other religious leaders among them, marched to Parliament demanding a law banning cow slaughter across the country. Led by the Bharatiya Jana Sangh Member of Parliament from Karnal, Haryana, Swami Rameshwaranand, a huge crowd of sadhus marched menacingly towards the Parliament House complex, clearly meaning to storm it. There was little security to protect Parliament, so the guards on duty hurriedly closed the gates. The infuriated agitators went berserk and started attacking government buildings on Parliament Street. The police then opened fire, killing eight sadhus. There was widespread condemnation of the police firing and the government's inept handling of the situation. Indira Gandhi, sensing the disquiet, sacked veteran politician Gulzarilal Nanda, who was then the home minister.

This was her first year in office and she was fighting on several fronts. Following the Indian Army's loss to China in 1962, Nehru had, according to his biographer – Marie Seton, an air of sad, sorrowing desolation about him. The issue of his successor was in the air and contrary to present-day perceptions, Indira Gandhi was not the obvious successor. In fact, in 1963, she had toyed with the idea of leaving the country and living in England, where her sons Rajiv and Sanjay were studying. She wrote in a letter to her friend Dorothy Norman 19 days before Nehru's death that she 'had to settle down outside India for at least a year and was looking for ways of earning foreign currency to do so'.[171]

Nehru himself was not grooming her as his successor; instead he supported her rejection of offers of parliamentary seats and made no plans for her future. When she became the Congress president in February 1959, Nehru's detractors had dubbed it the prime minister's bid to push his daughter into the coveted post. However, a large section of the Congress's leaders felt that she had earned her post through merit.

Indira Gandhi was the fourth woman to head the party and quickly proved her mettle by tackling the Kerala crisis, where the E.M.S. Namboodiripad government's sweeping land reforms and educational bills controlling private schools in the state had upset powerful sections of the society enough for them to demand his removal. She further established herself by recommending the creation of Maharashtra and Gujarat to end the linguistic troubles in the then Bombay state.

When Indira Gandhi's one-year term came to an end in February 1960, the CWC tried to persuade her to stand for a re-election, but she declined firmly, paving the way for K. Kamaraj to be elected president. Subsequently, she avoided assuming any formal political role but continued to protect her father from people she thought were fair-weather friends. She was also careful to not let her political and social work affect her bond with her children.

Destiny, however, willed otherwise. Nehru died on 27 May 1964. Within hours of Nehru's death, the Congress old guard, informally known as the 'syndicate', closed ranks to elect Shastri as Nehru's successor. Kamraj, a politician among politicians, preferred Shastri to the hardliner Morarji Desai.

According to Pupul Jayakar, a close friend and adviser of Indira Gandhi, before taking the oath of office and secrecy, Shastri had called on Indira Gandhi, offering her the prime ministership. 'Indira Gandhi refused,' Jayakar wrote, because 'she felt if she had become prime minister at that time, she would have been destroyed.'[172] Shastri subsequently offered her a ministerial assignment, insisting that without her presence, he would not have a stable government. She relented and took up the information and broadcasting portfolio.

In September 1965, Pakistan launched Operation Grand Slam in the Chamb sector of Akhnoor in Jammu and Kashmir. Indian troops quickly crossed into west Pakistan at three points aiming for Lahore. UN brokered a ceasefire agreement on 22 September, with both sides holding some of the other's territory at the end of the war. The Soviet Premier Alexei Kosygin invited both Shastri and Pakistan's President General Ayub Khan to Tashkent in Uzbekistan to work out a settlement in January 1966. The night Shastri and Ayub signed the treaty, Shastri suffered a massive heart attack and died.

Kamraj moved swiftly and started projecting Indira Gandhi as Shastri's successor. A number of senior Congressmen, led by Morarji Desai, were unwilling, but Kamraj saw a quality in Indira Gandhi that, according to him, others did not have, 'and he felt that she would win the elections in 1967'.[173]

Kamraj, considered a crafty politician, felt that Indira Gandhi's lack of experience and acceptability within the Congress would make her compliant and dependent on him. P.V. Narasimha Rao would later say that Indira Gandhi was supposed to be merely a 'vote-catching device' who, after the 1967 polls, would be forced to take a back seat with an experienced person being chosen to lead the country.[174]

Desai forced a leadership contest within the Congress Parliamentary Party. Nine days after Shastri died, a vote was held among Congress's elected members. At three in the afternoon, the presiding officer handed over the result to Kamraj in the Central Hall of Parliament. Kamraj announced the winner in chaste Tamil. Few members of Parliament or AICC office-bearers understood what the Congress chief had said. The suspense did not last long as someone excitedly declared in Hindi that Indira Gandhi had won 355 votes to Desai's 169.

Indira Gandhi rose in stature, and many among the Congress's old guard who had thought of manipulating her were in for a shock. Kamraj, who had played a great role in shaping her career, was also disappointed when he realized that she had a mind of her own and an independent style of functioning. At one juncture, Kamraj was heard describing her rather ruefully as 'a big man's daughter, a little man's mistake', referring to himself as a little man.[175]

Indira Gandhi was sworn in as prime minister on 24 January 1966, facing a sandstone statue of Buddha at the Rashtrapati Bhavan that had the words 'Be Without Fear' inscribed on it.

But there were many problems. The cow-slaughter issue forced her to set up a panel under retired Supreme Court chief justice A.K. Sarkar to see if a nationwide ban on cow slaughter was feasible. She daringly made RSS chief M.S. Golwalkar a member of the panel, along with the Shankaracharya of Puri, V. Kurien of the National Dairy Development Board and economist Ashok Mitra, among others. Kurien later wrote that Golwalkar admitted to him in so many words that the RSS had launched the November 1966 campaign to embarrass the government and with definite political objectives in mind.[176] The A.K. Sarkar committee's initial mandate was to submit a report in six months but it kept delaying until it was dismissed in 1979 by the Morarji Desai government.

In 1967, Indira Gandhi turned 50. For the first time, she decided to contest the 1967 general election from Raebareli constituency, from where her late husband, Feroze Gandhi, had won in 1952 and 1957. During her husband's election, she had campaigned for him extensively in the region. True to Kamraj's assessment, her personal charisma was phenomenal. She clocked over 25,000 km over 45 days of campaigning.

While Indira Gandhi's popularity ratings were high, the country was struggling on many fronts. The 1966 famine and drought were so severe that they led to food riots in some parts of the country; Mizo tribals were revolting, and a linguistic agitation was taking shape in Punjab. To make matters worse, a series of scurrilous posters surfaced in Delhi and other parts of the country, emphasizing her allegedly inauspicious stars and reminding people that the day she took oath as prime minister, an earthquake had struck and an Air India plane carrying scientist Dr Homi Bhabha had crashed; it was said that since she was a widow, she was inauspicious. This was decades before Internet-savvy social media trolls, but the content was similar.

The socialist movement was gaining ground in India with 'backward castes', such as the Yadavs, Jats, Reddys, Patels and the Marathas, becoming disillusioned with the Congress. Ram Manohar Lohia, a former Congressman, felt that the elections of 1952, 1957 and 1962, which the party had won with ease, had made voters believe that the Congress could not be defeated. To counter this, Lohia urged the fragmented opposition to field a single candidate against each Congress nominee. The 'Lohia formula' proved to be a success in the 1967 general election, making a huge dent in the Congress's seat.

The Socialist Party would manifest itself as a key opposition party in its different avatars such as the Janata Party and the Janata Dal.

The BJP also had leaders who were deeply influenced by Lohia's ideology. Lohia and the socialists felt that both Nehru and Indira Gandhi were not seriously committed to socialism, and though both talked a great deal about socialism, they had done little in practice to empower the working class. The socialists felt that big public sector institutions merely created another set of bureaucrats and industrialists with no grounding in the socialist ethos.

At a public meeting in Jaipur around the same time, Indira Gandhi hit out at former royals and took on Maharani Gayatri Devi, who had swept the 1962 Lok Sabha polls by a mammoth margin, winning 1,92,909 votes out of the 2,46,516 cast. Gayatri Devi, a glamorous queen, had fancied herself as Indira Gandhi's rival and worked hard to bring the Swatantra Party, which believed in free enterprise and closer ties with the West, close to the Right-wing Jana Sangh. Indira Gandhi asked the voters 'to go ask the maharajas and maharanis how much they had done for the people in their states when they ruled them and what they did to fight the British while they lived in luxury at the cost of the people'.[177]

The March 1967 general elections were, however, a blow to Indira Gandhi. The Congress managed to retain the Centre, winning 283 out of 520 seats, but it lost in nine states. The politically influential Uttar Pradesh slipped out of its hands within a month when Charan Singh left the Congress with a large chunk of MLAs to become the chief minister of a non-Congress coalition.

According to V. Krishna Ananth, the 1967 elections witnessed the unveiling of the fractures in the nation's social and political edifice, 'the unfolding taking many forms and shapes in the discourse'. What emerged in 1967 was the fragmented socio-political reality of India as a nation which had been stitched together in 1947. The 'experiments in alliances, coalitions and vote appeal on the lines of caste, region, etc.' had a far-reaching impact and continue to influence politics till date.[178]

Counter-Moves

Indira Gandhi preferred to respond to these developments with silence and surprising counter-moves. She split the Congress party to get rid of the old guard and announced far-reaching populist measures, such as the abolition of privy purses and the nationalization of banks.

The move to nationalize fourteen leading banks won the nation's heart. The 'Shoeshine Boys' Union' offered to shine for free the shoes of all AICC delegates as a show of their gratitude towards the party. The biggest bank that was nationalized at the time was the Central Bank controlled by the Tatas, with deposits of over ₹4 billion; the smallest was the Bank of Maharashtra, with deposits totalling ₹700 million.

Indira Gandhi struck a severe blow to other big business houses too – such as the Birlas who were running the United Commercial Bank; the Dalmia–Jains with Bharat Bank and its 292 branch offices; the Punjab National Bank set up by Dayal Singh Majithia, Lala Harkishan Lal, Lala Lajpat Rai and others; and some Gujarati entrepreneurs who had big stakes in Dena Bank. An economic survey of twenty leading banks of that era conducted by a chamber of commerce showed that 188 people who served as directors were also directors of 1,452 companies. The large funds they had used to acquire private profit and privileges were now open for public welfare; measures such as financing the rural sector of the economy to lend money to farmers and taxi-drivers for the purchase of tractors and cabs respectively became possible.

Indira Gandhi returned to power in the early polls of 1971, with the powerful slogan 'garibi hatao'. Emerging as a towering and powerful prime minister, she had her greatest moment of glory when Pakistan was split into two. The surrender of thousands of Pakistani troops in Dhaka and the creation of Bangladesh capped her triumph, earning her the title of 'Durga' from none other than Atal Bihari

Vajpayee of the Bharatiya Jana Sangh. India's decisive victory, in 1971, over Pakistan-restored national pride that had been damaged in 1962. President V.V. Giri awarded her the nation's highest civilian honour, the Bharat Ratna.

In an article titled 'Kiski Puja Kar Rahe Hain Bahujan? (Whom are the lower castes worshipping?)', Prem Kumar Mani, a Dalit, recalled that Vajpayee had referred to Indira Gandhi as 'Abhinav Chandi Durga' for defeating Pakistan. Communist leader S.A. Dange protested strongly, saying that Vajpayee did not know what he was saying and Indira Gandhi could not understand what she was hearing, and that they should know that Chandi Durga had massacred Dalits and the backward classes.[179]

Modesty may have prevented Indira Gandhi from accepting Vajpayee's compliment, but she admitted to Jayakar, her friend and biographer, that she had had some intimations of 'supernatural powers throughout the war and even previous to it, having had strange experiences'.[180] Jayakar thought that all doubt had left her and she was filled with a sense of euphoria that left little space for any other emotion.

The Pokhran nuclear tests in 1974, which made India the world's sixth nuclear power, further enhanced Indira Gandhi's stature in India and abroad. The annexation of Sikkim in 1975 turned her into a towering personality who could do no wrong.

A personality cult emerged around her. Conscious of her bitter experience with the Congress's old guard, she tried to take total control of the organization. Many powerful chief ministers were shunted out and replaced by her favourites. Among her favourites were Barkatullah Khan, who replaced Mohanlal Sukhadia in Rajasthan, and P.C. Sethi, who replaced S.C. Shukla in Madhya Pradesh. Indira also made deliberate attempts to control party funds, which were crucial for elections and all other political activities, making the party and the government dependent upon her for survival.

Emergency and the Sanjay Years

Earlier, in 1969, Indira Gandhi's younger son, Sanjay, returned from England, where he had trained at the Rolls Royce factory in Crewe. Sanjay, then 23, applied for a licence to manufacture a small and cheap car. When he turned out to be the lone applicant to have been granted a licence, charges of nepotism started doing the rounds. The matter was raised in Parliament, which saw Indira Gandhi pursing her lips and shrugging off the criticism. But there was more to follow. The Haryana government under Bansi Lal handed over 300 acres of land to establish Sanjay's car factory – for which some 15,000 peasants were evicted. P.N. Haksar, who was principal secretary to Indira Gandhi till 1973, was fired for opposing Sanjay's project.

On the other side of the political spectrum, this period saw the emergence of Jayaprakash Narayan, a freedom fighter who was living quietly in Bihar. JP, as he was popularly called, was a young man in 1921 when Nehru and Abul Kalam Azad had spotted him. He spent a considerable time in various British jails. His ties with Nehru turned sour soon after Independence, and he joined the rival Socialist Party. In 1973, JP wrote to several Members of Parliament seeking to protect individual rights and democratic values. He formed a body called Citizens for Democracy and became a sort of patriarch for disgruntled elements. Sanjay became a favourite target of his at the time, and some publications hostile to Indira Gandhi and the Congress published exaggerated stories about her son turning into a monster.

Sanjay Gandhi's rise also coincided with the emergence of a small but powerful clique within the Congress that often functioned parallel to the Prime Minister's Office. At Indira Gandhi's residence, a special telephone line was installed in Sanjay's room, where Indira Gandhi's additional private secretary Dhawan remained constantly in touch with chief ministers of Congress-ruled states, the police commissioner and the lieutenant governor of Delhi, and several influential party and government functionaries. The modus operandi was to make calls and issue instructions for and on behalf of the prime minister's son, although on many occasions Indira Gandhi was not even aware of Sanjay's growing unconstitutional clout.

On 12 June 1975, the Allahabad High Court declared Indira's 1971 parliamentary election from Raebareli null and void because of electoral malpractice. More importantly, it debarred her from holding any public office for the next six years. While she struggled to face the situation, her close adviser Siddhartha Shankar Ray came up with a proposal to invoke Article 352 of the Constitution and proclaim an internal emergency. On 25 June 1975, JP, Morarji Desai and other leaders held a public rally at Delhi's Ram Lila grounds asking her to step down. JP urged the people to join them in a non-cooperation movement. The following morning, Indira announced a national emergency in view of 'threats to national security'.

Opposition leaders were arrested, censorship was imposed, and a ban was soon announced on grassroots organizations, including the RSS and thirteen of its cover organizations. The declaration of the Emergency was not unheard of in developing countries like India. Even in Britain, the Edward Heath government had declared emergencies five times during its tenure from June 1970 to March 1974. In India too, an 'external' emergency had been declared during the 1962 and 1971 wars. But in the summer of 1975, there was nothing to justify it. Political scientists and scholars of that era felt that if individual states like Bihar were facing problems, a presidential decree would have sufficed.

In 1978, the Shah Commission, which was set up to examine the Emergency and its excesses, found that there was no evidence of a threat to the Constitution or to law and order that warranted such a declaration.

There were other bizarre events in the Sanjay Gandhi saga of the Emergency. At Connaught Place, New Delhi, government officials one day descended on a textile shop called Pandit Brothers; the 80-year-old owner of this shop was the uncle of Haksar, Indira Gandhi's former principal secretary who had opposed Sanjay

Gandhi's car project. It may have been just a coincidence but Haksar's
uncle had to spend a day in police custody. The reason cited by the
police was that the shop had towels and napkins that did not bear
individual price tags, though the bundles did.

Connaught Place also had a popular joint called Indian Coffee
House where journalists, writers, liberals and lawyers used to meet
regularly. Someone told Sanjay Gandhi that people at the coffee
house were criticizing the Emergency. One morning, the entire
coffee house was bulldozed.

Indira Gandhi, however, had a different take on her younger son.
After her defeat in 1977, noted filmmaker Khawaja Ahmad Abbas
had sought an appointment with the former prime minister. Abbas
gave specific instances of excesses, ranging from forced sterilization
to violence, but Indira Gandhi made no attempt to defend herself.
Instead, she praised Sanjay Gandhi's 'simplicity and sincerity' and
blamed her party chief ministers, the CWC and other AICC office-
bearers for 'building up a false image of Sanjay'.[181] She had also
written numerous letters to chief ministers of Congress-ruled states,
asking them not to accord state receptions, she claimed, but they
had insisted on lionizing Sanjay.

Significantly, during the Emergency, a constitutional amendment
was introduced. The Forty-Second Amendment, enacted in
November 1976, after the Lok Sabha's five-year term had expired,
purported to reduce the power of the Supreme Court and the high
courts. It also declared India to be a 'sovereign, socialist secular
democratic republic' – the earlier description was a 'sovereign
democratic republic' – and laid down the duties of Indian citizens
to their government. One of the main authors of this amendment
was D.K. Barooah, who as Congress president had immortalized
himself by coining the 'India is Indira, Indira is India' slogan. When
the Bill was brought in Parliament, A.R. Antulay, a barrister from
Lincoln's Inn, outdid Barooah in praising Indira Gandhi and called
for a 'fresh look at existing constitutional provisions like five-yearly
parliamentary polls'. As if there was a battle for excellence in flattery,

defence minister Bansi Lal tried to outdo both Barooah and Antulay when he told Indira Gandhi's cousin B.K. Nehru to change the provisions and 'just make her the President of India for life'.[182]

By January 1977, Indira Gandhi had realized that the Emergency would have to be revoked. She called for fresh elections, dissolved the already stretched Lok Sabha, released all political prisoners and braced for polls.

The Emergency, with all its limitations, had not done irreparable damage. Individual and political freedom existed within it, and political opponents were not eliminated. Even the most draconian provisions of the Forty-Second Amendment had not abolished the Supreme Court or ended the electoral process.

One reason for the Emergency's limited impact could be that the Indira–Sanjay Gandhi Emergency era had failed to usher in any significant social or economic reform to compensate for the absence of democracy.

That Congress MPs themselves voted to repeal much of the Forty-Second and other Emergency-era constitutional amendments when the Janata Party was in power also meant that the Congress could not get rid of its democratic ethos.

But Indira and Sanjay Gandhi's flirtation with dictatorship taught most Indians about the dangers to democracy. It educated them about demagoguery, the perils of hero worship, and about disregarding liberty and placing power in the hands of a few. It taught them that, like the fight against McCarthyism in the United States, vigilance was the constant price that citizens would have to pay to avoid a recurrence of what happened on a June day in 1975.

The RSS viewed the Emergency as the 'second freedom struggle'. Many years later, the BJP-led Shivraj Singh Chouhan government in Madhya Pradesh announced hefty monthly pensions (ranging from ₹8,000 to ₹25,000) for thousands of political activists who were detained under the Maintenance of Internal Security Act (MISA) and the Defence of India Rules (DIR).

Much of the Sangh's literature even claimed that it was the RSS and the Jana Sangh that had saved democracy. The role of peoples' movements has been underplayed in RSS journals and books, and a subtle attempt has been made to project the Sangh *parivar* (family) as the people who opposed the Emergency. Arvind Rajagopal, a scholar and the author of *Hindu Nationalism and Reshaping of Public in India*, thinks that the Emergency provided the Jana Sangh and the RSS with an element of respectability, which subsequently paved the way for its later avatar, the BJP, to enter the mainstream of Indian politics. Rajagopal feels that in the absence of any comprehensive history of the Emergency, the RSS successfully manufactured an account of democratic struggle that it claimed existed mainly due to the Sangh. According to him, Mahatma Gandhi's assassination had made the RSS a political pariah, but after the Emergency, acquiring political power was within their grasp. The importance of the Emergency in the growth of the RSS and the BJP needs to be emphasized, according to Rajagopal, because it helped them place Hindutva in a wider historical process rather than in fanaticism.[183]

Interestingly, the abrupt fall of the Janata regime also had a lot to do with the RSS. When Charan Singh and other members revolted against Morarji Desai, the socialist lobby raised the issue of 'dual membership', objecting to the Jana Sangh's presence in the Desai government as the Janata Party had a code for its members not to join any other organization whose objectives were at variance with its own. The Jana Sangh members in the Janata Party were linked to the RSS.

Defeat and Return to Power

The Congress's electoral defeat of 1977 was huge. Indira and Sanjay Gandhi both lost. In Uttar Pradesh, which had 84 Lok Sabha seats, the party drew a blank. There were similar stories from all over north India. Indira Gandhi could sense it coming. While campaigning in Raebareli, she had asked the London-based industrialist, Swraj

Paul, to check with BBC's Mark Tully how she was doing. Tully had bluntly presented a grim picture. At the dinner table, she had turned to Paul to ask about the BBC correspondent's assessment. Paul reproduced in a low voice what Tully had said in a much harsher tone. To his surprise, she was far from upset and remarked that Tully 'was correct in his assessment'.[184]

The Congress ended up with 153 seats in the Lok Sabha against the Janata Party's tally of 295. The Janata Party, comprising of the Congress (O), the Bharatiya Jana Sangh, the Samyukta Socialist Party and the Bharatiya Lok Dal, had hurriedly come into existence barely a month before the general elections and was a mix of socialist and Right-wing ideologies. The Jana Sangh, backed by the RSS, was an influential player and when the Janata Party government was formed, it had Vajpayee and L.K. Advani as senior ministers.

The Congress's first ever defeat since Independence saw an exodus from the party. Some senior party leaders, including then Congress president, K. Brahmananda Reddy, announced on the first day of 1978 that Indira Gandhi had been expelled from the party. She rallied around her a new band of loyalists. But the split cost her dearly. The former prime minister, who headed a faction called Congress (I) – Reddy's faction was called Congress (R) – lost the support of 76 of the 153 Congress members in the Lok Sabha. Her new party was homeless and it had also lost control of the party symbol of the cow and calf.

Indira Gandhi was, however, reportedly relieved to let go of the cow and calf, which had become a symbol of ridicule throughout the country: the cow was seen as Indira Gandhi herself and the calf as Sanjay. She decided to discard the symbol and asked for the old party symbol of a pair of bullocks, but the Election Commission had frozen the symbol by then. Buta Singh, who, as the AICC general secretary, had a room at 24 Akbar Road, petitioned to the Election Commission. Indira Gandhi was in Vijayawada with Narasimha Rao when Buta Singh was asked by the commission to pick an election symbol. The choices were an elephant, a bicycle and an open palm.

Unsure of which to pick, Buta Singh booked a call to seek Indira Gandhi's approval. The line was probably not clear or, perhaps, Buta Singh's accent was thick, but she kept hearing *haathi* (elephant), instead of *haath* (hand) when it came to the third option. She kept refusing even as Buta Singh tried to explain that it was not an elephant but the open-palm symbol that he was advising her to pick. An exasperated Indira Gandhi handed the telephone to Rao. In a matter of seconds, Rao, master of more than a dozen languages, understood what Buta Singh was trying to convey and asked him to call it a *panja* instead. A relieved Indira Gandhi took the receiver and wholeheartedly agreed. Although discarded then, the cycle and the elephant are alive and kicking after all these years – in Uttar Pradesh – as the symbols of the Samajwadi Party and the Bahujan Samaj Party.

By the time Indira Gandhi returned to power in 1980 by exploiting the Janata Party's inherent contradictions, ideological divides and one-upmanship, her zeal to promote secularism and socialism – watchwords throughout the early 1970s – was missing. She sought to cultivate the majority community's votes, accepting an invitation to launch the Vishwa Hindu Parishad's Ekatmata Yagna. This was the nascent VHP's first mass-contact programme, providing a sign that Hindu rituals and symbols could be effectively utilized for popular and political mobilization. A clear indication came from her loyalist C.M. Stephen, who declared in 1983 that 'the wave-length of Hindu culture and the Congress culture was the same'. Barely six months before her assassination, Indira Gandhi had sought to assure the majority community that 'the integrity of the country would be in peril if any injustice was one to them'.

RAJIV GANDHI

(1944–1991)

IF DEATH WAS ON INDIRA GANDHI'S MIND IN THE DAYS LEADING UP
to her assassination, her son too seems to have had some kind of
premonition about his untimely end. Journalist Neena Gopal, who
interviewed the then prime minister, moments before he was killed
by an LTTE suicide bomber on 21 May 1991 at Sriperumbudur
in Tamil Nadu, suggests that this was the case in her book, *The
Assassination of Rajiv Gandhi*.

Gopal recalls asking Rajiv Gandhi whether he felt his life was at
risk. Gandhi responded with a counter-question:

> Have you noticed how every time any South Asian leader
> of any import rises to a position of power or is about to
> achieve something for himself or his country, he is cut
> down, attacked, killed... [L]ook at Mrs [Indira] Gandhi,
> Sheikh Mujib, look at Zulfikar Ali Bhutto, at Zia-ul-Haq,
> [S.W.R.D.] Bandaranaike...

Gopal says that within minutes of making the statement hinting
that he was aware he was a likely target of dark forces at play, he
was gone.[185]

The journalist also quotes Chandran Chandrasekharan, a senior
RAW officer, as telling her later: 'We failed Rajiv Gandhi, we failed
to save his life.'[186]

One of Rajiv Gandhi's decisions as prime minister was that of
sending Indian armed forces to neighbouring Sri Lanka to end
militant insurgency there. The prime minister had been advised by
the Indian High Commission in Colombo, military commanders and
intelligence agencies to undertake the risky and adventurous mission.

Many Indian soldiers lost their lives but the Liberation Tigers of Tamil Eelam (LTTE) couldn't be tamed. The army was called back. But by then the LTTE had become a sworn enemy of Rajiv Gandhi.

Gopal insists that there were hundreds of intercepts between April 1990 and May 1991 showing the LTTE's intention to kill Rajiv Gandhi. The author quotes Col. Hariharan who had a small army of Jaffna Tamils keeping an eye on the LTTE for him, as saying that he was taken aback when he was given a cassette to listen to; from what his code-breakers told him, a plot was afoot to eliminate the prime minister. Some of the intercepted messages were: 'Rajiv Gandhi *avarund mandalai addipodalam*', 'Dump *pannidungo*' and '*Maranai vechidungo*'.[187] An approximate translation would be: Blow Rajiv Gandhi's head off; Eliminate him; Kill him.

It would indeed be a violent end for Rajiv Gandhi, whose unexpected rise to the post of the country's top executive was brought about by another act of violence – his mother's assassination at the hands of her own security guards.

The Beginnings

Rajiv Gandhi, MP from Amethi and Congress general secretary at the time, was in West Bengal when Indira Gandhi was assassinated on 31 October 1984 in Delhi. He heard the news on his way back to the national capital. As soon as he reached Delhi, P.C. Alexander, principal secretary to Indira, and other trusted aides told him the Union cabinet and the party wanted him to take over as prime minister. Alexander would later recall that at AIIMS, where Indira Gandhi had been rushed to, he had to tear Rajiv away from his wife Sonia Gandhi, who kept pleading with him not to agree. But Rajiv Gandhi believed it was his duty to accept the responsibility. It took Sonia many months to recover from the trauma of Indira Gandhi's assassination.

The young prime minister – Rajiv Gandhi was just forty then – quickly announced that general elections would be held ahead of schedule on 24, 27 and 28 December 1984. Gandhi's election campaign was aggressive and focused on Punjab separatists who were seeking a separate homeland as one of the key issues. The hidden agenda of the campaign was to somehow exploit Hindu insecurity and project the Rajiv Gandhi-led Congress as their sole saviour.

An immense sympathy wave in Rajiv Gandhi's favour won 414 of the 543 Lok Sabha seats for the Congress – a sweeping tally that both his mother Indira Gandhi and grandfather Jawaharlal Nehru had failed to achieve during their long tenures. It was a personal triumph for Rajiv Gandhi, who had travelled over 50,000 km by car, helicopter and aeroplane during 25 days of relentless campaigning. There was talk of a secret meeting between Rajiv Gandhi and the then RSS chief Balasaheb Deoras; there was speculation that this meeting had resulted in the RSS cadre supporting the Congress despite the presence of the BJP on the scene. The BJP, however, now denies that the Sangh, its ideological fulcrum, had any truck with the Congress.

The Opposition was badly bruised. The newly formed BJP managed to win just two seats. Party stalwart Atal Bihari Vajpayee lost to Madhavrao Scindia in Gwalior, while Rajiv Gandhi's childhood buddy and film star, Amitabh Bachchan, humbled the seasoned politician Hemwati Nandan Bahugana in Allahabad. At his campaign rallies, Bachchan had focused on Indira Gandhi's assassination and his friendship with Rajiv Gandhi. *'Jab maine Indiraji ke shareer ko inhi dono haaton mein uthaya...* (When I carried Indira Gandhi's body in my hands...),' he would say.[188]

The Congress's spectacular mandate had the media gushing over the new leader. *India Today* exclaimed that 'the results had demolished the myth of [Rajiv Gandhi being] a political novice', while *Time* magazine dubbed the results a 'mandate for change, for cleaning up and for efficiency'. *Newsweek* likened Rajiv Gandhi to J.F. Kennedy.[189] For the first and perhaps the only time, 24 Akbar Road, the AICC headquarters in New Delhi, was illuminated for three consecutive days in celebration of the party's victory.[190]

Rajiv Gandhi's rise had a massive impact on the Congress party too. Many veteran leaders who were close to Indira and Sanjay Gandhi found themselves left out in the cold. Rajiv Gandhi's *durbar* (court) was composed of a mix of technocrats, politicians, mavericks and time-servers. While there were advisers like P.V. Narasimha Rao and N.D. Tiwari, and professionals like P. Chidambaram and Mani Shankar Aiyar, there were also masters of political manipulation like Buta Singh, Arun Nehru and Sitaram Kesri. Some of his aides were from his alma mater, the Doon School, and some from Delhi's St. Stephen's College.

End of Innocence

Rajiv Gandhi had a scandal-free history when he took over and was dubbed 'Mr Clean'. But the image did not last as major controversies such as the Bofors, the Fairfax scandal and the HDW submarine deal would soon explode. For many, it was Bofors that marked the end of innocence for 'Mr. Clean'.

The Bofors scandal had erupted after a 1987 report on Swedish Radio claimed that the arms manufacturer Bofors A.B. had paid bribes to secure a defence contract. A firm called AE Services was named. Bofors was a complicated issue. In nutshell, it can be explained as follows: In 1986, the Indian army signed a contract to purchase the Bofors Howitzer. Nobody noticed until 1987, when the Swedish state radio claimed that Bofors had paid bribes to secure the contract. Swedish Radio's concern was not with India, but with Sweden where the Bofors company had been at the centre of a series of scandals.

When the Bofors payoffs issue was raised in Parliament, prime minister Rajiv Gandhi rushed to announce that not only had bribes not been paid but that no commissions had been given because the deal had no agents. When Swedish Radio confirmed that payoffs were indeed made, Gandhi started losing credibility and his image took a bad hit.

Aiyar, a close aide of Gandhi, wrote extensively defending the prime minister and foregrounding the role of Gandhi's cousin and other aide, Arun Nehru, in the Bofors deal. 'The next elections were more than three years away. If he (Rajiv Gandhi) were the beneficiary of the AE Service payment, there was no compulsion for him to terminate the account when it was terminated. What happened in August–September 1986 that might explain the termination of the Bofors–AE Services contract?'[191]

According to Aiyar, Arun Nehru, then the minister of state for power, was dropped from the council of ministers around the same time that the AE Services contract was concluded. In his words:

> As a relative of the prime minister and as a recognised leader of great influence in party and government circles, the falling out between Arun Nehru and Rajiv Gandhi was widely commented on in political circles and the media after Rajiv Gandhi failed to proceed to Srinagar in April 1986 where Arun Nehru was recovering from a severe heart attack. Bofors and AE knew as well as anyone else that Arun Nehru had ceased to be a person in good standing in the higher echelons of the ruling party. It was in this political context the AE Services contract was abruptly terminated.[192]

Arun Nehru (now dead) had denied Aiyar's charge that it was he who made Bofors an issue. He said:

> With the formation of the Jan Morcha we had begun opposing Rajiv[,] and details of Amitabh Bachchan's and [Amitabh's brother] Ajitabh Bachchan's flats had come out. Rajiv and those in the Congress went around saying that it was the handywork of Arun Nehru and V.P. Singh. But it was later revealed that someone else had revealed the Bachchan documents. However, since it was a political fight, we exploited all weak points that we found.[193]

The Bachchans later won a defamation suit against a Swedish publication for alleging that they had something to do with Bofors.

Many Congress activists still believe that it was Arun Nehru who had advised Rajiv Gandhi to open the locks at the Babri Masjid–Ramjanmabhoomi site in Ayodhya in February 1986, another controversial chapter in the long saga of the temple dispute that dragged on till November 2019.

Equally controversial was Rajiv Gandhi's move to challenge and overturn the Supreme Court judgment in the 1985–86 Shah Bano case. Mohammad Ahmad, a lawyer, had divorced Shah Bano, a 62-year-old childless Muslim woman from Indore, Madhya Pradesh. Shah Bano had fought a long legal battle seeking maintenance as she had no source of income. The court ruled that under Section 125 of the Criminal Procedure Code (CrPC), a divorced Muslim woman was entitled to receive maintenance from her husband. But certain sections of Muslim clergy in India opined that it was against the spirit of Islamic Sharia.

To this day, the Hindu Right and liberals criticize Gandhi for overturning the Shah Bano judgment, accusing him of minority appeasement and giving in to orthodoxy. Some contemporary historians believe that the opening of the locks to the Ramjanmabhoomi–Babri Masjid site for Hindu worshippers was Gandhi's 'soft Hindutva' aimed at countering backlash for supporting the Muslim clergy in the Shah Bano case. However, according to Wajahat Habibullah, IAS from the J&K cadre in Rajiv Gandhi's PMO, he later claimed in his book that the prime minister was not aware of the unlocking of Babri Masjid–Ramjanmabhoomi in February 1986. In his tell-all memoir – *My Years with Rajiv Gandhi: Triumph and Tragedy*, Habibullah said that when he asked the then prime minister whether he was involved in the decisions leading up to this unlocking, Rajiv Gandhi's answer was direct and instant, 'No Government has any business to interfere in matters like determination of the functioning of places of worship. I knew nothing of this development till I was told of it after the orders had been passed and executed.'[194]

Whatever be the reasons, political naivety did end up overshadowing many of his positive interventions, such as the priority he accorded to technology, education, infrastructure development and economic reforms.

S.S. Gill, author of *The Dynasty*, would later observe in his book that the tragedy of Rajiv Gandhi was not that he failed to redeem his promises but that he ended up aligning with the same forces that he had vowed to fight against.[195]

Failed Gambles

Rajiv Gandhi's 1984 victory was the first and the only time that a single party had captured over 50 per cent votes and had managed to acquire a brute majority in both Houses of Parliament. Yet, over the next four years, the Congress lost power in states despite making an 'earnest effort' to end trouble in Assam, Punjab, Jammu and Kashmir and Mizoram.

In Assam, Rajiv Gandhi's rule by Accord saw the Congress handing over power to the Asom Gana Parishad (AGP) in December 1985. The AGP's victory made Assam the fifth state to be ruled by a regional party and the eighth to be lost by the Congress.

In 1986, Laldenga was brought down from Britain and made the chief minister of Mizoram, which was given full statehood the following year. It had earlier been a Union Territory after being carved out of Assam in 1972.

The year 1986 also saw Rajiv Gandhi sign an Accord with Farooq Abdullah in Kashmir, leading to the exit of key Congress leader in the valley, Mufti Mohammad Sayeed, from the party. In protest, Mufti, who was a Union minister in Rajiv's cabinet, floated the Peoples Democratic Party (PDP), now led by his daughter Mehbooba.

In Punjab, secular and balanced Chief Minister Darbara Singh had been sacked by his political master, the previous prime minister

Indira Gandhi, in 1983. Rajiv Gandhi held state polls in September 1985 that saw the formation of the Akali Dal government.

Looking back, Rajiv Gandhi's gambles to forgo power did not make many of these Accords stable, though his moves were based upon realism and aimed at quelling unrest.

By the time Rajiv Gandhi was voted out of power in 1989, India's moral and administrative fabric had been corrupted to the core. The decline had begun during Indira Gandhi's tenure and the Emergency but by 1989, respect for law, human dignity and the rights of an individual were not even talking points in the country's administrative culture.

Defamation Bill

In 1988, Rajiv Gandhi introduced a defamation bill which sought to create new offences such as 'criminal imputation' and 'scurrilous writings'. But a successful nationwide strike by the newspaper industry and increasingly strident popular protests forced him to withdraw the legislation.

The same year, Salman Rushdie's *The Satanic Verses* was banned in India nine days after it was published in the UK in September 1988 (ahead of Ayatollah Khomeini's fatwa) on grounds of 'maintenance of the security of India' and 'maintenance of public order'. A number of Muslim MPs belonging to the Congress had written to Rajiv Gandhi seeking a ban, which was executed by the customs department under the Indian Customs Act.

The violence that broke out over *The Satanic Verses* also undermined Rajiv Gandhi's position among liberals and the majority community. In February 1989, twelve persons were killed in riots in south Mumbai. According to a Press Trust of India (PTI) report, the police fired at the rioters after people in the crowd opened fire on the police. The result was a three-hour battle, with rioters spilling across the crowded streets of the country's financial capital, burning cars, buses and motorcycles – even torching a police station.

When the controversy broke out, the Rajiv Gandhi government was already struggling for survival in the aftermath of the Bofors scandal. A National Front had been formed under V.P. Singh, Gandhi's former defence minister, while the government's move to 'discipline' a hawkish media through the infamous Defamation Bill boomeranged.

BABULAL GAUR
(1929–2019)

CONTROVERSY'S FAVOURITE CHILD, BABULAL GAUR, DIED IN BHOPAL IN 2019 a disillusioned man, waiting for a befitting post-retirement job that never came.

He was ninety when he breathed his last, just six years older – as he would have surely said – from the time when he was asked how old he was and had famously riposted: 'Only 84.'[196] It was a life lived to the fullest and littered often with comments that were politically incorrect, libelous, crude and outrageous; but we'll come to that later.

Almost half of those years were spent winning elections – ten times to be exact – from Govindpura, the constituency he represented in the Madhya Pradesh Assembly, including a brief stint as chief minister of the state. Gaur was first elected to the Madhya Pradesh Vidhan Sabha in 1974. He won again in 1977 and kept on winning till 2018 when he was benched because of his age.

He had been dropped from the Shivraj Singh Chouhan ministry in 2016 too, but he had a firm belief that his time was not up yet.

His astrologers had told that him he had 'rajyog' (destiny to rule) in his *kundli* (horoscope). So each time a Jagdish Mukhi, Banwarilal Purohit or Keshari Nath Tripathi (all BJP veterans) was rewarded with a term at sundry Raj Bhavans, Gaur would say the predictions of his astrologers was about to come true. 'I am not in a hurry to write my memoirs,' he would say.[197]

Gaur's original name was Baburam Yadav; he became Babulal Gaur after one of his teachers in Class IV in the school where he studied in Pratapgarh, Uttar Pradesh, praised his powers of concentration and renamed him. 'You read everything with *gaur* (concentration), so you should be called Gaur,' the teacher had reportedly said.[198]

Gaur not only read with concentration, he was a diligent writer too, evident from the 25-odd full-length, handwritten personal diaries that he kept. Ironically, it was these diaries that would be at the centre of an unusual and awkward test he faced late in life – a test of 'loyalty'. In 2016, the central BJP leadership reportedly asked Gaur, who was 87 then, to part with the diaries. Gaur said a senior Union minister had told him the diaries belonged to the party. The minister, known for his proximity to the RSS and the BJP, told Gaur that his ten terms as MLA, his ministerial posts and the chief minister's office were all the result of a single 'virtue': him being a disciplined soldier of the Bharatiya Jana Sangh and now the BJP.

Gaur was reluctant to 'gift' his diaries to the party. 'I have been writing these diaries for decades... [from] when I was a labourer in a mill and then as a Jana Sangh activist... I have poured my heart [out] in these personal notes. Parting with them is like parting with a part of me,' Gaur had told this writer. His style of writing, he said, had been simple. 'I have chronicled each and every event of the day that I considered significant. I wonder how my observations are of any interest to any institution or individual?'[199]

A cursory look at the diaries shows Gaur's keen interest in national and international politics. Some pages had pictures of world leaders along with press clippings and Gaur's observations in Hindi. On one page, Gaur had written his recollection of his experience visiting Malaysia. A lift operator at Petronas Towers, he had said, mistook him for Atal Bihari Vajpayee because he was wearing a *dhoti*.

There was another incident that Gaur never forgot. In September 2014, the BJP president then, Amit Shah, had turned to him at Bhopal airport and asked Gaur his age. '*Main sirf 84 saal ka hoon* (I am only 84),' Gaur had replied.[200] That was nine years more than the unofficial retirement age in the BJP from electoral politics. Gaur, who served as the chief minister of Madhya Pradesh in 2004 and 2005, before being replaced by Shivraj Chouhan, would keep rebutting the argument that age should act as a cut-off mark in politics. He would reel off names of leaders, such as Winston Churchill, Morarji Desai, Ronald Reagan and Nelson Mandela, to back his contention.

When the axe fell on his ministerial berth, Gaur claimed he had received feelers from Samajwadi Party leader Mulayam Singh Yadav, Janata Dal United's Sharad Yadav and Congress veteran Kamal Nath to switch loyalties. 'I told them flatly that I have no intention to cause embarrassment to the BJP leadership.' Gaur quoted Urdu poet Momin to explain his situation: '*Umar to sari kati ishq butan mein Momin, Akhiri waqt mein kya khak Musalman hongey.*'[201] (A rough English translation would be: 'You spent your entire life loving idols, how then would you become a Muslim at the end of life?')

Gaur would often wonder if the age factor in politics was democratic. 'The question is whether such a "rule" is valid. It goes without saying that the Constitution and law make no barrier on grounds of [old] age. A cursory look at old age leaders in India and abroad will tell a story on age and experience actually bringing an added advantage,' he once said.[202]

Gaur replaced Uma Bharti as the Madhya Pradesh chief minister in August 2004 after the saffron-clad leader had to step down following an arrest warrant in a riot case. In the little over a year that he ruled till late 2005, Gaur managed to upset the BJP's central leadership. When he had given a Madhya Pradesh government-owned B-200 King Air aircraft to Kamal Nath, the Union minister for commerce and industry then, to facilitate his attendance of a G-20 ministerial conference at Murree near Islamabad, he drew the wrath of the leadership.

BJP leaders of that era were even more furious that the Congress Union minister had returned the gesture by taking Gaur to Chicago to address investors. However, a full body search at a US airport had spoilt Gaur's mood so much that for weeks he kept giving a graphic account of how women security personnel had asked him to remove his clothes.[203]

Gaur loved sharing anecdotes, but they could sometimes border on risque. Gaffe prone as he was, he once regaled an audience in Bhopal by recalling a trip to Russia. A Russian leader's wife, Gaur claimed, had asked him how his *dhoti* remained in place without a belt or a zip. A minister then, Gaur had apparently said he could teach her the art of draping a *dhoti*, but in private, a pronouncement that left many horrified in the audience. His memories of that trip to Russia did not end there. Gaur recalled being kissed on the forehead by a woman. As if it was a joke, Gaur went on to say: 'If that had been noticed, I would not have got a ticket for the election at home.'[204]

This was possibly his least controversial attempt at humour. He was politically incorrect and crass on so many occasions that Madhya Pradesh BJP had stopped defending him.

Sometimes his remarks were not only politically incorrect, but also insensitive and potentially damaging. In June 2014, for instance, Gaur had triggered outrage when he described rape as a 'social crime', professing his belief that 'sometimes it's right and sometimes it's wrong'. The octogenarian had also said such crimes were difficult to prevent because rapists 'never reveal their intentions'.[205] The BJP had distanced itself from Gaur's remarks, saying his comments reflected his personal views. Months earlier he had also remarked that there were fewer cases of rape in southern India because women there dressed more 'decently' and were more religious.[206] Women in Chennai prefer 'full clothing', he had told a gathering after returning from the Tamil Nadu capital.[207] Even at the height of outrage in the country over the December 2012 gang rape in Delhi, Gaur had suggested that 'provocative dresses' worn by women was a factor. Speaking at an event in Bhopal, Gaur had said: 'Western values, films, television and provocative dresses are leading men to commit sex crimes.'[208]

On 29 June 2015, Gaur again came up with another controversial statement when he said: 'Drinking is a fundamental right and it is a status symbol too.'[209]

Earlier, in 2011, he had kicked up a controversy over a matter linked to sanitation. 'What should be done by Shudras is being done by a Brahmin,' Gaur had told a gathering. He was referring to the founder of Sulabh International toilets, Bindeshwar Pathak – a Brahmin from Bihar.[210]

TARUN GOGOI
(1936–2020)

TARUN GOGOI'S END CAME WHEN HIS PARTY NEEDED HIM THE MOST. AT the ripe old age of 84, Gogoi was trying to work out a grand alliance against the ruling BJP in Assam for the May 2021 Assembly elections when he died in hospital of multi-organ failure on 23 November 2020. The Congress veteran, a three-time chief minister who had helped his state return to normal after years of insurgency, had been undergoing treatment at Gauhati Medical College Hospital for post-Covid complications.

The Congress did stitch together a grand alliance but it failed. A report on the election defeat, submitted by former Maharashtra chief minister Ashok Chavan, attributed the failure to one key factor – the lack of a recognizable 'face'. Gogoi was that face of Assam – the 'turnaround man' who had led the Congress to three consecutive triumphs between 2001 and 2016.

Turnaround

Leading Assam From the Front is the title of Gogoi's memoirs, where he documented how he had taken over as chief minister at a turbulent time, when insurgency was at its peak, brutal killings dominated headlines and development had stalled. With empty coffers, the government could not pay its employees salaries for months together. Gogoi would remember the phase as follows:

> By 2001, indicators of development had fallen to an all-time low and insurgency was at its peak... When the history of Assam is penned, my three terms will show up both positives as well as negatives. There will be bouquets and brickbats, criticism and acclaim. But I will leave history to judge these years. I, as a son of the soil, am only content and gratified that I could take centre stage in the turnaround story.[211]

Dr Karan Singh, the former ruler of Jammu and Kashmir, while releasing Gogoi's memoirs, had referred to him as a great son of the Brahmaputra and commented,

> The manner in which the Chief Minister [Gogoi] handled a state like Assam[,] confronted with so much difficulties and complexities similar to that of Jammu and Kashmir, was quite extraordinary. For being the Chief Minister during the most difficult times with insurgency and various forces at

work and for bring[ing] about a turnaround in the situation, his place in the history is assured.[212]

In response, Gogoi had said, 'When [the] history of Assam is penned, my three terms will show up both positives as well as negatives. But, I will leave history to judge these years. I, as a son of the soil, am only content and grateful that I could take centrestage in the turnaround story,' drawing comfort that the biggest achievement of his government has been changing the mindset of the youth.[213] 'Today the youth of Assam are shining outside the state. They are feeling confident like never before. Assam's future is bright and the state is well poised to become one of the leading states of the country.'[214]

When Gogoi died on 23 November 2020, Congress president Sonia Gandhi said Gogoi's passing was a personal loss, while recalling his association with Indira Gandhi and Rajiv Gandhi, and describing him as 'Assam's most universally loved and venerated public figure'.

Gogoi came into prominence in 1976 when he was made the joint secretary of the All India Congress Committee and an office-bearer of the Indian Youth Congress under Ambika Soni's leadership. Indira Gandhi's younger son, Sanjay, had reportedly asked then AICC president Dev Kant Barooah to have a look at the young Gogoi. Barooah gave Gogoi the key responsibility of organizing the AICC's Guwahati session, where prime minister Indira Gandhi had famously said, 'Youth has stolen the thunder out of us.' This was a direct reference to the rise of son Sanjay and his core team, which included Gogoi, Pranab Mukherjee, Ghulam Nabi Azad, Kamal Nath and Ashok Gehlot.

Reporting for the *India Today* magazine, columnist Sunil Sethi had observed,

> Guwahati had never seen anything like it before. Five tumultuous days melted into cold nights as people from the remotest corners of the country poured in to witness or

participate in the greatest show in the country – the All India Congress Committee (AICC) session. Nearly 10 km out of the city, the once thickly forested bit of flat land known as Khana Para, was, by the touch of some magic wand, transformed into a glittering miniature township called Jawaharnagar. The entrance ticket here was the tricolour Congress party badge, emblazoned on a thousand banners and flags every inch of the way. The most significant event of the session was the emergence of the Youth Congress as a major force.[215]

After Independence, the Congress, under Jawaharlal Nehru and then Indira Gandhi, had made it a convention of sorts to hold sessions at newly created cities, such as Guwahati (where the Dispur area was named the state capital), Chandigarh, Faridabad, Bhubaneswar and Durgapur, to provide impetus to the party's growth and introduce the party's legacy to these places.

Apart from the emergence of Sanjay Gandhi's Youth Congress as a force, Gogoi bore witness to the 'Seven Sisters' being given shape through this event. This was the first time that the prime minister, Union ministers, chief ministers of various states and other powerful players had gathered in India's Northeast. The idea of the seven sisters – Assam, Meghalaya, Mizoram, Manipur, Nagaland, Tripura and Arunachal Pradesh – pooling their efforts and resources was deliberated extensively.

Gogoi also ensured that there was a cultural extravaganza to complement the outreach. While Indira Gandhi wore the traditional dresses of the northeastern states each day of the session – such as an Assamese silk sari, a Naga shawl and skirt and the Cargo dress from Meghalaya – cultural shows were held too – folk dances from each state alternating with other dance performances by some of India's best-known artistes, including classical dancers Yamini Krishnamurthy and Uma Sharma and tabla maestro Ustad Latif Ahmad Khan.

The bonhomie witnessed in November 1976 at Guwahati would be short-lived as, by March 1977, Indira Gandhi was out of power and would subsequently be ousted as Congress president, too – by many of the very people who had shared the dais with her at Jawaharnagar. A breakaway group was formed; it had Pranab Mukherjee, A.R. Antulay, Buta Singh, G. Venkatswamy and Gogoi as members. Indira Gandhi, who had by then shifted to her close associate Mohammad Yunus's 12 Willingdon Crescent residence in New Delhi, had to rebuild the party from scratch. Old-timer Shubhabrata Bhattacharya was there when Indira Gandhi handed over the first vehicle of the Congress (I) to treasurer Mukherjee and Gogoi. Mukherjee, Bhattacharya recalls, excitedly took the driver seat, inviting Gogoi to sit next to him. The idea was to drive till 24 Akbar Road, the new party office.

Just as Indira Gandhi returned to her residence after seeing off Mukherjee and Gogoi, the jeep broke down at Teen Murti Marg (Mother Teresa Marg now). Gogoi, Bhattacharya and others had to push and push hard till Mukherjee got the right momentum to accelerate.

For Gogoi, there would be no looking back. Sanjay's death and Rajiv Gandhi's elevation saw many Youth Congress leaders fall by the wayside. But Gogoi caught Rajiv Gandhi's eye, putting him in the league of Ahmed Patel, Digvijaya Singh and Tariq Anwar among others, and ministerial assignments kept coming, culminating in the record three consecutive terms as chief minister of Assam from 2001 to 2016.

Gogoi achieved a lot as chief minister, including breaking the backbone of many militant and separatist movements in the state – making Assam a lot more safe.

The Congress leadership's faith in Gogoi, from Sanjay Gandhi to the Sonia–Rahul era, would, however, prove costly for some. Aspirants like Himanta Biswa Sarma felt suffocated and switched loyalties to the BJP. Gogoi had accepted this fact candidly. Speaking to Assam's local media in March 2016, he had described Sarma – Assam's chief minister since May 2021 – as 'shani' (the planet Saturn, which is considered an ill omen), although the BJP leader was once his most trusted lieutenant. 'Yes, I was under the spell of Shani for several years,' Gogoi had said.[216]

Gogoi always considered himself an organizational man and remained deeply committed to the cause of the party. He was also equally concerned about what was happening in the rest of the country. Like lyricist-poet Salil Chowdhury, Gogoi's childhood was spent in the tea gardens of Assam where the bulk of the labourers were migrants from other states. This tea estate diaspora helped him understand and empathize with tribal people and those who came from socially and economically underprivileged backgrounds.

When Gogoi's son, Gaurav, who had gone to the USA for higher studies, returned to India and expressed his wish to enter politics, Gogoi instructed him to spend a few weeks with some of his friends from the 1970s, saying it would help him learn the complexities, paradoxes and intricacies of politics. This sort of schooling helped shape Gaurav's personality. At 38, Gaurav is not only the deputy leader of the Congress in the Lok Sabha but has also managed to become one of the few to be liked by the old guard as well as the younger leaders in the Grand Old Party.

Despite his long association with the Congress, Tarun Gogoi had firm roots in society and often asserted his 'Hindu' identity – like K. Karunakaran of Kerala. As the chief minister of Assam in 2012, he could sense the rise of the BJP and growing religious polarization in the wake of Badruddin Ajmal's hold over Muslims in the state.

On 20 April 2012, Gogoi had submitted a memorandum to then prime minister Manmohan Singh, seeking to grant Indian citizenship to Bengali-speaking Hindu migrants from Bangladesh. Gogoi would often take the credit for initiating the National Register for Citizens (NRC) to settle the unresolved citizenship issue of Bengali Hindus, Buddhists, and people who had crossed over to Assam in the face of persecution and torture after the partition of the country.

As chief minister, he would often say that he favoured having no cut-off date for Hindu migrants getting citizenship in the country. 'Even if a person [of Hindu lineage] takes refuge in Assam today, he should be given citizenship,' he would say.[217] The gamble proved costly, putting the Congress's electoral prospects under threat in the times that followed.

On 5 August 2020, when Prime Minister Narendra Modi laid the foundation stone of the Ram Temple in Ayodhya, Gogoi had remarked, 'The day of performing bhumi puja on 5th August, 2020, undoubtedly will be remembered as a day of great national importance, as it brings to an end the bitter conflict between the two parties of dispute belonging to two different religions.'[218]

Gogoi promoted sports facilities that helped Assam host the 33rd National Games in 2007. An avid golfer, Gogoi missed teeing off regularly when he was the chief minister. He developed a golf course near his hometown, Jorhat.

ABDUL JABBAR
(1956–2019)

ABDUL JABBAR KNEW HOW TO ARGUE HIS CASE. BUT THERE WERE TIMES when he wished he had the cartoonist's gift of caricature too. 'Had I been a cartoonist, I'd have made a cartoon,' Jabbar, convener of the Bhopal Gas Peedit Mahila Udyog Sangathan, an organization of survivors of the 1984 industrial disaster, had told author-journalist Priyanka Dubey a few years ago.[219] He added:

It would have shown all gas victims as a dead body lying in the open. And the gas rehabilitation department, the government, bureaucracy, judiciary, police, lawyers, CBI, writers, activists… I would have drawn them all as vultures and foxes tearing and eating up the pieces of that corpse. Everybody is feeding on the pain of gas victims. The victims were destroyed by the gas leak. But when they were running against time that cold December night, they had no idea that the real tragedy was waiting for them in the years to come.[220]

Jabbar passed away on 14 November 2019, hours before an air ambulance was to fly him from Bhopal to Mumbai for treatment at the Asian Heart Institute. He was 62. The tenacious activist, penniless after years of single-handed struggle for justice for the thousands of victims of the tragedy, died of a cardiac arrest. It spared Jabbar from accepting what would have been the only favour the state had sought to extend to him. Kamal Nath, who was chief minister of Madhya Pradesh then, former chief minister Digvijaya Singh and chief secretary S.R. Mohanty had acted swiftly to get all the clearances needed for Jabbar's treatment but destiny willed otherwise. The government, however, did bestow on him a belated honour. He was awarded a Padma Shri on the eve of the 2020 Republic Day.

This writer had met an ailing Jabbar earlier that year and told him about the facilities that super-speciality hospitals offer, but the activist seemed least interested.

Jabbar was neither a trained activist schooled at any institute of repute, nor was he a highly educated man. Moved as he was by empathy, he got involved in the efforts to help the gas tragedy survivors without too much forethought and it turned out to be a lifelong affair.

So even though many NGOs mushroomed – working with the gas survivors, presenting data and polished press releases – Jabbar chose to remain unsophisticated in comparison. Walking or depending on free rides, he mobilized crowds by word of mouth and sought donations from the survivors even if it meant receiving as little as ₹1 a day. His own financial position went from bad to worse, from precarious to penurious.

Jabbar remained rabidly opposed to big business houses – even when they offered to clear the huge stockpiles of toxic material – estimated to be around 350 tonnes – still lying at the now defunct Union Carbide factory in Bhopal. He would chuckle or laugh aloud each time Bhopal was declared one of the cleanest cities in the country by the Union urban development ministry.

In December 2017, Jabbar wrote to Prime Minister Narendra Modi requesting that the central government remove the toxic chemicals under the Swachh Bharat Abhiyan (SBA). 'It is inexplicable as to why the issue of the urgent need for cleaning up the highly toxic spots in and around the former pesticide factory of Union Carbide India Ltd (UCIL) at Bhopal is not a vital part of that (SBA) campaign,' Jabbar wrote. There was no response.[221]

According to official records, over 3,700 people died on the intervening night of 2 and 3 December 1984 when over 40 tonnes of poisonous methyl isocyanate gas leaked out of the storage tanks of the Union Carbide factory. But campaigners, like Jabbar, insist that the gas killed over 25,000 people and left another five and a half lakh injured or disabled.

In his 35-year crusade, Jabbar fought against every political regime – from the Arjun Singh government that was in power then to those headed by Motilal Vora, Sunder Lal Patwa, Digvijaya Singh, Uma Bharti, Babulal Gaur, Shivraj Singh Chouhan and Kamal Nath. He challenged and took on every government official he found apathetic to the plight of the victims, in the process becoming a presence disliked at government offices and hospitals. He resisted at all levels of the hierarchy.

The plight of the gas tragedy survivors no longer figures in the election manifestos of either the Congress or the BJP. The city too seems to care little. 'It is such a paradox,' Jabbar would say. 'Bhopal is identified across the world because of the gas disaster. Anywhere you go, the moment you mention that you are from Bhopal... people immediately empathize and ask questions about the gas tragedy. But the city itself is not concerned about its own people.' The people of Bhopal, he would rue, have no 'implicit or explicit sense' of being a concerned citizenry. Highlighting the seriousness of the matter, he said:

> The gravity of the situation can be judged from just one point. It is that Bhopal, after 35 years, has no record of those who were killed or disabled. Successive governments just never kept any records. If you pass through the lanes of Bhopal, you will never realize that this city has suffered almost a holocaust so recently.[222]

Jabbar received little or no support from residents of other parts of the city. His NGO, the Bhopal Gas Peedit Mahila Udyog Sangathan, kept producing hundreds and thousands of paper bags but local merchants, bakery owners and malls would not buy them even when a drive against plastic bags was on. Many of the city's Muslims, who supposedly doled away crores of rupees annually as part of their *zakat* (charity), were not too generous either. The clergy too did not issue a fatwa asking the faithful to donate money for the gas survivors.

Jabbar was opposed to both Hindutva hardliners and Muslim hawks. His opposition to those backing instant triple talaq was as vociferous as his dislike for the Sadhvi Pragya brand of politics.[223]

Each time the likes of Javed Akhtar and Shabana Azmi made it to the Rajya Sabha, Jabbar would rejoice, but funds from the Members of Parliament Local Area Development Scheme never came for the gas victims.

Jabbar had great faith in the Bhushans – the father-son activist-lawyers, Shanti and Prashant – and other rights-based activists, but when the Aam Aadmi Party, which itself had originated from an anti-corruption movement, looked for a nominee from Bhopal for the 2014 Lok Sabha elections, Jabbar's views were not considered. The ticket went to someone he did not approve of.[224]

Jabbar's worldview went beyond the gas victims; he had strong opinions on various world leaders – from Donald Trump to Abu Bakr al-Baghdadi. His views on economics made Dr Manmohan Singh and Arun Jaitley appear like birds of the same feather.

The crusader remained vehemently opposed to reforms, e-commerce and anything he though was anti-poor. In a way, his death marked the end of an argument.

JAYALALITHAA
(1948–2016)

AS A TEENAGER, A YOUNG TAMIL WOMAN DREAMT OF BECOMING A lawyer. Then, one day, along came a man whom the masses worshipped. This man, an actor hero-turned-politician, would take the beautiful young girl under his wing and mentor her. A time would come when she would become a star in her own right and the masses would worship the ground she walked on. Some would even prostrate themselves before her. Such was the thrall they were in.

Sounds familiar? Of course, it does. In Tamil Nadu's 'politics of adulation', Jayalalithaa would eventually score over her mentor M.G. Ramachandran (MGR, as the older actor was popularly known).

MGR, perhaps, had realized this too. Jayalalithaa, he would say, was an independent woman with a mind of her own, conceding – if only a tad grudgingly – that when voters even just saw them together, he would get an extra 40,000 votes, and if they spoke at election rallies and meetings together, that number would multiply. It was high praise from the matinee idol-turned-chief minister who ruled the hearts of a vast section of the people of Tamil Nadu for decades.

Most of those who support the All India Anna Dravida Munnetra Kazhagam (AIADMK), the party he founded in October 1972, are still hardcore MGR fans, drawn to the party because of his star appeal. The adoration would later widen to include Jayalalithaa, who joined the party in 1982. It was MGR himself who was responsible for according instant VIP status to his protégé, with his diktat to AIADMK activists that they should stand up to show their respect to her.

The relationship between the two would sour in a few years, though. In late 1984, when MGR was hospitalized in the US following a stroke, Jayalalithaa, a Rajya Sabha MP from his party since 1983, was convinced that she should take over the reins of Tamil Nadu. She approached Rajiv Gandhi, who was the prime minister then, and governor S.L. Khurana to appoint her as chief minister – a move that could not be executed eventually due to resistance from a section of the party. But Jayalalithaa had convinced Rajiv Gandhi that MGR's health would not permit him to discharge his duties. A furious MGR thus returned to remove her as the deputy leader of the party in Parliament.

When MGR died on Christmas Eve in 1987, his widow, Janaki Ramachandran, thought she would thrive on his legacy. She lasted barely 24 days in office. On the day of the vote of confidence, pandemonium had broken out inside the Tamil Nadu Assembly, prompting Rajiv Gandhi to dismiss the Janaki-led government and impose President's Rule. By the time President's Rule was over, the M. Karunanidhi-led DMK, had swept the polls and also settled the AIADMK succession battle in favour of Jayalalithaa, who had returned as the party's general secretary by then.

Old-timers recall that Janaki did not lack aggression, but her praise for MGR's archrival, Karunanidhi, cost her dearly. R. Mani, a senior Chennai-based journalist, says Janaki had sought Karunanidhi's support for the trust vote on 28 January 1988, and her praise for MGR's sworn enemy was seen as a blatant act of opportunism by AIADMK cadres as well as voters.[225] As a result, three years later, in 1991, the Jayalalithaa-led AIADMK would storm to power in Tamil Nadu – Jayalalithaa's alliance with the Congress helping her ride the sympathy wave following Rajiv Gandhi's assassination.

Days of Innocence Cut Short

Perhaps nobody could have foreseen her rise to stardom and through the political ranks a few decades before. Life may have taken a completely different trajectory for Jayalalithaa had she followed the path of her childhood fantasies. As a teenager, Jayalalithaa had dreamt of 'becoming a millionaire and a lawyer'. Like any other schoolgirl, Jayalalithaa had her personal heroes and would collect pictures of Hollywood actor Rock Hudson. She also had a crush on cricketers Nari Contractor and Mansoor Ali Khan Pataudi. 'I used to go for matches with binoculars just to look at Pataudi and Pataudi alone,' Jayalalithaa had told an interviewer in 1998.[226]

Born into a Tamil Iyengar Brahmin family in Melukote, Pandavapura taluka, Mandya district – then in the state of Mysore (now known as Karnataka) – Jayalalithaa was the granddaughter of the court physician to Mysore Maharaja Krishna Raja Wadiyar IV. Her father, Jayaram, a lawyer by training who never worked, squandered the family fortune and died when his daughter was just two years old. Jayalalithaa attended the Bishop Cotton Girls' School in Bangalore (now renamed Bengaluru) for some years, before moving to Mysore with her mother.

Jayalalithaa's mother Sandhya had perhaps never contemplated a film career for her daughter. But, she wanted her daughter to become an accomplished dancer. In Chennai, the young girl was put under the tutelage of K.J. Sarasa, a reputed dance teacher, but Jayalalithaa somehow was not very keen to learn dance.

Biographer Vaasanthi records that when Jayalalithaa had learnt enough, her *arangetram* was organized, in 1960, she was barely twelve then. Many film dignitaries turned up to see her debut performance, including Sivaji Ganesan, one of the most notable names in Tamil film industry. He is supposed to have praised young Jayalalithaa's performance and remarked that the girl was 'as lovely as a golden statue', wishing that 'she blossoms into a very popular film star'. Jayalalithaa and her mother were happy with his words but did not take them seriously. Both were determined that Jayalalithaa should not join the film world. 'Nor perhaps could Sivaji have imagined that this chit of a girl with "laddoo cheeks" would one day act with him as his heroine,' writes Vaasanthi.[227]

'A Mind of Her Own'

As we now know in retrospect, a starlet she did become. And how. She would go on to star with all the top names of the industry, but her longest and most popular co-star of course remained MGR. Their association lasted long enough for them to produce around 25 films together, and they would get to know each other so well that she followed him into politics eventually.

The MGR–Jayalalithaa relationship, though, would see both highs and lows – starting from their film career days itself. When the actor opted for a new heroine in 1970, an irate Jayalalithaa found a friend in Telugu star Shoban Babu. It was only in 1981 that her relationship with MGR would be revived, leading to her induction into politics a year later.

According to Valampuri John, writer, orator and former Rajya Sabha member, MGR was suspicious of Jayalalithaa and would monitor every move she made. Journalist Ajith Pillai claimed that MGR had realized she was an independent woman 'who acted on her own volition'.[228]

Jayalalithaa would confirm this in an interview published in *Savvy* magazine after being sacked as deputy leader of the AIADMK parliamentary party. She told the magazine:

> MGR has been a great influence in my life, I don't deny that. But now I am my own person. I have evolved. Hereafter, I am responsible only for myself. Never again will anybody influence me to such an extent that all my thoughts and actions and statements are influenced and made in a particular way just because someone else wants it that way.

MGR would, however, remain central to Jayalalithaa's political appeal even years after his death, underscoring the collective hold they had on people's memory. 'If I am here before you, it is because of MGR,' Jayalalithaa was heard telling voters in Chennai during the May 2016 Assembly elections. That was nearly three decades after MGR's passing.

MGR was the first film star to become the chief minister of a state in India, his song in *Enga Veettu Pillai* (The Son of our Home, 1965), virtually anticipating his future role in politics. 'If you follow me, the poor will never suffer. First Christ came and preached; then Gandhi came and preached; then the people have forgotten. Now I will set things right,' the song went.

Film and politics have a long and multi-dimensional history in Tamil Nadu. Since 1967, five of its eight chief ministers have been from the film industry, beginning with C.N. Annadurai. In his research article titled 'Politics and the Film in Tamil Nadu', Robert Hardgrave spotted what he called the 'politics of adulation' to explain why film stars entering politics were generally successful. In an otherwise diverse Indian society divided on the lines of ethnicity, class, caste, religion or linguistic affiliation, cinema acts as a binding force. Often, film stars provide a much more consensual and likeable alternative, and carry a myth around them.[229]

For MGR, art and politics were two sides of the same coin and Jayalalithaa would closely observe how her mentor portrayed himself as the 'protector' of the common man while conveying political messages through his films. Some Tamil politicians feel that Jayalalithaa's success in managing MGR, often described as the shrewdest among chief ministers, had convinced her that she could manipulate all categories of politicians.

Jayalalithaa's ties with the Nehru–Gandhi family, however, remained unstable. While she was not a major political player in the lifetime of Indira Gandhi, the actress had cordial ties with Rajiv Gandhi throughout 1985–1991. In fact, as prime minister, Rajiv would ignore protocol to call on Jayalalithaa at her Poes Garden residence each time he was in Chennai.

For the most part, the Jayalalithaa-led AIADMK remained a Congress ally, though the ties between the two parties would see more lows than highs after Sonia Gandhi's elevation as the All India Congress Committee chief. Among other things, Jayalalithaa and Sonia could never decide on a meeting place. The Sonia camp insisted that Jayalalithaa visit 10 Janpath, the Congress leader's residence in Delhi; the AICC chief wanted to avoid going to New Delhi's Tamil Nadu Bhawan in Chanakyapuri. Politician Subramanian Swamy finally found neutral territory at Ashoka Hotel in New Delhi, days after the Atal Bihari Vajpayee government fell by a single vote in March 1999. But soon, both Jayalalithaa and Sonia Gandhi had abruptly stopped talking. In the end, Sonia Gandhi felt betrayed when the AIADMK chief went back to join the BJP-led National Democratic Alliance, while Jayalalithaa had reasons to be upset with the former for failing to stitch together an alternative coalition.

However, when Jayalalithaa was unwell, Rahul Gandhi took leave from his Kisan Yatra in October 2016 to call on the ailing chief minister.

Jayalalithaa remained a cult figure for decades in Tamil Nadu's politics till her sudden death on 5 December 2016, at the age of 68, due to diabetes related complications. She is remembered as a *'puratchi thalaivi'* ('revolutionary leader'), revered as *Amma* (mother) by her party cadres, and it was not uncommon to see people prostrate before her at full stretch.

Extravagant Weddings and Other Controversies

Controversy was Jayalalithaa's constant companion, though. In 1995, when she was into her first term as chief minister, she declared that she was going to get her foster son married in style. V.N. Sudhakaran, the 28-year-old nephew of Jayalalithaa's friend and confidante V.K. Sasikala, married Sathyalakshmi, actor Sivaji Ganesan's granddaughter in a lavish and scandalously expensive wedding. A report on it in *India Today* read: 'A 2-km-long, illuminated baraat route, 10 dining halls, each seating a modest 25,000 persons and more diamonds than Elizabeth Taylor has seen, a 75,000 sq-ft pandal, saris worth more than what most people will earn this year, and an entire state machinery on wedding alert...' The Tamil Nadu Electricity Board (TNEB) had installed transformers to supply power to the site; Metrowater diverted water tankers to supply 7,00,000 litres of water; and government vehicles were employed to transport cut-outs of Jayalalithaa.

India Today's Chennai-based correspondent, G.C. Shekhar, made some rough estimates:

- The wedding hall and dining rooms cost ₹70 lakh.
- Decorations – cut-outs, hoardings and papier-mâché statues – and the illumination cost ₹50 lakh.
- Two lakh tamboolam (return gift) packets cost ₹16 lakh.
- VIP invitations included a silver plate with containers, a silk sari and silk dhoti – each worth ₹20,000. Over 1,000 VIPs invited.
- Lunch for the VIP guests cost ₹100 a head; each VIP was given bottled mineral water and a fresh hand-towel. Food for the 1,10,000 party activists cost ₹40 per head.

- Nearly 1,000 rooms at top city hotels were reserved for VIPs; average rent per room cost about ₹3,000.
- About 300 air-conditioned cars rented at ₹1,100 per day.

Even as some petitions were filed against the use of state machinery, Jayalalithaa and the entire political class remained unfazed, while national-level politicians, cutting across party lines, were present to bless the newlyweds. Among the guests were Sitaram Kesri, Lalu Prasad Yadav, Bhairon Singh Shekhawat, H.D. Deve Gowda, Ramakrishna Hegde, S. Bangarappa, Biju Patnaik, Janaki Ramachandran and Sharad Pawar.[230]

Jayalalithaa also faced corruption allegations, and her stints in jail tainted the otherwise almost perfect story of her career. She had allegedly amassed wealth beyond her known sources of income. Her death put an end to the corruption case against her – but the political void left behind drastically altered the state's politics and a trail of problems for her dear friend Sasikala.

Jayalalithaa's death served as a lesson for political parties led by a single person, especially in the absence of a succession plan or inner party institutions. Sasikala, who had performed the last rites of her friend, landed in jail – her hopes of succeeding Jayalalithaa as chief minister dashed by her being convicted as a wilful accomplice in the acts of corruption the former chief minister had been charged with.

It is natural to wonder what Sasikala's relationship with Jayalalithaa was like and how she came to meet such a fate due to the association. After all Sasikala did not have any overt experience in public life. In Vasanthi's gripping account of Jayalalithaa's life, *Amma: Jayalalithaa's Journey from Movie Star to Political Queen*, the author has sought to explore the factors that made the aloof and arrogant politician trust Sasikala so completely. 'Jayalalithaa had longed for a normal life of marriage and children, that she was not destined to have. Now at least there was a friend who heard her woes with sympathy. Who did not question her actions. Who did not argue with her,' she writes.[231]

Vaasanthi goes on to quote Jayalalithaa as saying:

> Sasikala never functioned as an extra-constitutional power centre. People must understand that a politician also needs someone to look after his or her home. A male politician has a wife at home and a woman politician has a husband or brother to take care of her personal matters. I have no one. It is only because Sasikala stepped in to take care of my household that I was able to devote my full attention to politics.[232]

If Sasikala's presence tells us that Jayalalithaa clearly kept those with patience and loyalty close to her, this is confirmed by the actions of O. Panneerselvam, who succeeded Jayalalithaa as chief minister after her death till he was replaced by another AIADMK nominee, Edappadi K. Palaniswami. Each time Jayalalithaa had to step down as chief minister following an adverse court ruling, Panneerselvam would serve as a standby.

An old video of Jayalalithaa, released by *The News Minute* after her death, showed her speaking in Tamil about youngsters joining the party and wanting immediate success. 'Joining a party, growing in the party, getting a position of great responsibility, is not like mixing Bru instant coffee. I'd like to tell you how O. Panneerselvam grew in the party,' Jayalalithaa says in the video. She then goes on to talk about Panneerselvam's political journey starting from 1977, when he joined the AIADMK as an administrative representative at the Periyakulam Ward 18, to the chief minister's post in 2001.

Last Rites

Even in death controversy would not leave Jayalalithaa, who was buried and not cremated. Before the funeral, it was thought that Jayalalithaa would be cremated and the ashes stored in an urn at the MGR memorial. It was also believed that Jayalalithaa wanted to be buried next to MGR. Apparently, she had, on some occasions, declared that her mentor had guided her life and career choices, and it was natural for her to pick a spot beside him as her final resting place. An unnamed source was quoted in *The Hindu* as saying, 'Amma is the third CM to have died in office. She was also buried in a manner similar to Anna and MGR. Simple.'[233]

Other explanations were offered too. Leaders of the Dravidian movement have largely been atheists and Jayalalithaa, too, fancied herself as beyond any caste or religious identity. Many towering Dravidian leaders such as Periyar, Annadurai, MGR and Karunanidhi (who died after Jayalalithaa) had all been buried with sandalwood and rosewater, so she was buried in a similar manner. T.N. Gopalan, a veteran journalist, however, told *The News Minute* website that some religious rituals were carried out by Sasikala and Jayalalithaa's nephew, J. Deepak, in the presence of Brahmin priests before the burial – reflecting the fact that Jayalalithaa had in fact been a practicing Iyengar, despite the appearances she would have liked to maintain. 'It may have been a question [of] carrying on MGR's legacy and being honoured in the same tradition. When Periyar was buried it was considered a sign of rebellion. But MGR wanted to be known as a disciple of Periyar and Anna, and that's why he had a burial,' he said, implying that this was also the case with Jayalalithaa. Besides, the burial would mean she would have a memorial to preserve her legacy for posterity.[234]

Others felt that had Jayalalithaa been cremated, the last rites would have had to be performed by a blood relative. Although Deepak was present at the funeral, Sasikala and other AIADMK stakeholders may have deliberately opted for a burial to avoid giving him the pride of place.[235]

In May 2020, the Madras High Court declared Jayalalithaa's nephew Deepak and her niece J. Deepa as her legal heirs, according to the Hindu Succession Act of 1956. The court classified them as Class II legal heirs, which means they can lay claim to their aunt's properties, worth over Rs 1,000 crore, as Jayalalithaa had no Class I or direct heirs.

Politics has, however, once again found its heir from filmdom – in Vijayakanth. Vijayakanth, a prominent actor-politician in the state and founder of the Desiya Murpokku Dravida Kazhagam (DMDK), is said to have modelled both his film and political careers after MGR and is even alluded to by some of his fans as Karuppu MGR ('dark-skinned MGR').[236] But the AIADMK badly missed Jayalalitha during April 2021 state assembly polls when it lost power to the rival DMK led by Karunanidhi's son, M.K. Stalin. The AIADMK leadership, wary of Jayalalithaa's close associate Sasikala, remained a divided house.

AJIT PRAMOD KUMAR JOGI
(1946–2020)

AJIT PRAMOD KUMAR JOGI'S JOURNEY STARTED WITH A POVERTY-stricken tribal childhood and then switched gears, taking him to the Indian Police Service, the Indian Administrative Service and eventually the high echelons of electoral politics as a member of the Congress party. It was a meteoric rise – the stuff that stories are woven around. But his political life was also one of contradictions and of unrealized potential, despite his three-year stint as chief minister.

In the caste matrix, Jogi had to struggle between identifying as a tribal and a Satnami dalit for most of his political life. Even after earning several reprieves from courts, as late as 2019, the

Chhattisgarh police registered a first information report (FIR) against him for alleged possession of a fake caste certificate.

Jogi was instinctively anti-caste, yet he chose upper caste leaders Arjun Singh, Pranab Mukherjee, and P.V. Narasimha Rao as his role models. All of his role models were masters in Machiavellian politics and often at the heart of Congress's fabled palace intrigues. Jogi himself was not a palace-manoeuvrer but he tried hard to cooperate with the different camps within the Congress. He also aspired to be a performer in the Congress's big-boy league, fancying himself to be a mass leader – which he was not. In spite of the presence of powerful mentors, he had to fend for himself till the end.

Finding his Foothold

Jogi was a man in a hurry from the beginning. He was the collector of Indore from 1981 to 1985 but was not content with being just a brilliant administrator. And luck seemed to smile on him when the intricate dynamics of the Madhya Pradesh Congress in the late 1980s prompted the prime minister and party president then Rajiv Gandhi to pick the 'outsider' Jogi for a Rajya Sabha nomination instead of looking at nominees recommended by Arjun Singh, the Shukla brothers, Shyama Charan and Vidya Charan, P.C. Sethi, Madhavrao Scindia and a galaxy of other leaders from that era.

Jogi joined Rajiv Gandhi's 'shouting brigade' in Parliament's Upper House. This was the time the former prime minister was facing an opposition onslaught over the Bofors scandal. Along with Ratnakar Pandey, Suresh Pachauri, S.P. 'Baba' Mishra and S.S. Ahluwalia, Jogi too developed a penchant for pouncing upon anyone who dared to speak against Rajiv or Sonia Gandhi.

After Rajiv Gandhi's assassination in May 1991, the group tried hard to prevail upon Sonia to take over the Congress. Rajiv Gandhi's death was a setback for Jogi and that was when he began to court Arjun Singh, P.V. Narasimha Rao, Pranab Mukherjee and Sonia Gandhi's private secretary Vincent George, successfully convincing each one of them that they had his complete loyalty. He would selectively use information to project himself as a 'utility' man. When Arjun Singh had a tiff with Rao, he viewed Jogi as his 'mole' in the Rao camp. Rao's crisis managers relied on Jogi for a similar role within Singh's camp. Jogi's brush with this power-play made him more ambitious.

By 1998 he had also become spokesperson of AICC, with daily and easy access to media persons who would troop into 24 Akbar Road every evening at 4 p.m. Always measured with words, Jogi was a popular spokesman. Reporters, however, saw a different man at Jogi's daily off-the-record briefings given inside the Congress headquarters and later at his Shahjahan Road residence. The passport to these briefings was strictly based on confidentiality and on the individual reporter's ability to reproduce the 'Jogi version'.

When P.V. Narasimha Rao got phased out, Jogi became a regular at the new AICC chief Sitaram Kesri's 7 Purana Qila residence. After several attempts, Jogi finally found a sympathetic ear. This rattled the Congress leader and Madhya Pradesh chief minister at the time, Digvijaya Singh. Jogi liked telling tales about 'Diggy Raja', whom he loved to hate, and often mixed facts with fiction and fantasy.

A reporter once narrated Jogi's tales to Digvijaya Singh, which led to a bitter confrontation between the two leaders. Jogi put Digvijaya Singh's landline call on speaker phone for the benefit of a select few media representatives. One could hear the chief minister telling him: 'Congress office *ki pavitrata, garima toh na kharab kar* (Don't violate the purity and dignity of the Congress office).'[237]

Jogi, Dileep Singh Bhuria (the Ratlam MP since 1980, who eventually shifted to the BJP), Aslam Sher Khan (hockey Olympian) and others tried to find a foothold in Madhya Pradesh politics but Digvijaya Singh was firm. When two groups of the ruling Congress clashed in Bhopal, Jogi accused the Digvijaya Singh camp of unleashing the 'suar maar bomb' – a bomb used by nomadic tribes for hunting wild boar.

Changing Fortunes

Luck finally smiled again on Jogi when NDA leader and the then prime minister Atal Bihari Vajpayee announced the creation of the new states of Uttarakhand, Jharkhand and Chhattisgarh in 2000. Jogi may not have had the support of a dozen Congress MLAs, but members of the Christian clergy, tribal leaders and thinkers reportedly lobbied hard for him to be made chief minister.

Chhattisgarh veteran Vidya Charan Shukla thought himself to be a favourite, but Sonia Gandhi was disinclined to oblige him. He had betrayed Indira Gandhi after the 1977 Lok Sabha election debacle and had been responsible for raising the Bofors bogey during Rao's time when he was minister for parliamentary affairs.

A crucial meeting was held at 10 Janpath to decide who would be Chhattisgarh's first chief minister. A handful of reporters saw Congress leaders coming out and Jogi bending to touch Digvijaya Singh's feet. By the time Jogi reached next door, 24 Akbar Road, he had his spin ready: 'We have been friends and colleagues. So whenever we meet, we try to rattle each other just like school-college boys do.'[238]

Years later, Digvijaya Singh would recall at Bhopal's Indian Coffee House that Jogi had promised 'lifelong' gratitude to him. However, '[i]t ended by the time Jogi's swearing-in took place in Raipur and I returned to Bhopal', Singh had said with his trademark chuckle.[239]

The creation of Chhattisgarh was painful for Singh in more than one ways. Even apart from the fact that a large chunk of Madhya Pradesh had been sliced out and a detractor was now at par with him as chief minister of a Congress-ruled state, Singh had to face some physical blows too. I was in Raipur on 1 November 2000, when Ghulam Nabi Azad, who was the AICC observer, gave me a statement, which was published in the *Telegraph* at the time: 'When we finalised the CLP leader's name in the forenoon, we thought our task was over. We were planning to watch Mission Kashmir till we realised we had a more important task – Mission Chhattisgarh.'[240] A fistfight had even broken out between supporters of Vidya Charan Shukla and Digvijaya Singh, resulting in the latter receiving some kicks and punches.

Jogi's tenure as the Chhattisgarh chief minister was lacklustre and by December 2003 the Congress was out of power.

Failing Health

At the height of his political career, Jogi met with an accident that proved to be, if not permanently disruptive, debilitating to a large extent. It certainly reduced his chances of a comeback. In April 2004, while campaigning for the Mahasamund Lok Sabha seat against Shukla, Jogi suffered a near-fatal accident. He survived but, for the rest of his life, was confined to a wheelchair.

During the 2014 Lok Sabha election campaign, Narendra Modi would mercilessly lampoon Jogi for his disability, calling him *apahij* (disabled).[241] He compared the Congress leadership with a Bollywood movie where a family introduced their beautiful daughter while finalising a marriage proposal but later switched sisters by bringing in the one with disability (Jogi) for the marriage ceremony,' reported the *New Indian Express*.[242]

Jogi was determined, nevertheless, to stage a comeback after stem cell therapy. He aligned with Bahujan Samaj Party leader Mayawati in 2018 after he floated an outfit of his own, the Janta Congress Chhattisgarh, in 2016. However, he died from a heart attack on 29 May 2020, aged 74. He had suffered a heart attack even before in 2005.

A.P.J. ABDUL KALAM

(1931–2015)

LONG BEFORE HE BECAME PRESIDENT, AS A VISITOR AT RASHTRAPATI
Bhavan one day, A.P.J. Abdul Kalam happened to glance through
the window while chatting with his host. He was spellbound. There
before his eyes was a panoramic view of the Mughal Gardens. 'I
wish I could walk on a full moon night in the Mughal Gardens,' he
mumbled. Kalam's host, the then President K.R. Narayanan, was
somewhat taken aback. 'You are most welcome to come here on a
full moon night,' Narayanan said after a pause.[243]

Kalam did come back – months later. And he stayed for five years.
An unconventional and independent-minded President, Kalam had
moments of uneasiness with both the NDA and the UPA regimes
during his tenure from 2002 to 2007.

Kalam was considered the 'People's President' as he did not
come from a political background. In 2002, the political equations
were such that neither the ruling BJP–NDA nor the Congress-led
Opposition had enough votes to get a nominee elected. It was said
that Samajwadi Party chief Mulayam Singh Yadav toyed with the
idea of Kalam as a 'consensus' man for Rashtrapati Bhavan. Prime
minister Atal Bihari Vajpayee, keen to strengthen his liberal image
following the anti-Muslim riots in Gujarat earlier that year, seized
the opportunity.

The former President, whose popularity outlived his stay at the
Rashtrapati Bhavan, was a widely respected rocket scientist. In fact,
even when he died on 27 July 2015, he was doing what he loved best:
igniting young minds. He was 83 at the time. Kalam collapsed while
delivering a lecture at the Indian Institute of Management (IIM) in
Shillong on a 'Liveable Planet Earth', where his target audience was
made up of 130 second-year students.

Credited with India's nuclear bomb and missile programme, he also shared his dreams for the nation in his popular book *India 2020: A Vision for the New Millennium*. Kalam set India three goals if it had to transform itself from a developing nation into one that is developed. 'One, you should be an economically strong nation. Secondly, you should be self-reliant in national security and its technologies. Third, you should have a high standing or a high status in the world forum.'[244] He relied heavily on Nobel laureate Amartya Sen's work. India, he says, would not achieve the 'developed status' without a major and continuing uplift of all Indians 'who exist today and the many more millions who would be added in the years to come. Vision 2020 has something for everyone. If somebody is a teacher, banker, doctor or a professional, they should devote a few days in a month to do something special, something that would make them feel proud and a poorer or suffering person's life a little better'.[245]

The directive for government officials and people working in PSUs from him was simple: 'Unleash your technological strengths. Transform yourself to service [read: serve] the people in your area.'[246] The private sector could create projects to uplift small-scale industries and fund research and development for persons who have a 'fire in them'. MNCs are expected to look at a one-billion-plus country as a long-term partner where they can create core competitive technological strength.

According to Kalam, poverty could be completely eliminated by 2020 through the continuous expansion of the domestic market, a growing tendency towards self-employment, the expansion of the wage economy, modernization of agriculture, technological upgradation, and integration of research and development. India would lead the world in software, media, financial services, food processing, drugs and pharmaceuticals.

As chairman of the Technology Information, Forecasting and Assessment Council, which generated the Technology Vision 2020 documents, Kalam provided guidance to several home-grown technology projects and major technology missions involving sugar and advanced composites and fly ash utilization.

Kalam said he had been deeply moved by what a ten-year-old had told him when she approached him for an autograph. 'What is your ambition,' Kalam had asked her. 'I want to live in a developed India,' the young student had replied.[247]

In addition to laying out his vision for the future, Kalam also addressed some burning questions through his writing and shed light on politics of the time. In *Turning Points: A Journey Through Challenges*, the 2012 sequel to his bestseller, *Wings of Fire: An Autobiography*, Kalam offers a vivid picture of Rashtrapati Bhavan's uneasy time with the governments of both Atal Bihari Vajpayee and Dr Manmohan Singh over the Gujarat riots, the office-of-profit controversy and the imposition of President's Rule in Bihar.[248]

Post retirement, the former President said that barely a month after moving into the Rashtrapati Bhavan in July 2002, he had virtually overruled the NDA government and visited riot-hit Gujarat. When he decided to tour Gujarat as his first major task, Kalam says, Vajpayee had asked him: 'Do you consider going to Gujarat at this time essential?' Kalam had told the prime minister: 'I consider it an important duty so that I can be of some use to remove the pain, and also accelerate the relief activities, and bring about a unity of minds, which is my mission, as I stressed in my address during the swearing-in ceremony.'[249]

Without identifying anyone, Kalam said that many fears were expressed, one of which was that the then Gujarat chief minister, Narendra Modi, might boycott his visit. Kalam avoids naming the home ministry, which was under L.K. Advani, but adds: 'At the ministry and bureaucratic level, it was suggested that I should not venture into Gujarat at that point of time. One of the main reasons was political.'[250]

Kalam claimed in the book that he was told that he would receive a cold reception and that there would be protests from many sides.

However, his experience was rather different, and he recounted it as follows:

> But to my great surprise, when I landed at Gandhinagar, not only the chief minister, but his entire cabinet and a large number of legislators, officials and members of the public were present at the airport. I visited twelve areas – three relief camps and nine riot-hit locations where the losses had been high.[251]

The book had no adverse comments on Modi. 'Narendra Modi, the chief minister, was with me throughout the visit. In one way, this helped me, as wherever I went, I received petitions and complaints[,] and as he was with me I was able to suggest to him that action be taken as quickly as possible,' Kalam wrote.[252]

At one relief camp, he recalled, a six-year-old boy walked up to him, held his hands and said: 'Rashtrapatiji, I want my mother and father.' 'I was speechless,' Kalam wrote. 'There itself, I held a quick meeting with the district collector. The chief minister also assured me that the boy's education and welfare would be taken care of by the government.'[253]

In his book, Kalam insisted he had problems with the Office of Profit Bill of 2006, which had sought to protect Sonia Gandhi from disqualification as MP from Raebareli. Gandhi resigned and got re-elected. Kalam says he did not find the Bill 'fair and reasonable' and took the unparalleled step of returning it to Parliament, instead of to the Union cabinet, for reconsideration. This was the first time a President had returned a Bill to the secretaries-general of the Lok Sabha and the Rajya Sabha. He later signed the Bill after it had gone through a joint parliamentary committee.

Kalam quoted the Manusmriti while speaking on gifts or profit: 'By accepting gifts, the divine light in the person gets extinguished.' He also quoted the Hadith (a saying of Prophet Mohammad): 'When the Almighty appoints a person to a position, He takes care of his provision. If a person takes anything beyond that, it is an illegal gain.'[254]

He said that after the surprise May 2004 election results, he had forwarded to various government agencies – 'without making any comment' – all the emails and letters he had received objecting to Sonia Gandhi staking her claim to form the government. Kalam, however, has clarified that had Gandhi staked the claim for herself, 'I would have had no option but to appoint her.'[255]

He said he was surprised when Sonia Gandhi arrived at the Rashtrapati Bhavan with Manmohan Singh. 'She showed me letters of support from various parties. Thereupon, I said that is welcome. The Rashtrapati Bhavan is ready for the swearing-in ceremony at the time of your choice,' Kalam wrote in his autobiographical sequel. 'That is when she told me that she would like to nominate Dr Manmohan Singh. This was definitely a surprise to me and the Rashtrapati Bhavan secretariat had to rework the letter (replacing Sonia's name with Singh's).'[256]

In his book, Kalam has also mentioned a purported episode involving Singh, a scene apparently so 'touching' that the former President does 'not want to describe it'. In October 2005, Kalam had told Prime Minister Singh that he would step down following the Supreme Court's adverse verdict on the dissolution of the Bihar Assembly. The apex court had described that year's 23 May presidential proclamation dissolving the Bihar House as unconstitutional and termed Kalam's decision 'malafide'. 'As soon as the verdict was known, I wrote a letter of resignation, signed it and kept it ready to be sent to the Vice-President, Bhairon Singh Shekhawat,' Kalam wrote, adding:

> The Vice-President was away. Meanwhile, the prime minister came to see me for some other discussion. I said I have decided to resign and showed him the letter. The scene was touching and I do not want to describe it. The

prime minister pleaded that I should not do it at this difficult time. He said that as a result of the furore that would be created, even the government may fall.[257]

Few details were known about this episode, although suggestions were then made that the prime minister turned 'very emotional'.

Kalam said the following 24 hours were extremely difficult for him:

Conscience is the light of the soul that burns within the chambers of the heart. That night I could not sleep. I was asking myself whether my conscience is important or the nation more important. The next day, I did my early morning namaz as usual. Then I took the decision to withdraw my decision to resign and not to disturb the government.[258]

Kalam claimed he had told Singh that the cabinet's decision to recommend the dissolution of the Bihar Assembly had not been presented properly in court:

I told him this once on the telephone and (the) second time personally. He mentioned that he would brief the lawyers to present the President's action supported by facts and (the) sequence of events. Ultimately, I was convinced that the lawyers did not put forth my side of actions as expected.[259]

Bihar had come under President's Rule on 7 March 2005, after the Assembly elections threw up a fractured verdict and no party or group was in a position to form a government. The Assembly was kept under suspended animation but Governor Buta Singh later recommended dissolution of the House.[260] Kalam was in Moscow when the Union cabinet decided to recommend dissolution of the Assembly, which had not had a single sitting. He wrote:

The call [from the prime minister] came at 1 a.m. Moscow time. I discussed the issues and raised the questions with the prime minister and I was convinced that even if I returned the cabinet decision, it would not matter because the decision would be somehow taken. Hence I decided to approve the dissolution.[261]

Kalam, who was in 1997 honoured with the Bharat Ratna, the republic's highest civilian award, is credited with playing a major role in the 1998 Pokhran-II nuclear tests, which were carried out during his stint as the chief scientific adviser to the prime minister and secretary of the Defence Research and Development Organization (DRDO).

The missile man had a passion for flowers too. Kalam had impressed Narayanan, his predecessor at the Rashtrapati Bhavan, and First Lady Usha Narayanan with his knowledge of flowers, their botanical names, life span and other details. The First Lady had even mentioned Kalam's knowledge of flowers in a television interview on the Mughal Gardens. Destiny ensured that the gardens would one day be part of Kalam's sprawling residence.

———

M. KARUNANIDHI
(1924–2018)

M. KARUNANIDHI, A VISIONARY, A SOCIAL REFORMER, AN AGENT OF change and political leader who served as the chief minister of Tamil Nadu on five occasions, passed away on 7 August 2018.

Originally a film scriptwriter, Karunanidhi's contributions to the state require several volumes. From his titanic battle against Indira Gandhi to his determined opposition to the imposition of Hindi as the national language, the DMK leader was a true democrat and believer in federalism. Like Prakash Singh Badal, he was one of the most towering regional satraps who opposed the Emergency bravely and faced as a consequence the Centre's dismissal of his elected government on more than one occasions.

Since the late 1940s, films and politics have had a long, multi-dimensional history in Tamil Nadu – arguably more than in any other Indian state. Since 1967, five of Tamil Nadu's seven chief ministers have been from the film industry. In his paper titled 'Politics and the Film in Tamil Nadu', you may remember, Robert Hardgrave remarked on the 'politics of adulation' to explain why film stars entering politics are generally successful. In an otherwise heterogenous society, where ethnicity, class, caste, religion and language all have the potential to create a divide, cinema is seen as a unifying factor.[262] Often, film stars provide a more consensual and likeable alternative to the average politician, and carry an aura around them that is awe-inspiring and fostering admiration.

For instance, Marudhur Gopalan Ramachandran, MGR as he was more popularly known, founder of the AIADMK and the first film star to become the chief minister of an Indian state, had sung a song in *Enga Veettu Pillai* (The Son of Our Home, released in 1965), whose lyrics, translated into English are as follows: 'If you follow me, the poor will never suffer. First Christ came and preached; then Gandhi came and preached; then the people have forgotten. Now I will set things right.' MGR's arch-rival in politics was the film scriptwriter M. Karunanidhi, head of the DMK.

Karunanidhi would also rise to become the chief minister of Tamil Nadu – five times, in fact. Following Independence, DMK was the first and at that time the only party that used films as a vehicle for political mobilization. During the late 1940s, leaders of the DMK even tapped the power of cinema to promote their ideology. Karunanidhi, for instance, wrote *Parasakthi* (The Goddess), which was considered the most controversial film in Tamil cinema. Released in 1952, it turned out to be a major success. The scriptwriter would say in retrospect, 'My intention was to introduce the ideas and policies of social reform and justice into films and bring up the status of the Tamil language as they were called for in DMK policies.'[263]

Over time, Karunanidhi, popularly called *Kaliagnar* (Artist), mellowed down quite a bit since those initial years. He started off as an atheist but eventually got bogged down by rituals and superstitions. His anger against the Brahminical order and the dominance of north India subsided with the passage of time. Similarly, his opposition to the imposition of Hindi also took a backseat with time. Karunanidhi used to often say before, 'If English that protects us like a shield, is banished, the Hindi sword will cut us to pieces.'[264] However, by the time the 2014 Lok Sabha polls were held, Karunanidhi could be seen telling voters in Chennai, 'Hindu, Muslim, Sikh, Isayi... *Apas mein bhai bhai*' ('Hindu, Muslim, Sikh and Christian – all are brothers'), or heard humming a line from the Hindi movie Chhalia, 'Hindu, Muslim, Sikh, Isayi – *sabko mera salaam*' (Hindu, Muslim, Sikh, Christians – my greetings to all!).[265] His gradual acceptance of the Congress as an ally and his almost blind desire to promote his sons, daughter and nephews in public life have left a blot on an otherwise outstanding political life.

Karunanidhi was rather charmed by Sonia Gandhi. By early 2004, he had pardoned her for the downfall of I.K. Gujral government at the Centre. Sonia Gandhi was formally not in politics in 1997 but her lieutenants Arjun Singh and Jitendra Prasad had played havoc with the Jain Commission of Inquiry that had probed the conspiracy angle of the Rajiv Gandhi assassination. Singh–Prasada had used the 10 Janpath bogey to make DMK ministers exit from the Gujral government, which was supported by the Congress from the outside.

The Jain Commission Report, selectively leaked in media, had hinted at a possible proximity between DMK and the LTTE, a radical separatist group of Sri Lankan tamils reportedly responsible for the Rajiv Gandhi assassination. The Jain Committee Report had recommended that Tamil Nadu chief minister M. Karunanidhi and the DMK party be held responsible for abetting Rajiv Gandhi's murder. The final report contained no such allegations.

The then Congress president, Sitaram Kesri, was sympathetic to Gujral and rather unwilling to pull the rug. Kesri, however, remained a mute spectator when the Gujral government fell, paving the way for the six-year rule of BJP leader Atal Bihari Vajpayee.

In this context, Karunanidhi had used some strong words against Congress and Sonia Gandhi, and conveniently parked himself as an NDA ally. For the next five years, Karunanidhi dictated terms and nominated his nephew Murasoli Maran and others in Vajpayee's council of ministers. The aura of Karunanidhi was such that the announcement of ministerial names and portfolios was made from the DMK office in Chennai rather than from New Delhi's Rashtrapati Bhavan or the prime minister's office in New Delhi.

Ironically, in April 2009, in an interview to NDTV, Karunanidhi made a controversial remark stating that Prabhakaran is 'my good friend' while also saying, 'India could not forgive the LTTE for assassinating Rajiv Gandhi'.

The row over a suitable place for M. Karunanidhi's burial and memorial in August 2018 once again brought into focus the various controversies over the burials and cremations of top politicians. The DMK had emotional reasons for insisting on a suitable memorial at Marina Beach. It succeeded in getting a place there. Yet many remembered that in 1975, when K. Kamraj, another former towering chief minister of the state, had died, Karunanidhi, the chief minister then, had denied the former Congress resident the honour of being buried near Anna Samadhi. A fight had broken out between DMK and Congress supporters over the burial site. Finally, space was allotted at another site near Gandhi Mandapam.

SITARAM KESRI

(1919–2000)

WHEN THE CONGRESS *PARIVAR* AWOKE TO THE NEWS OF SITARAM KESRI'S death one October morning in the year 2000, leaders and ordinary workers turned up in droves at the home of the man who had served the party for 65 long years. Among those present at the former Congress chief's 7 Purana Qila residence that day was his successor, Sonia Gandhi, who sat with the mourners. Former prime minister H.D. Deve Gowda, whose United Front government Kesri had pulled down in April 1997, was one of the earliest to show up.

The CWC met to pass a condolence resolution and Kesri's body was taken to Danapur, his hometown in Bihar. Senior leaders Motilal Vora, Ahmad Patel and Mohsina Kidwai accompanied the body. Laloo Prasad Yadav, who had a special rapport with Kesri, rushed from Bettiah to receive the body. The cortege was just setting out for Danapur when the Rashtriya Janata Dal chief reached the airport. Looking pale and tired, Yadav jostled with and shoved the crowd aside to lay a wreath on the body. Eyes welling up at the 'abrupt end', Laloo reportedly said: 'He was responsible for the rise of Dalits and backwards in Bihar and, for their cause, he often earned the displeasure of many, including his own party.'[266] A large number of Muslim and Dalit leaders had turned up at the airport, but there were few Congress ministers.

Local residents, mostly from backward castes, lined the Danapur–Patna road as the body was taken to Kesri's ancestral home where many of the late leader's classmates had gathered. A Danapur shopowner, who would often chide Kesri for his 'foolish involvement' in politics, said: 'He always eluded us, even in death.'[267] Kesri's body was taken to Sadaquat Ashram, the state party headquarters in Patna, and the last rites were performed at the Bansghat crematorium.

Sonia Gandhi lauded Kesri's contribution, saying the party valued his secular credentials and his fight for the downtrodden. 'We value his long contribution to the party. He was a secularist. Throughout his life he worked for the uplift of the downtrodden,' she said.[268]

Two-and-a-half-years before this, however, senior Congress leaders had bent every rule to evict Kesri from his post as party president. On 14 March 1998, the Congress's 24 Akbar Road headquarters was a mute witness to a coup that ensured the rather unsavoury exit of an 'elected' Congress president and the appointment of Sonia Gandhi as party chief.

Kesri, then in his 79th year, had arrived at the CWC meeting convinced that a party president could not be forced out. He did not know that before the 11 a.m. meeting, most CWC members had gathered at Pranab Mukherjee's house to endorse two crucial statements. The first was an ultimatum asking Kesri to step down; the second, a resolution replacing him with Sonia Gandhi. The moment Kesri stepped into the hall though, he knew something was amiss.

Loyalist Tariq Anwar was the only one who stood up to greet him. After Kesri sat down, Mukherjee began reading out a resolution 'thanking' him for his services.[269] A horrified Kesri shouted, '*Arre yeh kya keh rahe ho*? (What are you saying?)'[270] There were smirks on the faces of his colleagues. Kesri raved against the 'unconstitutional' meeting and stormed out, followed by loyalist Anwar. As he was getting into his car, he was heckled and some Youth Congress workers even tried to pull off his dhoti.

By the time Kesri exited 24 Akbar Road, the nameplate outside what used to be his room had already been replaced with a computer printout that read: 'Congress President Sonia Gandhi'.

When Kesri reached his Purana Qila residence, he was in no mood for his favourite pomeranian Ruchi's joyous welcome and ended up kicking her to shoo her away. Eyewitnesses recalled that the moment he kicked her, Kesri was overcome with remorse. The finest of biscuits – presented to Kesri during his tenure – were offered to the puzzled Ruchi.

Arriving journalists found the Congress veteran calmer. He bad-mouthed Mukherjee, Jitendra Prasada and Arjun Singh but his ingrained reverence for the 'family' prevented him from attacking Sonia Gandhi.

Kesri later told this writer he was hoping for a 'correction' from Sonia Gandhi after his ouster. When the new party chief arrived a few hours later to comfort him, Kesri rushed to greet her. Neither mentioned the 'coup'. Sonia Gandhi sought Kesri's blessings and guidance, and the old man puffed up with pleasure once again. By 7 p.m., he was singing paeans to the Nehru–Gandhis even as he promised to get even with Mukherjee, Prasada and Arjun Singh.

The face of the matter was that Congress had become disillusioned with 'chacha' (paternal uncle) Kesri after the 1998 general election, when it won only 141 seats. The party had asked 'nephews' Ahmad Patel and Ghulam Nabi Azad to persuade the old man to quit but Kesri had refused. Then Manmohan Singh, Mukherjee and A.K. Antony had called on Kesri and got him to meet Sonia Gandhi. On 9 March, five days before his ouster, Kesri announced he would resign to make way for Sonia Gandhi but soon changed tack. He said he wanted a meeting of the 1,300-member AICC, which would need over a month to arrange, before quitting.

Instead, on 14 March, Prasada hosted a lunch where 13 of the 17 CWC members signed Kesri's political death warrant. Patel, Prasada, Mukherjee, R.K. Dhawan, Arjun, Azad, Sharad Pawar, Vijaya Bhaskara Reddy, Antony, Manmohan, Meira Kumar, Oscar Fernandes and Madhavsinh Solanki signed the ultimatum to Kesri. J.B. Patnaik and Lalthanhawla approved it later. The 14 March resolution mentioned Kesri's 9 March announcement and said the 'confusion and state of uncertainty' had brought 'organisational work to a standstill'.

During the two-and-a-half-years more that he lived, Kesri would often say that 'Congress leadership *tapte hue suraj ke saman hai. Bahut pas jaoge to jal jaoge aur bahut door rahoge to thand se mar jaoge* (The

Congress leadership is like the blazing sun. Get too close and you'll be burnt, stay too far and you'll freeze to death).'[271]

The freedom fighter and former Union minister died a disturbed and disillusioned man, and never reconciled to his unceremonious ouster. There was much that he wanted to say but he suffered an asthma attack and then slipped into a coma.

The end came on 24 October 2000, a few weeks short of his 81st birthday. His faithful dog Ruchi died the same evening.

———

VINOD KHANNA
(1946–2017)

VINOD KHANNA HAD MONEY, CONVENTIONAL GOOD LOOKS, GLAMOUR and fame. But the 'sexy sannyasi' largely remained restless till he joined politics. Not that the actor's entry into politics was sedate. The very day he joined the BJP in December 1997, he was asked to contest from Gurdaspur, in Punjab, for the upcoming Lok Sabha elections in February the following year. Khanna had been taken aback. 'I didn't even know where Gurdaspur was!' he later told an interviewer. 'But I put my heart and soul into my constituency.'[272] Khanna would go on to win three more times.

Khanna's career in films started in the late sixties; his striking good looks and star appeal lifted him to the height of success, while his suave charm left the opposite gender smitten. He was linked to several top actresses of that era. By the late seventies, he had established himself as a formidable challenger to Amitabh Bachchan in the superstar sweepstakes. In many multi-starrer films where he shared the limelight with Bachchan – such as *Hera Pheri* (1976), and *Parvarish*, *Khoon Pasina* and *Amar Akbar Anthony* (all released in 1977) – Khanna was reportedly paid more than Big B.

Then one day in 1980, he walked away from it all. He had turned spiritual and was attracted to the philosophy of Bhagwan Rajneesh, alias Osho. He would initially visit Osho's ashram in Pune every weekend but soon announced his retirement from films. Over the next four years the 'sexy sannyasi', as he was called, would stay with Osho in Rajneeshpuram in Oregon in his quest for spiritual fulfilment. Khanna was Osho's gardener there, but was often also involved in cleaning the toilets and doing the dishes.

By the time he returned to India – and to films – Bachchan was not only an established superstar but had dabbled in politics too. By 1987, however, Bachchan had grown disillusioned, complaining of unease and a lack of affinity with politics. As the Bofors storm raged on India's political landscape, the actor resigned from Parliament and dumped his childhood friend Rajiv Gandhi, who was then the prime minister. That estrangement symbolized Gandhi's downfall. V.P. Singh, Gandhi's defence minister who had resigned and formed the Janata Dal, won the 1988 Lok Sabha by-election from Allahabad – from the seat Bachchan had vacated. The victory prompted the fragmented Opposition to unite and subsequently humble the Congress in the general election the following year.

Unlike Bachchan, Khanna remained low-key in the political arena although, along with Shatrughan Sinha, he joined the first set of Bollywood stars to become ministers in the central government. In July 2002, Atal Bihari Vajpayee made Khanna the Union minister of state for culture and tourism. The actor later served for a brief period in the ministry of external affairs too as a junior minister.

Khanna remained active in the Film and Television Institute (FTII) for four years between October 2001 and March 2005. The

UPA government under Manmohan Singh acknowledged Khanna's contribution and permitted him to continue as head of the general council of FTII up to a year after the BJP-led NDA had been voted out in the 2004 elections. Nearly a decade later, when actor Gajendra Chauhan faced protests as the FTII director, agitating students had cited Khanna's stint at the institute to drive home their point to officials in the information and broadcasting ministry: that they were not against a head with strong political leanings if the credentials were right.[273]

Khanna told an interviewer in 1998 that he had joined the BJP because he was a believer of Hindutva philosophy. 'I felt it was the right time and the right party to contest the election,' Khanna had said then, dispelling the notion that Shatrughan Sinha, who was already a BJP MP, had played a role in drafting him into the party. While Sinha later turned a dissident and left the party towards the end of Narendra Modi's first term as prime minister, Khanna remained a loyal soldier. 'My party's agenda is my agenda,' he would often say.[274]

Khanna helped the BJP end the Congress's hold on Gurdaspur when he defeated Lok Sabha MP Sukhbans Kaur Bhinder, the only woman in the country to have become a Member of Parliament six times – five times in the Lok Sabha and once in the Rajya Sabha. Sukhbans's husband, P.S. Bhinder, a former Deputy Inspector General (DIG) with the Delhi police during the Emergency, was considered close to Sanjay Gandhi.[275]

During his first election campaign, Khanna promised to turn the otherwise backward Gurdaspur, which shares its border with Pakistan, into Paris. The Congress had described Khanna as 'a star that appears by night and vanishes at day'.[276]

Despite the 'outsider' tag that was attached to him, Khanna won from Gurdaspur four times – in 1998, 1999, 2004 and 2014. The only time he tasted electoral defeat was in 2009 when he lost to Pratap Singh Bajwa. Khanna avenged that defeat in 2014. His death cut short his fourth stint as an MP. Khanna died on 27 April 2017, aged seventy – bringing the curtains down on a life that matched the world of reel in its flamboyance and unpredictability.

DILIP KUMAR
(1922–2021)

THERE ARE STARS EVEN BIGGER THAN HIM, BUT NO ONE IS A BETTER actor. Thus wrote Lord Meghnad Desai, his biographer, minutes after Dilip Kumar's death on 7 July 2021, at the age of 98. His death was mourned in the entire subcontinent, with fans and distant relatives even in Peshawar offering a Ghaibana Namaz-e-Janaza (funeral prayers in absentia) for the actor. He was born on 11 December 1922, in his ancestral home in the Qissa Khwani Bazaar area of the city, the capital of Pakistan's Khyber Pakhtunkhwa province.

Pakistan's Prime Minister Imran Khan took to Twitter to pay tribute to the actor:

> Saddened to learn of Dilip Kumar's passing. I can never forget his generosity in giving his time to help raise funds for SKMTH [the cancer hospital Imran had built in Lahore in the memory of his mother] when the project was launched. This is the most difficult time – to raise first 10% of the funds & his appearance in Pak & London helped raise huge amounts.

'Apart from this, for my generation Dilip Kumar was the greatest and most versatile actor,' Imran Khan added.

India's Prime Minister Narendra Modi too described him as a 'cinematic legend' and termed his death a 'loss' to the world of culture. 'Dilip Kumar ji will be remembered as a cinematic legend. He was blessed with unparalleled brilliance, due to which audiences across generations were enthralled. His passing away is a loss to our cultural world. Condolences to his family, friends and innumerable admirers. RIP,' Modi tweeted. He also spoke to Dilip Kumar's wife, the veteran actress Saira Banu.

The actor, who matched Hollywood great Marlon Brando, Japanese superstar Toshiro Mifune or Italian legend Marcello Mastroianni as far as having a huge fan following is concerned and idolized Ingrid Bergman and James Stewart, will always be remembered for the depth and integrity he brought to each character played on screen. The thespian, whose birth name was Mohammed Yusuf Khan, would develop a style of acting that was natural, meditative and minimalist, which suited the melancholic characters he played. The legendary filmmaker, Satyajit Ray, was so mesmerized by Dilip Kumar's performance that he had once described him as 'the ultimate method actor'.

From his 1944 debut movie *Jwaar Bhata* to his last film *Qila* (1998), the actor, who was the son of a fruit merchant and had no formal training in acting, essayed a whole gamut of roles which told the story of India as it unfolded – including the prosperity as well as the challenges the nation would face.

He would also have a stint in Parliament, from 2000 to 2006, as a nominated member of the Rajya Sabha, the Upper House of the Indian legislature. His first contact with politics, however, had come much earlier. Years before he became a star, Dilip Kumar (Yusuf Khan then) had spent a night in Yerwada Jail, fasting with Mahatma Gandhi's followers. World War II was still on, and he was employed as a manager in an army canteen in Pune, Maharashtra, when he made a well-rehearsed speech on why India should fight for its independence even as it chose to remain unaligned in the war. The police arrested him from the army club for airing anti-

British views, handcuffed him and hauled him off to jail where he was lodged with satyagrahis.

In his autobiography titled *Dilip Kumar: The Substance and the Shadows*, the actor recalled:

> I exchanged pleasantries with my fellow inmates and they told me that Sardar Vallabh Bhai Patel was in one of the cells and they were all on a hunger strike along with him. I don't know why but I too felt I should fast with them. So I refused the food that was brought for me on an unclean plate.[277]

He was released the next morning.

The actor would remain a staunch Congress supporter throughout his life, which was perhaps natural given his family's political leanings. Dilip Kumar once told journalist Pankaj Vohra in an interview that his father, Ghulam Sarwar Khan, and grandfather, Haji Mohammed Khan, were both Congress activists in Peshawar before Independence.[278]

He himself was deeply influenced by Jawaharlal Nehru and his career would peak between 1947 and 1964, when 36 of his 57 films were made, coinciding with Nehru's tenure as prime minister. In fact, throughout the Nehruvian era, Dilip Kumar would play a range of popular characters that reflected the Nehruvian ideology and optimism, which inspired Indian youth in the early days after Independence. Lord Meghnad Desai, a well-known economist in his own right, would highlight this in his biography of the actor, *Nehru's Hero: Dilip Kumar (2004)*. 'Dilip Kumar was the greatest actor not just in Hindi cinema but on a global scale. He was the most popular actor through the Fifties, Sixties and Seventies,' said Desai. 'His style of acting, his sense of dress, his gait and his mannerisms were copied by many of the younger actors who entered the film industry in the Sixties onwards. He was universally respected for his decency and for representing Nehru's Idea of India.'[279]

The Nehruvian idea of secularism was extremely close to the young Dilip Kumar, who would often attend Nehru's political rallies. According to journalist-editor Vir Sanghvi, if one were to look for an example of the success of Indian secularism, Dilip Kumar would have fitted the bill perfectly. 'He has been a truly patriotic Muslim. And India, in turn, has honoured him by treating him as a legend in his own lifetime,' Sanghvi says.

But the legend had his share of discomfort, too – starting, of course, with his name. It is not a coincidence that so many stars of that period played down their Muslim parentage, because the studios believed then that in the India of that era, it helped if people thought you were a Hindu or seen as one. In Kumar's own words, the actress, producer and owner of Bombay Talkies Studio, Devika Rani, was instrumental in giving him the screen name, sometime in 1943.

Friendships and Politics

Dilip Kumar had a few friends in politics, other than Nehru; barrister-politician Rajni Patel was the closest among them and Shiv Sena founder, Bal Thackeray, the oldest. The third politician who finds mention as a friend in the thespian's autobiography is Maharashtra strongman Sharad Pawar.

No less interesting was Dilip Kumar's run-in with Thackeray, the late Shiv Sena supremo, over an honour the Pakistan government had bestowed on the Peshawar-born actor in 1998–99. In his book, *Bal Thackeray and the Rise of the Shiv Sena*, journalist-author Vaibhav Purandare has recorded the fact that the beer session on the terrace of Matoshree (Thackeray's residence) that evening ended when Dilip Kumar accepted the Nishaan-e-Imtiaz from Pakistan. Thackeray went public saying in Hindi, 'Abhi chana bhi hain, beer bhi hain, lekin Dilip Kumar ke raste badal gaye (The beer and chana are still here, but Dilip Kumar has gone elsewhere).'[280]

Dilip Kumar had once explained why he had limited friends in politics. 'My involvement in politics would be limited to the pre-election campaigns that I would take part in,' he said.[281] Of course, he campaigned for Congress candidates till as late as the 1999 Lok Sabha elections, but did not care to remember their names once the meeting was over. The only election campaign he recalled vividly was his first. That was in the year 1962 when Nehru called him on the phone from Delhi and asked him to canvass in favour of the Congress candidate from North Bombay, V.K. Krishna Menon. It was a tough contest for Krishna Menon, Nehru's trusted aide, who was pitted against the socialist warhorse, Acharya J.B. Kriplani. The prime minister was aware of the formidable challenge his Marxist friend faced from the Praja Socialist Party candidate, but also knew how popular Dilip Kumar was. While thinking of asking Dilip Kumar to campaign for the Congress, the prime minister may have recalled how he had got the actor's 1960 film *Ganga Jamuna* cleared, overriding the censor board's objections to its dacoit-based theme. Memories of his first meeting with Dilip Kumar on the set of *Paigham* in 1959 in Madras may also have flickered on Nehru's mind. 'Yusuf, I heard you were here and I decided to drop in,' Nehru had remarked then, stretching an arm around Kumar's shoulder.

Nehru's gesture of affection towards Dilip Kumar that day had taken everyone present by surprise. Ahead of the prime minister's scheduled visit, the set had been abuzz for two days with everyone talking about an event earlier in Delhi where Nehru was the chief guest and Vyjayanthimala was the centre of attraction as the evening's main performer, so they were expecting the prime minister to greet the actress Vyjayanthimala first.

A year after this fortuitous meeting with Nehru, Dilip Kumar had been forced to call on the prime minister to seek his intervention for getting his ambitious film, *Ganga Jamuna*, cleared. The meeting had resulted in a go-ahead for not only Dilip Kumar's film but also all others held up until then, much to the chagrin of the Information and Broadcasting minister then, Dr B.V. Kaskar.

Writer-journalist Sanghvi thinks that the *Ganga Jamuna* episode had a communal angle too, since, according to him, the censor board's reluctance to clear the film had something to do with Dilip Kumar's real-life identity as Yusuf Khan. Sanghvi wrote about the matter in 1999:

> The censors gave the game away when they objected to Dilip Kumar's last words in the movie. Just before his character died, he said, 'Hey Ram'. That had to go, said the censors. Why, asked Dilip Kumar. Because those were Gandhiji's last words. But surely, any Hindu would think of Ram when he was dying. Yes, said the censors, any Hindu would... There is no doubt that Dilip Kumar believes his religion had something to do with it.[282]

Dilip Kumar stayed loyal to Nehru throughout and when the Prime Minister sought his help for campaigning, he had readily obliged. 'I obeyed Panditji at once, my love and respect for him being next only to the affection and admiration I had for Agha ji (Dilip Kumar's father),' the actor would say.[283]

Dilip Kumar's first interaction with Rajni Patel would take place in 1962, during one of his visits to the Congress office. Patel, a fundraiser for the Congress in the sixties, didn't know who Dilip Kumar was when they met at the party office in Mumbai in 1962. Kumar was already famous by then after hits like *Devdas*, *Mughal-e-Azam* and *Ganga Jamuna*. The actor was waiting for Krishna Menon when a well-dressed man had come up to him and introduced himself, saying; 'My name is Rajni. I practice law for a living.' 'I am Yusuf,' Dilip Kumar had replied, 'I don't do anything for a living.'[284]

Later, an apologetic Rajni Patel had confessed that he was not a movie buff and had not been inside a cinema for ages. 'Rajni Patel and I became close friends as our meetings became regular and purposeful from then onwards. His intellectual sharpness was complemented by his caring nature and the principles he stood for,' Dilip Kumar would recall.[285]

The actor addressed several election meetings for Krishna Menon, who won the North Bombay seat comfortably. Dilip Kumar would subsequently campaign for Congress candidates more frequently in Maharashtra, though he did not contest elections himself. According to the thespian, both he and Rajni Patel saw politics as a means to serving the common people. 'Both Rajni and I could have won elections and been in the fray as active politicians but that thought was far from my mind and his,' he would say.

Instead of fighting elections, they both chose to leverage their political connections. One example of that was the Nehru Centre built in Bombay, as Mumbai was known then, befitting the cosmopolitan stature of the country's financial capital. Spread over 20,000 square feet of space, the Nehru Centre consists of a planetarium, an auditorium for 1,000 people, an experimental theatre space, art galleries, a library and a research centre.

This centre was Dilip Kumar's idea, which Rajni Patel had pursued with great vigour in the 1970s with the then prime minister, Indira Gandhi. At the time, Rajni Patel had taken over as Bombay Regional Congress Committee head and also built a reputation of being Indira Gandhi's principal bagman. This was the time when Bombay was witnessing a construction boom. Patel spotted opportunity and, in collaboration with leading builders, developed what today ranks as the world's most expensive piece of real estate: Nariman Point and the residential enclave across the bay, Cuffe Parade.

Dilip Kumar had known Pawar since the time the politician was in the Youth Congress. A protégé of the late Y.B. Chavan, Pawar was also close to Rajni Patel and hence had become known to Kumar. The actor had also campaigned for Pawar during elections to the Maharashtra Assembly from Baramati in 1967.

A Surprise

In 1980, Rajni Patel would spring a surprise on his close friend. Dilip Kumar was then holidaying at Mahabaleshwar, a hill station 220 km from Bombay, when Patel woke him up one day to announce that he and Maharashtra chief minister Sharad Pawar had decided to appoint him the sheriff of Bombay. 'For a moment I thought it was a prank. I was about to laugh it off when Rajni explained that there was no going back for me as the news had been officially given to the media and I could myself hear it if I switched on the Radio,' Dilip Kumar would recall.[286]

Dilip Kumar had declined offers for the post of sheriff a couple of times earlier when he had just begun shooting for Manoj Kumar's *Kranti* (1981). But Rajni Patel and Sharad Pawar assured him that the new job would not interfere with his shooting schedule.

The news of the appointment had created a ripple in the media; this was the first time that an actor was being given the position which, although apolitical, was an important post. Kumar would later say that his stints as sheriff and as a Rajya Sabha member were significant for him only for the opportunity they gave him to do some good social work. 'I was able to make a contribution to deserving causes from the government funds at my disposal. I derived immense pleasure from the contributions I made over the years. I provided finances to build primary schools in rural Maharashtra,' he would recall.[287]

But there was a tinge of regret, too. Dilip Kumar said he was once pressured by a political friend to give away a prized piece of land near his residence at posh Bandra so that the city's municipal corporation could develop the plot into a park. 'Unfortunately, the sad story is that the same land has remained underdeveloped and unattended till this day,' Dilip Kumar recorded it in his autobiography.[288]

Ambassador of Peace

The Mumbai riots of 1993 had greatly upset Dilip Kumar; his faith in India's secularism shaken by what he would describe as 'irreligious and ungodly bestiality'. 'In the name of religion, religion itself is abused and defiled,' the disillusioned actor, who had provided shelter and succour to Muslim riot victims of Mohammad Ali Road and Bhindi Bazaar, told Anupama Chopra.[289] He added:

> All religions promote thoughts of fellowship, kindness, and consideration. But what is taking place is irreligious and ungodly bestiality let loose on the innocent people. The poor people. They are spread in thousands all over the city with no adequate shelter, no provision for food for themselves or their children. *Bas* ('That's all), period. No more talk about this. It makes me sick.[290]

Tim McGirk of the *Independent* had quoted Dilip Kumar as saying, 'If I were to make a film of the violence, I would know just the title. The Rage in Heaven. How about it?' Dilip Kumar had told the journalist. Further, he added:

> It's bad out there, still. A mob had encircled one slum and they were trying to starve to death the Muslims inside. They hadn't eaten for three days. Twice we tried to break through with a police escort and we were forced back. Finally, we were able to get in with a large police posse.[291]

The brutality had prompted leading film personalities to take out a procession of over 10,000 peace-loving citizens of Mumbai through neighbourhoods ransacked, looted and gutted by fire. Some went on a hunger strike beside a statue of Mahatma Gandhi; others including actress Shabana Azmi frequently visited areas that were badly affected, while Dilip Kumar led a delegation of prominent film personalities to Delhi, to plead with the prime minister, P.V. Narasimha Rao, to save Mumbai from being engulfed by religious hatred.

Dilip Kumar enjoyed warmth and affection from a large number of political figures cutting across party lines; among them was BJP veteran Atal Bihari Vajpayee, who tried to make use of the actor's goodwill on the diplomatic front. According to Pakistan's former foreign minister Khurshid Mahmud Kasuri, Dilip Kumar had urged the then prime minister, Nawaz Sharif, to end the post-Kargil war hostilities. In his book *Neither a Hawk nor a Dove: An Insider's Account of Pakistan's Foreign Policy*, Kasuri has claimed that after the Kargil War broke out (in May 1999), India's prime minister had called up his Pakistan counterpart, Sharif, to express regret that while he (Vajpayee) had been received in Lahore with such warmth (earlier that year), Pakistan had wasted no time in trying to occupy Kargil. Kasuri then goes on to say that Vajpayee told Sharif that he would like him to talk to someone sitting next to him. 'Sharif was astonished to hear the voice of Dilip Kumar (earlier Yusuf Khan), who was originally from Peshawar, tell him:

> Mian Sahib, we did not expect this from you since you have always claimed to be a great supporter of peace between Pakistan and India. Let me tell you as an Indian Muslim, that in case of tension between Pakistan and India, the position of Indian Muslims becomes very insecure and they find it difficult to even leave their homes. Please do something to control this situation.[292]

Controversial Legacy?

When Dilip Kumar's end came on 7 July 2021, due to pleural effusion – excess fluid between the layers of the pleura outside the lungs – a series of adulatory write-ups appeared in the media. But one article, by actor Naseeruddin Shah, was particularly harsh in its tone and tenor. Shah tried to kick up a row, lamenting how 'much more Dilip Kumar Saheb could and should have achieved while he lived'. He also questioned 'whether his [Dilip Kumar's] example as a star was worthy of emulation and whether he helped push the envelope toward progress or whether he facilitated the downward spiral of popular Hindi cinema into total star-centricity in which it wallows today'.[293]

Shah seemed unimpressed that Dilip Kumar 'never passed on the benefit of his experience, didn't bother to groom anyone, and apart from his pre-1970s performances, left behind no significant lessons for future actors'.[294]

There were more unkind cuts. Shah alleged that Dilip Kumar kept himself in public view through a strategy 'designed to place him above his peers', saying, 'What he was truly matchless at was in creating a demand for himself, sometimes at the cost of the film he was in – a legacy that weighs heavier on the Hindi film fraternity than his finely nuanced performances.'[295]

While industry peers ignored Shah's comments, Mohammad Asim Siddiqui, a movie buff and professor of English at Aligarh Muslim University, chose to respond. Professor Siddiqui pointed out that learning from the experience of others was a kind of open resource available to everyone in any field: 'The lessons are there for everyone to learn if they watch his films, or for that matter, films of any great actor which, of course, includes Naseeruddin Shah's many films.'[296]

Siddiqui argued that Dilip Kumar had himself learnt the art of acting by watching Hollywood films and observing the natural style of industry seniors, such as Ashok Kumar, while also benefiting from tips given by filmmaker S. Mukherjee and director Nitin Bose, whom he considered his mentor. 'But he knew that he had to develop his own style, a natural style, not modelled on anyone,' Siddiqui wrote, adding that one might grudge their success, but the fact remained that it was fans who made stars out of actors, by flocking to theatres, liking their performances even in ordinary films and expecting them to play certain roles which they, rather than the stars, might like.[297]

About Dilip Kumar's alleged interference in script and direction, Siddiqui insisted that it was largely due to his desire for perfection – a point made by famous directors and actors like Pran, Manoj Kumar and Subhash Ghai too. 'How many actors would try to spend months learning to play sitar from an ustad like he did when doing a song sequence in *Kohinoor*? Certainly, today's accomplished actors like Aamir Khan who put their heart and soul into their films have a model in Dilip Kumar,' Siddiqui wrote.[298]

Dilip Kumar, the AMU professor added, 'has been emulated by a lot of actors because he set the benchmark for acting.'[299]

LALDENGA
(1927–1990)

HAVILDAR IN THE INDIAN ARMY. SECESSIONIST. INSURGENT. FUGITIVE across the border. First chief minister of Mizoram. Laldenga's life might read like an adventure novel, but nothing captures his legacy better than the sobriquet he has been bestowed with: 'Father of the Mizo Nation'. It is a befitting tribute to the man who once wrote, 'In the house of India there lives an unhappy man. His name is Mizo.'[300]

While Mizoram never became a separate nation, Laldenga did ensure a distinct identity for his land – that of a full-fledged state. Unfortunately, he did not live long to enjoy the fruits of his long struggle. Not long after he joined mainstream politics, ending years of underground armed resistance to become chief minister, death cut short the life of what many believe was the 'greatest Mizo' to have ever lived.

Laldenga was born on 11 June 1927 at Pukpui village, Lunglei district, in the southern part of Mizoram. He served as an army *havildar* before taking over as the secretary of a voluntary organization, the Mizo Cultural Society, at Aizwal in 1955. By 1961, the cultural society had turned political and re-christened itself as the Mizo National Front (MNF). Laldenga's demands for an independent state became popular after the great famine of the late 1950s, when starvation stalked the Lushai or Mizo hills following *mautam*, or the flowering of the bamboo, an ill omen that supposedly signals high fertility among rats, which are known to overwhelm standing crops and stored grain. The cyclic ecological phenomena is unique to Mizoram and Manipur and supposedly occurs every 48 years. Records show that the Lushai (or Mizo hills) were struck by *mautam* in 1862 and 1911.

Laldenga's MNF had an armed wing called the Mizo National Army (MNA), which received arms, funding and training from both China and Pakistan. The MNA often launched militant attacks on the Indian armed forces and government establishments in Aizawl and Lunglei. Laldenga became a wanted man after the MNF, on 1 March 1966, declared 'independence' from the Indian Union to establish an independent Mizo nation called 'Greater Mizoram'. At one point, the secessionist movement in the Mizo hills turned so grave that prime minister Indira Gandhi resorted to air raids by the Indian Air Force (IAF) across key locations in the state. Till date, this remains the only instance of the IAF carrying out bombings within the country's civilian territory.

B. Raman, a distinguished Indian Police Service officer who worked with India's external intelligence agency, the Research and Analysis Wing (RAW), as well as its internal counterpart IB, months after the 1966 airstrikes, had testified before a panel that the air strikes had only served to draw more people towards joining the insurgency. The candid admission was substantiated by former chief minister Zoramthanga, who admitted to the media that he too had joined the MNF and the rebellion after the bombing of Aizawl in 1966.

Human rights activist Nandini Sundar, who conducted extensive interviews with Mizos who had lived through that turbulent decade, recorded that many remembered the period with horror and, even years later, had vivid memories of army search operations, starvation and a regime of curfews, their identities reduced to roll calls and a piece of paper. Separated from their fields, their homes and their forests, Mizo villagers described themselves as objects. 'In Mizoram, the grouping was called khokhom, which literally means driving villagers here and there; a term that sums up a world of terror, like the Palestinian Nakbah or catastrophe to refer to the forcible evacuations of 1948,' Sunder wrote in her paper titled, 'Interning Insurgent Populations: The Buried Histories of Indian Democracy'.[301]

Laldenga's resistance to the Indian state also captures the chequered story of the integration of the Northeast – the states of Arunachal Pradesh, Assam, Manipur, Meghalaya, Mizoram, Nagaland, Tripura and Sikkim – with mainland India. It's a tale littered with oversights and course corrections about a region, now enclosed by Bangladesh, Bhutan, China (Tibet) and Myanmar, and whose only domestic, overland link with the rest of the country is a narrow corridor.

Throughout the colonial period, the Northeast was treated separately and differently from other regions of British India. This history and legacy of separation and isolation from the rest of India created a problem when the time came to integrate different regions of the country after Independence.

Jawaharlal Nehru, a statesman and a visionary battling on many fronts, failed to respond sensitively to the intricate realities of the Northeast. When Nehru set up the first States Reorganization Commission, headed by Justice Fazal Ali, in 1955, fourteen states were created on the basis of language. In the Northeast, however, only Assam state was approved. The demands of minority groups for a Nagaland state to be created out of Assam and for separation of Mizo areas from Assam were not met.

In the months of fighting and ambush attacks that followed, Mizoram bled. There were allegations of burnings, killings and rape. In 1974, the Human Rights Committee set up by retired brigadier T.

Sailo submitted a memorandum to Indira Gandhi. The memorandum listed 36 cases of rights violations, with details of the army officers alleged to have been involved in the violations.

Things became worse when the MNF 'dagger brigade' began to assassinate former party leaders who had surrendered. Laldenga, who had by then gone into exile, issued notice to non-Mizos to leave the state.

With the fall of East Pakistan in 1971, Laldenga's men scattered to Myanmar. Laldenga moved to Karachi but, pragmatic to the core, he could sense that the army junta in Pakistan was not strong enough to help his cause. He then started sending feelers to the Indian government, seeking an honourable position for himself in any future setup. S. Hasanwalia, a senior RAW officer, is said to have met Laldenga in Zurich in 1975 to sell him the idea of peace talks. From then on, the peace bandwagon began to move on along a distinctly neat course, culminating in the historic peace accord in 1986.

All through, Laldenga had bargained long and hard with three successive prime ministers – Indira Gandhi, Morarji Desai and Rajiv Gandhi. He was supposed to meet Indira Gandhi on 31 October 1984, but the meeting never happened. She was assassinated the same day by her own bodyguards. In Rajiv Gandhi, who succeeded his mother as prime minister, Laldenga found a man who understood him and Mizo aspirations. Rajiv, who was eager to resolve endemic problems in several states met Laldenga on 15 February 1985. Laldenga, who had arrived from London, demanded concessions relating to tribal laws and customs and trading rights. In return, the MNF agreed to cut off contact with other insurgent groups in the Northeast.

Rajiv Gandhi's point man R.D. Pradhan, who was the Union home secretary then, signed the Mizoram Accord that made the Union Territory a full-fledged state on 20 February 1987. The accord was also signed by Laldenga and the then chief secretary of Mizoram, Lalkhama. It would be one of the several accords the Rajiv government would sign with leaders of troubled states, such as

Punjab, Jammu and Kashmir and Assam. The accord ended years of violence and insurgency in Mizoram and, over the next two decades, the state would become the most peaceful in the country. In 2013, it even overtook Kerala as the state with the highest literacy rate in India.[302] After the accord was signed, 572 underground Mizo rebels surrendered. Over 100 were absorbed in the India Reserve Battalion, about 70 in the Mizoram Armed Police and another 100 or so in the state government.

A lesser-known but important aspect of the Mizo Accord was the signing of a confidential agreement between the Congress and the MNF. This agreement was inked on 25 June 1986, exactly five days before the signing of the Mizo Accord, taking care of Laldenga's demand to install him as the chief minister of Mizoram. The state's first elections were held with the sitting Congress chief minister Lal Thanhawla stepping down to become the deputy chief minister. The MNF went on to win the Assembly elections in 1987 and Laldenga became the first chief minister of a full-fledged Mizoram state. However, his reign at the top was short-lived as he was soon toppled following defections from his party in 1988.

Laldenga died a couple of years later in London on his way home after undergoing treatment for lung cancer in New York. After a state funeral, his remains were buried at Treasury Square, the city centre of state capital Aizawl.

'He fought for a better Mizoram, our dignity and rights against the dominance of superpowers. He imbued the true spirit of Mizo nationalism among us, and his sacrifices led us to the path of peace, harmony and development,' K. Vanlalvena, general secretary of the Mizo National Front, told the *Indian Express* correspondent, John Zothansanga.[303]

MAULANA HUSSAIN AHMAD MADANI
(1878–1957)

AT A TIME WHEN ISIS (ISLAMIC STATE OF IRAQ AND SYRIA) FIGHTERS AND leaders are spreading beyond Iraq and Syria to other regions of the world, India, which hosts the second largest Muslim population in the world, has had negligible exposure to the dreaded and radical proto-state. The Observer Research Foundation's IS tracker project, which tracks and studies the activities committed in the name of ISIS by Indian actors, indicates that presence in the country is low-key, even though a small section of India's Muslims – who are either misguided or brainwashed – has the potential to subscribe to extremist and violent ideologies in the guise of faith. In contrast, there are many more recruits from other countries among ISIS ranks. As per US intelligence and CIA reports of 2018, there were over 30,000 foreigners in ISIS, including 3,400 from western European countries. From Germany alone, there are over 950 people who reportedly joined the ISIS.

Away from the glare of mainstream media, a protracted ideological battle is being fought almost on a daily basis between radical, fundamentalist organizations like the Popular Front of India (PFI) which, in the name of human rights, indulges in many anti-social and anti-national activities. On the other hand, the PFI's jaundiced views and its violent activities are being bitterly opposed by Muslim organizations like the Jamiat Ulema-e-Hind which stand for composite culture and pluralism.

The strong ideological and theoretical foundations of organizations like the Jamiat Ulema-e-Hind, firmly rooted in Islam, are acting as a bulwark against the fissiparous tendencies of other groups. In 2019, the Jamiat completed hundred years in public life, batting for composite nationalism and the rejection of the two-nation theory.

It had opposed the Muslim League's demand for Pakistan and since 2001, is effectively using the renowned Islamic seminary, Darul Uloom Deoband, to issue comprehensive fatwas declaring terrorism as un-Islamic.

Several research scholars and academicians have recorded the Jamiat's contribution in propagating moderate Islam in India. Call it an irony of fate, but some elements and individuals view the Deoband school of thought as some kind of ideological fountainhead of extremism.

The Jamiat owes its staunch nationalistic flavour to its mentor Maulana Hussain Ahmed Madani, a great son of India. A scholar of repute who participated in the country's freedom struggle, he was jailed for eight years at home and abroad. Maulana Madani was given the title of Shaikh ul Arab wal Ajam (The sheikh of Arabs and Non-Arabs). One of his famous remarks in pre-Independence India was, 'All should endeavour jointly for such a democratic government in which Hindus, Muslims, Sikhs, Christians and Parsis are included. Such a freedom is in accordance with Islam.'[304]

Madani passionately advocated the idea of composite nationalism and the joint struggle of all religious communities against the British. He justified inter-communal unity and cooperation on the basis of the Quran and the hadiths (sayings of Prophet Mohammad). At a time when ideas of religion-based nationalism were being advocated by the Hindu Mahasabha and the Muslim League, Madani advanced 'the theory of territorial nationhood', saying that it is 'not necessary that a nation, to be a nation, should share the same religion and culture'. Madani and Muslim clergy of that era were described by Peter Hardy as representing 'a sea change in the kind of assumptions Ulama were wont to make about the nature of solidarity of the Islamic community'.[305]

During the turbulent years of the 1930s and 1940s, Madani passionately wrote, argued and campaigned for the position that Muslims could live as observant Muslims in a multi-religious, multicultural, pluralistic society where they would be full citizens of an independent, secular India.

Madani vehemently opposed the creation of Pakistan and the logic of the two-nation theory. He argued that India had had an Islamic presence from the beginning of human history, that the blessed soil of India was the repository of centuries of deceased holy men, and that India was Indian Muslims' 'only and beloved' home. In his endeavour, Madani fought with both the Hindu Right and Muslim separatists, always giving an intellectual and scholarly basis for his line of thinking.

The central theme of Madani's political ideology was 'mutahaddah qawmiyat' or the mutual co-existence in one nation of Muslims and Hindus with the objective of non-interference in each other's affairs and mutual respect for each other's traditions and privileges, says Rizwan Malik.[306] Malik completed his doctorate in 1995 from the Department of South Asian Studies at the University of Toronto on 'Mawlana Husain Ahmad Madani and Jamiat-e-Ulama (1920–1957): Status of Islam and Muslims in India'. Mutahaddah qawmiyat has also been translated as 'composite nationalism'.

Madani's criticism of the two-nation theory was based on his assumption that Muslims did not constitute a qawm (nation) different from non-Muslim Indians. He argued that in the Quran and in the practice of Prophet Muhammad, the term 'qawm' had a non-religious connotation. Indian Muslims were part of the worldwide Muslim ummah and could not be restricted to a territoriality based on Muslim nationality. Madani had a rather fierce and engaging debate with poet Allama Muhammad Iqbal on whether the identity of a nation depends upon its land or religion.

This was the time when Jinnah's demand for Pakistan and the two-nation theory were gaining currency among a section of Muslims. Madani spoke candidly in December 1937 at a political meeting in Delhi. He said: 'In the current age, qawmeen [nations] are based on autaan [the plural of watan/homelands], not religion.'[307]

He said people living abroad made no distinction between whether a person was 'Muslim, Hindu, Sikh or Parsi', but viewed them as 'Hindustani'. He reiterated, as he often had before, that all Indians were viewed with contempt because of being in bondage to colonial rule. The following day Urdu newspapers, *al-Aman* and *Ehsaan*, (soon followed by others) reported that Madani had said that not 'nation', but *millat* (a term commonly linked to religious community) depended on territory. Poet Iqbal was quick to dismiss the distinction between *millat* and *qawm* as a philological quibble irrelevant to his fundamental concern. Instead, he unleashed a war of sorts when he penned a poem 'Hussain Ahmad' in *Armaghan-e-Hijaaz*, his book of verses in Persian saying, *'Hanooz Nadand Rumooz-E-Deen, Warnaza Deoband Husain Ahmad! Aen Che Bu-ul-Ajabi As Saroad Bar Sar-E-Minbar Ke Millat Az Watan AstChe Bekhabar Za-Maqam-E-Muhammad Arabi Ast.'*[308] (Rough translation: The Ajamites [non-Arabs] do not yet know the fine points of our faith; Otherwise Husain Ahmad of Deoband! What is this foolhardiness? A sermon-song from the pulpit that a nation by a homeland be! From the real position of the Arabian Prophet, how sadly unaware is he!)

Madani responded to Iqbal. He justified his *mutahaddah qawmivat* on theological grounds – that is, on Prophet Muhammad's covenant with the Madinites (residents of Madina). The Prophet had said that all Madinites – whether Muslim or non-Muslim – belong to one community (*qawm*). Madani regarded it as a legally valid precedent for the justification of a Muslim alliance with Hindus in India to confront the British.

Iqbal finally had to accept Madani's point that a *qawm* includes believers and non-believers. The Prophet, Madani pointed out, had rejected those of his own lineage, like Abu Lahab who had denied Islam. The Prophet in short was not an Arab patriot but a leader of co-religionists.

Madani was clear in his mind that as per Islamic principles, it was permitted for Muslims to join hands with non-Muslims and form a sort of united front on the basis of *wataniyat* (nationalism), *nasal* (race), *rang* (colour) or *zabaan* (language) to defeat a bigger enemy.

In the context of disruption of communal unity, Madani used to often quote the Quranic verse, the '*Sura-e-Ittesaal*', which says, 'Get ready as many horses and forces against the enemies of Islam so that you may put into them the fear of God and your power.' Madani used to further explain the verse saying, '[U]nity is essential for Muslims of India because Hindu–Muslim unity is the only deterrent for our enemy; only with this at our command can we inspire fear in him and melt his stony heart. As such this unity is not only legitimate but necessary.'[309]

In independent India, Madani wanted a central law to curb communalism and religious fanaticism. Muslims, on the other hand, he used to advise, should produce literature in different languages, bringing the message of welfare and good for entire humanity. He used to often repeat saying how the Prophet had addressed himself to entire mankind, not to Muslims alone. He stressed the need for reforming textbooks by including in them a description of different cultures and the living conduct of all religions, and not of one community or sect alone as was the case with other existing textbooks at the time.[310]

Madani was all for democratic participation in the electoral process. He said:

> In the independent republic of India, election is the final
> word of government formation. Muslims have made a
> significant contribution to the making of this decision. It is
> the obligation of Muslims to realise their own importance
> and give evidence of being enlightened, patriotic and alive
> to the national good.[311]

The life and times of Maulana Hussain Ahmad Madani continue to deeply influence Muslims in India. During the Partition of the country, Madani, several other Muslim religious leaders and sufis belonging to various sects and orders prevailed upon millions of Muslims to stay on in India. Several United Province districts bordering Punjab had a substantial Muslim population. Madani and his associates sat on the banks of river Jamuna to prevail upon Muslims not to migrate to Pakistan.

After Independence, the new government, led by Jawaharlal Nehru, tried according him several honours and recognitions, such as a Rajya Sabha nomination and the Padma Vibhushan, but Madani politely turned it down and resumed teaching at the Deoband seminary. At the time of his death in 1957, his mortal remains were draped in the tricolour, with prime minister Nehru and many of his cabinet colleagues leading the procession. He was accorded a state funeral with full honours.

PRANAB KUMAR MUKHERJEE
(1935–2020)

LIKE MADHAVRAO SCINDIA, PRANAB MUKHERJEE WILL GO DOWN IN history as one of the finest prime ministers India did not have. Instead, the high priest of the Congress became the custodian of the Constitution.

Pragmatic to a fault as he was, Mukherjee first expressed his dream of occupying Rashtrapati Bhavan way back in 2001. In an interview, he candidly spoke of why he would never become the prime minister of the country or the chief minister of West Bengal. Mukherjee, a Rajya Sabha member at the time, had cited three chief reasons for this: one, his poor command over Hindi; two, he lacked the leadership qualities of Jawaharlal Nehru, Indira Gandhi, Atal Bihari Vajpayee, Jyoti Basu, Rajiv Gandhi and Mamata Banerjee; and three, his inability to win a Lok Sabha seat. (Mukherjee however did subsequently win his first Lok Sabha seat in 2004.) When pressed to speak about his qualities, Mukherjee blushed before responding that as a student of Indian politics, he had always dreamt of becoming the President of the republic someday.[312]

That day would arrive over a decade later in July 2012 when Sonia Gandhi announced his name as UPA's nominee for the Rashtrapati Bhavan in recognition of his service spanning over five decades. Sources close to Gandhi said that unlike 2007, when the Congress president had requested him to write a public statement ruling himself out of the race for Rashtrapati Bhavan, this time around she had decided to reward his loyalty, political acumen and distinguished service to the party and the nation.

In 1977–78, when most Congress stalwarts had deserted Indira Gandhi in the face of electoral defeat, Mukherjee stood by her and even served as the treasurer of Congress (Indira) when a handful of party office bearers set up office at 24 Akbar Road in New Delhi. It was a testing time for Indira Gandhi and her party. She was herself 'homeless' at the time; her Mehrauli farmhouse was only half built and she was therefore forced to stay at the residence of Mohammad Yunus with Rajiv, Sonia, Sanjay, Maneka, two grandchildren and five dogs.

When Indira Gandhi staged a comeback in 1980, Mukherjee emerged as her key troubleshooter. In 1984, he was rated as one of the five best finance ministers of the world by *Euromoney* magazine. His trust quotient was so high that on a few occasions Gandhi would let him handle key assignments such as the task of prevailing upon three senior ministers: R. Venkataraman, P.V. Narasimha Rao and N.D. Tiwari.[313] Mukherjee's former cabinet colleagues recall the ease with which he used to bring about a consensus in the cabinet, making the prime minister's job that much easier. Mukherjee was a Rajya Sabha MP from Gujarat from 1979 to 1985. During this stint, he rose to become Indira Gandhi's number one man and also developed closeness to noted businessman Dhirubhai Ambani. Indira Gandhi had also used Mukherjee's assistance to secure the resignation of a reluctant A.R. Antulay in 1982 following charges of a corruption scandal, of which he was later cleared. Mukherjee also acted as Gandhi's enforcer in Andhra and other states where chief ministers were replaced successively.

Mukherjee served the people and his party with utmost humility, and this was eventually rewarded. When Narasimha Rao became prime minister, Mukherjee continued to call him 'PV' in private, but in the cabinet and during other formal meetings, he always addressed him as 'Mr Prime Minister Sir'. When Manmohan became the Reserve Bank of India governor, Mukherjee held the finance portfolio. But when the economist became prime minister in May 2004, he saw Mukherjee addressing him as 'Mr Prime Minister Sir.' Mukherjee would eventually have the ultimate satisfaction of hearing Manmohan Singh address him as 'Mr President Sir' when he moved to the Rashtrapati Bhavan.

The Rajiv Gandhi Era

Before this could come to be, though, there were some turbulent times in store for Mukherjee. Following Indira Gandhi's assassination, Mukherjee's ties with Rajiv Gandhi hit the nadir. The man who was number two in the Indira Gandhi's cabinet was expelled from the party in 1986. Sources close to Mukherjee insisted that it was a case of misunderstanding.

Mukherjee was with Rajiv Gandhi in Bengal when news of the attack on Indira Gandhi reached them. The duo returned to New Delhi in an aircraft together. One version of what followed suggests that overwhelmed by grief, Mukherjee went to the aircraft's toilet and wept. He then chose to sit at the back of the aircraft because his eyes were red. But his opponents within the Congress accused him of 'plotting and scheming' against Rajiv Gandhi.[314] Another version has it that when Rajiv Gandhi had posed a 'theoretical question' about who would take over as the 'caretaker prime minister', Mukherjee had stressed on seniority, which was later construed as his desire to occupy the coveted chair.[315]

A little before the 1984–85 poll results, the Mukherjee camp had predicted that if the Congress under Rajiv Gandhi got more than 300 seats, the veteran leader would not find a place in government. The premonition came true. It was perhaps Arjun Singh who broke the news to him. According to those present at Rashtrapati Bhavan, Mukherjee put on a brave face and smiled as he stood next to Rajiv Gandhi. Next to him were three debutant members of Parliament: actors Amitabh Bachchan, Vyjayanthimala and Sunil Dutt. A cynic present there could not help commenting, 'His [Mukherjee's] performance was so good, he could have got a job in Bollywood.'[316] Soon after, Mukherjee left the Congress to float his own political party, the Rashtriya Samajwadi Congress (RSC), which would later merge with the Congress party in 1989.

On 26 April 1986, Pranab Mukherjee was sitting with veteran party leader Kamlapati Tripathi when lightning struck. In the month of April it is not unusual for Delhi to witness gushy dust storms, but lightening was a bit strange. When the telephone rang, Tripathi's daughter-in-law, Chandra, picked it up. Then she turned pale. Looking at a somewhat poised Mukherjee, she informed her father-in-law that Mukherjee had been expelled from the Congress for six long years. Although until a year and a half ago Mukherjee was officially designated the number two in the Indira Gandhi cabinet, none of his party leaders had hitherto bothered to inform him about this development. The expulsion order was not even signed by any AICC functionary but by a lowly office secretary.[317]

Tripathi had a daily tussle with prime minister Rajiv Gandhi in the subsequent period. In protest, Tripathi did what had become the Varanasi-born leader's second most favourite daily pastime, after performing elaborate pujas: writing a copious letter to Rajiv Gandhi.

These letters were written in bold language and were demanding in nature, articulating the concerns of the in-house old guard dissidents.

Mukherjee turned defiant. He told *India Today* in its 15 May 1986 edition, 'I have been a proud Congressman. [... N]obody can take my contribution away. [...] To those who think I have no power base, I can only say that I will remain an activist. I believe in the Congress ideology, and in whatever way I can, I will propagate that.'[318]

While Tripathi and Vasant Dada Patil (the former Maharashtra chief minister, who was the governor of Rajasthan at the time) turned vocal, a handful of party leaders (namely A.P. Sharma, Shyam Sunder Mahapatra, R. Gundu Rao, Mayawati Tripathi, Sripat Mishra, Deep Chand Bhatia and Ashok Bhattacharya) joined Mukherjee's RSC. A national convention was held in January 1987 at Vithalbhai Patel House in New Delhi, where an alternative, 16-point programme was announced to take on Congress president Rajiv Gandhi. Gandhi revoked A.P. Sharma and Gundu Rao's suspension in May 1987 in order to cut losses.

In electoral terms, Mukherjee was badly mauled at his home turf, West Bengal. His party had contested over 200 seats in the March 1987 state Assembly polls and lost everywhere. Even five sitting Congress MLAs who had defected to the RSC lost their deposit. Led by Jyoti Basu, the Left alliance won 251 seats leaving the Congress with 40 in a house of 294. The magnitude of the defeat was so severe that Mukherjee turned conciliatory towards the Rajiv Gandhi-led Congress.

At the time, Rajiv Gandhi was himself struggling and facing battles on many fronts. Bofors and a range of other scandals had badly dented his 'Mr Clean' image. V.P. Singh, Arun Nehru and Arif Mohammad Khan had turned rebellious, forming the Jan Morcha.

In the first part of his memoirs titled *The Turbulent Years: 1980–1996*, Mukherjee profusely thanked Sheila Dikshit for his 'ghar wapsi'. 'I learnt later that two individuals, Santosh Mohan Deb and Sheila Dikshit, lobbied with Rajiv to bring me back to the party. I did not know her personally at that time,' wrote Mukherjee.[319]

Sheila Dikshit, then known as the daughter-in-law of Congress veteran Uma Shankar Dikshit, had won the Lok Sabha polls from Kannauj, Uttar Pradesh, in December 1984. Rajiv Gandhi had subsequently made her the parliamentary affairs minister. She used to distribute chits to ministers and MPs, giving them talking points to cover in debates. She was also actively working with the Jawaharlal Nehru Birth Centenary Panel, which gave her some proximity to Rajiv and Sonia Gandhi, and many chief ministers of Congress-ruled states.

In his autobiographical account, Mukherjee has deftly dealt with the vexed issue of his differences with Rajiv Gandhi. In one place he wrote, 'To return to the question of why he dropped me from the Cabinet and expelled me from the party, all I can say is that he made mistakes and so did I. He let others influence him and listened to their calumnies against me. I let my frustration overtake my patience.'[320]

Mukherjee also admitted that he failed to sense Rajiv Gandhi's unhappiness and the hostility of those around him. 'However,' he said, 'I remained engrossed in my work, as is my usual way. Many of my actions, all without malice or ill-intent, were used by my detractors to project me as someone unwilling to accept Rajiv's leadership. Petty things were blown up into huge issues.'[321]

Mukherjee cited an example from an interview he gave on 31 October 1984, in which he had stated that the economic policies of the government would continue. This was a time Indira Gandhi was dead and Rajiv Gandhi had taken over as the new prime minister while Mukherjee was finance minister. 'It was interpreted as questioning the authority of the prime minister. While I had given the interview to quell any uncertainty about India in the international markets following the assassination of Mrs Gandhi, it was portrayed as presumptuous and unmindful of Rajiv's authority.'[322]

In the second part of his memoirs, Mukherjee explained why he was dropped from the Rajiv Gandhi cabinet. 'When I was dropped from the cabinet [in December 1984], I was not even 50 years old. But we were clearly of very different backgrounds and temperaments,' he writes.[323] 'Rajiv was a reluctant politician. He was forced by circumstances to become prime minister at the age of 40. He was ahead of his times. He wanted rapid change and saw the old guard in the Congress as an obstacle to his vision. He was forward-looking, tech-savvy and welcomed foreign investment in India as well as an enlargement of the market economy. In contrast, I was a conservative, conventional political leader who favoured the public sector, a regulated economy and wanted foreign investment only from NRIs.'[324]

Mukherjee says in the book that he was often asked whether he bore a grudge against Rajiv Gandhi. Referring to an interview Rajiv Gandhi had given to Aroon Purie of *India Today* just before his assassination in May 1991, he said he learnt from the interview that many things had been said about them that weren't true.[325]

According to Mukherjee, his proximity to the Congress old guard, such as Kamlapati Tripathi and Vasantdada Patil, had angered Rajiv Gandhi.[326]

Mukherjee then goes on to quote from T.N. Ninan's interview of Rajiv Gandhi taken in May 1986 to indicate why he was expelled from the Congress. He quotes Gandhi as saying:

> I thought a few people were going beyond the limits of normal... what should I say... freedom of action within the democratic processes of the party, especially when elections in the party are due[,] so that all the feelings could be vented in the election process. So we took some action.[327]

Mukherjee quotes verbatim from Ninan asking Rajiv Gandhi:

> TNN: Did Pranab overestimate his real strength and therefore become a fall guy, because he is prominent and he doesn't really have a following? So if you pick on him you get the message across?

Rajiv : We picked the four or five people who we thought were making... trying to destabilise the party...who were going beyond the limits of democratic freedom in the party. And we took action. There is no...sort...of...further motivation than that.[328]

Mukherjee too had given an interview in April 1986 to journalist Pritish Nandy, Editor of the *Illustrated Weekly of India*. The magazine carried a twelve-page story titled 'The Man Who Knew Too Much', which created a furore in political circles. The report implied that Mukherjee knew something which would harm the party.[329] Mukherjee said when he was expelled from the Congress on 26 April 1986, nobody from the party leadership had bothered to inform him.

Eventually, Mukherjee did return and win back Rajiv Gandhi's confidence in 1988 and went on to hold several ministerial portfolios and important positions in the party under the leadership of P.V. Narasimha Rao, Sitaram Kesri and Sonia Gandhi.

Later Years in the Congress

The hot and humid evening of 22 May 2004 saw a somewhat relaxed Mukherjee when the United Progressive Alliance (UPA) ministry under Manmohan Singh was sworn in. As television channels went wild speculating about who was going to get what portfolio, Mukherjee sat quietly at his Talkatora Road residence in New Delhi, reportedly going through various reports on the functioning of the Union home ministry. Kashmir had seen a terror attack a few hours before and some news channels, confident that they were interviewing the next home minister, even aired some comments from Mukherjee on the attack. Later that night, however, Mukherjee was given the defence portfolio. In political circles, there is an errant impression that the defence portfolio somehow ranks below home.

Eyewitness accounts said there was an air of disbelief at Talkatora Road. Mukherjee, however, remained unfazed. He reportedly took barely a few seconds to grasp the news. When he returned from the washroom, he told his assistant in a measured voice: 'Connect me to the defence secretary.' By the time he shifted out to North Bloc at Raisina Hills as finance minister, Mukherjee telephoned his successor A.K. Antony and said, 'I am giving you all my sleepless nights.'[330] Experience had taught Mukherjee that in the slippery corridors of power there is no time to ponder over unfulfiled possibilities or remain a prisoner of one's desires.

For reasons unknown, Sonia Gandhi–Pranab Mukherjee relations have always been shrouded in mystery. There is a probably erroneous and over-simplistic assumption that the Congress chief at 10 Janpath did not trust Mukherjee fully. Insiders, though, always insist that Sonia Gandhi had a healthy regard for Mukherjee and greatly valued his input. When she took over as Congress chief in 1998, she got upset when she learnt that former prime minister P.V. Narasimha Rao had made a submission before the Constitution review panel, set up by the Atal Bihari Vajpayee regime under Justice M.N. Venkatachaliah with the well-known Sonia Gandhi-baiter of that era, P.A. Sangma. Fearing foul play, the Congress had decided to boycott the panel's meetings. However, instead of issuing a statement against Rao, Sonia Gandhi turned to Mukherjee and dispatched the veteran leader to gauge Rao's mood. The Chanakya of Indian politics told Mukherjee that he had done nothing wrong. He had gone to clear Indira Gandhi's name in the context of the accession of Sikkim. Rao had apparently told the panel that it was grossly wrong to view Indira Gandhi's move to induct Sikkim as an Indian state as one that had played havoc with constitutional provisions. Sonia Gandhi quickly gave Rao a clean chit, saying she had always held him in high regard and her mother-in-law too had had great regard for Rao.

Mukherjee's relations with Sonia Gandhi had evolved over the years. He was instrumental in plotting an 'unconstitutional coup' on 5 March 1998 against the then Congress president Sitaram Kesri to ensure Sonia Gandhi could formally take over the party.

In the third edition of his memoirs, *The Coalition Years: 1996–2012*, dedicated to the Indian voter, Mukherjee recalled how Jitendra Prasada and Sharad Pawar were vociferously seeking a change of leadership in the Congress.[331] Mukherjee admitted that there was no provision for the removal of the Congress president in the party constitution, but said he had studied it minutely to find a solution. 'The Congress constitution has a provision, article XIX-J which says that, in the event of an extraordinary situation, the CWC can resort to appropriate solutions not mentioned in the constitution, subject to ratification by the AICC within six months,' Mukherjee wrote.[332] Subsequently, a plan was hatched at Mukherjee's Talkatora Road residence, in the presence of many CWC members, to operationalize the oust-Kesri campaign. When the CWC meeting was held on 5 March 1998, Kesri was asked to step down. The veteran refused and adjourned the meeting, but Mukherjee, who was AICC general secretary then, presided over the meeting and moved a resolution inviting Sonia Gandhi to take over.

He was also Sonia Gandhi's closest advisor when Sharad Pawar, P.A. Sangma and Tariq Anwar revolted against her on the ground of her foreign origins. It is believed that the drafts of all letters by Sonia Gandhi of that era were prepared by Mukherjee. In fact, Sonia Gandhi's admiration for the Bengali babu dates back to Indira Gandhi's dinner table conversation, when the former prime minister used to narrate anecdotes of Mukherjee's wit and scholarship with relish. Like Indira Gandhi, Sonia Gandhi too regarded him as a living encyclopaedia and an authority on a range of subjects – from food processing to culture to diplomacy to social policies.

It may have been mere coincidence that when Mukherjee's memoirs were released by the then vice-president Hamid Ansari, Sonia and Rahul Gandhi, Dr Manmohan Singh and a large number of other influential party leaders stayed away. From the party's side, Dr Karan Singh and P.J. Kurian attended.

The third part of Mukherjee's memoirs was a delightful recollection and an authentic account of the country's politics particularly during the UPA years. However, like most autobiographical accounts, Mukherjee's version of events and personalities is subjective and often lacks accurate portrayal. For instance, his reluctance to join the Manmohan Singh government in May 2004 appears to be an afterthought. This vital piece of information was invisible when Sonia Gandhi declined and Manmohan Singh was named as the prime minister on the evening of 17 May 2004. Mukherjee was actually multitasking at that point of time – from trying to persuading Sonia Gandhi to 'honour' the 2004 mandate, to bringing in alliance partners on board, firming up ties with the Left parties and preparing numerous drafts that ranged from letters to Rashtrapati Bhavan and allies and providing inputs for Sonia Gandhi's central hall speech. He was going about it clinically like a seasoned Congress manager.

It's worth recalling how Mukherjee had performed similar duties in 1991 when his long-standing friend P.V. Narasimha Rao was being sworn in. When Rajiv Gandhi died and Rao became prime minister, he turned to Mukherjee for assistance with cabinet formation. Smoking the finest Havana cigars gifted by a friend, Mukherjee stayed up most of the night to prepare an exhaustive list for Rao. Perhaps modesty prevented him from inserting his own name when he sent the final list to the then President R. Venkataraman. Mukherjee was subsequently made deputy chairman of the Planning Commission.

As an insider, Mukherjee was privy to lot of information and developments in the grand old party. In 1999, when the Vajpayee government fell by one vote and an unsuccessful bid for an alternative government was made, Sonia Gandhi had Manmohan Singh on the reserve bench. This aspect had agitated two persons much more than Mukherjee. Madhavrao Scindia hated it the most. His administrative acumen, personal charisma and proximity to Rajiv and Sonia Gandhi had been utterly disregarded by 10 Janpath. The other aggrieved soul was Arjun Singh, a maverick in popular perception, but a Sonia Gandhi loyalist who had sacrificed his otherwise promising political career fighting her proxy battle against Rao. As a veteran, Mukherjee should have known that when she discounted Scindia and Arjun, his chances of making a cut were nil.

It is elementary to know why Manmohan was chosen in 2004, instead of Mukherjee and Arjun Singh (Scindia was dead by then). After the P.V. Narasimha Rao experiment, 10 Janpath was wary of appointing a politician as the Congress prime minister heading a coalition government. Though Sonia Gandhi was officially not in politics and played little role in Rao's appointment as Congress president and prime minister after Rajiv Gandhi's assassination, she was alive to the games Rao and his team had played, which ranged from tinkering with core principles of secularism, socialism, probity in public life and handling of the Congress organization. She did not want a ghost of that era during UPA. In that sense, the denial of the prime ministerial chair was not a reflection on Mukherjee but of her general distrust towards the political tribe.

Manmohan Singh, on the other hand, proved exceptional. For ten long years, the prime minister consciously avoided building a coterie or having favourites. He didn't even toy with the idea of contesting Lok Sabha polls from Jallandhar even though the Badals and Akalis were prepared to support him informally. As prime minister, Singh appointed and removed ministers dutifully in recognition of the fact that the political leadership was with Sonia Gandhi. She was the vote-catcher and leader of the Congress. One may have disdain for such an approach but that's how it was.

A word about Mukherjee lamenting the exit of Trinamool from UPA in the second phase is perhaps in order here. It must be remembered that the entire Mamata Banerjee story during 1990s, including her exit from the Congress, has many elements and characters. Everyone knows how the likes of Somen Mitra and others were backed and propped up to drive Mamata Banerjee out of the Congress. Mukherjee and Banerjee may have subsequently brought peace but history and its sequence of events can't be altered as per one's convenience.

In an interview to *India Today*'s Editor M.J. Akbar in 2010, Pranab Mukherjee had predicted that he would not see himself serving under Rahul Gandhi. Mukherjee, then Union finance minister and key trouble shooter for the UPA government led by prime minister Manmohan Singh, had said that he will not be in the next cabinet if the then Congress general secretary Rahul Gandhi becomes prime minister. 'My goodness, what would be my age? I am already 75. There is a limit beyond which you cannot go. Rather, I have overstayed my wicket,' Mukherjee, who held a unique distinction of working with four Congress prime ministers (Indira Gandhi, Rajiv Gandhi, P.V. Narasimha Rao and Manmohan Singh) had said.[333]

Former President Mukherjee, agreeing to be the chief guest at the RSS headquarters in Nagpur on 7 June 2018, drew a fair amount of criticism. But, I feel, it should be seen more as RSS's constant attempt to broaden its base and appropriate iconic figures. Contrary to popular perception, the chequered history of RSS-Congress relations have had patches of cosy relations and proximity that brought dividends to both sides.[334]

As President, Mukherjee earned the dubious distinction of rejecting a record 37 mercy petitions filed by death row convicts that sent them to the gallows. Those hanged during his tenure included Mumbai terror attack convict Ajmal Kasab, Parliament attack convict Afzal Guru and 1993 Mumbai serial blasts convict Yakub Memon.

By the time his term in Rashtrapati Bhavan ended in July 2017, Mukherjee had built up a reputation as a preservationist, setting up a garage-turned-museum in the Bhavan, where its old treasures such as a portrait of Lord Irwin, the walking stick of V.V. Giri and other items were dusted, restored and granted a proud audience.

ARUN NEHRU
(1944–2013)

Few, least of all Arun Nehru, would have anticipated such a public putdown. But there was no stopping Priyanka Gandhi Vadra as she ripped into her uncle's vote bank, calling him a betrayer and a backstabber. That was in 1999, in Raebareli – sometime before the Uttar Pradesh constituency voted in the Lok Sabha elections that year.

Fourteen years later, on 26 July 2013, when Priyanka, her mother Sonia, brother Rahul Gandhi and husband Robert Vadra attended Arun Nehru's funeral in Delhi, death seemed to have reconciled two branches of the family that had witnessed a bitter estrangement a quarter century ago. Arun Nehru, 69, had passed away at a Gurgaon hospital the day before the funeral. In death, he had ceased to be the minister who had tarnished his boss Rajiv Gandhi over Bofors and joined his opponents. He was once more the loyal cousin – albeit now no more – who had helped Rajiv Gandhi make up his mind about becoming the prime minister after Indira Gandhi's assassination in 1984.

It had all been very different during the 1999 Lok Sabha elections when Arun Nehru, great-grandson of Motilal Nehru's elder brother Nandlal, contested from the Nehru–Gandhi pocket borough of Raebareli on a BJP ticket. Priyanka Gandhi Vadra's public attack on her uncle came as she campaigned for Congress candidate and family loyalist Capt. Satish Sharma. She told voters at a rally:

> I have a complaint against you. A man who committed treachery while he was in my father's ministry, who stabbed a brother in the back – answer me – how did you let such a man in here? How did he dare come here? [...] I spoke to

my mother before coming here. She told me not to speak
ill of anyone. But I am young; who shall I speak my mind
to if not to you?[335]

The process of reconciliation began only when Sonia and her
children visited Arun Nehru in the hospital. Around the same time,
this writer had asked Arun Nehru about the rapprochement with
Sonia Gandhi. 'We are a family and we continue to be a family,' she
had replied curtly, adding, 'However, I do not wish to talk about
it, please.'[336]

Contrary to common perceptions, Rajiv Gandhi did not draft Arun
Nehru into the Congress. When Indira Gandhi won from Medak and
Raebareli in the 1980 Lok Sabha polls, she had vacated the latter seat
and asked Arun Nehru, then in the middle of a successful corporate
career, to contest the seat.

That summer, the death of Indira Gandhi's younger son Sanjay
had set off an intense tug-of-war between his widow Maneka and
Rajiv Gandhi to fill the vacuum. Arun Nehru teamed up with Shivraj
Patil and brought fifty party MPs to Indira Gandhi, urging her to
pick Rajiv as Sanjay's successor.

Four years later, minutes after Indira's assassination in October
1984, Arun Nehru had arrived at the All India Institute of Medical
Sciences to see Sonia Gandhi hysterical with fear for the lives of
her children. When Arun Nehru rushed back to 1 Safdarjung Road,
he was stunned to see that there was not a single security guard
to protect young Rahul and Priyanka Gandhi. He brought them
back from school and sent them to the Gulmohar Park home of
Teji Bachchan, mother of Rajiv Gandhi's friend and Bollywood
star Amitabh.

Rajiv Gandhi was in Bengal at the time. The moment he arrived
in Delhi, Arun Nehru told him that 'there is no question of having
an interim prime minister', clearly alluding to Pranab Mukherjee's
comments about a precedent.[337] Mukherjee, seen as the number two
in the Indira Gandhi government, had brought up the example of

Gulzarilal Nanda who had twice been interim prime minister – the first time after the death of Jawaharlal Nehru and then after Lal Bahadur Shastri died. Years later, after the cousins had fallen out, Arun Nehru had told a reporter from *Onlooker*, 'Rajiv wanted that job badly... Rajiv told me that he did not want an interim prime minister, but instead he himself wanted to be sworn in as PM straightway.'[338]

Arun Nehru emerged as Rajiv Gandhi's most trusted aide. Many in the Congress believe that it was he who had advised Rajiv Gandhi in 1986 to open the locks to the Ramjanmabhoomi–Babri Masjid site in Ayodhya for Hindu worshippers. Arun Nehru's supporters insist that the idea of playing the 'soft Hindutva' card – aimed at countering a backlash against the Congress for supporting the Muslim clergy in the Shah Bano case – had come from the then Congress chief minister of Uttar Pradesh, Veer Bahadur Singh.

It was the Bofors controversy that ultimately caused bad blood between Arun Nehru and Rajiv Gandhi. After being dropped from the ministry and expelled from the Congress, Arun Nehru had joined V.P. Singh's Jan Morcha in 1987 and later became a Janata Dal minister before shifting to the BJP.

Mani Shankar Aiyar, who was a close Rajiv Gandhi aide, wrote in the *Sunday* magazine, 'The falling out between Arun Nehru and Rajiv Gandhi was widely commented on in political circles and the media after Rajiv Gandhi failed to proceed to Srinagar in April 1986 where Arun Nehru was recovering from a severe heart attack.'[339]

Arun's death removed one of the last surviving players from the Bofors controversy. Italian businessman Ottavio Quattrocchi had died less than a fortnight earlier in Milan.

ATAL BIHARI VAJPAYEE

(1924–2018)

IF POLITICS IS THE ART OF ALWAYS TAKING CREDIT, THEN FORMER PRIME minister Atal Bihari Vajpayee was an aberration. Because he instead gave credit where it was due, whether it was a friend or an adversary. As a democratically elected prime minister, one of the lasting legacies of the late BJP leader would be his healthy respect for rivals, including Congress stalwarts from Jawaharlal Nehru to Sonia Gandhi.

Yet he could be unsparing in his criticism too. Vajpayee is said to have attracted the attention of independent India's first prime minister when he demanded a special session of Parliament in the middle of the India–China War in 1962. Nehru conceded and debated the issue even though he was on the defensive. Till the end, however, Vajpayee, never hesitated to praise 'Panditji', either at home or abroad.

In fact, when Vajpayee became the foreign minister of the Morarji Desai government in 1977, he asked officials to restore a portrait of Nehru on the wall behind the foreign minister's table and chair. Some overzealous babus had removed the portrait as the first non-Congress government came to power at the Centre.

Earlier, when Bangladesh was created in 1971, Vajpayee had also described Indira Gandhi as 'Abhinav Chandi Durga' for defeating Pakistan in the war. The comparison with the demon-slaying goddess had helped the Congress prime minister cultivate a larger than life image. She would later admit to her friend and biographer, Pupul Jayakar, that she had had some intimations of 'supernatural powers throughout the war and even previous to it, having had strange experiences.'[340] The remark, however, had generated a lot of heat.

In his article titled '*Kiski Puja Kar Rahen Hain Bahujan?*' (Who are the lower castes really worshiping?), Dalit activist Prem Kumar Mani recalled how communist leader S.A. Dange had protested against the comment.[341] 'Atal Bihari fails to understand what he is saying and Mrs Gandhi fails to understand what she is hearing,' Dange had reportedly said. 'Both must understand that Chandi Durga was a slaughterer of the Dalits and backward sections.'[342]

Even though the criticism may have been valid, the fact of Vajpayee's graciousness remains. Another instance of it came on 26 December 2004, three days after P.V. Narasimha Rao's death. Vajpayee, who had turned eighty the previous day, was in his hometown, Gwalior, to participate at a writers' meet when he chose the occasion to make an important disclosure, crediting the former prime minister for being the 'true father' of India's nuclear programme. Sounding a tad emotional, Vajpayee revealed that when he assumed the prime minister's office in 1996 (a thirteen-day stint), he had received a paper from his predecessor, urging him to continue the country's nuclear programme. 'Rao had asked me not to make it public. But today when he is dead and gone, I wish to set the record straight,' he said. In his typical style, he said: 'Rao told me that the bomb is ready. I exploded it. I did not miss the opportunity.'[343]

Vajpayee said he never blamed the Congress on this count. 'They, too, wanted a strong India to counter Pakistan and China. In foreign policy matters, they never lacked commitment,' he said.[344] Yet barely ten years later, his party's leadership would consistently blame the Congress for all the ills plaguing the country.

Vajpayee, though, had reason to have a healthy regard for the Congress leadership. In 1994, when Pakistan was making a big issue about alleged human rights violations in Jammu and Kashmir at international fora, Rao had sent Vajpayee as the leader of the Indian delegation to that year's session of the Human Rights Commission at Geneva. The image of a triumphant Vajpayee hugging Salman Khurshid (India's junior foreign minister then) after returning from

Geneva on the *India Today* magazine cover is still etched in many minds.

This is not to say that Vajpayee did not have his share of bitter political battles with the Congress. He did, for instance, lock horns with Rajiv Gandhi over many issues – such as Bofors, the Shah Bano controversy and the Ayodhya dispute. But when the latter was killed in a bomb explosion at Sriperumbudur in May 1991, Vajpayee called noted interviewer Karan Thapar to disclose that Gandhi had done him a favour once.

Rajiv Gandhi, he recalled, was the prime minister when he came to know that Vajpayee was suffering from an acute kidney ailment and required treatment abroad. Vajpayee told Thapar that Gandhi called him up one day to say he was including him in India's delegation to the UN. 'He (Rajiv) hoped I would use the opportunity to get the treatment I needed. I went to New York and that's one reason I am alive today,' Vajpayee told Thapar in a TV interview.[345]

Years later, while speaking in New York in 2002, Vajpayee similarly mentioned a gesture by Sonia Gandhi after terrorists had attacked the Indian Parliament on 13 December 2001. Sonia Gandhi, he said, had telephoned him to ask: 'Where are you, are you okay? I am okay, are you okay too?'[346] Sonia Gandhi was then leader of the Opposition and Vajpayee the prime minister. 'This is the greatness of Indian democracy,' Vajpayee told his audience. 'We have differences in our politics but the whole world also believes that India is moving unitedly ahead.'[347]

Vajpayee also returned the Congress' favours when he could. In some ways, for example, Vajpayee was instrumental in helping Sonia Gandhi become an astute politician.[348] Vajpayee had chosen her to head an Indian delegation to the USA in June 2001. It turned out to be a milestone of sorts for the leader of the Opposition who was otherwise still hesitant and diffident as a politician.

Sonia Gandhi's elevation as India's representative to the UN AIDS Conference caused heartburn within the BJP–NDA and reportedly left health minister C.P. Thakur sulking. Thakur had been hoping to lead the delegation.

A high point came for Sonia Gandhi when she had a one-to-one meeting with the US vice-president, Dick Cheney. In a series of meetings and press interactions during the trip, she consciously avoided bringing in domestic politics or her ideological differences with the BJP, preferring to focus on the theme of national consensus on tackling poverty and disease and stabilizing the population. She gradually developed a lot of respect for Vajpayee.

Both Priyanka and Rahul Gandhi had the highest regard for the former prime minister. In private conversations, Rahul Gandhi would often rue that he did not get much of a chance to interact and learn from Vajpayee.

SULTAN SALAHUDDIN OWAISI
(1931–2008)

IN THE LAST SCENE OF *GARM HAVA* (HOT WINDS), THE ICONIC FILM ABOUT the post-Partition plight of Muslims in India, Salim Mirza and his son Sikander run into a massive demonstration. The father and son are leaving Agra – and India – for good, disillusioned by the ostracism they had been facing, collective socioeconomic assault of changed attitudes and loss of means of survival, courtesy the reluctance of banks to give loans.

The rally draws nearer as the *tonga* approaches the Agra Cantonment Station. What happens next lifts the film beyond the immediate and into the future as father and son realize that the flag-waving protesters are no different from them. They too want jobs and opportunities. Sikander jumps off the tonga first, then Salim, as the two join the crowd demanding a better deal for the dispossessed. The train to Attari, near the border of Pakistan, is forgotten. The final scene brings a sense of hope as we see Salim accept his situation and take charge of his life afresh.

Unfortunately, life doesn't always play out like movie endings. The 1974 film about the plight of a North Indian Muslim family may have ended on a positive note but a sense of uncertainty dogging the community and its inadequate political representation (despite being the country's second-largest community) have been twin blots on an otherwise vibrant democracy.

Figures don't lie: of the 540-odd MPs in the 17th Lok Sabha, only 27 are Muslim. The highest representation from the community was seen in the year 1980, when Parliament's Lower House had 49 Muslims. The corresponding figures for other years show that little has changed over the past seventy years: 21 Muslim MPs in 1952, 24 in 1957, 23 in 1962, 29 in 1967, 30 in 1971, 34 in 1977, 46 in 1984, 33 in 1989, 28 in 1991, 29 in 1996, 32 in 1999, 36 in 2004, 30 in 2009 and 23 in 2014.[349]

It is this sense of alienation in their own country that led to the rise of the Owaisis of the All India Majlis-e-Ittehadul Muslimeen (AIMIM), one of the few 'Muslim' parties in Indian politics. What the Owaisis did was tap into the discontent, fed by a long history of communal riots, unemployment and appalling socioeconomic indicators – as made obvious by the Sachar Committee Report. Today, that feeling of estrangement has been exacerbated further by the selective use of law and arrests of innocent people on charges of sedition.

AIMIM thrived under its self-styled commander, or 'Salar', Sultan Salahuddin Owaisi. Salahuddin was AIMIM's first elected representative. From municipal corporation to Parliament, he did not lose any election in his fifty years of public life. More significantly, he played a pivotal role in the run up to key events such as the Babri

Masjid demolition and the Shah Bano case, which saw the Rajiv Gandhi government overturn a Supreme Court judgment relating to alimony for a divorced Muslim woman. Salahuddin Owaisi headed the Babri Masjid Action Committee, served as a senior functionary of the All India Muslim Personal Law Board and seldom missed an opportunity to champion the cause of Muslims in India.

Salahuddin Owaisi believed that the state could never ensure quality education and health, and set up many medical and educational institutions in and around Hyderabad. He was a deft fundraiser who would raise money through crowdfunding, donations and religious charities. The money would then be liberally distributed after any communal riot to restore the livelihoods of survivors so that they could be rehabilitated with confidence. This concept of supporting people with people's money, and not relying on the state's help, made AIMIM popular among small traders, service providers and marginal workers.

The Beginnings

AIMIM, initially known as Ittehad-e-Bainal Muslimeen, had been founded to promote the socioeconomic and educational development of Muslims. The organization took shape as a political entity in 1938, with Nawab Bahadur Yar Jung being elected the president of the MIM (the suffix 'All India' was added two decades later in 1958). Salahuddin Owaisi would have been barely seven, but those were momentous days and the young boy would see important events – some of them disconcerting – unfold before his eyes.

MIM had aligned with the Muslim League in those pre-Independence days when India was divided into areas directly held by the British and the 565 princely states, which were under Indian rulers who had entered into alliances and agreements with the British to let them have a decisive say in defence and military affairs and revenue-sharing in exchange for a degree of independence. Some of the notable princely states were Hyderabad, Mysore, Gwalior, Baroda, Patiala, and Jammu and Kashmir.

Hyderabad, founded in 1724 by the first Nizam-ul-Mulk, was the richest and the biggest among the princely states. The Nizams, counted among the wealthiest in the world, were patrons of literature, art and architecture, and Hyderabad saw enormous growth, both culturally and economically, till 1948, when the Indian government began securing the accession of princely states into one polity.

Unlike the Scindias and the Holkars, however, the Nizam of Hyderabad remained defiant, insisting that Hyderabad, a landlocked state with an area of over 82,000 square miles, retain its identity as an independent Muslim dominion. The bravado would prove costly when the Indian Army launched Operation Polo in September 1948, led by Sardar Vallabhbhai Patel, the then minister of home affairs and deputy prime minister. The 'Police Action', as the operation was called, forced the Nizam to step down.

The Nizam's case on the ground wasn't helped by the private militia, the Razakars, organized by a wily man called Qasim Rizvi. By the early 1940s, Rizvi took control of the MIM and wielded considerable influence in the Nizam's court. Rizvi had tried to buy arms and ammunition from the French and had even approached America. Later cable communications revealed that Rizvi had sought to buy 6,00,000 rifles, an equal number of revolvers and 3,00,000 light and heavy machine guns from the German weapons the French had seized during World War II. Rizvi had reportedly communicated that if France could not supply the weapons, the Nizam's regime had offers from Sweden, Belgium and the Netherlands. Rizvi later fled to Pakistan, leaving the Nizam and the MIM in the lurch.

The present-day AIMIM has sought to erase the Rizvi chapter from its history and makes no mention of the period between 1948–57, when its earlier avatar the MIM became defunct. While describing the party's history, the AIMIM website abruptly jumps from 1948 to 1960 – the year it contested civic polls in Hyderabad for the first time in independent India. The website says: 'After the turbulent days of Military Action, euphemistically known as Police Action, that hastened the accession of erstwhile Hyderabad State (Nizam's Dominions) to the Indian Union on 17th September 1948, the MIM ceased to exist.' The 'vision document' of the present-day AIMIM reiterates its allegiance to the Indian Constitution and secular democracy.[350]

The MIM's revitalization as AIMIM has since remained a story of the Owaisis. Maulvi Abdul Wahed Owaisi, Salahuddin's father, was an eminent lawyer. Undeterred by the atmosphere of fear and the miserable condition of a section of Muslims in Hyderabad, he took up the onerous task of organizing the community. His message of hope soon caught the imagination of the people. So did his courage; here was a man who was not afraid of taking on the might of the establishment. The clean-shaven *maulvi*, eulogized as the Fakhr-e-Millat (Pride of the Community), rebuilt the party, brick by brick, taking immense pains to propel it to its stated goal – to create a platform to unite Muslims.

Abdul Wahed Owaisi loved his title – an excusable vanity given the position of eminence he enjoyed within his community. His successors too would bask in the adulation: Salahuddin as Salar-e-Millat (Commander of the Community), his grandson Asaduddin as Naqeeb-e-Millat (Leader of the Community) and his other grandson Akbaruddin as Habeeb-e-Millat (Darling of the Community).

Like the Thackerays of Mumbai, the Owaisis too emerged as top leaders in the region where they had settled. While the Thackerays were from Madhya Pradesh and made Mumbai their home, the Owaisis came from Ausa, Latur, in Maharashtra – part of the Nizam's territory before 1948.

Abdul Wahed Owaisi steered the party for seventeen years, from 1958 till his death in 1975. Salahuddin Owaisi, who matured under the shadow of his father, sensed that several issues bothered the

Muslims of Hyderabad. The first was the fear of the new government, which consisted of ministers and key officials known to hate the Nizam and the Majlis. The second was majoritarianism in the newly created state of Andhra Pradesh. The third fear was about what the future held, a sense of uncertainty that refused to go away against the backdrop of a difficult past.

Mingling with the Masses

Salahuddin Owaisi quickly grasped that the key was to understand the pulse of the people, which meant mingling with the masses. Abdul Wahed and Salahuddin Owaisi would travel by public transport and roam the streets of the old city from morning till lunch, meeting people. They would stick to this routine for years. Every time some communal trouble flared up, the father or son would be the first to reach the affected area. They had realized how important it was to be at the spot in difficult situations and made it their policy to be physically present during such situations. Throughout the 1970s, whenever incidents of communal violence broke out in Hyderabad, the combative attitude of the Owaisis created a sort of power balance between the two communities. For common Muslims this was a reassuring development. Scared and insecure for so long, they now felt that there was somebody who understood their pain and was ready to fight for them. This had another effect too: it often discouraged rioters and scuttled their plans of widespread violence.

Some believe that the Owaisis' foray into electoral politics, and the leverage they enjoyed with district authorities, played a major role in controlling and ending riots in Hyderabad.

If Abdul Wahed Owaisi's lasting legacy was redefining AIMIM's aims and objectives, accepting the principles of the Indian Constitution in letter and spirit, Salahuddin Owaisi's success was in providing legitimacy to the party and ensuring its democratic participation.

Salahuddin Owaisi had many firsts. In 1960, he was elected from the Mallepally division in the city civic polls. The AIMIM won 24 divisions to emerge as the main opposition party. Two years later, he became the first Owaisi to win an Assembly election, becoming in the process the party's first legislator. He won from Pathergatti constituency in Hyderabad town, trouncing Masooma Begum, who was a cabinet minister in the Congress ministry headed by Damodaram Sanjivayya. There would be no looking back as Owaisi would go on to represent various Deccan constituencies till 1983, eventually contesting the parliamentary elections in 1984 from Hyderabad. His winning streak continued till 1999. In 2004, the baton passed to his son Asaduddin Owaisi, who has won the Hyderabad Lok Sabha seat in every election since then.

When Abdul Wahed Owaisi died in 1975, Salahuddin became the AIMIM president. Under his leadership, the Majlis would hold public meetings around the year in Hyderabad; the 'Jalsa Halat-e-Hazara' gatherings served the purpose of keeping AIMIM cadres and sympathizers abreast of contemporary local and national sociopolitical developments, their implications for Muslims and the options available to them. Virtually anyone and everyone present at the meetings would speak up. The meetings had a far-reaching impact, and not merely in terms of increasing the political consciousness of AIMIM cadres and sympathizers. The gatherings ensured that the Owaisi perspective always had the upper hand when compared to the combined effort of television channels, state-run radio, Urdu newspapers and other media.

Salahuddin Owaisi's idea of self-reliance was not confined to distributing donations and charity, or setting up private hospitals and educational institutions. If Muslims were to be equal partners in the country's progress, they needed to be properly trained. So Owaisi established an Industrial Training Institute, using the rent he received from the Andhra government for the construction of a fire station at the AIMIM office at Darussalam, Hyderabad.

In 1978, when the M. Chenna Reddy government was in power in Andhra Pradesh, Owaisi succeeded in establishing SETWIN (Society for Employment, Promotion and Training in Twin Cities – of Hyderabad and Secunderabad). SETWIN ran skill-development courses in screen-printing and repairing refrigerators, air-conditioners, TV sets and other electronic goods. The training institute helped many youths get employment in the Gulf nations, bringing about a significant change in people's lives – both in terms of financial solvency and confidence.

Salahuddin Owaisi enjoyed a blow-hot-blow-cold relationship with major political parties, including the Congress. In an acknowledgement of the strength and influence of AIMIM, prime minister Indira Gandhi had visited the party's Darussalam headquarters in 1980. By the time Owaisi entered national politics in 1984, he had sensed a role for himself on a much larger canvas.

In the aftermath of the 1987 massacres in Hashimpura and Maliana, and in Moradabad seven years earlier, Salahuddin Owaisi realized that Muslims in Uttar Pradesh were becoming increasingly despondent. Resentment was brewing in Bihar too, where Muslims account for a sizeable chunk of the population. But Owaisi had little connection with the two northern states and his Urdu, with a Hyderabadi diction, was far from perfect. However, an opportunity knocked on his doors soon.

In Parliament, Salahuddin Owaisi met Syed Shahabuddin, a belligerent 'Leftist' who had quit the Indian Foreign Service to join politics and had become an articulate voice of the community. Destiny had willed that the lawyer-turned-teacher-turned-diplomat would join politics and take a Right-ward turn to represent orthodox Muslim interests. Owaisi was quick to join Shahabuddin in opposing a Supreme Court judgment granting a divorced Muslim woman, Shah Bano, the right to alimony from her former husband. As Muslim politicians mounted a campaign to get the verdict overturned, the Rajiv Gandhi government with its absolute majority came up with a law that diluted the judgment and restricted the right of Muslim divorcées to alimony from their former husbands to only ninety days after the divorce.

The Shah Bano controversy and the government's move suited the protagonists of the Hindutva movement just fine. They argued that the government was appeasing the Muslim community. Rajiv Gandhi panicked. What followed was a 'balancing act': the unlocking of the Babri Masjid in 1986 allowed Hindus unrestricted access to the disputed site in Ayodhya.

Babri Panel

The Ayodhya dispute, or the Ramjanmabhoomi–Babri Masjid Title Dispute, (now settled in favour of Ramjanmabhoomi) was a vexed political, historical and socio-religious debate that centred on a plot of land in Ayodhya, Uttar Pradesh – supposedly the birthplace of Lord Ram, the legendary warrior king. Many believed that the Babri Masjid was built in 1528 by Mughal emperor Babur's lieutenant Mir Baqi after demolishing a temple at the site.

The protracted legal battle turned political when a hawkish Vishwa Hindu Parishad began a campaign for the construction of a Ram temple in Ayodhya and the BJP decided to join in, with all-out political support. The Muslim side closed ranks, forming the Babri Masjid Action Committee.

Shahabuddin made Owaisi an active player in the Babri Masjid–Ramjanmabhoomi case. In Owaisi, Shahabuddin found his 'Deccan support', material help and a man who could counter his Muslim rival, Ibrahim Sulaiman Sait of the Indian Union Muslim League (IUML). Sait was a giant of a leader and the IUML had much better credentials to represent the interests of southern Muslims having been part of the United Democratic Front (UDF) in Kerala.

Shahabuddin was not the lone beneficiary of Owaisi's largesse. Zafaryab Jilani, lawyer and founder member of the Babri Masjid Action Committee, fondly remembers Owaisi's hospitality at 34

Ashoka Marg. In an interview to *The Print*, Jilani recalled that whenever he needed to stay in Delhi to pursue legal matters related to the Babri Masjid case, the Owaisi clan would make arrangements for him, among other Muslim plaintiffs in the case, there. 'This kothi on Ashoka Road has been with the Owaisis since 1984. Salahuddin had told us that "whenever you need to come to Delhi for matters related to the Babri Masjid case, my house will always be open for you",' Jilani recalled Owaisi as telling him. 'Here, all kinds of lodging and food arrangements have always remained available for me as well as my associates. A room in this house has been especially reserved for us.' Salahuddin Owaisi's son Asaduddin, Jilani added, continued the tradition.[351]

The Babri imbroglio had some ugly moments too for Owaisi. After the mosque was demolished in December 1992, the Congress government at the Centre, then headed by P.V. Narasimha Rao, tried to win over its critics. There were allegations in Hyderabad that the Congress-led Andhra government had given a plot to the AIMIM to set up an educational institution. Mohammed Amanullah Khan, leader of the four-member AIMIM in the Andhra Pradesh Assembly, challenged Owaisi's policies and dared him to make public his position on the Babri demolition. Owaisi threw him out of the party for 'inciting indiscipline'.

When Salahuddin Owaisi's end came in 2008, the then Andhra chief minister Y.S. Rajasekhar Reddy led his cabinet colleagues in paying their respects to the 76-year-old leader.

Praise also came from others, ideologically poles apart, a reflection of the respect Owaisi commanded across political divides. 'Despite the ideological differences, I can tell you that Salahuddin Owaisi was a great political leader,' said BJP central minister G. Kishan Reddy, who was then a member of the Andhra Assembly.[352] Kishan Reddy also recalled that when he was elected to the state Assembly in 2004, at the age of 44, Owaisi had called him over the phone to congratulate him. 'I was very happy that a veteran leader like Salahuddin Owaisi remembered a young MLA like me,' Kishan Reddy said.[353]

Tributes poured in from the Left too. Gaddar, the popular poet and balladeer, described Owaisi as a 'great leader' of the Muslim community. 'One call by him was enough to establish peace in the city,' Gaddar said.

Asaduddin Owaisi

While Salahuddin Owaisi consolidated the Owaisis' hold over the AIMIM, his elder son Asaduddin, who joined the family profession of law and politics, expanded the party's base beyond Hyderabad and Telangana, the new state carved out of Andhra Pradesh in 2014. By the time the Bihar Assembly elections were held in October 2020, AIMIM had made serious inroads in the state, marking a significant shift in the voting pattern of Muslims – especially in the Seemanchal region where the party won five seats. Asaduddin Owaisi, a barrister from London's Lincoln's Inn, had sensed that after the anti-citizenship law (CAA) stir, a section of Muslims were disillusioned with 'secular' mainstream political parties.

As Naqeeb-e-Millat, Asaduddin Owaisi understood that the community was apprehensive after the revocation of Article 370 in Jammu and Kashmir, the Ayodhya verdict, legislation against interfaith marriages and police investigations into the Delhi riots. Any further drastic changes in law and administration could change their lives inexorably.

Asaduddin has also developed a penchant for forging alliances with Dalit outfits like the Mayawati-led BSP and Prakash Ambedkar's Vanchit Bahujan Aghadi (VBA). The attempts to reach out come at a time the Congress has looked particularly vulnerable with its past baggage – 58 major riots before Godhra (2002), 'unlocking' of the Babri Masjid site, flip-flop on Muslim Personal Law, minority character for AMU and the legal infirmness of seemingly pro-minority measures.

The rise of the Hindu Right seems to have given AIMIM more space and opportunities. But it's also true that AIMIM's success in Seemanchal has a dangerous potential: of Muslims leaning towards

Islamic politics wherever they are numerically superior, although there are only a few such regions in the country.

Going back in history, the Muslim League and the Hindu Mahasabha had both sold their respective visions of the Two Nation Theory, according to which Hindus and Muslims constituted separate nations and could not coexist. Islamic scholars like Maulana Hussain Ahmed Madani and Maulana Abul Kalam Azad had opposed this line of thinking, saying there was a qualitative difference between the Urdu words: *qawm* and *millat*. *Qawm* implies common national heritage of Hindus and Muslims – the age-old socioeconomic ties and synchronicity. *Millat* has a more simplistic definition of a community.

Asaduddin Owaisi, like his grandfather and father, kept saying that as a political entity, AIMIM has the right to further its cause and expand its base. Muslims too have the freedom to vote and reject those who are unable to counter majoritarianism. AIMIM's Seemanchal (Bihar) model, however, did not augur well for secular democracy, secular parties or for Muslims in India.

~

RAM VILAS PASWAN
(1946–2020)

NOT FOR NOTHING DID THEY CALL HIM 'MAUSAM VAIGYANIK' (WEATHER scientist). It was an appellation tossed dismissively at him by a friend-turned-rival, but to Ram Vilas Paswan's credit, he seldom read the political *mausam* (weather) wrong, the astute politician that he was. It was this uncanny knack of trusting his instincts and ending up on the side of the eventual winner that perhaps galled Lalu Prasad Yadav, who had come up with the sarcastic moniker for his fellow politician from Bihar.

Paswan's windsock abilities were on display early when, sometime in 1968, he had reportedly asked a friend for advice on a possible career choice. 'Should I be the government or its servant?' Paswan, then barely 22, is said to have asked the question to Lakshmi Narain Arya. This was when Paswan had got an offer to take up the job of a deputy superintendent of police (DySP) in Bihar.

'Yeh toh aapke upar nirbhar karta hai, aap government ban-na chate hai ya servant ban-na chahte hai (You need to figure whether you want to be the government or its servant),' Arya recalls telling him, lobbing the decision back to Paswan's court.[354]

Needless to say, Paswan never joined the police. Instead of becoming a DySP, he entered politics and went on to win eight Lok Sabha elections, serving as a minister in governments headed by V.P. Singh, H.D. Deve Gowda, I.K. Gujral, Atal Bihari Vajpayee, Manmohan Singh and Narendra Modi, underscoring his acceptability to leaders across the political spectrum.

Paswan's electoral journey began in 1969, when he entered the Bihar Legislative Assembly as a member of the Samyukta Socialist Party. He defeated Congress old-timer Mishri Sada by 700 votes in Alauli, a reserved constituency. He was still a young man – only thirty – when he made the transition from Bihar to national politics. In 1977, Paswan would ride the anti-Emergency wave to enter Parliament by a record 4-lakh-plus margin of victory from Hajipur. That would be the first of his many Lok Sabha election victories during his political career that spanned over half a century. Today, the flood-prone Saharbanni, Paswan's ancestral village in Bihar's Khagaria district, is known as *'mantri tola'* (residence of a weighty minister), thanks to its famous son.

Paswan's biographer, Sobhana Nair, remembers him as someone who was in equal measure a participant and a spectator in the power matrix of Lutyens' Delhi. 'And he wore many hats – a Dalit leader, a socialist, a liberal and also a political opportunist,' she says.[355]

It was this political opportunism that also made Paswan a perpetual prisoner of the trappings of power and robbed him of the status of a catalyst. Paswan fancied himself as a rebel, a social reformer and proudly called himself a follower of Babasaheb Bhimrao Ambedkar, the architect of the Indian Constitution who led a crusade against untouchability. In his early years, Paswan would even describe himself as a 'Maoist' and believed in the Ambedkarite critique of Hinduism. By the late 1970s and the early 1980s, Paswan was considered a Dalit icon. He had formed the Dalit Sena in 1983, an organization that worked for the emancipation and welfare of the oppressed castes. However, his subsequent political compromises diminished his role and stature as a Dalit messiah, even as Kanshi Ram and Mayawati and their Bahujan Samaj Party emerged as more powerful and potent votaries of the cause of the Scheduled Castes.

Academic Badri Narayan felt that Paswan himself was to blame for this, as his appeal among the Dalits remained largely confined to within his own caste – the Dusadhs – and his home state of Bihar. 'The Chamars (31.3 per cent among Bihar Dalits) and Dusadhs (30.9 per cent) are close to each other in number in Bihar and have impressive populations. Yet, Paswan remained a Dusadh leader, first and foremost,' Narayan says.

Paswan played an important role in the V.P. Singh government (1989–90) and conferred the Bharat Ratna, India's highest civilian honour, on Ambedkar posthumously, declaring the late leader's birth anniversary, April 14, as a national holiday. He was also instrumental in getting the Mandal Commission recommendations implemented in 1990. Paswan was then minister of welfare and insisted on early implementation of reservations on the lines suggested by the Mandal Commission, despite nationwide protests from upper-caste youths opposed to quotas in government jobs and education.

Still, Paswan's standing among Dalits remained restricted, which had perhaps something to do with his conciliatory approach every time caste violence erupted between the upper castes and Dalits – represented by the Ranvir Sena and the ultra-Maoist communist outfits respectively.

What some criticized as conciliatory, others saw in Paswan's approach the rare quality of affable dignity. Abdul Khaliq, a former IAS officer, thinks that the Lok Janshakti Party (LJP) leader was a quintessential politician, an efficient minister, dignified, soft-spoken and completely devoid of administrative self-importance. Khaliq had worked closely with Paswan, first as a bureaucrat and later as a political activist when he left the civil service to join the LJP. 'Government officials who had the privilege of working with him will vouch for his razor-sharp mind and affable style,' Khaliq wrote in the *Indian Express* two days after Paswan's death on 8 October 2020.[356]

Khaliq, who was the secretary-general of the LJP, also contests claims that Paswan was a weathervane and invariably manipulated his way into the alliance that formed the government of the day. In defence of his political master, he wrote:

> Pray, which party in the country has not accommodated conflicting ideologies to wrest power? None! Paswanji understood the importance of using political power responsibly and was not shy about seeking it. As one of the foremost leaders of the most oppressed group of citizens, he has used his stints in various governments to protect and advance their interests.

Astute and Accommodating

Paswan joined hands with the Bharatiya Janata Party twice but kept his Muslim constituency in good humour too. When the anti-Muslim riots broke out in the Narendra Modi-ruled Gujarat in 2002, Paswan had tendered his resignation to the Atal Bihari Vajpayee government at the Centre. Before that, Paswan had teamed up with

Bengal's future chief minister Mamata Banerjee to block a proposed NDA legislation that sought to bar people of foreign origin from holding high offices. The proposal had been mooted at the Vajpayee government's first cabinet meeting in 1999. Paswan's gesture had earned him a lot of goodwill from his neighbour at 10 Janpath.

Sonia Gandhi and Paswan had been neighbours since the early 1990s. When Rajiv Gandhi was assassinated on 21 May 1991, a crowd had gathered at the Janpath roundabout near Paswan's house raising slogans against former prime minister V.P. Singh. It was Singh – Rajiv's associate-turned-rival – who had withdrawn Rajiv Gandhi's security. Paswan had to flee when the angry mob attacked his 12 Janpath residence and burnt furniture. Sonia Gandhi, despite struggling with the devastating personal tragedy and a bout of asthma, reportedly had the presence of mind to summon her long-time aide, R.K. Dhawan, and Captain Satish Sharma, one of Rajiv's flying club buddies who was close to the family, to ensure that nothing untoward happened.

There would be more instances of bonhomie with Sonia Gandhi. At an *iftar* she hosted on 11 December 2001, at her party's 24 Akbar Road headquarters, the Congress president had two surprise guests. Paswan and Sharad Yadav, both ministers in Vajpayee's cabinet, had attended the *iftar* and mingled with Congress bigwigs, triggering talk of a radical political realignment. That would fructify in 2004 when Paswan joined the Sonia Gandhi-led United Progressive Alliance under Manmohan Singh's prime ministership.

Paswan was among a handful of leaders who could move around insurgency-affected Jammu and Kashmir without an armed escort. As late as 2016, when Narendra Modi was the prime minister, Paswan had boldly pitched for a '*mahasanghatan*' (a grand alliance) of India, Pakistan and Bangladesh, with a common currency and open trade – à la the European Union.

Journalist and biographer Sobhana Nair thinks Paswan's strength lay partly in his pleasant, accommodating and helpful nature. If he could oblige a fellow politician, even if the person were from the opposing side, or assist a journalist in trouble, he would go out of his way to help. His doors were always open and he never stood on ceremony, she says.[357]

In 1999, Paswan had voted against the Vajpayee government on the floor of the Lower House for its 'communal politics'. While that government had fallen in its 13th month, Paswan would again join the subsequent government that Vajpayee would form. As mentioned earlier, he would again resign from Vajpayee's cabinet to protest the 2002 Gujarat riots, though, ostensibly because of the then Modi-led state government's failure to protect the minorities.[358] Modi is not known to be too forgiving towards those who had opposed him in 2002, but Paswan proved to be an exception. When Modi moved from Gujarat to Delhi, Paswan would be rewarded for returning to the NDA fold with ministerial berths – in 2014 as well as in 2019.

Paswan's Final Days and His Heir

In November 2019, Paswan, who had been eager to see his son succeed him, appointed Chirag the president of the LJP. It would, however, be a short tenure for Chirag at the party's helm.

Paswan did not live to see the outcome of the acrimonious Bihar elections of 2020, when Chirag tried to wreak the revenge that his father could not on Nitish Kumar and his Janata Dal (United) [JD(U)]. The LJP fielded candidates against all the JD(U) nominees but not against the BJP. This was when the BJP and the JD(U) were allies. The election outcome was such that both Chirag and the LJP faced irrelevance as the BJP–JD(U) edged out the RJD–Congress combine.

AHMED PATEL

(1949–2020)

LEGEND HAS IT THAT THE EXIT OF NIZAM-UL-MULK FROM EMPEROR Mohammad Shah's court had hastened the disintegration of the Mughal empire. The ruler had earned the title 'Rangeela' (The Colourful One) on account of his overindulgence in women and wine. Mulk, a vizier, had tried to reform the administration. After failing to do so due to king's indifferent attitude, in 1724, Mulk had marched south to found the state of Hyderabad in the Deccan and assumed the title of Nizam.

Ahmedbhai Mohammadbhai Patel, AICC treasurer, political secretary and crisis manager – all rolled into one – was involved in every decision that Congress president Sonia Gandhi took from 1998 till October 2020. Patel, self-effacing as he was, was no Nizam-ul-Mulk but his death, on 24 November 2020, marked the end of an era for the Grand Old Party.

Ahmed Bhai, as he was popularly known, had systematically cultivated people across the spectrum – from the highest echelons of influence to the grassroots. Despite remaining the quintessential backroom politician who scrupulously shied away from the limelight, he wielded much power and clout. However grudgingly, Sonia and later Rahul Gandhi would have to accept his indispensability.

Sonia Gandhi took a shine to Patel's style of functioning, which was temperamentally closer to her heart. She admired the way he managed contradictions. In May 1999, Sharad Pawar had revolted against Sonia Gandhi, citing her foreign origins. Within the next five months the Maharashtra Assembly polls were held, where the Congress and Pawar's newly formed Nationalist Congress Party

(NCP) fought separately against the formidable Shiv Sena–BJP alliance. The fractured mandate had given the Congress 75 seats and the NCP 58 in the 288-member Assembly. Patel swung into action and worked out the 'basics' with NCP's Praful Patel. A pragmatic Sonia Gandhi gave her nod on the ground that Pawar himself had no problem teaming up with a Sonia Gandhi-led Congress to form a government with the help of Independents.

Next, Ahmed Patel ensured that Vilasrao Deshmukh was made chief minister. As a gesture of gratitude, the Maharashtra chief minister helped Patel build a personal rapport with industrialists such as Mukesh and Anil Ambani, Ratan Tata, Anand Mahindra, Adi Godrej, Sajjan Jindal, Uday Kotak, Deepak Parekh, Gautam Singhania and Baba Kalyani. Later, in 2005, in Haryana, Patel backed Bhupinder Singh Hooda, who remained forever indebted to him for it. There was no dearth of Congress chief ministers who remained grateful to Patel's behind-the-scenes machinations and support.

Patel was at work again in November 2019 when the Shiv Sena fell out with its ally, the BJP. In the initial few days, the official Congress line was to scoff at the prospect of forging an alliance with the hawkish Sena. The Kerala unit of the party even went on record to express its reservations. Back in the 1990s, the Sena had levelled some serious allegations against Patel in the Rajya Sabha, prompting him to announce his withdrawal from public life if the charges were proved correct. Nearly two decades later, there was no trace of that past bitterness. Patel took a flight to Mumbai to stitch an alliance in place, with the help of Pawar.

To the outside world, Patel remained somewhat of an enigma. But those familiar with the Congress culture found him to be an asset. He was affable, attentive and had a relatively clean image – all key traits of a consummate backstage player. Add his determination and drive, and it is easy to understand why he was so vital to the party.

Also, in Patel, the Congress high command saw someone capable of at least deciphering two fellow Gujaratis, current Prime Minister Narendra Modi and Home Minister Amit Shah. It was an open secret that in August 2017, Patel was not keen on an unprecedented fifth term in the Rajya Sabha (nobody in the Congress gets five terms in Parliament's Upper House). But Sonia Gandhi, the party boss then, had reportedly forced his hand, pointing out that he alone was capable of matching Shah and the entire might of the BJP.

As party treasurer, Patel's job was not only to mobilize funds but also marshal crowds and support from within the ranks, even when Rahul Gandhi's luck did not favour him in the 2019 general election and the majority of Assembly polls held that year. It would not be an exaggeration to say that there is not a single state in the country where Patel was not personally known to the majority of district-level Congress functionaries and elected representatives. His ability to mobilize resources (read: money, crowd, private jets and other logistics at less than an hour's notice), while being as discreet as possible, was well known. And so he was called in to deliver at this moment of need for Rahul Gandhi and the party.

Patel was also a crucial link for Rahul Gandhi to court potential allies like Mamata Banerjee, Mayawati, N. Chandrababu Naidu and a range of other non-NDA, non-UPA regional players. In Congress circles, Patel's ability to reach out to the bureaucracy, media and business houses was part of in-house folklore. It is said that the low-key Congress veteran had a huge stock of 'I owe you' vouchers from virtually every walk of life. More significantly, most of these vouchers were seldom exchanged.

Contrary to popular perception, though, Patel did not always have a hassle-free run within the Congress; another veteran, Ghulam Nabi Azad, acted as a counter-balance to him in the party. When Sonia Gandhi took over as Congress chief in March 1998, Patel was made AICC treasurer. But a year into it, he had a massive tiff with her private secretary, Vincent George. Patel resigned in a huff and for a brief period was in the doghouse without any assignment.

He even left for his home state where he held a massive rally in Bharuch to signal his willingness to start afresh, even if independently of the Congress. When Madhavrao Scindia got wind of it, he, along with another veteran, Motilal Vora, helped Patel restore his ties with 10 Janpath. For Patel, it was an important lesson in realpolitik.

Patel returned as Sonia Gandhi's political secretary, while Vora took up the job of AICC treasurer (the two remained joint signatories on AICC bank accounts). The episode led to a firm bond among the three. Patel remained grateful to Vora till he breathed his last.

The high office of political secretary was, however, not without its hurdles as Sonia Gandhi had another political secretary in Ambika Soni. Leaders from rival camps, such as those led by Arjun Singh, Jitendra Prasada and Vincent George, and the likes of family retainers M.L. Fotedar and R.K. Dhawan kept Patel on his toes.

But this was also a fascinating period for those who chronicle politics. Patel forged quick, temporary and need-based alliances with Arjun Singh, Prasada, Pranab Mukherjee, Ambika Soni and K. Natwar Singh. He was given a room at the party's 24 Akbar Road headquarters but, for some tactical reasons, seldom occupied it, preferring to function from his 23 Mother Teresa Marg residence. Within a few months, Sonia Gandhi had rejigged the AICC secretariat, drafting Soni into the office of the Congress president and appointing Patel to the important post of political secretary.

UPA Years

The UPA years too were far from smooth. The high-level 'core group' would meet every Friday through the ten years (beginning from 2004) that the alliance was in power, and Patel would be in attendance with the then prime minister Manmohan Singh and Union ministers A.K. Antony, P. Chidambaram and Pranab Mukherjee (till the latter moved to Rashtrapati Bhavan in 2012). Patel's mandate was to give Sonia Gandhi critical points and feedback on how the allies felt about the performance of the government under Singh. Often, at these gatherings, Patel had skirmishes with the other leaders, as Gandhi and Singh watched on. Despite lacking administrative experience and not always matching the cerebral prowess of

Mukherjee and Chidambaram, Patel often stood his ground and won rounds of appreciation. Closer scrutiny would reveal a lot of hard work that would often continue till early in the morning, when he would offer *fajr* [dawn] prayers.

The next big hurdle for Patel came during the Rahul Gandhi era, in March 2015. Rahul had left on a foreign trip, unwilling to end his sabbatical until some influential Congress leaders were 'sidelined'. This was a time when leaders close to Rahul sought to pin all the blame for the Congress's problems (and also the party's humiliating defeat in the 2014 general election) on Patel, Vora and Janardan Dwivedi – who were dubbed the Congress's Brahma, Vishnu and Mahesh.

Patel and the old guard had dug their heels in, pointing out that Mohan Gopal, Deep Kaul and Jairam Ramesh, along with AICC general secretaries Madhusudan Mistry, C.P. Joshi, Ajay Maken and Mohan Prakash, had been given all powers during the 2014 Lok Sabha polls but failed to deliver. Finally, Rahul Gandhi returned from a suspenseful sabbatical, ending an agonizing and embarrassing chapter for a majority of Congress members. Perhaps his mother had made it clear to him that he had to take Patel, Vora and other members of the old guard along.

Apparently, Rahul Gandhi used to find Patel's adherence to realpolitik distasteful and unprincipled. But Sonia Gandhi could sense that her son and his team's experiments with the NSUI and the Youth Congress had delivered nothing. By 2017, Rahul Gandhi had been compelled to make peace with Patel, who returned as the party treasurer – arguably the most important post after the party president.

Back in the saddle, Patel quickly delivered. Backing grassroots leaders with proven abilities, he ensured that Rajasthan, Madhya Pradesh and Chhattisgarh were added to the Congress's kitty in the face of the Modi–Shah juggernaut. The combined efforts of Patel and his chosen general secretary, Ashok Gehlot, almost delivered Gujarat too.

It is said that the Gandhis are the glue that holds the Congress together. Yet, party insiders know that it was Patel who really held it together. Unless the Congress quickly recovers and puts in place effective alternatives, Patel's demise may just prove to be a body blow to the already tottering party.

Patel's absence will be felt the most as the Congress and the Gandhis struggle to project a united face. There is every possibility now that disgruntled Congress leaders – the so-called Group of 23 or G-23 – and some regional satraps will get more vocal and proactive and contemplate life beyond the existing ecosystem.

In her condolence message, Sonia Gandhi described Patel as an 'irreplaceable comrade' who would be missed by both her and her son. It was an apt description. Backed to the hilt by Sonia Gandhi, Patel was the go-to person within the party for almost two decades; a telephone call from him to any chief minister of a Congress-ruled state would make them – be it Capt. Amarinder Singh, Ashok Gehlot or V. Narayanasamy – say or do whatever the Congress high command wished to hear or execute. Ditto was the case with leaders of non-BJP political parties, corporate honchos, media houses, religious heads and NGOs. In the process, many compromises had to be made but on most occasions, workable solutions prevented things from getting unsavoury.

Not Aggressive Enough

One charge against Patel was that he lacked killer instincts. It is part of Congress folklore that Patel had vetoed aggressive – legal and political – moves against Narendra Modi over the 2002 Gujarat riots that left around a thousand people dead. Modi was Gujarat's chief minister when the riots broke out. When the Congress-led UPA wrested power at the Centre in 2004, some legal eagles in the party and some ministers in the Singh government had advocated a stronger line against Modi. But Patel had reportedly convinced Sonia Gandhi and Singh to let the 'law take its own course'. A minuscule section of the Congress grudged that against Patel but the parliamentarian from Bharuch remained convinced till the end that the move would have been counter-productive and hampered the smooth sailing of the UPA.

It was not that Patel had a soft spot for the BJP or the Sangh *parivar*. In fact, he had suffered significantly at their hands. Until 1989–91, when Gujarat saw the unprecedented rise of the Vishwa Hindu Parishad in the wake of the Ramjanmabhoomi movement, Patel had represented Bharuch three times as Lok Sabha member – in 1977, 1980 and 1984. But he lost the 1989 election following a sustained communal campaign against him.

Patel was a popular figure who was locally addressed as 'Babu Bhai'. However, the VHP at the time reportedly changed his name from Babu Bhai to 'Ahmed' in every graffiti, poster or banner to emphasize his religious identity. Patel lost by 18,909 votes and painfully described his electoral loss as a 'a defeat of secularism, rather than mine'. He used to be the only Muslim Lok Sabha member from Gujarat. Given this history, it should be clear that Patel's advice to convince Sonia Gandhi was probably just him being pragmatic.

Although he lost relevance in electoral politics after this, Patel was not disheartened and continued to stay relevant. After he entered the Rajya Sabha in 1993, Patel developed a comfort level with the then prime minister P.V. Narasimha Rao who was then having functional problems with 10 Janpath. Rao used Patel as an effective backroom channel of communication with Sonia Gandhi – a ploy that even Sitaram Kesri employed during his stint as Congress president. In this sense, after the Rajiv Gandhi era, each time a new Congress president took over, Patel would be at the centre of the party's internal power play. By the time Rahul Gandhi took over as the 87th AICC chief in December 2017, some of his contemporaries would say off the record, 'New CP (Congress president), same AP (Ahmed Patel)'.

Through the UPA years, Patel was the fourth-most powerful man in the establishment after Sonia Gandhi, then prime minister Singh and senior minister Mukherjee. In the party, Patel was seen as a bridge between the old guard and those who claimed proximity to Rahul Gandhi.

Unlike many other Congress leaders, Patel never tried to become a central minister. But his 23 Mother Teresa Marg home was considered a power centre. Access to Patel's house was restricted. Multiple entry and exit doors, chambers and seating arrangements revealed the pecking order of the visitors to his residence, where the fate of Congress chief ministers and state party functionaries and candidates for elections, from Parliament to civic bodies, were often decided. Getting an appointment with Patel was not easy unless one received a call from a landline number. The appointment would invariably be late at night.

Ticket-seekers are known to have tracked Patel down at various places, including mosques where he offered Friday prayers. A god-fearing person who performed Hajj in 2011, Patel was known for not missing praying five times a day. He observed Ramzan fasts and recited the Quran every morning. At one point, Patel had to change mosques every week to escape those seeking favours.

Despite being so very in demand, Patel had in fact been looking to retire from active politics since 2014. But every time he broached the topic, Sonia Gandhi had summarily rejected his request on the ground that as a loyalist he had no choice but to accept the high command's diktat.

I met him last in February 2020. The inevitable question had come up during the course of the conversation: why not write his memoirs, since he had witnessed so many momentous events from up close and been privy to confidential matters of state? Academics, journalists and future researchers would benefit from such a treasure trove of information.

Patel was quick to reject the suggestion. 'These [secrets],' he had said, 'will travel with me to the grave.'[359]

RAJESH PILOT

(1945–2000)

RAJESH PILOT'S PROMISING CAREER CAME TO AN ABRUPT AND TRAGIC END when the jeep he was travelling in collided head-on with a bus in his Lok Sabha constituency of Dausa, 90 km from Jaipur, on 11 June 2000. Pilot was on his way to catch a flight to Delhi and sources said he was at the wheel. The man said to be always in a hurry was apparently driving at breakneck speed, and had overtaken his escort vehicle at a blind spot, when the jeep collided with the Rajasthan Road Transport bus around 4.45 p.m.

Pilot was rushed to SMS Medical College Hospital in Jaipur, but did not survive. The Indian Air Force pilot-turned-politician had suffered multiple injuries to his head, chest and face. He was 55 and in the prime of his political career.

A former minister for internal security, Pilot had earlier enjoyed Z+ security, which had recently been downgraded. There was no talk of foul play but newspapers had received an anonymous fax on the night of his death, which pointed an accusing finger at a controversial godman. The mahant concerned was a key witness before the Jain Commission that had conducted a probe into Rajiv Gandhi's assassination.

Some, like Mahant Sewa Dass Singh, president of the Pheruman Akali Dal, came out openly in demanding a probe into the events leading to the collision. 'This is not a simple accident. His security was downgraded very recently despite threats to his life,' Sewa Dass Singh had said.[360]

Congress president Sonia Gandhi rushed to Jaipur on a special flight. Among the passengers was Pilot's widow, Rama. A huge crowd of Pilot's supporters thronged the hospital as news of his death broke. Many were in tears. Politicians cutting across party lines, relatives and friends had rushed to Pilot's 10 Akbar Road residence in Delhi, but there was no one to accept the condolences.

Forever a rebel, Pilot was known for his outspokenness. He had previously opposed former prime minister P.V. Narasimha Rao and former party chief Sitaram Kesri and was even planning to take on Sonia Gandhi in the upcoming organizational elections when his life was cut short. His sudden end created a void in the Congress, which had few charismatic leaders from outside the Nehru–Gandhi family. That void has remained two decades after his death.

Pilot, whose original name was Rajeshwar Prasad, was born into a poor family in Ghaziabad on 10 February 1945. After he lost his army father Jai Dayal Singh at an early age, Pilot was brought up by his brother, who sold milk in affluent Delhi localities. Pilot's autobiography, *Flight to Parliament*, narrates how he rose from selling milk to MPs on chilly winter mornings to becoming an MP himself in 1980.[361] The previous year he had quit the Indian Air Force where he had risen to the rank of squadron leader.

Pilot's first ministerial break following his change in career – which coincided with the change in name too – came in 1985 when Rajiv Gandhi made him minister of state for transport. Pilot would later go on to hold the communications, home (internal security) and environment portfolios in the Narasimha Rao government between 1991 and 1996. He was an able parliamentarian, a strong votary of probity and ethics in public life, and was bitterly opposed to the Congress's alliance with Jayalalithaa and Rabri Devi.

Throughout the late 1980s and the 1990s, Pilot remained popular with the middle class for his politically correct stand on issues, clean image and efficiency. But he also loved to take on the high and the mighty and enjoyed the media attention it generated. An example of how he could step on powerful toes came on 25 February 1993, when the BJP organized a demonstration near Parliament. The wounds of the Babri Masjid's demolition were still fresh and Pilot, as a junior minister in the internal security ministry, had ordered unprecedented bandobast (preparations) to thwart any possible attack on mosques in the area. The day passed off peacefully and Pilot boasted that had he been in charge of security on 6 December 1992, instead of S.B. Chavan, his senior in the internal security ministry, the mosque would not have been demolished.[362]

The same year saw Pilot taking on the likes of party colleagues Arjun Singh, Sharad Pawar, Madhavrao Scindia and Kamal Nath too. He ordered a probe into an alleged nexus between politicians and the underworld following a report by a committee. None of them had been named in the report but Pilot, it seemed, wanted to score political points against them.

Pilot later turned on the heat on self-styled godman Chandraswami, who was close to prime minister P.V. Narasimha Rao. Chandraswami, a *tantrik*, had powerful friends, including international arms dealer Adnan Khashoggi, the Sultan of Brunei and Margaret Thatcher. He also had equally well-placed enemies. In 1995, when the Congress under Narasimha Rao was in power, Chandraswami was wanted in connection with a series of cases, but nobody could act against him because of his high connections. Pilot got him arrested. It was more than a coincidence that in the subsequent cabinet shuffle, Pilot was shunted out of internal security to look after forests and the environment.

An outspoken man, who often punched above his weight, Pilot had always aimed high. His unfulfiled bid to take on Sonia Gandhi in the organizational elections was not the first time that he had nursed such ambitions. In 1991, when Rajiv Gandhi was assassinated and a clueless Congress was looking for a successor, Pilot had thrown his hat into the ring, projecting himself as a young leader fit to step into Rajiv Gandhi's shoes. Unlike Arjun Singh, Pawar, Scindia and Shankar Dayal Sharma, Pilot had little locus standi in terms of experience, either in the organization or in the government, where he was a junior minister. He was not even a cabinet minister at the time. His candidature was more in the nature of positioning for the future.

Today, scores of Congress activists, at all levels of the hierarchy, rue Pilot's absence. Had he been there, they say, the '*doodhwala*' (milkman) could have taken on the *'chaiwala'* (tea vendor/Narendra Modi).

JITENDRA PRASADA
(1938–2001)

FIRST IT WAS AN OFFICER PAR EXCELLENCE WHO DIED IN TRAGIC circumstances. Barely seven months later, a gentleman joined him, leaving a huge void in the Congress.

Rajesh Pilot and Jitendra Prasada had very little in common. Pilot was a born challenger, rebel and fighter who came up through the ranks to take on the high command. Prasada was an aristocrat, a backroom player adept at planning and plotting. Yet, towards the end, they came together to revive internal democracy in the country's oldest political party. But destiny had other plans for both of them. Pilot met with a fatal accident in June 2000. On 9 January 2001, Prasada suffered a brain haemorrhage that proved fatal. He died a week later.

Prasada was a key aide to Rajiv Gandhi and P.V. Narasimha Rao, political secretary to both leaders when they were prime minister. He also served as the AICC vice-president, Uttar Pradesh Congress chief and was a CWC member.

But 'Jiti Bhai', as Prasada was fondly called, defied tradition and surprised his friends and foes alike when he decided to take on Sonia Gandhi in the organizational polls that concluded in November 2000. No amount of persuasion, pleas, advice or alluring had worked to change his mind. Prasada had done the unthinkable in the Congress *parivar*; he had challenged a member of the Nehru–Gandhi family.

To some it was ironical that Prasada himself became a victim of palace intrigue – an art he had mastered as an understudy of the wily Hemvati Nandan Bahuguna, and later as political secretary to Rajiv Gandhi and P.V. Narasimha Rao. The AICC grapevine has it that Prasada was led up the garden path by some of his contemporaries who encouraged him to file the nomination against Sonia Gandhi, convincing him that she would invite him for a rapprochement.

The game plan appeared good on paper, except that the call from 10 Janpath never came. The old guard cautioned her against hosting a tea party, pointing out that it would be seen as a sign of weakness. The loyalist had no option but to turn a rebel.

Coming from a close aide of Rajiv Gandhi, Prasada's provocation had, however, rattled the Sonia Gandhi camp. Leaving nothing to chance, the leadership ensured that Prasada's threat was wiped out. While the final tally showed Prasada getting just above one per cent of the votes against Rajiv Gandhi's widow, Prasada's contribution would always be acknowledged in the history of the Congress. He might not have been a towering personality like Subhas Chandra Bose, who had defeated Mahatma Gandhi's nominee P. Sitaramayya in the 1939 Congress organizational polls, but Prasada succeeded in pricking the conscience of millions of party workers.

During his whirlwind electioneering against Sonia Gandhi, Prasada was greeted with locked doors at the party offices in Jaipur, Lucknow, Patna, Hyderabad, Bengaluru and Chennai. Yet, he maintained a solemn and dignified posture, refraining from launching any personal attacks against Sonia Gandhi, despite being egged on by known Sonia-baiters like the Samajwadi Party and the Nationalist Congress Party. Whenever journalists asked him to comment on Sonia Gandhi, Prasada would say with a smile: '*Arrey bhai, hamein Congress mein rahna hai* (I intend staying in the Congress). She is our leader.'

Prasada's chequered political career, spread over four decades, saw many ups and downs such as the downfall of the Congress in Uttar Pradesh in the wake of the Mandal and Ayodhya movements. Till his death, however, he was optimistic about the future of the Congress in the state. 'People,' he would say, 'are looking up towards us but we are failing to win their confidence. That is the real challenge before the Congress.'[363]

Prasada was born on 12 November 1938 into an aristocratic family in Shahjanpur that had another claim to fame. His great grandmother was Nobel laureate Rabindranath Tagore's niece. Born as Sudakshina Thakur, she married Sir Jwala Prasada, the zamindar of Shahjahanpur and an Imperial Civil Service (ICS) officer. Theirs was the first inter-caste marriage in the Rohilkhand region. The name given to her after the wedding was Purnima Devi. She was daughter of Tagore's brother Hemendranath Tagore. Rabindranath Tagore said to have spent considerable time in Shahjahanpur with niece Purnima in Prasada House. The Prasada family still has a collection of Tagore's cursive paintings.

'Baba Sahib', as Prasada was fondly called by Uttar Pradesh Congress leaders and workers, entered politics in 1970 as a Member of the Legislative Council in Uttar Pradesh. He was elected to the Lok Sabha for the first time in 1971 and repeated the feat in the 1980, 1984 and 1999 elections from Shahjahanpur.

OTTAVIO QUATTROCCHI

(1938–2013)

ON 13 JULY 2013, THE MAN WHO KNEW THE TRUTH ABOUT BOFORS DIED in Milan, Italy. Ottavio Quattrocchi, aged 73, had suffered a stroke.

Quattrocchi, called Mr Q by many in the media and his critics, was a close friend of Rajiv and Sonia Gandhi. By his own admission, he was in regular touch with Sonia Gandhi until 1993 when the prospect of arrest prompted him to shift base to Malaysia.

Quattrocchi was a representative of Snamprogetti, a Milan-based Italian multinational company involved in engineering and construction projects. The beginning of his association with India coincided with the year Rajiv and Sonia Gandhi got married. Quattrocchi had come to India briefly in 1964 but had left for Nigeria, returning again later only when he began work on his first Snamprogetti project, the Madras Refinery.

His wife, Maria, was described by friends as the 'driving force' behind her husband's rise. Maria was said to have forged a close association with Sonia Gandhi and often took her mother out shopping when her family from Italy visited New Delhi. The younger two of the four Quattrocchi children grew up playing with Rahul and Priyanka Gandhi.

The Quattrocchis were also regulars at the Sunday brunch served at the Gandhi residence. The gathering always included Amitabh and Jaya Bachchan, Suman and Manjulika Dubey, Mohan and Nirmal Thadani, Michael and Usha Albuquerque, Sunita and Ramesh Kohli, Deep Kaul, Romi Chopra, Arun and Nina Singh, and Satish and Sterre Sharma. Rajiv and Sonia Gandhi would giggle and crack jokes with their circle of friends and spend quality time with them. Sonia Gandhi would often opt for Kashmiri cuisine or simple Indian meals served in *thalis* (large metal plates), consisting of dal, two vegetable preparations, salad and a non-vegetarian dish. The exclusiveness of the gathering led to a lot of heartburn and rumour-mongering among those not included in the prime minister's 'inner circle'.

Throughout Rajiv Gandhi's tenure, from 1984 to 1989, there were allegations that Quattrocchi was so influential that ministers and senior bureaucrats would stand up when he visited them. It was also alleged that he could get ministers and bureaucrats sacked if they snubbed him. When Ramchandra Rath, a former Youth Congress chief and close associate of Sanjay Gandhi, had to step down as fertilizer minister in the government, the Delhi grapevine had it that this was the price he paid for keeping Quattrocchi waiting. Rath later claimed he was having lunch with the then Odisha governor. 'I didn't know who he was at the time.'

But many others, including Congress politicians, business leaders and bureaucrats, remember Quattrocchi as a good-humoured, social person who loved entertaining the high and mighty. He was the archetypal middleman: expansive, earthy, full of laughter and fond of showing off in an ingratiating manner.[364] 'He was full of bureaucratic gossip, name-dropped constantly and made no secret of his proximity to the Gandhi family,' recalled a former Union minister who asked not to be named.

In 1986, the Swiss arms manufacturer, Bofors, had landed a $15 billion contract to supply Howitzer guns to India. Quattrocchi was alleged to have served as a middleman in the deal, in which kickbacks were said to have been paid to Indian politicians and defence officials. The scandal cost Rajiv Gandhi the general election in 1989.

Quattrocchi left India for Malaysia on 29 July 1993. The CBI tried, but failed, to get him extradited to face trial in the Bofors case.

The CBI chargesheet, filed in 1999 when the NDA was in power, accused Quattrocchi of serving as a conduit for bribes. His wife Maria and the Bofors representative in India, Win Chadha, were also named. Chadha died in 2001. The CBI said Quattrocchi's AE Services received $7.3 million and Win Chaddha's Svenska Inc. received $27 million from A.B. Bofors for securing the contract from the Rajiv

Gandhi-led government. It said Quattrocchi had deposited the money in Swiss banks for the benefit of certain Indian public servants.

In 1993, Quattrocchi had faxed a signed, three-page news release that originated from Kuala Lumpur but appeared to have been routed through a source in Delhi. In it, he had put forth his denial and strongly defended the Gandhi family. He described Rajiv Gandhi as a 'noble soul'. The Italian denied having ever dealt with Bofors. 'I have never had any dealings with Bofors. I never received any money from Bofors, either in the gun deal or any other deal,' he said.[365]

Quattrocchi had also said that he had no plans of returning to India. Asked whether he was still friendly with the Gandhis, he shot back: 'Whether I maintain links with the Gandhi family or not is my private affair; why should I tell anybody about it? But once I am a friend of somebody, I remain a friend. Be it good or bad times.'[366]

His counsel had told the Supreme Court that Quattrocchi was prepared to come to India if promised he would not be arrested.

In March 2011, a Delhi court discharged Quattrocchi from the payoffs case, bringing the curtains down on a major chapter in the 25-year-old controversy.

<hr>

HAZARILAL RAGHUVANSHI
(1930–2020)

HAZARILAL RAGHUVANSHI HAD A DREAM: BEFORE HAIRLESS HUNKS TAKE over the world, men will pause and reflect on the timeless elegance of the growth beneath the nose. Someone did pause – and the person was no less than Pakistan President Pervez Musharraf. So impressed was Musharraf with Raghuvanshi's walrus moustache that he invited the leader from Madhya Pradesh to be a Pakistan army 'regular'. It was in jest, of course, but the Congress veteran's moustache had clearly made a mark. For Raghuvanshi, Musharraf's comment was the ultimate compliment. 'Few accessories,' he would say later, 'convey wisdom and mystery better than an impressive moustache.'[367]

Raghuvanshi, the former deputy speaker of the Madhya Pradesh Assembly and a minister in successive Congress governments starting with the 1980 Arjun Singh regime to the Digvijaya Singh government in 2003, died on 9 April 2020 at the ripe old age of 93. Raghuvanshi was a minister in successive Congress governments, starting with the 1980 Arjun Singh regime in which he was minister of state to the Digvijaya Singh government and continuing up to 1998 when he was a prominent state cabinet minister. His moustache's moment of glory had come thirteen years earlier in 2007, when he visited Islamabad as part of a team of Indian presiding officers for a convention of the Commonwealth Parliamentary Association held there between 25 and 27 March. When the Indian panel members called on President Musharraf, Raghuvanshi had instantly drawn the former Pakistan Army chief's attention. The Delhi-born Musharraf could not resist asking him, 'What are you doing in the Madhya Pradesh Assembly? Why don't you be a Pak regular?'[368]

Fellow delegate Ishwardas Rohani, a former BJP leader and the speaker of the Madhya Pradesh Assembly then said that although made in jest, the comment said a lot about Raghuvanshi's moustache. 'It was a genuine compliment, I guess,' Rohani said.[369]

Raghuvanshi had taken the opportunity to invite Musharraf to visit Bhopal. 'He readily agreed, saying "please send an invitation",' the Congress leader recalled.[370]

About his favourite topic, the moustache, Raghuvanshi said he had had to shave it off only twice since 1948 – when he lost each of his parents.[371] 'It had to be done in keeping with Hindu rites,' he had explained, pleased that his prized possession lending gravity to his visage had braved customs and scissors. In an age when the clean-shaven look seems to have lopped off the machismo of the moustache, the Congress veteran and former minister considered himself to be an exception. '[A] moustache deserves to be celebrated, not scorned,' Raghuvanshi would often say, stroking his walrus undergrowth.[372]

Not everyone agreed with him. The stubble is in but for the trendy, urban male, a hairy bush is no longer a mark of virility. Droopy or aliesque, where the long, narrow, pointed ends curl upwards; handlebar or toothbrush, walrus or pencil, the heyday of the moustache is over. And there's no need to split hairs over a losing battle, say those against the moustache.

Family sources say until the age of eighty plus, Raghuvanshi would still do hundred sit-ups a day, eat five parathas dipped in ghee for breakfast and insist that a moustache is an important part of one's personality. Yes, it takes time and a few trials to settle on a particular style but once finally adopted, there's no going back.

He had one regret, though – that is, apart from the fast withering support for whiskers. Neither his son nor his grandson sported a moustache. He had tried every trick in the book, including a long period of sullen silence when he avoided talking to them, but without success.

The old man is dead but for him, it's long live the moustache.

KANSHI RAM

(1934–2006)

ONE OF KANSHI RAM'S FAVOURITE EXPRESSIONS WAS THAT HE WANTED a *majboor* (desperate or weak) government, and not one that was *mazboot* (strong), till Dalits had reached the pinnacle of power. That was in the early 1980s when thousands of Dalit masses would travel miles on foot or rickety bicycles to hear their hero speak.

Bahujan Samaj Party founder Kanshi Ram, fondly addressed as 'Manyavar', 'Saheb' or 'Bahujan Nayak', remains one of India's most iconic political figures even years after his death in October 2006. Today, his popularity among the weaker sections of society is, perhaps, a tad more than that of Bhimrao Ambedkar, who is considered the father of the Indian Constitution. If Ambedkar, a constitutional expert, gave the Dalits full socioeconomic and political rights in the country's supreme legal document, Kanshi Ram's legacy has provided socially marginalized people, particularly those in northern India, an independent and powerful political identity.

Of course, it wasn't a smooth run for the man who redefined the Dalit movement in the country with his extraordinary organizational skills. For one, Kanshi Ram's 'pragmatic approach' towards politics led to tensions within the movement. While he never criticized Ambedkar, Dalit leaders from Maharashtra, for instance, could not reconcile themselves to the absence of Ambedkar's ideals-based ideology in Kanshi Ram's methods. It is a different thing that the Republican Party of India (RPI), which evolved out of the Scheduled Castes Federation that Ambedkar led, has not been able to follow the path the Dalit icon had shown. A faction of the RPI is currently an ally of the BJP, while the other faction, consisting of Ambedkar's son Prakash, allied with the hawkish All India Majlis-e-Ittehad-ul-Muslimeen (AIMIM) led by Asaduddin Owaisi in 2018 Maharashtra state Assembly polls. (More on the AIMIM in the chapter on Salahuddin Owaisi).

Born on 15 March 1934, in Pirthipur Bunga village near Punjab's Ropar district, Kanshi Ram was a Ramdasia Sikh belonging to the Chamar caste, which had been brought into the fold of Sikhism during the time of the fourth Guru, Ram Das. Kanshi Ram's family was not prosperous, although they did own some land and a small tannery.

Biographer Badri Narayan, who has pieced together an immensely readable book, *Kanshi Ram: Leader of the Dalits*, through interviews with family members and peers, claims that it was an incident of caste discrimination in the year 1960 that had ignited in the young Kanshi Ram the desire to mobilize Dalits into a socially powerful force. Kanshi Ram, a BSc graduate from Ropar University, was then working at the Explosive Research and Development Laboratory (ERDL) in Pune. It so happened that the ERDL had reportedly removed the holidays meant for Ambedkar Jayanti and Buddha Jayanti, and allotted them to mark the birth anniversaries of Bal Gangadhar Tilak and Gopal Krishna Gokhale. When one employee refused to report for work on Ambedkar's birth anniversary, he was removed from service. Kanshi Ram had protested but escaped disciplinary action because he successfully mobilized other employees and even met the then defence minister, Yashwantrao Chavan, who reversed the holiday order.[373]

The ERDL episode made Kanshi Ram read up Ambedkar's writings, particularly the *Annihilation of Caste*, as he set out in search for pride in his caste identity. He would later write to his family announcing that he was snapping all ties with them, convinced that familial attachments would compromise his dedication towards the Dalit cause. His biographer Badri Narayan says this was also the reason Kanshi Ram never married.

By 1964, Kanshi Ram had become an activist, social crusader and a political player while serving the government. He had initially thought of joining the Ambedkarite RPI and, later, the Dalit Panthers in Maharashtra, but figured out that there were too many factions of both groups.

Ambedkar, who believed that Dalit parties would one day marginalize the 'Brahminical forces', had formed the Republican Party of India in 1956, seeking a better political deal for the Dalits. But factionalism had reduced the RPI to such a state that, by 1970, it was bargaining with the Congress for a mere two seats in Ambedkar's native state of Maharashtra.

Kanshi Ram, an astute observer of poltics and society, had also realized that infinite academic debates on the relevance of Marxism and Buddhism to the Dalit cause often blurred the political focus needed for organizing a movement. So he remained focussed on mobilizing Dalit masses into a cohesive force and, in 1971, formed the SC/ST/OBC Minorities Communities Employees Association. The outfit would soon be renamed as the All India Backward and Minority Communities Employees' Federation (BAMCEF), a unique organization that largely consisted of educated Dalits who were government employees. BAMCEF was sort of a think tank, talent bank and financial bank, all clubbed into one, with the overarching objective of uniting Dalits. It was during this time that Kanshi Ram spotted an enterprising and industrious schoolteacher named Mayawati, who would go on to become his right-hand person and, eventually, the face of the Bahujan Samaj Party (BSP).

By 1981, Kanshi Ram had come up with another outfit, the Dalit Soshit Samaj Sangharsh Samiti (DS-4), a quasi-political party that sought to mobilize the weaker sections through mass awareness *jagrans* and cycle rallies. The BSP, conceived of as a 'mission', was formed in 1984. By then, Kanshi Ram had decided that only by capturing state power – for him, the 'master key' – could the Dalit movement bring about fundamental changes in society. And so, at every public meeting, Kanshi Ram would ask for 'one note' and 'one vote'; a symbolic fund-collection drive to arouse the self-respect of the historically downtrodden coupled with his appeal for political commitment to the cause.

From the early 1980s, Kanshi Ram had been targeting other Dalit leaders, particularly Babu Jagjivan Ram of the Congress and Ram Vilas Paswan of the Janata Party (subsequently, the Janata Dal). He advanced an interesting thesis that formed part of a book he wrote in 1982, provocatively titled *The Chamcha Age: An Era of the Stooge*. The word 'chamcha' (stooge/sycophant) occurs frequently in the 158-page book.[374] As my columnist friend Vivek Kaul has tried explaining, elsewhere, the closest English word for the *desi* word *chamcha* is sycophancy. But sycophancy doesn't have the same depth as *chamchagiri* does.[375]

Historian and writer Ramachandra Guha, too, has tried explaining *chamcha* and *chamchagiri* in an essay titled *A Short History of Congress Chamchagiri*, part of his immensely readable book, *Patriots and Partisans*.[376] Kanshi Ram's use of the term *chamcha* for Dalit leaders betraying the Ambedkarite cause, such as Jagjivan Ram and Ram Vilas Paswan, was a potent tool that found instant appeal among Dalits in Uttar Pradesh.[377]

As for the difference in ideologies between Kanshi Ram and Ambedkar, Badri Narayan thinks it had much to do with their diverse educational backgrounds. He argues:

> While Ambedkar studied at Columbia University and was trained in Western knowledge tradition, Kanshi Ram was born in a small village in Punjab and trained in the school of Pune's Dalit politics. Because of Ambedkar's western training, his ideological ingredients were derived by seeing Dalits in the context of history. Kanshi Ram's political arguments in favour of Dalits on the other hand merged historical and mythological contexts. This is because he understood the mythology and folk-based culture and society of U.P. Kanshi Ram initially tried to follow Ambedkar's path that had been adopted in Maharashtra. However, he changed course and asserted that although Dalit politics got its grounding in Maharashtra, it grew

and was nurtured on the soil of U.P. Ambedkar called the politics of emancipation of marginalized groups the 'Dalit movement'; while Kanshi Ram preferred to term it the 'Bahujan movement', avoiding the use of the word 'Dalit'.[378]

When this author met him in 1989, Kanshi Ram had a fountain pen in his hand. 'I want it to turn upside. The Bahujan Samaj (Dalits and tribals) is at the bottom of the pyramid,' he had said, pointing towards the nib. *'Main yeh vaiwastha badlna chahta hoon* (I want to change the power equations drastically).'

That was shortly after Kanshi Ram had lost Lok Sabha elections from two constituencies; East Delhi, where he fought against H.K.L. Bhagat, a powerful minister in the Rajiv Gandhi government, and against Rajiv himself at Amethi. Kanshi Ram had finished third in both the seats.

His initial forays into politics were not successful. The Kanshi Ram-led BSP kept losing elections throughout the 1980s. In 1985, the BSP got a mere 2.4 per cent of the total votes polled in the Uttar Pradesh Assembly elections. In the subsequent by-elections held in March 1987, the BSP had polled an impressive 26.7 per cent. Kanshi Ram had fought the 1988 Lok Sabha byepolls from Allahabad, a seat vacated by megastar Amitabh Bachchan following the Bofors uproar. Pitted against the combined opposition candidate, V.P. Singh, a future prime minister, and the Congress's Sunil Shastri, Kanshi Ram had lost but managed to poll over 72,000 votes. 'You can guess the tremendous growth of my support base from the fact that during the December 1984 general election, my candidate got just 1,716 votes in Allahabad,' Kanshi Ram had told Bhaskar Roy of the *India Today* magazine.[379]

'Jiski jitni sankhya bhari, uski utni hissedari (The greater a community's numbers, the greater its political representation),' was another of Kanshi Ram's·potent slogans.

In the 1991 Assembly elections in Uttar Pradesh, the BSP, pitted against the Samajwadi Party, the Congress and the BJP, managed to get just twelve seats in a House of 425. The BJP, under Kalyan Singh, won 221 seats – eight more than the majority mark of 213. Kanshi Ram got into backstage negotiations with arch-rival Mulayam Singh Yadav, who had formed the Samajwadi Party. This was a turbulent period in Uttar Pradesh, where caste-based reservations based on the Mandal Commission's recommendations had led to euphoria among the backward classes, while the December 1992 demolition of the sixteenth century Babri mosque in Ayodhya, considered to be the birthplace of Lord Ram, would sharply divide the electorate on communal lines. When fresh Assembly elections were called in 1993 following the dismissal of the Kalyan Singh government, Kanshi Ram and Mulayam Singh stunned their opponents by announcing an electoral pact. The two parties represented a huge vote bank, comprising Yadavs and Dalits. It didn't take long for the Muslims to realize that this was a winning combination which they could not afford to ignore. The turnout of Muslim voters was 70 to 80 per cent, the highest ever in the state. Dalits, too, had voted enthusiastically, sensing a chance for the BSP to share power with Mulayam Singh. The combine won 176 seats, just one short of the BJP's tally, proving wrong the widespread prediction that the BJP would be the only party able to form a government. The Samajwadi–BSP combine made inroads into every region of the state.

The alliance didn't last long and soon, by 1995, the Samajwadi Party and the BSP became bitter rivals. Things got so bad that on 2 June 1995, Kanshi Ram's protégé Mayawati had to lock herself inside her suite in Lucknow's state guesthouse, because it had been surrounded by a violent mob of Samajwadi workers following the BSP's withdrawal of support to the Mulayam Singh government. Mayawati, who had 40 MLAs with her, bolted the room from inside, while chief minister Mulayam Singh, reportedly keen to win over some BSP legislators, allegedly ordered that electricity and water supply be snapped in the guest house. A headcount revealed that five BSP MLAs were missing. As Mayawati made frantic calls to Union home minister Shankar Rao Chavan, Samajwadi workers screamed abuses and hurled threats at her. Kanshi Ram was nowhere to be seen.

Barely 24 hours later, Mayawati created history when she was sworn in as the first Dalit chief minister of Uttar Pradesh. Kanshi Ram had pulled a bigger surprise than the 1993 tie-up with the Samajwadi Party – getting L.K. Advani and Atal Bihari Vajpayee to agree to extend the BJP's support to Mayawati. Mayawati remains the only Dalit woman to have become chief minister till date.

'Politics is all about pragmatism, realism and stability,' was all that Kanshi Ram would say later, allowing himself a smile, when asked about what had transpired behind the scenes.

Mulayam Singh, reduced to a mere spectator, sat next to Kanshi Ram at the midnight swearing-in. They did not acknowledge each other's presence.

Prime minister P.V. Narasimha Rao, who was away in France, described Mayawati as a 'miracle of democracy' while addressing captains of trade and industry in Paris, marvelling at how a woman from the most neglected section of society had assumed the powerful office of chief minister in India's most populous and politically significant state.

It did not require a clairvoyant to predict a tempestuous marriage ahead for the BSP and the BJP. By October 1995, the two had parted company and Mayawati was out of power. Kanshi Ram turned to the Congress for the July 1996 Assembly elections in Uttar Pradesh. The timing of the alliance was close to the 1996 general elections in which the Congress had been locked in a grim battle against a resurgent BJP and aggressive regional parties. When the BSP–Congress alliance was announced in New Delhi, Narasimha Rao, who was the prime minister then as well as the Congress's president, had sounded a bit cagey when asked about the seat-share arrangement. Kanshi Ram, sitting next to Narasimha Rao and Uttar Pradesh Congress Committee chief Jitendra Prasada, was vocal, spelling out the terms of the accord. He said the BSP would contest 300 of the 425 Assembly seats in the state and the Congress the remaining 125.

While Narasimha Rao maintained a stoic silence, Prasada, a key architect of the alliance, had tried to look the other way.

After the Congress's 1996 Lok Sabha defeat and the UP Assembly poll debacle, an AICC panel headed by party veteran K. Karunakaran had gone on a fact-finding mission to Uttar Pradesh and observed rather dryly that district-level offices in Gorakhpur, Basti, Bahraich and dozens of other places had remained intact but the boards/signposts outside had changed from the Congress to the BJP.

There would be no looking back for the BSP and, under Kanshi Ram's watchful supervision, Mayawati would serve two more times as Uttar Pradesh chief minister till her mentor's death in October 2006. She would become chief minister again in May 2007 and complete her full five-year term for the first time, before moving to the Rajya Sabha in April 2012.

One of Kanshi Ram's lasting legacies is Dalit empowerment and inspiring in Dalits assertiveness – something they had long lacked. The most significant and visible effect of that was the way Uttar Pradesh's feudal social structure got neutralized, ending decades of Congress rule that had treated Dalits as a benign patriarch would. Substantial numbers of Dalit voters became important for 'socialist' and backward-class leaders who had a history of subjugating the Dalits. From the later part of the 1980s, Dalit voters started coming out in large numbers to exercise their franchise in the 'Jat belts' of western Uttar Pradesh where they were once not allowed to vote.

During her brief tenures as chief minister between 1995 and 1997, Mayawati rounded up as many as 1,45,000 rowdies, criminals and goondas who were known to intimidate Dalits. In their study titled *Dalit Assertion and Bahujan Samaj Party*, Vivek Kumar and Uday Sinha have observed that Dalit women would outnumber men at public meetings and rallies that Mayawati addressed. Dalit women, the authors concluded, were freer than upper-caste women and often closely identified with Mayawati – a woman like them who came from a socially underprivileged background similar to theirs.[380]

On 11 May 2007, the 'miracle of democracy' was seen paying her respects to herself. At the Prerna Sthal temple inside the BSP headquarters at Lucknow, Mayawati stood in silence for a minute before three tall deities, statues of B.R. Ambedkar, Kanshi Ram and herself. As she stepped out of the temple, it began to rain. Some Lucknow residents, who had been sweating in the 40°C heat that day, took it as 'divine approval' for the change of guard in Uttar Pradesh, which had just voted out Mulayam Singh's Samajwadi Party in the elections that summer. Two days later, Mayawati would assume charge as chief minister for the fourth time.

Inside the temple, a flash of memories must have come to Mayawati's mind. It was sometime in 1977; Mayawati was just out of college, busy preparing for the civil services exams and teaching at a school when she met Kanshi Ram for the first time. Her future mentor had told her that while she aspired to be a DM (district magistrate), she would become a chief minister one day if she followed his path. Kanshi Ram, who had seen Mayawati controlling the masses, sought single-minded devotion from her and promised her that, in return, once she became chief minister, she would have immense 'control' over hundreds of IAS officers – and not over DMs alone.

When Kanshi Ram died, his funeral rites were performed according to the Buddhist tradition, with Mayawati lighting the pyre. 'I heralded a new tradition of social change by lighting the pyre of Kanshi Ram,' Mayawati said after performing the seventh-day ritual for her late mentor. 'In Buddhism, there is no difference between a boy and a girl in performing rituals.'

Kanshi Ram had planned to embrace Buddhism on 14 October 2006, the 50th anniversary of Ambedkar's conversion, but he died five days before it could happen.

'Saheb Kanshi Ram and I had decided that we would convert and adopt Buddhism when we get an "absolute majority" at the Centre,' Mayawati had explained after Kanshi Ram's death. 'We wanted to do this because we could make a difference to the religion by taking along with us millions of people. If we convert without power then only we two will be converting. But when you have power you can really create a stir.'[381]

Kanshi Ram may not have been able to convert and he did not ever control power directly, but he did create a stir nonetheless – the echoes of which resonate even today.

P.V. NARASIMHA RAO
(1921–2004)

EVEN IN DEATH P.V. NARASIMHA RAO KEPT AWAY FROM THE HEADQUARTERS of the party he had once headed. The former prime minister's 9 Motilal Nehru Marg residence in Delhi was barely 200 metres away from the Congress's 24 Akbar Road headquarters, but Rao had not once visited the office after being forced to step down as party chief eight years earlier, a few months after the 1996 Lok Sabha electoral rout. On 23 December 2004, his body was not about to do so either.

The following morning, the flower-decked army gun carriage carrying Rao's body was to have been kept briefly at the Congress office so that the party's rank and file could get a last glimpse of the late leader considered to be the architect of India's economic reforms. But the gun carriage could not make it past the main gate, where it was kept for nearly 40 minutes as prime minister Manmohan Singh, Congress chief Sonia Gandhi and several ministers paid their last respects and offered wreaths. According to senior journalist Dr Sanjaya Baru, who was Prime Minister Dr Manmohan Singh's media advisor then, Sonia Gandhi's political secretary Ahmed Patel had asked him to convey to Rao's sons that the funeral should be held in Hyderabad instead of Delhi.

Rao's body, accompanied by his family members, was later flown to Hyderabad on a special flight that evening. Sonia Gandhi deputed All India Congress Committee (AICC) treasurer Motilal Vora and general secretary Ashok Gehlot to accompany the body. Among others on the flight were minister of state Prithviraj Chavan, the designated minister for the state funeral, as well as several Union ministers from the then undivided Andhra Pradesh, including S. Jaipal Reddy, K. Chandrasekhar Rao, Renuka Chowdhury and Panabaka Laxmi.

The Impact of Ayodhya

Rao remained a staunch Congressman throughout his career that spanned over six decades but died an ill and bitter man, seven months after the Sonia Gandhi-led UPA came to power in 2004. Already isolated since 1996, when Rao was first removed as leader of Congress party in Parliament and then sacked as Congress president, he spent the last few years of his life blaming both his party and the Bharatiya Janata Party (BJP) for the single-most controversial event that blotted his reign – the December 1992 demolition of the Babri Masjid in Ayodhya. While he accused some of his party colleagues of making him a scapegoat, he held the BJP responsible for destroying his otherwise impressive political career. In his book, Ayodhya 6 December 1992, published after his death in 2006, Rao has argued on a singular point – that the BJP scuppered a possible solution to the temple tangle to keep the pot boiling.[382]

Known to be measured with his words, he observed that till August 1992, his talks with 'apolitical' sadhus and sannyasis on how and where a Ram temple could be built in Ayodhya 'without breaking the law or upsetting communal harmony' had been proceeding quite well. Then abruptly, he said, the Vishwa Hindu Parishad-backed sadhus broke off the talks. Four months later, the sixteenth century mosque was demolished by hordes of *kar sevaks*.[383]

'Why did they (the sadhus) go back on their promise (to explore all avenues towards a peaceful settlement of the dispute),' Rao wondered in his book and then offered a plausible explanation: 'It was clear that there was a change of mind on their (the sadhus') part, or what is more likely, on the part of the political forces that controlled them.'[384]

Without naming the BJP, he wrote: 'These forces deliberately wanted to get out of [a] friendly situation which the sannyasis were getting into with me and which, if left to itself, would have made the mandir issue wholly apolitical.' He added: 'This subtle aspect of the Ramjanmabhoomi matter is very important and brings home the undeniable fact that while Hindu masses were swayed by their devotion to Ram and their intense desire for the temple, the political forces behind the issue could not care less for the temple – they only wanted to retain a long-term, vote-rich communal issue for as long as they could.'

Old-timers would recall that till August 1992, Rao had been in constant touch with the top Nagpur-based leadership of the Rashtriya Swayamsevak Sangh, the BJP's ideological fulcrum, to try and resolve the Ayodhya dispute amicably.[385]

While Congress leaders such as V.N. Gadgil and Vasant Sathe acted as his personal emissaries, several sadhus and *sants* of that era – including Mahant Avaidyanath, Vamdeo Maharaj, Ramchandradas Paramhans, Mahant Nrityagopal Das, Swami Paramanand, Swami Chinmayananda and Pejawar Swamiji – were regular visitors to 7 Race Course Road, New Delhi, Rao's prime ministerial residence. Rao had also sought help from many apolitical saints, such as Jain *muni* Acharya Sushil and his spiritual guru based in Ramtek (Maharashtra), to prevail upon the Sangh-VHP to go slow on Ayodhya.

According to Rao, the demand for the Ram temple was not for just one shrine in Ayodhya, the administrative headquarters of Faizabad district in Uttar Pradesh. Rao wrote:

More had been lined up, so that the agitation could be kept
alive even if the issues of one or two specific temples were
settled. The number was three (Ayodhya, Mathura, Kashi)
and for good measure, in the unlikely event of all three
temple issues being settled amicably, there was a never-
ending store of more than 3,000 controversial temples lined
up all over the country![386]

The Ayodhya dispute had from the beginning been the Congress's
Achilles' heel. India's first prime minister Jawaharlal Nehru had been
dragged into the temple imbroglio in December 1949 when idols
were surreptitiously placed inside the Babri mosque. Nehru had asked
the Uttar Pradesh Chief Secretary then, Bhagwan Sahay, to restore
the status quo. But K.K. Nayar, who was the deputy commissioner of
Faizabad then, wrote lengthy letters ruing that he had failed to find
'any Hindu even among Congressmen', who was ready to support
the removal of the idols.[387]

The Indian Civil Service officer said that each time he visited
the site, he was greeted with the slogan: 'Nyaya anyay karna chhor
do; Nayar, bhagwan ka phatak khol do (Stop talking about justice or
injustice; Nayar, open the door towards the deity).'[388]

Nayar later became a Lok Sabha MP of the Jana Sangh, the
forerunner of the BJP.

Decades later, in 1986, when Rajiv Gandhi was the prime minister
and the Congress was in power in Uttar Pradesh, the fast-paced
events that lead to the opening of the lock had surprised even the BJP,
which highlighted the Congress's role in a White Paper published
after the Babri Masjid was demolished. Under the heading, 'The case
for opening the lock – a contrast', it asked sarcastically:

How is it this case moved at such a speed? How did the
government acquiesce in this case? How did the Faizabad
court allow the appeal (to open the lock) in two days when
the Hindus had been pleading for 37 years? How did the

Doordarshan cameras click the opening of the lock within an hour of the court order? All these questions have one answer, the government is not against such things and they can, and do, happen.[389]

From 1986 to 1989, Rajiv Gandhi, his home minister Buta Singh and the chief ministers of Uttar Pradesh at the time, first Veer Bahadur Singh and then N.D. Tiwari, kept trying to bring the Ayodhya issue to the centrestage. In 1989, the government even allowed the *shilanyas* (foundation ceremony) at the site. Somehow, each of these measures boomeranged.

Rao, who had watched this period from close quarters before becoming a central figure himself, articulated his dilemma in his book. He said the BJP's 'pseudo religious movement' could not have sustained itself on a purely religious plane and needed a political reaction to flourish. 'I cannot escape the uneasy feeling that we Congressmen (while in government) supplied it with just that.'[390]

He also cited several government records and statements to suggest that the *shilanyas* Rajiv Gandhi had allowed took place on 'disputed' land.

The demolition left Rao a disillusioned man. He wrote that while the Kalyan Singh government in Uttar Pradesh and the BJP were largely responsible for the 'wanton vandalism', he believed that his Congress colleagues in the ministry too had been guided by 'political and vote-earning' considerations. 'They had already made up their mind that one person had to be made historically responsible for the tragedy... They got a stick to beat me with. I understood it.'[391]

Rao said brave words were uttered after the demolition and some Congress figures even tried to look like sages who knew everything beforehand. 'I must say that this is a pose, because having been authors of the crisis and enacted the whole drama of destruction, those responsible wanted to have some specific role assigned to themselves in history, something even wrongly to be proud of,' he wrote without naming party leaders who, he claimed, had a vested interest in holding him responsible for the Babri outrage.[392]

Rao said that when he explained these finer points to his cabinet colleagues, they did not help him. Instead, they made him a scapegoat. 'It was me that they demolished,' he rued.[393]

When Babri masjid fell on 6 December 1992, Rao found himself isolated in the cabinet meeting that took place in the evening of that fateful day. Dr Manmohan Singh, who had taken over as finance minister, tried to stand by Rao. Nehru–Gandhi family retainer M.L. Fotedar, who was union health and family welfare minister then, is said to have chided Manmohan for backing Rao. 'I told him (Manmohan), "Kindly keep quiet."' Fotedar had told an interviewer later.[394]

Rajiv Gandhi's Death

Destiny, however, had something more in store for Rao. On 21 May 1991, having declined Rajiv Gandhi's offer to contest Lok Sabha as part of the Congress election campaign, Rao was busy packing his books to move back to his birthplace Warrangal in Andhra. Rao would perhaps have even shifted out of Delhi much before had a technician turned up to assist him with packing a bulky computer system he had recently acquired. The news of Rajiv Gandhi's gruesome assassination on that fateful night at Sriperembudur stunned everyone and caused a huge void in the political arena.

There was no clear mechanism for succession in the Congress. The Gandhi family hold had dismantled the post of number two in the party. Indira Gandhi, forever suspicious, had taught her son Rajiv Gandhi an important lesson – to keep regional satraps at bay and not to promote anyone not part of the Nehru–Gandhi clan. As prime minister, leader of the Opposition and leader of the Congress, Rajiv Gandhi may have spent hours and days cutting regional satraps to size, but many still nursed the ambition of becoming prime minister instead of him. His sudden death brought their ambitions into play.

One among those vying for the prime ministerial post was Sharad Pawar from Maharashtra, who had a knack of striking deals with his foes. Then there was N.D. Tiwari, a seasoned Brahmin leader from Uttar Pradesh who was considered a politician among politicians. The Madhya Pradesh leader Arjun Singh was known for his political skills and as a chief minister, gave Rajiv Gandhi a hard time by constantly disobeying him. When Gandhi asked him to step down following his indictment in a court case, Singh rebelled and forced Gandhi to strike a deal with him. There were also the Karnataka chief minister Veerendra Patil, his Andhra counterpart M. Channa Reddy and others who were kept at arm's length. To counter these leaders, Rajiv Gandhi had promoted a set of courtiers who lacked a mass base of their own to powerful positions, including Buta Singh, Ghulam Nabi Azad and Jitendra Prasada – who were informally given the title 'rootless wonders' by their own partymen.

Rajiv Gandhi's death altered everything. Sonia Gandhi, Priyanka Gandhi and a handful of party leaders may have been mourning a personal loss, but for the regional satraps, courtiers and the majority of Congress MPs, the succession issue was most important. Those in the fray were hell-bent on winning the key position. While the kingmakers and courtiers were honing their skills to get their favourites the top job, the moneybags too were openly promising party leaders and MPs that they would be suitably rewarded if their favourite won the race.

This was not the first time that Congress was faced with a leadership issue. In 1984, when Indira Gandhi was assassinated, Congressmen saw young Rajiv Gandhi as the heir-apparent. Rajiv Gandhi's selection was, however, not too smooth. Pranab Mukherjee, who had served as Indira Gandhi's unofficial number two, projected himself as a likely successor. His miscalculation cost him dearly, forcing him to leave the party and float his own outfit.

Eighteen hours after Rajiv Gandhi's assassination, the Congress Working Committee (CWC), the apex decision-making body of the party, consisting of twelve members and two permanent and four special invitees, met at 24 Akbar Road, the Congress party's headquarters. According to the Congress constitution, the party's most senior general secretary should head such meetings, but there was little or no agreement on the seniority of the general secretaries. Finally former Union minister Pranab Mukherjee, who was not in the succession race, proposed Rao's name to chair the meeting. Rao was non-controversial and readily accepted by all groups and factions. In fact, Rao was often seen at 10 Janpath at the time escorting foreign dignitaries, who had come to participate in Rajiv's funeral. There was no one who could handle the situation except for Rao and Natwar Singh, both of whom had exposure with many heads of the state and leaders from African nations. Rao, who had served as country's external affairs minister between 1980–84 and again in 1988–89, had personally known and interacted with many visiting dignitaries and was therefore thought of as well-suited for the job.

At the end of the meeting, the CWC unanimously requested Rajiv Gandhi's widow to take over as the AICC chief. The party collectively ignored the fact that Sonia Gandhi was not even a 'char anna' member of the Congress party. A *char* (four) anna (the rupee was divided into annas before conversion to the metric system) membership fee was a prerequisite for anyone joining the party. Mahatma Gandhi, who is credited with giving the Congress a mass base during India's freedom struggle, had envisaged the concept of *char* anna membership. No thought was given to Sonia Gandhi's leadership qualities or her unfamiliarity with the complexities of the political system.

These deliberations had took place while Rajiv Gandhi's body had not even been buried. The CWC's decision was communicated to Sonia Gandhi by a group of party leaders consisting of Ghulam Nabi Azad, M.L. Fotedar and Pranab Mukherjee among others. A day later, Sonia Gandhi issued a small statement refusing to accept the post. It said, 'The tragedy that has befallen me and my children does not make it possible for me to accept the presidentship of the Congress.'

After protracted behind-the-scenes manoeuvring, Rao, 71 then, emerged victorious. Congress' in-house kingmakers M.L. Fotedar and Sitaram Kesri preferred Rao over Arjun Singh and Sharad Pawar. A mock election was arranged. The venue was 24 Akbar Road. Several rooms were converted into polling stations where MPs were asked to cast their vote under the watchful eyes of senior leaders like A.K. Antony, Sharad Pawar and P. Shiv Shankar. Rao polled more than 95 per cent of votes. Barring a handful of diehard Pawar supporters, everyone voted for him.

Five years of Narasimha Rao's premiership (1991–96) saw many highs and lows. Rao was India's first 'accidental' prime minister, and a path-breaking one. He took charge of the national government and restored political stability, assumed leadership of the Congress and proved that there was hope beyond the Nehru–Gandhi dynasty, pushed through significant economic reforms and steered India through the uncharted waters of the post-Cold War world. Rao not only ruled a full term but his policies ushered in a new era and gave a new direction to national politics. He was an unlikely prime minister but a seminal one. The country's economic crisis 1991 was a consequence of bad economic management of the past.

One among Rao's many contributions was the trust he openly put in economist Dr Manmohan Singh, who was made finance minister during 1991–96 despite him not having political experience or clout. Rao trusted Manmohan's economic acumen. As prime minister, Rao gave Manmohan full support to clear the 'cobwebs of unnecessary control' that had impeded economic development and decreed that 'the world has changed, and the country must also change'.[395]

Manmohan was Rao's personal choice. On the morning of 22 June 1991, a Saturday, Manmohan received a telephone call at his Bahadur Shah Zafar Marg office of the University Grants Commission. Rao, who was scheduled to take his oath as prime minister that afternoon, was on the line. He asked Manmohan directly, 'What are you doing there? Go home and change, and come straight to Rashtrapati Bhavan.'[396]

Rao's otherwise glorious tenure was marred by allegations of corruption, demolition of Babri masjid, communal violence, factionalism within the Congress and the Grand Old Party finally losing its primacy in country's politics.

Trouble with Sonia Gandhi

A section of Congressmen who were in the thick of things during the Rao era feel that midway into his tenure as prime minister, Rao was reluctant to facilitate the return of a member of the Nehru–Gandhi family in the Congress. Rao was of the view that Sonia Gandhi, lacking in experience as she was at the time, may become a 'puppet' in the hands of some of his archrivals within the party.

It has been said that Rao's inept handling of the Ayodhya dispute, his focus on economic reforms, the tardy probe into the Rajiv Gandhi assassination case under his rule, and the allegations of corruption he faced contributed for creating a deep wedge between 10 Janpath (Sonia Gandhi's residence) and 7 Race Course Road (prime minister's house). In retrospect, these appear to be contributing factors but the real reason seems to have been Sonia Gandhi's own assessment that Rao was systematically trying to undermine the Nehru–Gandhi legacy. Rao even developed a coterie of sorts, consisting of Matang Singh, Bhuvnesh Chaturvedi, Vidya Charan Shukla, M.S. Bitta and others, who conspired against known baiters such as V. George, K. Karunakaran, Arjun Singh, M.L. Fotedar, Natwar Singh and others.

Both Gandhi and Rao were reticent persons, and when he took over as prime minister, the two hardly spoke to each other, preferring to deal with Wajahat Habibullah and Ramu Damodaran. Habibullah, an IAS officer of the 1967 batch from the Jammu and Kashmir cadre, was drafted as the chief executive of the Rajiv Gandhi Foundation (RGF), headed by Sonia Gandhi, while Damodaran was private secretary to Rao.

Despite all this, within days of taking over as prime minister, Rao made a gesture that deeply touched Sonia Gandhi. He was appointed as a trustee of RGF. There was a tussle as to where the first RGF meeting should take place. Sonia Gandhi was keen to have it at 10 Janpath, but some persons close to Rao raised the issue of protocol. Habibullah and Damodaran saved the situation when the latter explained to Rao that Sonia Gandhi was in no mental condition to visit 7 Race Course Road, as it used to be Rajiv Gandhi's office. Sensitive to her feelings, he called Sonia Gandhi informing her that he would be coming over to 10 Janpath. Unfortunately, the outside world misconstrued Rao's gesture as a mark of the country's prime minister paying obeisance to a private citizen.

Their relationship, however, would soon be strained by Rao's move to deny a Rajya Sabha nomination to Sonia Gandhi's private secretary Vincent George in January 1992. The Congress was to select party nominees for the Rajya Sabha from Karnataka, and some senior party leaders ganged up against Margaret Alva, who was seeking an unprecedented fourth successive term. They nominated George, even though he actually hails from Kerala. Rao was hesitant to clear George's name, despite the fact that almost all the party bigwigs, particularly K. Karunakaran and Arjun Singh, were keen that he be nominated. There was no word from Sonia Gandhi either in favour of or against George. As Rao was leaving for Russia, he called on her to inquire if she wanted George to be in the Upper House. Sonia Gandhi made it clear that if the party wanted to give a ticket to George, the decision should be based on merit and in keeping with political considerations. Following this exchange, Rao chose to deny George the nomination. When the list of candidates was faxed from abroad, George had been denied a ticket and Alva's name was on the list.

This issue, although seemingly insignificant, became a major factor in the distrust that characterized the relationship between 10 Janpath and 7 Race Course Road over the next four years (1992–96). Sonia Gandhi's private secretary, it was claimed, became hostile towards Rao. George was singularly responsible for widening the gap between the two, and he had a role to play in the events that finally led to the split of the party in 1995 when the All India Indira Congress (Tiwari) was formed.

Disgruntled leaders and party activists, unhappy with the Narasimha Rao regime, began to be given audience with Sonia Gandhi. George would call up MPs saying that Gandhi was free to meet them between 5 and 7 p.m. on particular days. The message was clear; they were welcome to air their grievances to her. Congressmen readily obliged George, and the queues outside 10 Janpath were never small.

The outside world would never fully understand the importance of Vincent George. His role was either exaggerated as some kind of super boss or downgraded to that of a petty clerk. The truth was different. For ten long years, between 1991 and 2001, before he was finally sidelined, George had the distinction of having constant access to Sonia Gandhi. He was in charge of arranging meetings – be they with senior leaders or grassroots workers, industry and other bigwigs or supporters from the villages – and tracking down party leaders. His supporters even today boast of 'George Sahib' being able to find any party leader within half an hour – a distinction that no one in the party could match. He was loyal, hardworking and efficient, and he never exceeded his brief.

Constant effort was made to keep conveying to Sonia Gandhi that all was not well under the new government. For instance, in 1994, an independent TV producer prepared a capsule on the Congress campaign for the Assembly elections of Andhra Pradesh and Karnataka. The presentation was made to Rao and his close associates, but it was rejected on the grounds that it focused on the party's glorious past, starting with Nehru and going on to glorify Indira and Rajiv Gandhi. Hours later the producer was given an audience with Sonia Gandhi to narrate how he was discouraged from highlighting the family's contribution.

Sonia Gandhi may have had her own views on various issues facing the country, but George's role was significant. George facilitated the access of a large number of Congress leaders and MPs who wished to drive home the same point to her – that the Congress would lose its character if she did not intervene. She seldom spoke, but her willingness to hear out all those unhappy with the prime minister was indication enough to these visitors that she did not approve of Rao's style of functioning.

Rao died eight months after Sonia Gandhi-led UPA came to power in 2004. During those days of isolation, illness and perhaps indignity, he used to admit that the Babri demolition of December 1992 had destroyed his otherwise impressive political career.

In 2020, Sonia Gandhi finally acknowledged Rao's contributions. Marking his birth centenary and the 29th anniversary of the first union budget presented on 24 July 1991 by the Rao regime, she praised Rao's contribution to the country and the Congress. Some in the Congress felt it was merely a ploy not to let either the BJP or the ruling Telagana Rashtriya Samiti usurp Rao's legacy.

Sonia Gandhi also wrote a letter saying, 'P.V. Narasimha Rao was a much respected national and international figure. The Congress party takes pride in his many accomplishments and contributions. The birth centenary of Rao is an occasion to recall and pay tribute to a most scholarly and erudite personality, who after a long career in state and national politics, (became) the prime minister of the country at a time of grave economic crisis.'[397]

N.T. RAMA RAO

(1923–1996)

THE AIRCRAFT HAD JUST LANDED AT THE BEGUMPET AIRPORT. AFTER the plane glided to a halt, a tall gentleman with a pleasant, smiling face emerged at the door. Then his expression changed. A little distance away, on the tarmac, stood Tantuguri Anjaiah, the Congress chief minister of undivided Andhra Pradesh, a garland in his hands. With him was his entire cabinet, waiting to welcome the AICC general secretary who was on a 'private' visit to the state.

The year was 1982. The Congress was back in power at the Centre and the dark clouds of the post-Emergency rout seemed a distant past.

As the crowd of Congress leaders surged forward to welcome him, Rajiv Gandhi's face turned grim. Anjaiah, however, failed to read the change in Gandhi's mood. By the time the Andhra leaders were through with their welcome, the otherwise sober Gandhi had lost his cool. Those within earshot heard him call Anjaiah, a sixty-plus veteran from a less privileged section of society, a 'buffoon'.

The rash of arrogance did not end there. This was a time that Indira Gandhi's residence and office was packed with mavericks, and courtiers who excelled in palace intrigue. In order to cut others down, Indira Gandhi's key advisors often ill advised her against Congress chief ministers who were not according importance to a 'coterie' around the prime minister. Some of them convinced her to sack Anjaiah. The humiliation was complete. 'I came by the grace of Madam, I am going under her orders,' Anjaiah would say as he left. 'I don't know why I came and why I am going.'[398]

Anjaiah wasn't the only one in the dark. His party too had no inkling of what was coming; the repercussions of the airport humiliation and the veteran's unceremonious exit would extend beyond the state's power corridors.

The 'insult' of the 'Telugu *bidda*' (Telugu son of the soil) turned into ammunition in the hands of Nandamuri Taraka Rama Rao (popularly called NTR), an actor who had just arrived on the political scene. In the 1983 Assembly elections, NTR's newly created Telugu Desam Party would go on to power the '*atmagauravam*' (self-respect) plank.

NTR was not the first matinee idol to storm a Congress citadel; that distinction goes to Tamil Nadu's Maruthur Gopalan Ramachandran, more famous as MGR. But NTR's rise was sudden and spectacular – more so because he did not have a well-established political party. He also did not have the benefit of tutelage under a veteran, like MGR had C.N. Annadurai, or training as a Congress activist. Nor did he have the backing of a potent Dravidian social and political movement like MGR had in Tamil Nadu. Undivided Andhra Pradesh had come into existence barely three decades ago, following revolutionary freedom fighter Potti Sreeramulu's fast unto death demanding for a separate state made up of the Telugu-speaking districts of Madras Presidency.

The creation of new states based on linguistic and regional aspirations has been a tricky and volatile subject in India because of the numerous demands for smaller states made by a large variety of regional and linguistic groups across the country. But Sreeramulu's 1952 hunger strike had managed to pressure the then prime minister Jawaharlal Nehru to set up the first States Reorganization Commission to recommend the redrawing of boundaries of states and other territories in the following year.

After undivided Andhra Pradesh was formed in 1953, the Indian National Congress won every election held in the state for the next three decades up to 1983. Indira Gandhi and the Congress were so firmly rooted in undivided Andhra Pradesh that even in 1977, when she lost the post-Emergency parliamentary elections, the state had given her and the Congress all of its 41 out of 42 Lok Sabha seats. The following year, in the 1978 state polls, the Indira faction of the

Congress had returned to power, winning 175 of the 294 seats in the Assembly.

It was against this backdrop that NTR spearheaded his political campaign in undivided Andhra Pradesh in 1982–83, a campaign that probably had no precedent in India's political history.[399] According to NTR's biographer and journalist S. Venkat Narayan:

> Between June 14 [1982], when Rama Rao set out on the first phase of campaign tours, and January 3 [1983], when he arrived in Tirupati to make the last speech of the campaign, he had travelled for a total of 70 days, reaching every nook and corner of the state and covering a total distance of 35,000 km. [...] He was seen and heard by an estimated 3 crore people – a record for the history books. No man had travelled in the state so extensively in living memory; no man had spoken so eloquently, articulating the frustrations and aspirations of his people; no man was received with so much warmth, love and affection; and no man had so electrified so many people with his oratory and swayed the emotions of his people so much that they could do anything for him. Not since Mahatma Gandhi, anyway.[400]

NTR came from an extremely modest background. As a young man in Vijayawada struggling to make ends meet, he would cycle long distances every day to supply milk to households, hotels and other business establishments. He would even try his hand at running a mess in Mumbai that served mouth-watering Andhra recipes – *chepala pulusu, gongura* chicken, *arupu podi, pulihora, majjika annam, majjiga chaaru, chamagadda vepudu,* cabbage *senagapappu vepudu, allam pachad* and so on – but without success.

Back in Vijayawada, he dabbled in tobacco, beedi and cigarette trade, and worked as a court attendant for a monthly salary of ₹64. He tried running a printing press too. A graduation in Arts finally got him a job as a sub-registrar in the revenue department, but by then he had made up his mind to try his luck in the film industry.

His first role was as a police officer in *Mana Desam* (1949), for which he was paid ₹500. Wide-shouldered, flamboyant and with a proud, hawkish face, NTR made as good a villain as he did a hero in the 292 movies he acted in between 1949 and 1982.

A major factor in the shaping of brand NTR was the roles that he essayed. He played nearly every important god, including Krishna (17 times) and Ram, and even Karna as the hero in *Daana Veera Soora Karna* (1977) at a time when such interpretations were not the norm. In fact, he had played Duryodhana and Krishna too in that film. One of his films, *Shri Venkateshwara Mahatyam* (1960), evoked such reverence that his followers erected makeshift shrines inside movie halls so they could offer prayers before and after the screening.

According to biographers Chandrahas and K. Lakshminarayana, the fine line between reality and myth surrounding his life had blurred. For instance, while *Mayabazar* (1957) was being shot, the entire studio came to a standstill when NTR appeared on set as Lord Krishna. That was the first time he was playing Krishna. Crew members rushed to touch his feet and some even offered *aarti*. He blessed them all.[401]

When NTR entered politics, the owner of a certain transportion business called Chowdary (who went only by this name) was so devoted to him that he put 40 trucks at his disposal to ferry fans for the leader's first public rally. Chowdary did not charge a single paisa. For some reason, he didn't even hang around to meet his idol.

NTR was nearing 60 when he acted in *Bobbili Puli* (The Lion of Bobbili, 1982), his last film, which would pave his entry into politics. In the film, he had played the role of an army officer who turns into an idealist fighting against a corrupt government. The film was still drawing crowds to theatres across Andhra when he launched his Telugu Desam Party. His son-in-law N. Chandrababu Naidu, a minister in the Anjaiah cabinet and a rising star in the state Congress, along with the (late) Y.S. Rajasekhara Reddy, helped him build the TDP organization.

NTR drew unprecedented crowds wherever he travelled in the run up to the 1983 Assembly elections. According to one estimate, even in those days when 24x7 television news was still far away and nobody had heard of social media platforms, NTR ensured that he was seen and heard by over 3,00,00,000 people. He refurbished a 1940 Chevrolet convertible, named it 'Chaitanya Ratham' (chariot of awakening) and mobilized the entire state of undivided Andhra Pradesh, bringing tinsel-world techniques to politics. His *Chaitanya Ratham* was fitted with rotating floodlights and loudspeakers. The actor would climb on to the top through a hatch to address the masses and use the van's interior to relax. On an average, he logged 120 km every day, always stopping and addressing gatherings of fifteen persons and more.

He often shaved, bathed and washed his own clothes by the roadside and ate with people sitting cross-legged on the floor, redefining the concept of election campaigning – as later perfected by Lal Krishna Advani and Narendra Modi. The political class of the NTR era, however, remained dismissive of his innovative techniques, dismissing them as celluloid fads. Today, all politicians swear by the effectiveness of road shows.

The Telugu press was in a tizzy. The state's largest-selling paper, *Enadu*, was already on board, with its owner Ramoji Rao becoming a staunch supporter. Each day, *Enadu* would carry a story on NTR stopping by a roadside shop to have a plate of piping hot *idli*, *pesarattu* and coffee.

Kambhampati Rammohan Rao, a diehard supporter and member of the Rajya Sabha, accompanied the TDP chief. He would later tell *The Hindu* newspaper how people would wait for a glimpse of their icon. Rammohan Rao would recall:

> *Maa Telugu thalliki malle poodanda* (A garland of jasmine
> flowers for Mother Telugu) was the signature tune of the

TDP. The song had an electrifying effect on the people. The response to the tour was overwhelming. He would be late by 24 hours, sometimes even 72 hours, but people would wait. They would camp on the roadside, bringing along cots, stoves and utensils just to make sure they did not miss him.[402]

Dasu Keshav Rao of *The Hindu* remembers NTR being so focused on the campaign that he did not return to Hyderabad until the elections had been announced. 'In the process, he missed the marriage[s] of two of his sons!' Rao wrote, recollecting that the leader's eldest son Nandamuri Harikrishna drove the *Chaitanya Ratham*.[403]

On the campaign trail, NTR spoke on the Congress government's corruption and decay and 'Delhi's tendency to change chief ministers like puppets'. By the time Indira Gandhi reached Andhra to campaign for her party, the battle had already been lost. Her party, Gandhi realized, had no chance. A majority of Congress MLAs had not nursed their Assembly constituencies well, hoping that Indira Gandhi's charisma would see them through. NTR, on the other hand, had done his arithmetic well.

Helped by the young and crafty Chandrababu Naidu, the TDP chose many educated persons from different walks of life, people who had a clean image and the desire to serve as a public representative. NTR also tried to sew up strategic pre-poll alliances with non-Congress players such as the Left parties, the Janata Party and the Sanjay Vichar Manch led by Maneka Gandhi. By the time the Assembly polls were held, only Maneka Gandhi's outfit was on board.

The Left had grossly underestimated NTR's appeal and had demanded 150 seats out of the 294 as part of any deal. But both NTR and Naidu were clear that the TDP would contest on a majority of seats so that, if the verdict was favourable, it could form a government on its own strength.

One of NTR's election campaign promises was that rice would become available at ₹2 per kilogram. He was greeted with derision by the Congress but voters took the offer. That was the time when the Union government had classified rice into three categories: common, fine and super fine. Their market prices were ₹2.50, 2.80 and 3 respectively. NTR promised to sell all three varieties at ₹2 per kilogram. The TDP swept to power, winning 202 seats, while the Congress finished with 60 from the House of 294.

The verdict left Indira and Rajiv Gandhi deeply upset; both saw the defeat as a personal setback. A plot was hatched and, under instructions from 'Delhi', Governor Ram Lal dismissed the NTR government in 1984.

NTR himself was away, in the US, for a health check-up when the Congress propped up a TDP rebel, N. Bhaskara Rao. NTR rushed back and took charge of the situation, but not before switching to wearing black as a first step. He then succeeded in getting the support of 17 opposition parties across the country and paraded a majority of party MLAs outside the Rashtrapati Bhavan. Bhaskara Rao lasted merely 31 days as chief minister; NTR was back in the saddle again.

The move to dismiss the NTR government was just one such instance of non-Congress state governments being toppled during Indira Gandhi's two innings as prime minister. The first United Front government – a political coalition in West Bengal which included Jyoti Basu's CPI(M), the CPI and the Bangla Congress – was dismissed under controversial circumstances eight months after it was formed in March 1967. The dismissal was executed by then Governor Dharma Vira, whose appointment as the Centre's representative in Bengal had been opposed by the Left. In November 1967, Vira rejected Basu's majority claim without a test, leading to the imposition of President's Rule. In Tamil Nadu, M. Karunanidhi's government was dismissed on 31 January 1976, after the DMK leader had openly challenged the Emergency.

Under Rajiv Gandhi's prime ministership too, the country saw several topple dramas – from Kashmir to Karnataka. Rajiv Gandhi's home minister, Buta Singh, who functioned as the virtual number two in the government, had the reputation of being Gandhi's 'axe man'. Between 1985 and 1989 he toppled so many state governments that Gandhi once told him in jest, 'Buta Singhji, *ab aap kirpan andar rakhiye.* (Buta Singhji, now please sheathe your *kirpan.*)'

Finally, it was the Supreme Court's 1994 landmark verdict in the S.R. Bommai case that would end the arbitrary use of Article 356 of the Indian Constitution. The bench of judges issued strict guidelines on the imposition of President's Rule after the matter reached the top court following the dismissal of the Bommai government in Karnataka.

Once back as chief minister, NTR introduced several 'first of its kind' welfare measures, earning a place in the hearts of Telugu-speaking people. Many believe that NTR's rise also consolidated the exclusive identity the Telugu community had earned, breaking away from the misnomer tag of 'Madrasis' in other parts of the country and outside. NTR zealously emphasized Telugu culture and language.

His lesser-known achievement, according to biographer Venkat Narayan, was that he convinced Indira Gandhi that economically and politically strong states could make a strong Centre.[404] Indira Gandhi's earlier stance was that strong states implied a weak Centre at the federal level.

NTR fought many titanic battles with the Centre. He was the first to take up the cause of amendments in the Hindu Succession Act to ensure equal property rights for women in 1986. He introduced educational reforms and laid the foundation for the Telugu Ganga project to provide drinking water to Madras city, apart from irrigating the dry land of the Rayalaseema region.

NTR's bond with Andhra Pradesh was so strong that in the 1984 parliamentary elections, held after Indira Gandhi's assassination, the Congress won a three-fourths majority in the Lok Sabha but failed to encash sympathy votes in Andhra. The TDP won 30 of the 42 Lok Sabha seats in the state, becoming the principal Opposition party in the House.

By 1987, Rajiv Gandhi's 'Mr Clean' image had taken a beating over Bofors, while Shah Bano and other controversies had given the otherwise dispirited opposition a chance to strike back, and many called for NTR's move to national politics. Soon, the chief minister of undivided Andhra Pradesh emerged as a key player in the games V.P. Singh, Devi Lal and Chandra Shekhar played among themselves. But there was also a flipside to that as the impression that he was neglecting his home state began to gain ground. A bout of indifferent health followed too. The Congress captured power in the 1989 elections in Andhra, pushing him to the opposition benches. But he bounced back in 1994 in spite of fellow 'Telugu bidda' Congress veteran P.V. Narasimha Rao being the prime minister.

It would be NTR's last hurrah. On 26 August 1995, nine months into his third term as chief minister of Andhra, his son-in-law and trusted lieutenant Naidu rebelled against him. Naidu defended his coup, saying he had been forced to act against his father-in-law because of NTR's second wife Lakshmi Parvathi's growing influence in party affairs and the state government. Lakshmi Parvathi was NTR's biographer, and he had married her in 1993, much against his family's wishes.

On that August day, Hyderabad saw the 72-year-old actor running amok on the city's streets with a metaphoric dagger in his back to demonstrate that he had been betrayed and backstabbed. Suddenly, NTR was a nobody; his fall as dramatic as his spectacular rise. Virtually all members of his family and most of the TDP's 200 legislators deserted the chief minister. Life had, ironically, panned out exactly as NTR would often say, 'What is destined to happen will happen. Victory and defeat are like light and darkness.'[405]

In *The Other Side of Truth*, a book published in 2009, NTR's other son-in-law Daggubati Venkateshwara Rao says that NTR was so enraged by Naidu's revolt that he had asked his actor-son Nandamuri Balakrishna to 'go and murder Chandrababu' for betraying him.[406] NTR even wanted Balakrishna to show him the sword stained with Naidu's blood.

Rao, who subsequently fell out with Naidu, claims that from the beginning, Naidu had wanted to become the chief minister and TDP president by ousting NTR. To substantiate his claim, Rao has quoted K. Rosaiah, a senior Congress leader who later served as the governor of Tamil Nadu, as saying that Naidu nursed a grudge against his father-in-law from the time NTR had launched the Telugu Desam Party in 1982. Rosaiah claims that Naidu had approached Indira Gandhi and told her that he wanted to contest against NTR 'But she said she was not in favour of any such thing and asked the party not to encourage him to do so,' Rao has quoted Rosaiah as saying in the book.[407] Rao has also given a detailed account of what happened on 26 August 1995:

> On that day when I landed at the Begumpet airport, about 40 TDP MLAs surrounded me asking me to come to Viceroy Hotel. But I went home only to find Chandrababu Naidu, Harikrishna and Balakrishna sitting there and waiting for me. [...] Chandrababu took me aside and told me that he will take over as the chief minister and party president. He told me that I will be made the deputy chief minister and Harikrishna will be appointed as general secretary of the party.[408]

When Rao came out of the room, Harikrishna and others asked him what he and Naidu had discussed. 'I told them everything. Harikrishna was unhappy and demanded that he should be made a minister. I told him that he can become the deputy chief minister and I was not interested in joining the cabinet.'[409]

Rao says two of NTR's sons sided with Naidu and two sons and a daughter (Rao's wife Purandeswari) were with NTR. He also admits that despite his wife's pleas not to join Naidu, he had gone to the Viceroy Hotel (the centre of the revolt). 'I committed an unforgivable sin,' Rao says in the book.[410] Rao had returned to the NTR camp a fortnight later and stayed with his father-in-law till the actor's death.

The disillusioned leader died in January 1996, allegedly for want of good medical care.

Naidu's own version of August 1995 came to light 16 years later in 2011 when he told scribes in Hyderabad how he had revolted against NTR to save the party and the state. A *'dushta shakti'* (evil force) he said, referring to Lakshmi Parvathi, had tried to destroy the party, and he had to protect it from this 'evil force'. In his words:

> I never thought even in my dreams that I will revolt against NTR. For me, NTR was not just a father-in-law, but a god whom I worshipped. But he was facing problems, having come under the influence of the 'evil force', and hence we were left with no other option to save the TDP. [...] We tried all means to check her (Lakshmi Parvathi's) influence and save the party but failed. Then, left with no option, we had to effect a leadership change and form the government (in 1995) in a democratic manner with the support of more than 200 MLAs.[411]

As an actor-politician, NTR joined the league of MGR, Karunanidhi and Jayalalithaa – several notches above the Bollywood stars who joined politics. 'Bollywood people are not interested in politics. No one became [a] CM overnight. They [NTR, MGR and Jayalalithaa] all had to work hard for it,' Kannada actor and three-time MP Ambareesh Amarnath told journalist Priya Sahgal of *India Today* who narrated the conversation to the author.

For biographers Chandrahas and K. Lakshminarayana, who belonged to the civil services and had the benefit of working under NTR, a large part of his political life, much like his existence and his public persona, had to do with the concept of identity. NTR, they say, tried to develop his own distinctive style, both in front as well as behind the camera, as he tirelessly advocated Andhra's distinct cultural identity.

NTR, according to the two biographers, also loved to refer to himself in the royal plural; hated newspapers to the extent of making it a virtue not to read them, and rarely lost his shit in public. Incidentally, his victory was the first election that future psephologist and TV news czar Prannoy Roy got wrong.

When NTR died, Narasimha Rao, who was the prime minister then, described him as 'a man of many parts – a learned and deeply religious person, a very fine and powerful actor who swayed millions of people, a forceful orator and above all, a man of the masses.'[412]

S. JAIPAL REDDY
(1942–2019)

S. JAIPAL REDDY WAS AN IDEOLOGUE. AN IDEOLOGUE WITH A PRAGMATIC approach. Contradictory? Not really. After all, Rene Descartes did say: 'It is not enough to have a good mind. The main thing is to use it well.'[413] Jaipal Reddy, who often cited the seventeeth-century philosopher's scientific method, practised that dictum throughout his political life.

This pragmatism was evident when in the early 1970s he introduced the controversial godman Chandraswami to P.V. Narasimha Rao, who was then the chief minister of Andhra Pradesh. In her immensely readable book, *Gurus: Stories of India's Leading Babas*, Bhavdeep Kang writes that Jaipal Reddy, who always insisted upon being a rationalist and an agnostic, realized in 1972 that Chandraswami knew everything he wanted to ask.[414]

It was pragmatism, perhaps, that later helped Jaipal Reddy hop from the Nehruvian Congress to the Janata Dal *parivar*, abuse and challenge the dynasty to his heart's content, and then become a camp follower of the one-family dominance.

Jaipal Reddy had fought against Indira Gandhi from Medak in 1980 when the former prime minister was on her comeback trail. Indira Gandhi had given up Raebareli and, till her assassination in 1984, represented Medak, now in Telangana.

Cut to 4 November 2001: a cricket match had been scheduled outside the Jawaharlal Nehru Stadium between 10 Janpath and the media when journalists spotted a familiar figure with walking aids. Jaipal Reddy, polio-stricken since childhood, had turned up to watch the match. By then a Congress spokesperson, he had heard that Rahul Gandhi, who had still not joined politics, and his brother-in-law, Robert Vadra, would be playing for the 10 Janpath team.

Jaipal Reddy, who had a way with words (some of his critics used to say he had read through the entire Oxford English Dictionary five times by the time he was in the seventh grade), would explain his political somersaults in his own inimitable style: 'I left the Congress in protest against the temporary aberration of the Emergency; I rejoined the Congress because I regard theocratic fascism (represented by the Sangh parivar) as a very much long-term aberration.'[415]

About breaking ties with the Janata parivar, he would say: 'I stood like the Casabianca (sic) boy on the burning deck until the deck itself collapsed.'[416]

Jaipal Reddy remained chief spokesperson for the Congress for many years but avoided commenting upon internal party dynamics even in off-the-record conversations. He loved describing himself as the 'external affairs' person of the Congress.

A decent man by nature, he never mentioned Rajiv Gandhi's rather uncharitable comment about him at the height of the Bofors controversy. Rajiv Gandhi had dismissed Jaipal Reddy's consistent and stringent attacks, saying, '[H]e (Jaipal Reddy) doesn't have a leg to stand on.'[417]

Jaipal had a love–hate relationship with N.T. Rama Rao. He had once described the actor-politician as a 'fake sannyasi with a fetish for drama'.[418] NTR had reportedly offered him a place in the Andhra cabinet in 1984 but Jaipal Reddy, then a Janata Party MLA, had politely declined, saying: 'I can be your guide, adviser or well-wisher, but not a member of your cabinet.'[419]

Jaipal Reddy earned a reputation as an efficient minister even though the major part of his career was spent on the Opposition benches. When the United Front government appointed him information and broadcasting minister, Jaipal Reddy shaped and oversaw the road map for the Information Age that was knocking at the door.

As Union minister for culture under Manmohan Singh, he was often invited by Sonia Gandhi to narrate the history and significance of various monuments and heritage sites. It is believed that Jaipal Reddy's ability to deftly mix history, religion and philosophy invariably prompted Sonia Gandhi to extend the appointment for long durations.

Jaipal Reddy's book, *Ten Ideologies: The Great Asymmetry between Agrarianism and Industrialism*, was released by Manmohan Singh in 2018 in the presence of academic Pratap Bhanu Mehta and a host of political leaders from across parties, such as Sharad Yadav, H.D. Deve Gowda, Sitaram Yechury, Prakash Karat, P. Chidambaram and Jairam Ramesh. Mehta had then wondered whether the social bonhomie at the book release would translate into 'political unity' in the 2019 Lok Sabha elections.

After 23 May 2019, Jaipal Reddy was a disillusioned man. He could not fathom how a large section of voters could reject Nehruvian secularism. Jaipal died soon after on 28 July 2019. He was 77.

MUFTI MOHAMMAD SAYEED

(1936–2016)

MUFTI MOHAMMAD SAYEED WAS AN ARDENT BRIDGE PLAYER AND KNEW the art of reading his partners well. The only time Sayeed was beaten in the game was in 2005 when his three-year chief ministerial term as part of the coalition arrangement with the Congress was ending in J&K. Sayeed counted on his goodwill with the then prime minister Dr Manmohan Singh and AICC chief Sonia Gandhi to get another term in office. His close associate M.L. Fotedar had already told him that a majority of CWC members were in favour of his continuation. But when the CWC met in October 2005 to discuss the power rotation arrangement, aspirant Ghulam Nabi Azad raised the issue of a possible rebellion from party MLAs from the Jammu region, forcing Sonia Gandhi and Manmohan Singh to decide in favour of Azad. Fotedar later termed the development as a case of 'loss of golden opportunity'.[420]

As chief minister between 2002 and 2005, Mufti Sayeed had undertaken major initiatives to bring peace and tranquillity in the valley. His political mobilization had brought the common Kashmiri into the mainstream and had created a conducive environment for Indo-Pak dialogues. However, by the time Azad-led Congress–PDP completed term, J&K was in flames over Shri Amarnath Shrine Board controversy and economic blockade between the Jammu region and the Valley.

The Congress–PDP alliance of 2002 was stitched together thanks to three former prime ministers who had worked overtime to bring the two sides together. P.V. Narasimha Rao, V.P. Singh, I.K. Gujral and Manmohan Singh (who later became prime minster) had prevailed upon the Congress to give the first chance to Sayeed.

During most part of his political life, Sayeed had remained

a Congressman. He had won the 1989 Lok Sabha polls from Muzzafarnagar, Uttar Pradesh, and even contested from Katihar, Bihar, in 1996.

Sayeed held many posts during his lifetime, including that of the home minister of the country, but he coveted the chief minister's post the most. Throughout 1980s and 1990s, arch-rival Farooq Abdullah used to joke that Sayeed had a suit tailored for his swearing-in at a shop on Residency Road in Jammu, 'and it's been gathering dust there for decades.'[421]

Sayeed's relations with the Nehru–Gandhi family were far from stable. In 1985, when Rajiv Gandhi had become prime minister, he had made Sayeed the Union minister for tourism. But when Gandhi signed a pact with Farooq Abdullah, Sayeed resigned from the Union cabinet and joined V.P. Singh's Jan Morcha. In his resignation letter, he cited the 1987 Meerut riots as a cause of his disappointment with Gandhi and the Congress.

Sayeed retuned to state politics when he rejoined the Congress in 1996 but he did not like the Congress culture under Sitaram Kesri. When Sonia Gandhi took over as Congress chief in 1998, Mufti floated his regional People's Democratic Party (PDP) the following year. He told Sonia Gandhi that there was a vacant political space in Kashmir, which had been occupied by the religious Right-wing Muslim United Front in 1987.

By the time Narendra Modi-led BJP won the 2014 Lok Sabha polls and J&K polls were held, the bridge player was ready to lean towards a partnership with the BJP. In death, he ensured smooth succession for his daughter Mehbooba.

Sayeed was a generous host. In New Delhi, his annual 'wazwaan' feast was most sought after. Exquisite mutton preparations such as *gustaba, rista, tabakmas* and *yakhini pulao* would often throw up such heavenly aromas in the air that crows, vultures and kites would hover around for hours.

NARAIN DUTT TIWARI
(1925–2018)

NARAIN DUTT TIWARI WAS REGARDED AS A POLITICIAN AMONG POLITICIANS – one of the best not to have become prime minister. As luck would have it, Tiwari lost the 1991 Lok Sabha elections to a little-known former newspaper vendor, Balraj Passi, by a margin of 5,000 votes from Nainital, his home district. The Congress's prime ministerial candidate Rajiv Gandhi had been assassinated in the midst of the elections, but Passi's giant-killing act ended Tiwari's aspirations for the country's top executive job. P.V. Narasimha Rao succeeded Rajiv Gandhi as the AICC chief and became prime minister.

Tiwari's greatest drawback was, perhaps, his lack of a killer instinct. He could not muster the courage to either revolt against Rajiv Gandhi during 1989–91, when Indira Gandhi's son faced credibility problems within the Congress, or take on Rao during 1993–95, the period after the Babri Masjid demolition. He did, however, join hands with Arjun Singh to form the breakaway All India Congress (Tiwari) in 1996 but lost in the general election that year from Jhansi.

What might put Tiwari's political life in perspective was the other names that were mentioned in the same breath as his: P.V. Narasimha Rao, R. Venkataraman and Pranab Mukherjee. The four, including Tiwari, were addressed as PV, RV, ND and Pranab. Each rose to the pinnacle of their political career except for Tiwari. Rao became Congress president and prime minister, Venkataraman and Mukherjee made it to the Rashtrapati Bhavan, but Tiwari failed to make the cut despite being a chief minister four times and a central minister for decades.

What must have surely rankled was the sobriquet he earned for frequent visits from Lucknow to Delhi as chief minister of Uttar Pradesh: 'New Delhi Tiwari'. Only, the throne of New Delhi would forever remain out of his grasp.

Politics can be cruel, even more so in memories that persist. Tiwari was considered Sanjay Gandhi's lackey by a section of media, purported to have picked up and carried the Kolhapuri shoes of Indira Gandhi's arrogant son.[422]

There was, however, more to Tiwari's disrepute than just politics. Known as a 'ladies' man' for his colourful lifestyle after the death of his first wife Sushila in 1991, he often ended up courting controversies. His last appointment in public life as governor of Andhra Pradesh saw the former freedom fighter make an inglorious exit from the Hyderabad Raj Bhavan after private news channels showed a person who appeared to be him in sexual encounter with three women. Tiwari denied that it was him in the video but ultimately had to resign. Despite his purported dalliances, Tiwari's gentlemanly attributes and grace stood out. It was said that there was no big town in the country where Tiwari did not have a female companion but he never flaunted his prowess or named them.[423]

His decision to marry Ujjwala Sharma, a divorcee, in 2014 at the age of 89 – following a six-year-long paternity suit that he lost – was not mocked but appreciated even in the otherwise conservative circles of Uttar Pradesh and Uttarakhand, the two states he had ruled in the course of his political career.

Rohit Shekhar, a little-known lawyer in his late twenties, had in 2008 filed the paternity suit against Tiwari. Rohit Shekhar claimed that he came to know about his 'natural' father when he was twelve or thirteen and, since turning eighteen, had repeatedly sought but been denied his 'status'. The politician acknowledged his association with Shekhar's mother Ujjwala, but challenged the petitioner on several grounds, including the jurisdiction of the court and 'limitation'. Shekhar, he said, should have filed the suit within three years of turning eighteen.

Tiwari had met Shekhar's grandfather, Sher Singh, a minister of state in the Indira Gandhi government, when he was the president of the Indian Youth Congress in 1967. The following year, Ujjwala had been appointed joint secretary of the women's wing of the Youth Congress, then headed by Nandini Sathpathy.

According to Tiwari, Shekhar was born while Ujjwala was married to another man, B.P. Sharma. The legal presumption, he contended, is that a child born to a married woman is the legitimate child of the husband. Tiwari also insisted there was no special statute or provision in the Criminal Procedure Code or the Evidence Act to empower courts to order DNA tests.

When the matter came up in court, Sharma submitted that between 1970 and 1979, he and Ujjwala did not have 'sexual access' to each other. The judges, while sanctioning the DNA test, underscored the need for an offspring's quest for biological roots. 'The protective cocoon of legitimacy, in such case, should not entomb the child's aspiration to learn the truth of his paternity,' the court had observed while citing England's Family Reforms Act, 1969 and 1987.[424] The court also noted that there was 'legislative inactivity' in India's domestic laws and that both the UN Declaration of Human Rights and the Convention of the Rights of the Child were applicable in the case as India had ratified these international instruments. Rohit Shekhar won the suit in 2014 after the DNA test – probably the first such case involving a prominent political figure in the country.

Within two months the young man, who stood by Tiwari till the leader's last breath, had influenced him to marry his biological mother Ujjwala, a noted Sanskrit scholar and classical singer. Tiwari had described Ujjwala as an 'unchaste woman' when the case was still going on, forcing Rohit Shekhar to approach the court again to stop slurs against illegitimate children and ban the use of words and phrases such as 'bastard', 'illegitimate' and 'unchaste woman' in legal proceedings.[425]

Through his council, Rohit Shekhar, himself a lawyer, had petitioned, 'I want to remove disparaging references to children born outside of wedlock and any language that describes women who have children outside marriage as unchaste or promiscuous. How can these words be permitted in a court of law?' According to him, 'In my opinion, there are no illegitimate children, only illegitimate fathers.' He was deeply disturbed that his mother was described in a disparanging manner and submitted to the court, 'The paternity fight was a fight for my mother's dignity. *Maa ka sammaan chahiye tha mujhe* (I wanted my mother's dignity to be protected).'[426]

In the subsequent turn of events when Tiwari lost the paternity suit and had a major rethink, he tied the knot with his old flame, Ujjwala, at 'Arohi', 1 Mall Avenue, Lucknow, on 15 May 2014.[427]

Invitees to the wedding saw Tiwari dressed as a groom and Ujjwala, then 66, as the bride. To chants of Vedic hymns, Tiwari and Ujjwala took the seven *pheras*, exchanged garlands and vowed to spend the rest of their lives in love, peace and harmony.

Rohit Shekhar and Ujjwala, both accomplished singers, are said to have comforted an ailing Tiwari in his years of illness. Tiwari would ask them to sing the raga Durga that helped him sleep like a child. Tiwari died in October 2018 at the age of 93. A few months later, on 16 April 2019, Shekhar too passed away under unfortunate circumstances. He was barely forty and was trying to project himself as Tiwari's legal and political heir.

Towards the end of his life, Tiwari had joined the BJP and Shekhar had been lobbying hard for a party ticket from the Kumaon region. But he was told to wait till the 2022 Assembly elections. The move to switch loyalties to the BJP was not easy, either for Shekhar or his father. But Tiwari's family had reportedly been cut up with the Gandhis for rejecting an invitation to grace the veteran's 91st birthday in 2016. The celebration had been planned in Haldwani, Uttarakhand, but Rohit Shekhar, Ujjwala and Tiwari had sent word through informal channels that they were prepared to be in Delhi just in case Rahul Gandhi was willing to make an appearance. Nothing materialized. Shekhar was seen visiting an ailing Jayalalithaa in Chennai around that time.

MADHAVRAO SCINDIA
(1945–2001)

THE DEATH OF THE 'PEOPLE'S MAHARAJA' ON 30 SEPTEMBER 2001 LEFT the Congress poorer on many counts. Madhavrao Scindia was not only young, charismatic and efficient, he was also a hero of sorts and the party's link to the great Indian middle class, despite belonging to a royal family himself. He was able to do so by introducing fast and comfortable trains, such as the Shatabdi Express between Delhi and many state capitals, and by installing a computerized reservation system that reduced the serpentine queues at ticket counters.

Born on 10 March 1945 in Mumbai, Scindia lost his father at an early age. He did his schooling in Gwalior and got his Master of Arts degree from Oxford University before taking the plunge into electoral politics in 1971, winning the Guna Lok Sabha seat.

When Scindia was first elected to Parliament in 1971 as an Independent candidate and joined the Congress during the Emergency, his decision had led to a confrontation with his mother Vijayaraje Scindia, who being part of the Sangh *parivar* was bitterly opposed to Indira Gandhi. Scindia, however, seldom reacted to his mother's occasional outbursts against him. 'Yes, it used to pain a lot,' Scindia had said.[428] However, the mother-son relationship improved a little before the Rajmata's death. When Vijayaraje slipped into a coma at Delhi's Apollo Hospital, Scindia would spend hours sitting next to his mother. Scindia, though, remained largely loyal to the Congress.

Within the Congress, there was no dearth of leaders who still feel that Madhavrao, like Sardar Vallabhbhai Patel and Pranab Mukherjee, was probably one of the best prime ministers India never had. His rise was cruelly cut short by fate – at the same time as when the Congress was on the trail of a comeback. When he died on 30 September 2001, Madhavrao was barely fifty-six and less than three years later, in 2004, a Congress-led coalition came to power.

'...Madhavrao Scindia would have been Prime Minister if he had lived,' K. Natwar Singh, eighty-nine, diplomat turned politician, had insisted on 10 March 2020, when Jyotiraditya Scindia had switched loyalty from the Congress to the BJP.[429]

Within the party, Scindia evoked mixed responses. Some were in awe of his royal lineage and dashing personality, while others felt insecure and saw him as a threat. To a large number of Congress leaders, the maharaja was warm and friendly, someone who always smiled and had no airs. 'It was impossible for anyone not to be charmed by him. There was something about him that drew people closer to him,' recalled Salman Khurshid, former Uttar Pradesh Congress chief.[430]

As railway minister, Scindia became a household name for introducing the computerized reservation system and the Shatabdi trains. His reputation as an efficient administrator grew further till he resigned as civil aviation minister, taking moral responsibility for an air crash.

Scindia favoured probity in public life. He was agitated when his name figured in the Jain hawala case, because of which he resigned from the Congress in 1996. Subsequently, in the same year, Scindia formed the Madhya Pradesh Vikas Congress in protest against his name figuring the hawala case. 'It was a battle to restore my honour,' Scindia had said after merging his outfit with the parent organization in 1997.[431] However, he refrained from commenting on P.V. Narasimha Rao, who was seen as his bête noire.

He was also a leader who could speak extempore on issues ranging from caste politics and the nuclear missile defence system to the finer points of *Lagaan*, a film he adored. Scindia loved to talk about the bowling action of Kachra, a character in the film, and how the protagonist, portrayed by producer and lead actor Aamir Khan, and his team had humbled the British on screen.

Scindia would also often narrate anecdotes. Once, late into the night, he said, he had been stopped by a policeman in London who asked for his identity. When Scindia said he was the maharaja of Gwalior, the policeman retorted, 'Well, if you are maharaja of Gwalior, I am pasha of Iran.'[432]

Scindia may now be best known for his involvement in politics, but he wore several hats – as a cricketer, golfer, connoisseur of art, culture and films, and a celebrity among Delhi's glitterati. In fact, it is a wonder that he still found the time to pursue politics for at least 12 hours a day.

It was Scindia's passion for politics that got him to board the ill-fated aircraft that crashed near Mainpuri that September day in 2001. Scindia was 56 and at the prime of his career. As the Congress's deputy leader in the Lok Sabha, it was not Scindia's duty to shore up the party's prospects in Uttar Pradesh where his camp follower, Kanpur MP and state party chief Sriprakash Jaiswal was trying to revive the Congress in the heartland. But, as a 'loyal Congress worker', the maharaja of Gwalior had taken it upon himself to chip in. Perhaps he felt duty-bound to tour the state. 'I do not wish to speculate on Congress prospects in UP but, as a loyal soldier, I want to contribute as much as I can,' he would say, reminding his friends and followers for the last time of what a loyal and noble soul he was.[433]

C.K. JAFFER SHARIEF
(1933–2018)

SHERBET, *CHAI* AND SAMOSAS FOR THE 'SYNDICATE'; VITAL INSIDE
information for Indira Gandhi. That, in a nutshell, sums up C.K. Jaffer
Sharief's unique role in the events leading to the Congress's 1969 split.
An apparently disinterested presence, he was also a secret participant
in the intrigue. Sharief would eventually rise high in a long political
career, leaving behind his modest background. He would go on to
win seven Lok Sabha elections and become the Union minister for
railways – all the while employing to good use his skills as a gatherer
and purveyor of information.

The veteran from Karnataka died of a heart attack at a private
hospital in Bengaluru on 25 November 2018. He was 85.

Sharief's association with politics started with him running errands
for the towering Lingayat leader S. Nijalingappa, who was the chief
minister of Karnataka and president of the AICC then. This is where
Sharief first put his information-gathering skills to good use.

A group of Congress chief ministers and CWC members – known
as the 'Syndicate' – were conspiring to dislodge Indira Gandhi as
prime minister. Sharief's primary loyalties lay with Gandhi and
not with his boss, Nijalingappa. Thus Gandhi had prior and inside
knowledge of every move the Syndicate was making.

Sharief would prolong his stay each time he entered the
assembly of elders or Syndicate members carrying sherbet, *chai* or
samosas. As part-time driver of the AICC chief, Sharief was also
privy to conversations that Nijalingappa had in the rear seat of his
Ambassador.

When Nijalingappa eventually expelled Indira Gandhi from the
Congress in 1969, leading to the split in the Grand Old Party, an
emotional Gandhi insisted that membership in the Congress was her

'birth right'. 'Nobody can throw me out of the Congress. It is not a legal question, nor one of passing a resolution to pronounce an expulsion order. It is a question of the very fibre of one's heart and being,' she had said.[434] The forewarned leader eventually succeeded in retaining the support of 310 of the Congress's 429 members in Parliament.

Sharief was ready with his inputs again in 1983 when Indira Gandhi was locked in a battle with actor-politician N.T. Rama Rao (NTR) in the then undivided Andhra Pradesh. The Assembly elections that year were a watershed in Indian politics as a new political outfit – the Telugu Desam Party led by NTR – defeated the Congress.

Before the polls, Buta Singh, who had been home minister in both Rajiv and Indira Gandhi's governments, was confident of victory and had been giving the prime minister daily 'feedback' on the party's bright prospects. Sharief was then the minister of state for railways. Apparently acting on his own, he instructed the Railway Protection Force (RPF) to give inputs about the polls. The RPF had its own network of spies and agents, and Sharief would pass on confidential information thus collected to Indira Gandhi. He is said to have also shared the RPF inputs with two senior journalists, Shubhabrata Bhattacharya and Louis Fernandez, who were writing for the *Sunday* magazine and the *Telegraph* newspaper respectively.

On the day of the result, Indira Gandhi was hardly surprised when NTR's party stunned the nation. The Telugu Desam won 201 of the 290 Assembly seats and NTR became the first non-Congress chief minister of the state.

As minister of state for railways, Sharief had a running feud with A.B.A. Ghani Khan Choudhury who had scant regard for his junior's humble background.

When Sharief became the cabinet minister for railways under P.V. Narasimha Rao, he started using his ministerial saloon in goods trains instead of passenger trains, perhaps preferring the privacy and the slow speed. Sharief later fell out with Narasimha Rao and it was said that the prime minister would wonder why Sharief was turning into a 'Mir Jafar'.

Like he did during Indira Gandhi's time, Sharief would again carry many tales to an otherwise apolitical Sonia Gandhi. Narasimha Rao would eventually reduce Sharief to a minister without portfolio but by then Sharief's loyalties lay firmly with Sonia Gandhi.

CAPTAIN SATISH SHARMA
(1947–2021)

THE YEAR WAS 1963. A BOY, 16 YEARS OLD, WAS CYCLING TO THE DELHI Flying Club in Safdarjung when a black Hindustan 14 car pulled up beside him. 'Hop in,' the driver said.

Young Satish Sharma looked incredulous. The car's occupant was Rajiv Gandhi, grandson of the then prime minister Jawaharlal Nehru. Rajiv Gandhi got down, opened the boot, shoved Sharma's cycle in, bundled the cyclist into the passengers' seat and drove off to the flying club.

That chance meeting, according to *India Today*'s Inderjit Badhwar and Prabhu Chawla, would be the beginning of a long friendship between the two future Indian Airlines commercial pilots, a bond that pre-dated their entry into politics and would remain till death intervened.[435]

Rajiv Gandhi had a wide circles of friends in the Indian Airlines but two men – 'Cappy' Capt. Sharma and H.R. Singh, an Indian Airlines pilot ring leader of sorts – stood out. Singh would later fall out with

Rajiv Gandhi when Maneka Gandhi had to leave Indira Gandhi's residence months after Sanjay Gandhi's death in an air crash. But Sharma stayed on, almost like a shadow to Rajiv Gandhi when he entered politics in 1981 after the death of his younger brother.

Sharma, who trained as a pilot in Kansas City, Missouri, would also chuck a lucrative job to join politics in 1983, eventually becoming an MP and later a minister. All the while he wore his loyalty to the family of his assassinated friend on his sleeve. He passed away on 17 February 2021, his death snapped a precious link, especially for Sonia Gandhi, with the life and times of her late husband Rajiv and mother-in-law Indira Gandhi.

Cockpit Bond

Sharma, who was born in Secunderabad, in the present-day state of Telangana, and Rajiv Gandhi had often flown Dakotas together – a proximity that, he would later say, had firmed up their bond and made it all-weather and turbulence-proof. 'When you've seen someone in the cockpit for those many years, you really get to know the guy,' Sharma had told an interviewer. 'I've seen him [Rajiv Gandhi] tackle the worst of weather, going through thunderstorms and lightning bolts, and I always marvelled at his coolness.'[436]

Sharma came from a wealthy family. He was raised by his maternal grandfather, Amarchand Sharma, who had left Punjab for Secunderabad to become one of the biggest contractors in the then undivided Andhra Pradesh. Amarchand Sharma had built India's first siphon spillway dam, Sarla Sagar, in the state he migrated to.

According to M.L. Fotedar, staunch Indira Gandhi loyalist who died a few years ago, Priyanka Gandhi Vadra might have had a different name, 'Sharika', had Sharma not been close to Rajiv Gandhi. Apparently, Indira Gandhi had wanted to name her granddaughter after the Nehru family deity Sharika Bhagwati (Ashtadash), the goddess with 18 arms, a manifestation of Shakti. Around the same time, Sharma's Dutch wife Sterre, who was pregnant too, gave birth to a daughter. The couple approached Indira Gandhi to name their newborn baby. Fotedar has quoted her as saying, 'Sharika was on my mind, and I simply could not resist mentioning it so their child was given the name!'[437]

Sterra, daughter of John Jenzar who was *Time* magazine's former bureau chief in Brussels and subsequently the International Monetary Fund's permanent representative to the United Nations, had previously worked as a fashion designer for a Dutch company. In the 1980s, she had opened a children's boutique in New Delhi's Archana Arcade. Within a year she had opened another store – 'Balloons' – in the national capital's plush South Extension.

Sharma became a key member of Rajiv Gandhi's durbar along with Vijay Dhar (son of Kashmiri politician and diplomat D.P. Dhar), hotelier Lalit Suri, Amitabh Bachchan (Rajiv Gandhi's childhood buddy) and Arun Singh (Rajiv Gandhi's classmate at the Doon School). When Rajiv Gandhi became the prime minister, Sharma's primary job was to look after the leader's parliamentary constituency, Amethi, and act as an interface between the constituents and the MP. He would often accompany Sonia Gandhi to Amethi to distribute medical supplies, undertake other welfare activities and listen to the people's grievances. Sonia Gandhi would avoid making political speeches, restricting herself to asking people to vote for Rajiv Gandhi. '*Patiji ko vote dijiye* (Vote for my husband),' was one of her favourite sentences and she would giggle after saying it – to the amusement of everyone present.[438] In 1986, Sharma was drafted into the Rajya Sabha.

Old-timers recall that Sharma was Rajiv Gandhi's key troubleshooter and how the prime minister would ask Vincent George, his personal assistant at the time, to put him through to Sharma. 'George, get me Satish,' used to be a constant command from Rajiv Gandhi. Whether it was dealing with angry MLAs in Amitabh Bachchan's constituency, Allahabad, or mediating between dissidents and the chief ministers of Bihar and Odisha (Orissa then), Congress leaders of that era remember Sharma for his 'hands-on' approach. Sharma also had the controversial job of distributing party funds and liaising with ministers for 'resource mobilization' during Assembly and parliamentary elections.

Sharma had access where even other close associates of Rajiv Gandhi were not allowed in thanks to the strict demarcation between 7 Race Course Road and the adjoining 5 Race Course Road that served as Rajiv Gandhi's office and residence respectively. Even IFS officer Mani Shankar Aiyar and senior IAS officer Wajahat Habibullah, who were in the Prime Minister's Office and had both studied with Rajiv Gandhi at Doon School, and other close associates like Sam Pitroda and P. Chidambaram, were not allowed inside Rajiv Gandhi's family quarters. But Sharma would shuttle between 7 and 5 Race Course Road. The unhindered access aroused the jealousy of many prominent leaders who claimed proximity to Rajiv Gandhi. Sanjay Singh, the former Raja of Amethi, was one such leader who disliked Sharma.

Sharma remained among a handful of persons, such as Suman Dubey, Amitabh Bachchan, Arun Singh, Mohan Thadani and Michael Albuquerque, who were considered Rajiv Gandhi's personal friends and would occasionally be seen having meals at the prime minister's residence along with their spouses. Like Madhavrao Scindia, he did not have to go through Fotedar, R.K. Dhawan or Vincent George to meet Gandhi.

On most days, though, Sharma would invariably walk across to Hotel Ashoka in Chanakyapuri and occupy the last table, away from public glare. He would quietly have soup and a sandwich, pay and return to work at 7 Race Course Road.

Under the Glare

Things were moving smoothly for Rajiv Gandhi when one day, 16 April 1987, a Swedish radio station made a startling broadcast, alleging that artillery manufacturer Bofors had paid kickbacks to secure an arms contract signed with the Indian government the previous year. Many around Rajiv Gandhi faced the glare and V.P. Singh, who was the prime minister's bête noire, constantly targeted his former boss as well as Sharma.

Singh, who became prime minister in 1989, alleged that a 10-acre plot Sharma had acquired on the Delhi–Haryana border, adjoining Rajiv Gandhi's family farm near Chhatarpur village, had been given to him at a 'throwaway' price. Janata Dal, the Left parties and the BJP also made a big issue of Sharma allegedly importing 3,000 kg of 'Italian marble tiles' for the swimming pool that was constructed at his farm.

Sharma denied all these allegations, insisting that his land transactions had been 'completely above board', and that the charges against him were part of a pattern to 'attack anyone close to Rajiv'.[439] As for the swimming pool tiles, Sharma claimed that they were gifted to him by his father-in-law in New York and that he had paid customs duty of ₹1.9 lakh for them to be transported. Further, he added, 'The tiles are ceramic, not marble. And I could have bought them in India for ₹60,000.'[440]

MP from Amethi

In September 1991, a few months after Rajiv Gandhi's assassination, the Election Commission announced by-elections for the Amethi Lok Sabha seat that the late leader had represented. The Congress's in-house shouting brigade, often called the Sonia brigade, swung into action. Ratnakar Pandey, S.S. Ahluwalia and Suresh Pachauri openly asked prime minister P.V. Narasimha Rao to call on Sonia Gandhi and persuade her to contest from Amethi amid a 'Sonia lao' (draft Sonia in) campaign. Sonia Gandhi was not interested. Instead, she and her children, Rahul and Priyanka, decided to go on a tour of Europe and America. When Rao heard of Sonia Gandhi's travel plans, he immediately called on her. The meeting lasted an hour. Sonia Gandhi made it clear that she had no intention of contesting from Amethi. When Rao reportedly told her that there was a view in the party that Sharma should be fielded, Sonia Gandhi told the prime minister that the ticket should be given on merit and in keeping with political considerations.

Sharma got the ticket, with the Rao camp giving the impression that Sonia Gandhi had recommended him. Sharma's own statements corroborated this view. Taking a leaf from the Ramayana, he said, like Bharat, he was keeping the seat secure for his Bhaujai (sister-in-law). He succeeded in convincing the Amethi electorate that his candidature had Sonia Gandhi's blessings and that she would soon be contesting the polls to look after Amethi. That would not happen till 1999. In fact, in the 1998 parliamentary elections, Sharma lost from Amethi to Sanjay Singh, who had joined the BJP.[441]

Sharma, however, got elected again to the Lok Sabha in 1999 from Raebareli, while Sonia Gandhi won from Amethi. The victory in Raebareli must have been all the more sweet as Sharma defeated BJP's Arun Nehru, Rajiv Gandhi's cousin and his arch-rival in the prime minister's inner circle from 1984 to 1987. Arun Nehru, who had fallen out with Rajiv Gandhi after the Bofors controversy, had joined V.P. Singh's Jan Morcha in 1987 before shifting to the BJP.

Sharma owed his success to Priyanka Gandhi, who had delivered a brutal putdown of her uncle while campaigning for Sharma. '*Mujhe aap se ek shikayat hai. Mere pita ke mantri mandal mein rehte hue jisne gaddari ki, bhai ki peeth mein chhura mara – jawab dijiye – aise aadmi ko aapne yahan ghusne kaise diya? Unki yahan aane ki himmat kaise hui?* (I have a complaint against you. A man who committed treachery while remaining in my father's ministry, who stabbed a brother in the back – answer me – how did you let such a man in here? How did he dare come here?)' Priyanka Gandhi had asked while addressing a gathering at Raebareli.[442]

'*Yahan aane se pehle maine apni maa se baat ki thi. Maa ne kaha kisi ki burai mat karna. Magar main jawan hoon, dil ki baat aap se na kahun to kisse kahun?* (I spoke to my mother before coming here. She told me not to speak ill of anyone. But I am young; to whom shall I speak my mind if not to you?)' Priyanka Gandhi had added.[443]

So telling was the impact of her speech that even a seasoned orator like Atal Bihari Vajpayee failed to undo the damage. Vajpayee, who was the prime minister then, had visited Raebareli a day after Priyanka's speech. In his trademark style, he took a dig at Priyanka Gandhi, saying he was 'scared' to visit Raebareli as it seemed to be someone else's *'ilaqa'* (territory). But it was too late: Arun Nehru's fate had already been sealed.

Sharma was Union minister for petroleum and natural gas from 1993 to 1996 during the Narasimha Rao era. By 1996, he had come under a cloud following a complaint by H.D. Shourie, director of the NGO Common Cause. Shourie had alleged that ministry officials showed favour to certain allottees while sanctioning petrol pump and gas agencies, thereby abusing their official position as public servants. A case of criminal conspiracy and criminal breach of trust by a public servant under the Indian Penal Code and the Prevention of Corruption Act was registered against Sharma and the allottees. According to the political grapevine of that era, a close aide of Sharma who nursed a grudge against the minister had leaked the details to Shourie.

Sharma did not become a Union minister during the ten years of UPA rule although he continued to get Rajya Sabha nominations from Uttarakhand and Uttar Pradesh. Perhaps probity-conscious Gandhis did not want to make him a minister after the petrol pump scam.

But the Gandhis' sense of belonging and gratitude was evident at Sharma's funeral in New Delhi. A barefoot Rahul Gandhi was a pallbearer as Satish Sharma's body was being taken for cremation. T.S. Singh Deo, a cabinet minister in the Chhattisgarh government, tweeted that Rahul had cancelled his political plans for the day to be present for the last rites of Satish Sharma. Deo remembered, 'It was Capt. Sharma who gave Rahul ji the first tour of every nook and corner of Amethi before his first election [in 2004].'

VIDYA CHARAN SHUKLA
(1929–2013)

WITH VIDYA CHARAN SHUKLA'S DEATH, THE COUNTRY LOST A POLITICIAN who was a master of power-politics and intrigue, and was responsible for the iron-fist handling of the media during the Emergency.

Shukla, aged 84, died in New Delhi on 11 June 2013 after battling for his life for days after the gruesome Naxal attack at Sukma in Chhattisgarh on 25 May 2013. Shukla was a veteran warhorse who served many regimes: first, under Indira–Sanjay Gandhi, then Rajiv Gandhi–V.P. Singh–Chandra Shekhar and finally, P.V. Narasimha Rao. After trying his luck unsuccessfully in state politics, Shukla returned to the Congress for one last time, only to get critically wounded while participating in the party's 'parivartan yatra', organized to drive the BJP out of power. He was shot thrice. For hours, the old man was left bleeding until help finally arrived. While he was still conscious, Shukla was witness to a remarkable act of loyalty. His bodyguard Praful Shukla died before his eyes trying to shield his master.

The son of Pandit Ravi Shankar Shukla, a towering freedom fighter and the first chief minister of central province, young Vidya Charan Shukla was a budding industrialist when he was struck by a strong desire to join politics. His elder brother Shyama Charan was equally keen, pleading with Jawaharlal Nehru and Pandit Ravi Shankar Shukla to join politics. But Shukla would not relent. When he died in 1956, Nehru drafted both his sons Shyama and Vidya Shankar Shukla in Congress. Nehru advised Vidya Shankar Shukla to contest for the Lok Sabha, while his brother confined himself to state politics – a division that the brothers observed till the year 2000, when the Chhattisgarh state was formed and Vidya Shankar Shukla failed to become its Congress chief minister. He had revolted and contested unsuccessfully against Ajit Jogi.

Vidya Shankar Shukla achieved both fame and notoriety as a close aide of Sanjay Gandhi during the Emergency. Along with Bansi Lal, Sidharatha Shankar Ray, Om Mehta, Yashpal Kapoor and R.K. Dhawan, he was considered as key character during the 21-month long period that saw the Indira Gandhi regime severely curtailing civil liberties and suspending elections. There were several instances where Shukla was accused of 'high-handedness'.[444]

Indira Gandhi's cousin, Nayantara Sahgal, was not arrested during the Emergency but on one occasion, her sister was told by the then Bengal chief minister Siddhartha Shankar Ray, 'We could pick her up under MISA any day.'[445] MISA, which stood for the Maintenance of Internal Security Act, was dreaded by everyone during the Emergency. Nayantara later wrote that Shukla, who was then heading the information and broadcasting ministry, had told her mother (Nehru's sister) Vijayalaxmi Pandit 'with a concealed sense of satisfaction' that Nayantara would not [be] able to write about politics. Nehru's sister quickly retorted that politics was not the lone subject that Nayantara was capable of writing about.[446]

Freedom fighter and noted industrialist Ramkrishna Bajaj had also found himself at the receiving end of his high-handedness. Bajaj, a Gandhian who loved to describe himself as 'Gandhi's coolie', was constantly harassed throughout the Emergency. Shukla, along with Om Mehta and Ambika Soni, had reportedly tried to take control of Vishwa Yuvak Kendra, an apolitical youth training and development centre in the heart of Delhi. Bajaj, never a man to take quick offence, sought help from Indira Gandhi, with whom he had shared a childhood friendship, and Nehru–Gandhi family retainer Mohammad Yunus. But the harassment did not end. Bajaj realized that the harassment was a deliberate policy to browbeat the Bajajs into submission. Shukla subsequently advised him to resign as a Kendra trustee and hand over the entire trust to Sanjay Gandhi. Bajaj then took the matter up with Indira Gandhi who spent six hours with him during her visit to Wardha, where she was to see an ailing Vinoba Bhave. On board the plane, Bajaj asked her in Hindi, *'Aapki mujh se koi narazgi hai kya?* (Are you angry with me for something)?' To which she replied, *'Haan, shikayeten to hoti hi rahti hain* (Yes, there are always some issues).'[447] The industrialist tried to draw her attention towards the Kendra issue but the prime minister chose not to respond.

Even as the Kendra issue failed to be resolved, income tax sleuths raided 114 Bajaj residential and business establishments across the country on 18 May 1976. As many as 1,100 officers raided factories and residences in Mumbai, Pune, Bengaluru, Chennai, Kanpur, Kolkata and elsewhere. The income tax department did not even spare Bajaj's mother, 84-year old Jankidevi, who was leading a secluded life having renounced all worldly possessions since the demise of her spouse, Jamnalal, in 1942. Bajaj later learnt that his close association with Viren Shah (who later became the governor of Bengal under the BJP–NDA rule) and his politician brother Kamalnayan's move to leave Indira Gandhi in 1966 were being held against him. As an olive branch, Bajaj was asked by Shukla (on behalf of Indira Gandhi) to persuade Vinoba Bhave to dissuade him from going for a fast against cow slaughter. Indira Gandhi was very keen to get the Gandhian endorsement of the Emergency – something that the apolitical Bhave kept avoiding giving. He was persuaded to describe the Emergency as a *'anushasan parva'* (disciplinary phase) but most of his supporters and followers joined Jayprakash Narain's movement against Indira Gandhi anyway.[448]

Shukla was also accused of clamping down on violence in Hindi films during the Emergency, on the ground that it could trigger off civil unrest. When Ramesh Sippy's *Sholay* was being released, writers Salim–Javed were tense if the film would pass the censors but actor Amitabh Bachchan's association with Gandhis came handy. Vidya was prompted to clear it with minor cuts.

Singer Kishore Kumar was banned from appearing on All India Radio and Doordarshan, and the likes of Pran and Dev Anand too suffered. They had reportedly offended the Shukla and the Sanjay Gandhi brigade by refusing to say a few words in appreciation about the Youth Congress and Sanjay Gandhi on government-run television and radio a day after Delhi witnessed a 'Geeton Bhari Sham'. The programme had ostensibly been held primarily to raise money for Sanjay Gandhi and Rukhsana Sultana's controversial family planning programme in 1976.

When Indira Gandhi lost power in 1977, Shukla deposed before the Shah Commission of Inquiry owning up his decisions. As a result, internal politics in the Congress forced him to resign.

Shukla returned to the national scene again when V.P. Singh revolted against Rajiv Gandhi over the Bofors issue in 1987. He then went on to become a leading light of Jan Morcha but when V.P. Singh became prime minister, his name was missing from the cabinet list. Shukla, however, served as a minister in the short-lived Chandra Shekhar regime.

After Rajiv Gandhi's death, Shukla was drafted back into Congress by P.V. Narasimha Rao. The prime minister used Shukla's services to checkmate his rival, Arjun Singh. It was at this stage that his aggressive and Machiavellian role reportedly created a rift between Rao and 10 Janpath, from where an apolitical but keen observer Sonia Gandhi kept tabs on politics. Shukla added fuel to the fire when he told Lok Sabha that controversial Bofors papers were on their way to India. A group of Congressmen claiming loyalty to Sonia Gandhi, gheraoed Rao, seeking Shukla's ouster. Rao did not sack Shukla but somehow nobody talked about the Bofors papers again.

Noted London-based lawyer Sarosh Zaiwalla claimed that during that period, Shukla had visited London and met him at his country house in Sussex to discuss and stress on the need for Sonia Gandhi to stay away from politics.[449] Zaiwalla had handled Amitabh Bachchan's Bofors libel suit and stopped a biopic on Sonia Gandhi at her behest.

AMAR SINGH
(1956–2020)

DURING HIS CHEQUERED POLITICAL AND SOCIAL LIFE, AMAR SINGH courted the high and mighty – Madhavrao Scindia, Mulayam Singh Yadav, Adi and Parmeshwar Godrej, Tina and Anil Ambani, Sanjay and Manyata Dutt, Sridevi and Boney Kapoor and most famously, the Bachchans. Yet virtually no one was with him in the end. Up above, if Amar Singh gets to hear the many who are waxing lyrical about him now, he would let out a rich, throaty chuckle.

Amar Singh's life had begun as the son of a small-time trader. His father Harish Chandra Singh had moved from Azamgarh to Aligarh, and subsequently to Kolkata. He was a modest trader of the once famous Aligarh locks in Bara Bazar, a hub of Marwaris in Kolkata. Amar Singh was taught at convent school where he became friends with Shyam Bhartiya, who later married the daughter of noted industrialist K.K. Birla, Shobhana.

Amar Singh had once told Aditi Phadnis (Political Editor at *Business Standard*) in an interview:

I was born and grew up in a three-room flat on 202 Chittaranjan Avenue. There were five of us and only one bathroom. I still remember the torture in the mornings when all of us used to queue outside the toilet. Since then I have an obsession with big bathrooms. Every room in my Greater Kailash House has a bathroom. I've seen those days; I left home because I didn't want to continue with my father's trading business. I had nothing. Proud fathers get suits stitched for their sons. I paid for my first suit myself, when I was 28.[450]

The journey from Kolkata to Delhi was not at Amar Singh's bidding. The young politician in him was keen to dabble in Kolkata municipal politics siding with Subrata Mukherjee. Since Mukherjee and Somen Mitra were arch-rivals, Mitra's animosity turned so intense that Singh had to flee Kolkata. He could return to the city only after giving an undertaking that he would not indulge in municipal politics. The initial setback in politics made Singh turn to Birla and the Shyam–Shobhana Bhartia household that gave him a big foothold in Delhi. The Bharatias introduced him to Madhavrao Scindia, who was a big leader of the Congress in that era. But when a Rajya Sabha seat failed to materialize, Amar Singh soon shifted to the Samajwadi Party (SP), where he befriended its chief Mulayam Singh Yadav.

Author, journalist and TV news anchor Priya Sahgal, who interviewed Amar Singh on several occasions, thinks when the socialist met the socialite [Amar Singh], they learnt that party was both a noun and a verb. Sahgal witnessed a gala affair at New Delhi's Ashoka Hotel (during the United Front government). A party was being thrown to celebrate the launch of Sahara India TV and also Kerry Packer's venture capitalist firm. 'From elephants to BMWs, all made their way up the driveway, as did Anil Ambani, Amitabh Bachchan and other Bollywood notables, the entire Parliament of Delhi including the then Congress president, Sitaram Kesri. It was also a statement that Amar Singh had arrived.'[451]

His close relationship with the Bachchans and their eventual falling out perhaps most drew the attention of the public. In February 2020, he sought forgiveness from Amitabh Bachchan and was said to have sent him an emotional video. There are some friends of Amar Singh who feel that the gesture was unilateral and perhaps unwarranted. According to them, the Bachchans had dropped him long ago. Amar Singh could not get over the fact that he was not invited for Big B's 70th birthday bash. 'Even his [Amitabh Bachchan's] spot boys were called, but not me,' he told one interviewer.[452]

Like many mortals, Amar Singh had a weakness for wealth, power and celebrity. A manipulator par excellence, he loved flaunting his extraordinary skill in performing dubious deals or pulling the proverbial rabbit out of a hat when someone was in trouble. For instance, he is said to have bailed out Amitabh Bachchan from near bankruptcy when his business venture Amitabh Bachchan Corporation Limited (ABCL) went bust. During the short tenure of Chandra Shekhar as prime minister in early 1991, he was also believed to have secured ABCL relief from hefty tax liabilities. In fact, Singh was known to say *'Paploo fit ho gaya!'* [the trick has worked] whenever he fixed something using various means and tricks. However, Amar Singh resented being called a 'political fixer'. Once when a journalist described him as such, Singh quickly dragged him to court for defamation, filing suits in Kolkata, Uttar Pradesh and Delhi courts, before finally making peace.

Amar Singh has also been accused of many gory deeds – from preventing Sonia Gandhi's rise to the prime ministerial post in 1999 to mustering crucial support for the Manmohan Singh government in 2008, when the UPA regime appeared to be in danger over the India-US nuclear deal. He took great pride in owning up to most of these accusations. But he always denied driving a wedge between Amitabh Bachchan and Sonia Gandhi. That was one charge he was wholly innocent of, he insisted. He would passionately argue that the Bachchan–Gandhi relationship dated back to a time before his birth. At one point he said:

> I have no authority or competence to comment on the ties of two great families. Only they are competent to comment on each other. All I know about Amit*ji* is that he is a man of great dignity, depth and emotion, and he's convinced that there's respect only for utility and no place for emotion.[453]

In private conversations he would say that the Gandhi–Bachchan fallout had been the result of human failings, ego clashes and one-upmanship.

Amar Singh appeared in Amitabh Bachchan's life after Rajiv Gandhi's death in 1991, and soon became the star's 'brother' and eyes and ears. For years Amar Singh acted as a shadow of the actor and his family. When Bachchan was issued a flurry of tax notices during the UPA-I tenure, he issued a veiled warning: The Samajwadi Party general secretary warned the Congress that his party could use the actor in the 2007 Uttar Pradesh Assembly election. Amitabh Bachchan distanced himself from Amar Singh's statement suggesting that the actor could stage a political comeback. Amar Singh clarified: 'I did not say he will enter politics. I said if you continuously keep humiliating someone, he could be compelled to join politics.'[454]

In 2006, Amar Singh was able to prevail upon Amitabh to let his wife Jaya Bachchan continue in politics, despite husband Amitabh's deep misgivings. This was when Jaya had faced disqualification from the Rajya Sabha in March 2006, following a petition before the Election Commission accusing her of holding an office of profit as the chairperson of the Uttar Pradesh Film Development Corporation. Singh also got Amitabh to campaign for the Samajwadi Party. For many years he hovered around the family with Hanuman-like devotion.

Between 2010 and 2012, the Bachchans fell out with Amar Singh. Delhi and Mumbai's social circuits claimed that the fallout coincided with the politician's own banishment from the capital's darbar. The bitter spat began when Jaya Bachchan insisted on keeping her Rajya Sabha seat after Singh was shunted out of the Samajwadi Party. Jaya Bachchan's decision to ignore Singh's advice reportedly had the support of her daughter-in-law Aishwarya.[455] It was then that Amitabh Bachchan forced the two sides to retreat into dignified silence; he himself vowed never to speak anything about Singh in public or in private.

During that two-year period, another controversy from the past – the 2008 cash-for-vote allegations made following the trust vote in Parliament – returned to haunt Singh. He was arrested and sent to Tihar Jail in 2011. Although he was eventually acquitted, Singh remained bitter about the fact that none of his influential friends visited him in prison. He should have known better.

Jaya Bachchan once told Amar Singh: 'You will be very disappointed, as you are more giving than any one of us [the Bachchans]. If you expect any reciprocity, you will be a very sad person.' Singh may have understood the full import of her remark in his last days.[456]

Had he pondered some more, he would have remembered another older gem from Jaya Bachchan pronounced at Sidhaur in Barabanki District way back in October 2004. The occasion was an Assembly by-election and she was seeking votes for the Samajwadis. She said: '*Mere devar Amar Singh sach mein Thakur hai. Jo kehte hain woh karte hain. Aap Samajwadi Party ko vote dijiye. Yeh log vaade aur rishte nibhana jaante hain.* (My brother-in-law is a real Thakur. He does what he says. Please vote for the Samajwadi Party because these people know how to keep promises and relations.)'[457]

When she said this, Jaya Bachchan had the Gandhis – once close friends of the Bachchans – in mind. Speaking bitterly of the past, she remembered Rajiv and Sonia Gandhi thusly: '*Jin logon ne humko rajniti mein aage badhaya, unhone beech mein hi hamara saath chhod diya. Saath tab chhoda jab hum taqleef mein the. Yeh log hamesha dhokha dete hain.* (Those who brought us into politics left us midway. They left us when we were in a crisis. They are known to betray people.)'[458]

In May 2015, Amar Singh had to vacate his 27 Lodhi Estate bungalow – once the hottest address in New Delhi, visited by the rich and the powerful, including the Bachchans.[459] 'Mr Bachchan, according to me, is contrary to *baghban* (gardener), the role he played onscreen. Off-screen, he is *bagh-ujar* (someone who uproots a garden), at least emotionally. I am saying this on record,' Amar Singh had later complained.[460]

There was more to follow. He told a newspaper:

> Remorse is for human beings, not for the house. Families
> like the Bachchans, if there was a death in the house, they

would have my and my wife's names on the cards as family members. For the wedding of their sons and daughters, they used to print cards referring to us as family. I also treated them as family. I don't regret doing anything for them. Whatever you do for the family, you don't regret. [...] I regret the way they treated me opportunistically. But I maintain that a good human being can be a bad actor and a good actor may not necessarily be a good human being.[461]

Towards the end, the man who had once been a king had been reduced to a pawn on the chessboard of life.

ARJUN SINGH
(1930–2011)

Hazaaron khwahishen aisi ke har khwahish pe dum nikle...
Bahut nikle mere armaan, lekin phir bhi kam nikle.

[Thousands of desires, each worth dying for;
many of them I have realized, yet I yearn for more.]

—Mirza Ghalib

ARJUN SINGH, VETERAN CONGRESSMAN, ABLE PARLIAMENTARIAN, three-time chief minister, Union minister and governor, did yearn for more but the one crown that would have been the apotheosis of his long political career remained elusive. Seven years after he faced his biggest disappointment, he was gone, taking with him an unfulfiled ambition and tantalizing secrets that would never be known.

Arjun Singh's eventful life, with its fair share of controversies, came to an end on 4 March 2011, hours after his exclusion from the CWC as a regular member. Congress chief Sonia Gandhi's token gesture of retaining him as a permanent invitee to the party's highest decision-making body had little bearing on him. He was already too disillusioned and ill to acknowledge it.

It was an unremarkable exit for someone who had emerged from the boondocks of Madhya Pradesh politics to come within sniffing distance of the country's highest position of elected authority.

Arjun Singh rose from a small principality in the backward Rewa region and cut his political teeth as an understudy to Dwarka Prasad Mishra, a writer and Madhya Pradesh chief minister who had outwitted Indira Gandhi in the party's internal tussle for power and control. Dwarka Prasad Mishra – whose son Brajesh Mishra was to later serve as principal secretary to prime minister Atal Bihari Vajpayee and as national security adviser – not only defied Indira Gandhi but had also succeeded in consolidating support among party legislators, thereby saving his chair at a time Congress chief ministers used to be at the mercy of the central leadership. Not for nothing was he called the Chanakya of Madhya Pradesh politics. Arjun Singh, however, did not take long to outshine his mentor; tales of the protege's deft manoeuvres soon replaced similar stories involving Mishra.

A man of few words, Singh had loyalists in the party across the country and was known to lavish favours on his confidants in return for their unflinching allegiance. He was a strong votary of power politics and was credited with the view that power could overcome many handicaps.

After Sonia Gandhi refused to join politics following Rajiv Gandhi's death in 1991, Singh set his sights on the pinnacle of Congress politics. He became a diehard Sonia Gandhi loyalist in the hope that one day 'Madam' would recognize his devotion and worth, and reward him by helping him become the most powerful man in the country, perhaps even prime minister.

Arjun Singh believed the many astrologers and self-styled godmen who had been telling him for long that the planetary combinations in his *kundli* (natal chart) pointed to a *rajyog* (the destiny to rule). 'Leave it to us and we will place all the stars in your favour,' a prominent godman from Madhya Pradesh had told him.

Singh would tell his associates he had been an AICC vice-president, chief minister, governor and a central minister; the only blank in an otherwise glittering resume was the post of prime minister.

That crown too would come his way, he firmly believed – even more so after he survived a massive heart attack in 1989. Doctors at Hamidia Hospital in Bhopal had almost given up on him when a call from Rajiv Gandhi ensured a timely airlift to Delhi's Escorts Heart Institute. Surely, he reckoned, there was a 'divine design' behind his survival.

The date 18 May 2004 proved to be a turning point for Singh when Sonia Gandhi declined the prime minister's chair hours after a Congress-led coalition had defeated Vajpayee's National Democratic Alliance (NDA). Congress's secularism had won; the party had regained its past glory and a Gandhi was at the helm of affairs – but another Singh, a Sikh, became prime minister instead.

Arjun Singh never reconciled to Manmohan Singh's stature but felt no bitterness towards him either. His sense of loyalty towards the Nehru–Gandhi family also did not permit him to go public against Sonia Gandhi. But his dream was over. Minister for human resources – a post he had held earlier too – was hardly adequate recompense for a man who aspired to become prime minister.

In the years that followed, Singh sacrificed his promising political career, spurned rapprochement offers from P.V. Narasimha Rao, left the Congress, formed his own outfit, returned to the parent organization and plotted successfully the downfall of two coalitions, one headed by I.K. Gujral and the other by Vajpayee.

Years later, weeks before he fell ill in January 2011, old-timers would recall that the veteran who had by then been marginalized would often flip through the empty pages of his appointment diary. If there were any visitors, they heard him speak of 'coalition compulsions', 'age factor' and 'change in political culture, values and ethos' – his own take on why he was no longer relevant in Sonia Gandhi's Congress.

But if anyone thought Arjun Singh would fade away from memory without a ripple, they were soon jolted out of such delusions. In his autobiography, *A Grain of Sand in the Hourglass of Time*, Singh hit back from beyond the grave at his old party rival, P.V. Narasimha Rao, in the context of the Babri Masjid demolition and former Union Carbide chief Warren Anderson's escape from India after the Bhopal gas tragedy. He also accused Rao, a former prime minister who died in 2004, of questioning the right of the Nehru–Gandhi family to always head the Congress, while buttressing his own image as a loyalist; not a line in the book though is critical of Indira, Rajiv, Sanjay or Sonia Gandhi.

In his memoirs, Arjun Singh claims that Rao, who was the prime minister then, had directed him not to visit Ayodhya on 4 December 1992, two days before the mosque was demolished. Rao, Singh says, asked him to meet Uttar Pradesh chief minister Kalyan Singh in Lucknow. 'You don't say anything from me, but make all the enquiries on how his (BJP) government is preparing to protect the Babri mosque,' Singh has quoted Rao as telling him.[462]

After the meeting, Singh had called Rao and told him it was not possible to gauge the exact situation in Ayodhya without going there. An alarmed Rao is purported to have told him: 'How can you go when the chief minister is requesting you not to go?'[463] It was at this point, Singh says, that he realized the 'entire rigmarole' had been enacted to prevent him from visiting Ayodhya. 'The prime minister insisted that I should not go to Ayodhya because my presence there could create a situation that the government of Uttar Pradesh would exploit and may create disturbances... I was in a fix...because openly defying the prime minister had certain adverse implications,' Singh explained.[464]

He said he even toyed with the idea of resigning over the phone, so that he would not be under any obligation to obey Rao.

> At this juncture, Jitendra Prasada (Rao's political secretary) entered my room. He started persuading me to obey the prime minister and keep away from Ayodhya. I pointed out to him that 'we would all cut a very sorry figure by having come to Lucknow and then backing out at the last moment'.[465]

Singh described his meeting with Rao, which took place on the morning of 5 December 1992:

> I reported verbatim the details of my conversation with Kalyan Singh... When I had finished, the prime minister asked me: 'What is your own assessment of the situation?' I replied: 'You did not allow me to move out of Lucknow, so what assessment can I give you?' He then tried to probe further: 'No, no, I know you have your sources and I want to know what is the shape of things to come.' I then told him very frankly that the Babri mosque was going to be demolished. This news definitely shook him and he wanted to dispute my claim, but, on second thoughts, he kept quiet. In a somewhat agitated frame of mind, he started thinking aloud about the repercussions if the mosque were to be brought down. He then suddenly exclaimed that this would have 'a very bad impact on the Congress Party', which was stating the obvious. I could not contain myself and told him bluntly that 'we have turned a blind eye' to the machinations of the BJP and the other pro-Hindutva

outfits. He then queried: 'When could this (demolition) happen?' I responded: 'This could happen any day.' Even I did not realize that the Babri mosque would be demolished the very next day.'[466]

Rao's purported outburst against the Nehru–Gandhi family came a year and a half before the Babri demolition. Arjun Singh says that a few days after Rajiv Gandhi's May 1991 assassination, he had approached Rao along with party seniors M.L. Fotedar and Sitaram Kesri, and suggested that Sonia be asked to take over the leadership. 'He [Rao] burst out in anger and virtually yelled out words to the effect [of] whether it was essential that the Congress party should be treated like a train where the compartments have to be attached to an engine belonging to the Nehru–Gandhi family or were there other alternatives?' Singh writes, adding that Rao's outburst left him dumbfounded.[467]

Another time Rao's 'unexpected outburst' left him surprised was when as prime minister Rao returned from the US sometime in early 1992. 'I am not afraid of anyone as President George Bush Sr is now behind me,' Rao is purported to have said.[468] 'I was very surprised by this unexpected outburst because the matters we were discussing had no relevance whatsoever to President Bush,' chronicles Singh, who was then the human resources development minister and served as the 'number two' in the Rao government. '[Rao] seemed to have been emboldened after his meeting with President Bush and felt that [the] latter's support would see him through all difficult situations.'[469]

Arjun Singh was the Madhya Pradesh chief minister when, in December 1984, a gas leak from the Bhopal Union Carbide factory killed over 3,000 people. Anderson, Carbide's US-based chief, arrived in Bhopal on 7 December and was arrested, but bail was arranged hurriedly. Within hours, a state government-owned Cessna flew him to Delhi, from where he took a flight home, never to return. The Cessna's pilot S.H. Ali and others have claimed that a 'call' from a powerful person in Delhi had prompted the local administration to let Anderson off. Arjun Singh says it was Rao, who was the Union home minister then. 'I came to know later that the Union Home Secretary, R.D. Pradhan, upon the instructions of the Union home minister P.V. Narasimha Rao, had telephoned Brahma Swaroop (state Chief Secretary) to ensure Anderson's release,' Singh says.[470]

In 2010, he issued a statement absolving Rajiv Gandhi and implicating Rao in Anderson's escape.

The autobiography also seeks to set the record straight on allegations of Arjun Singh's own 'disappearance' from Bhopal when the deadly gas was wreaking havoc on the intervening night of 2 and 3 December. According to him, hours after the leaking methyl isocyanate gas left a trail of death in the Madhya Pradesh capital, this is what happened:

> [L]ate in the morning of December 3, 1984, I quietly took off from Bhopal in a plane and landed in Allahabad, about 550 km away. I went to my old school, St. Mary Convent, where with the permission of the principal, I sat in the chapel to pray for the welfare of my people and gain moral courage to act personally in the face of monumental catastrophe.[471]

Late Abdul Jabbar, then the convener of the Bhopal Gas Peedit Mahila Udhyog Sangathan, an organization of gas victims, had said that Arjun Singh's explanation was difficult to fathom. 'How can a chief minister go to pray 550 km away when citizens were dying right, left and centre?' he wondered.[472] That night, Jabbar recalled, angry protesters had raised the slogan, 'Gas *nikli adhi raat*, Arjun *bhaga raaton raat*'. Translated, the slogan would read: 'Gas leaked at midnight; Arjun ran away under the cover of darkness'.

Jabbar said that as far as he remembered, Arjun Singh had reportedly been advised by the local administration to stay away after the lethal gas had leaked from the Union Carbide factory in one of the world's worst industrial disasters. 'Why did he wait for 25 years to tell this?' Jabbar had added, alleging that Singh's explanation in his autobiography was an 'afterthought'. Jabbar also questioned Arjun Singh's claim that it was Rao who was to blame for Anderson being allowed to leave India after visiting Bhopal on 7 December.[473]

Arjun Singh's disappearance was raised before Rajiv Gandhi, too, when the then prime minister visited Bhopal on 4 December. Gandhi had asked Singh to clarify but the chief minister had suggested setting up a commission of inquiry to address all issues, including his alleged disappearance. A commission, under Justice N.K. Singh, was appointed but it was folded up within nine months even before it had made any progress.

In his memoirs, Singh claims that when he broached the subject of Anderson's arrest with Rajiv Gandhi, the prime minister had kept mum. Singh gives an account of his meeting with Gandhi on December 6:

> At one of the hospitals (in Bhopal) that we visited, Rajiv took
> me aside to brief me. It was something rather confidential,
> which, naturally, I could not have shared with anyone.
> Everyone later wanted to know what did he say? What
> was it all about? What were his instructions or his brief?

Nobody would ever know. 'Well even today I cannot reveal what he told me,' Singh said. 'It is a state secret that I shall carry to my grave.'[474]

BUTA SINGH
(1934–2021)

BUTA SINGH, WHO TOOK PRIDE IN BEING A RAJIV GANDHI LOYALIST, DIED at the age of 86 in New Delhi on 2 January 2021. He was virtually the number two in Rajiv Gandhi's cabinet – a reckless demolition man who dismissed state governments almost at will. Yet, the veteran who was privy to many state secrets died bitter and disenchanted. 'I am thoroughly disillusioned. Loyalty is no longer a premium,' Buta Singh had said a few years ago when this writer met him at his 11-A Teen Murti Marg residence.

'I fought many battles, built the Congress party, did everything to ensure that the party's flag remains high. But now I feel I am no longer relevant,' the former Union minister had added, without taking any names. 'I have many, many memories but it looks like there is nobody to care for loyalty.'

What kind of memories? A teasing smile had played through the bitterness. Yes, he had a lot to say about the circumstances in which former Madhya Pradesh chief minister Arjun Singh had let the Union Carbide chief, Warren Anderson, escape on 7 December 1984, four days after the lethal gas leak killed thousands in Bhopal. 'I know the exact role played by Arjun Singh. But why should I say anything? Is anyone going to listen to me?' he said.

Buta Singh came from an extremely modest background in Mustafapur, a village near Jalandhar, before going on to do his master's in history from Mumbai's Khalsa College. A Marxist in his student days, he was an avid reader of Bolshevik literature, and his first job was as a proofreader for a communist organ – the *Phoolwari* magazine. When he heard the news of Joseph Stalin's death in 1953, he is said to have wept bitterly.

But it would be on an Akali ticket that he would take his first steps in politics. Buta Singh was working as a sub-editor for *Akali Patrika* when the Shiromani Akali Dal fielded him from the Moga seat in Punjab in 1962. When the Akalis split, Buta Singh joined the Master Tara Singh group but did not stay long. Soon after, he was introduced to Indira Gandhi and joined the Congress, which would be his home for the next few decades.

During the Rajiv Gandhi era, Buta Singh rose to function as the virtual number two in the government, upstaging two senior ministers – P.V. Narasimha Rao and P. Shiv Shankar. He had more access to Rajiv Gandhi than any other Congress leader. To be fair to Buta Singh, he did not have any ambitions to become 'Caesar' or a 'Rasputin', but he loved his reputation as Rajiv Gandhi's hatchet man.

He did, after all, always have a penchant for going for the kill, sometimes regardless of the consequences. Buta Singh was barely seven when his uncle once pointed to a hornets' nest, saying it was a beehive full of honey. Two days later, Buta Singh's sister Pritam Kaur heard the boy screaming. He had tried getting to the nest and was attacked by a swarm of hornets. He fell from the tree and broke his leg.[475]

Buta Singh became home minister in 1986 and toppled so many state governments that in 1988, Rajiv told him in jest, 'Buta Singhji, *ab aap kirpan andar rakhiye*. (Buta Singhji, now please sheathe your kirpan.)'[476] The allusion was to the change of guard in a host of states, including Madhya Pradesh, Jammu and Kashmir, Tripura, Rajasthan and Bihar.

Buta Singh had tried his hand at resolving the Ayodhya dispute too. Along with the then chief minister of Uttar Pradesh, N.D. Tiwari, Buta Singh had organized the *shilanyas* (foundation ceremony) at the Ramjanmabhoomi–Babri Masjid site in 1989 and was the architect of Rajiv Gandhi's Lok Sabha campaign that year, which was launched from the bank of the river Saryu in Ayodhya with the promise of a 'Ram Rajya'. The measures boomeranged and the Congress fell short of a simple majority.

Buta Singh's in-house rivalry with Giani Zail Singh played havoc in the politics of their home state, Punjab. The Orwellian future may not have materialized in 1984 but in Indian politics, the year marked the loss of morality, innocence and secularism. Punjab was most affected when the state brazenly turned a blind eye to everything that was decent, civil or ethical. The stage for wrongdoings in Punjab was actually set in October 1983 when Darbara Singh, the secular and balanced chief minister of Punjab, was made to resign by his political master, prime minister Indira Gandhi. Both Buta Singh and Zail Singh (who later rose to become President of India) played a dubious role in propping up Jarnail Singh Bhindranwale.

In the Congress after Rajiv Gandhi, Buta Singh lost his glory and political clout prompting him to keep changing political loyalties; he joined the BJP in 1998 and then returned to the Congress in 2002.

In the 2009 parliamentary elections too, after he was denied a Congress ticket, Buta Singh contested as an Independent candidate from Jalore, Rajasthan, and lost. He would, however, again reunite with his old party towards the end of his life and insist that he had been with the Congress all along. This wasn't entirely untrue. Earlier, Buta Singh was among the few who stood by Indira Gandhi after the Congress split in 1977–78.

Buta Singh was the AICC general secretary when the Congress moved into its 24 Akbar Road office in 1978. The party was facing an acute shortage of manpower, resources and vehicles. Buta Singh had solved the vehicle crunch at the time. He had friends in Delhi, including some with flourishing transport businesses in the national capital. One such friend was Jagjit Singh of the Tourist Taxi Service at Janpath. Jagjit Singh let the Congress use his fleet of yellow and white cabs.

At times, both Indira and Sanjay Gandhi counted on Buta Singh's proximity to Jagjit Singh to avail vehicles. On most occasions, Jagjit Singh would turn down Buta Singh's request to pay for the cabs. When Indira Gandhi returned to power later, she would remember Jagjit Singh's help and give him a ticket from an Assembly segment near Chandigarh where the Mohali township has now come up.

Further, when the party was out of power in 1978, it was also badly in need of money. Once again, Buta Singh's innovative thinking helped. As a matter of practice, all visiting party leaders were requested to 'donate' money for the new party. MPs and leaders from the south always obliged with ₹100 or more. Those from Uttar Pradesh and Bihar were somewhat stingy, sometimes donating as little as ₹10 or ₹20, which Buta Singh would accept with humility and graciousness.

He was made the governor of Bihar in 2004, but his Machiavellian habit of treating state governments with disdain landed him in a controversy. Buta Singh had recommended the dissolution of the Bihar Assembly in 2005 but the move was sharply criticized by the Supreme Court. The apex court ruled that Buta Singh had acted in haste and misled the Union cabinet because he did not want Nitish Kumar's Janata Dal (United) and the BJP to form the government.

On 26 January 2006, Buta Singh sent a fax to the President at the time A.P.J. Abdul Kalam saying that he was resigning from the post of governor. Once the dust had settled down, Sonia Gandhi and Manmohan Singh appointed him chairman of the National Commission for Scheduled Castes in 2007, according to him a cabinet berth and a palatial house in Lutyens' Delhi.

Buta Singh courted other controversies too. In the year 2000, judge Ajit Bharihoke of a special court convicted Narasimha Rao and Buta Singh in the JMM bribery case. The charge against them was bribing MPs belonging to the Janata Dal (Ajit) and the Jharkhand Mukti Morcha in return for votes in favour of the minority Congress government during a no-confidence motion in the Lok Sabha in 1993. The decision was later overturned and both Narasimha Rao and Buta Singh were cleared of the charge in 2002.

BALASAHEB THACKERAY

(1926–2012)

UNLIKE MOST POLITICIANS OR PARTY SUPREMOS, BAL KESHAV THACKERAY (popularly known as Balasaheb Thackeray) never held a public office or contested an election. What set him apart from the rest, was not limited to this though. He also held an unwelcome record: that of getting disenfranchised. Simply put, he lost the right to vote or fight an election for a few years – a dubious distinction for someone who had made politics his life's calling.

That was sometime in the mid-nineties. Less than twenty years later – in 2012 – the then Congress government in Maharashtra would order a state funeral for the 'Tiger'.

Forgotten in the frenzy of grief was the blemish of disenfranchisement. Only a 'superstar' could have pulled off such a posthumous cover-up. As columnist Vir Sanghvi had once said: there was only one superstar in Mumbai, and that was Balasaheb Thackeray.

For Sanghvi, who lived in Mumbai for a considerable period of time, a measure of Thackeray's political significance was his sheer longevity;[477] despite straddling a career across four decades, from 1966 to 2012, his influence never ebbed. The Shiv Sena boss continued to be the uncrowned king of Mumbai, dominating politics, business and Bollywood (the city's fabled filmdom) in a way no other politician had ever done.

He remained in a league of his own, without ever becoming an elected representative – unlike other regional stalwarts like N.T. Rama Rao, M.G. Ramachandran, Jayalalithaa, Mayawati and Mamata Banerjee, or long-entrenched state rivals who defied the Congress and rose to become chief ministers. Thackeray was different: a king who did not need a throne to wield power. It of course did help that his party's street-smart aggression worked in perfect sync with its radical Hindutva ideology and parochial objectives.

The other thing that worked in sync, also to his favour, was Thackeray's ironical pen and the increasing disenchantment among Maharashtra's youth. It was 1966; Indira Gandhi was the prime minister and Sharad Pawar was yet to emerge on Maharashtra's political scene – dominated at the time by communists and labour unions. This was also a time when migrants from south Indian states, particularly Tamil Nadu, called the shots in the metropolis, while Marathi-speaking youth – the 'sons of the soil' – remained unemployed, pushed to the margins in their home state.

Thackeray, who came from a Marathi-speaking Kayastha family from Madhya Pradesh, was bitter too. He was employed as a cartoonist with the *Free Press Journal* in Mumbai, but had reportedly been denied a promotion by a 'south Indian clique'. The forty-year-old left his job to start a satirical weekly, *Marmik*, which would culminate in the launch of the Shiv Sena. *Marmik* would highlight the recruitment of non-Maharashtrians in both government and private industries with the headline: '*Vaacha ani gappa basa*' (Read and keep quiet). Soon, south Indians were targeted with the war cry '*Bajao pungi, bhagao lungi*' that Thackeray had coined. Not only did he know how to express the dominant sentiment through his pen, he was also adept at reading the popular pulse.[478]

The magazine was the perfect vehicle of expression for Thackeray, whose style was influenced by Sir David Low, one of the great political cartoonists and caricaturists of the last century.

On 1 May 1966, an editorial in *Marmik* decried the Maharashtra government's support for industries whose owners recruited labourers from outside Maharashtra, questioning the rightness of creating employment for migrants while local people were jobless. In the same issue, Thackeray had published a list of officers at a government fertilizer company. The list showed that only three officers were from Maharashtra while the rest were from other states, which, Thackeray argued, was an insult to Maharashtrians.

It was against this backdrop that the Sena came into being – an ideal setting for the man with an anglicized surname. (Thackeray's father Keshav, an admirer of British novelist William Makepeace Thackeray, had changed the family's original surname Thakre to Thackeray.)

To Thackeray's credit, he did not fail to seize opportunities. Author and commentator Kumar Ketkar agrees with Sanghvi's assessment that Thackeray was a bigger showman than actors Raj Kapoor, Amitabh Bachchan or Rajesh Khanna. Ketkar saw Thackeray as a born actor who knew how to be funny, smart, sardonic and then, suddenly, inspiring, while the absence of any ideology, except for radical Hindutva, Ketkar said, helped the Sena thrive on mindless action. Thackeray would always tell Shiv Sainiks not to read. He himself was dismissive of all social, political and economic theories which, he said, were all bunkum. Ketkar further stated that Thackeray had a disdain for the trappings of power and never wanted the responsibility that came with it.[479]

Thackeray considered Adolf Hitler to be his role model and would often say that he wanted to be the Hitler not only of Mumbai or Maharashtra but of the entire country. It was, perhaps, this authoritarian trait that prompted him to support Indira Gandhi's Emergency. In an editorial in *Marmik* on 31 August 1975, he wrote that imposing the Emergency was the only way to handle situations created after an unrest; however, he did caution against enforcing it for too long.

'Hitman' to Cult Figure

Thackeray's rise is also a telling commentary on how the Congress, which excelled in propping up regional players to cut to size its own regional satraps, paid the price for its Machiavellian designs. In the Sena's initial years, the Congress would use and manipulate

Thackeray and his nascent party to 'fix' Morarji Desai, V.K. Krishna Menon and several other influential players.

In her biography of Thackeray titled *Hindu Hriday Samrat: How The Shiv Sena Changed Mumbai Forever*, author Sujata Anandan has recorded that the Shiv Sena was then derogatorily referred to as the 'Vasant Sena' after the legendary Congress leaders Vasantrao Naik and Vasantdada Patil, both of whom provided the party credibility by accepting its demand for employment of 80 per cent local people in business establishments.[480] Both Naik and Patil detested the dominance of Gujarati, Parsi, Sindhi and Bohra Muslim enterprises in Mumbai and Maharashtra. That suited Thackeray just fine, and he played the role of the Congress's hitman till like Jarnail Singh Bhindranwale, in the mid-1980s in Punjab, he too became a cult figure.

This was also when the Congress government in Maharashtra was worried over the communists gaining a foothold in the industrial units of north Mumbai. The Shiv Sena's job was to fight the communists – by any means necessary – and to protect the Congress bastion.

One such election where the Shiv Sena helped out the Congress was in 1967. Congress stalwart Krishna Menon had been denied a party ticket and was therefore contesting as an independent candidate from the Bombay (now Mumbai) North-East parliamentary constituency. His campaign was highlighting his proximity to Jawaharlal Nehru. His campaign posters read 'Nehru's vision, Menon's mission' and showed Menon within a Nehru silhouette.

Indira Gandhi, who was fighting to isolate Menon, instructed her key aides to get the former defence minister defeated at 'all costs'. Thackeray, the Shiv Sena and *Marmik* swung into action, campaigning for the Congress nominee, S.G. Barve. A day before the vote, *Marmik* published a cartoon that showed Menon with two foreign girls, his hands around their shoulders. The caption insinuated that they were why Menon wanted to be the defence minister. Barve won the election.

Thackeray had a brush with the law in February 1969 when he was arrested on the charge of starting a riot. Sena workers had tried to stop the then deputy prime minister Morarji Desai's car at Mahim to hand him a memorandum demanding the merger of Belgaum, Karwar and Nipani with Maharashtra. Desai's driver panicked and accelerated the car, injuring several Sena activists in the process. Angry *sainiks* then began rioting and the violence lasted four days. The situation was so bad that the army had to be brought in. Sixty-nine people died in the agitation. Thackeray, Manohar Joshi and Dattaji Salvi were arrested and sent to Yerwada jail in Pune and later to Arthur Road Jail in Mumbai. They were released after 100 days by the Congress government, reportedly after 'instructions from the top'.

Such violence by Sena workers would unfold again and again under Thackeray, as the party upped its aggressive campaign against south Indians, communists, Muslims, Biharis and north Indians in Mumbai. Apart from the 1969 violence, the party has been accused of instigating several other riots in Maharashtra, including the Bhiwandi riots in 1984 and the 1992–93 violence in Mumbai.

Many have wondered how Thackeray was able to mobilize youths so easily. But that was where his real strength lay: his ability to recognize the existence of a large number of unemployed, frustrated youths who were willing to indulge in violence at the slightest provocation, provided they were bailed out.

The Shiv Sena supremo is also credited with popularizing '*dahi handi*' contests, a community event to celebrate Janmashtami, and making it as popular as the Ganesh Utsav and Dussehra.

Later in his life, Thackeray avoided mingling with supporters but made up for it with occasional *darshans* from the balcony of his heavily guarded Bandra home, *Matoshree*, and by giving rabble-rousing speeches at his famous Dussehra rallies. Seated on a throne with multiple images of a tiger, Thackeray virtually lorded over Mumbai for years, receiving political leaders, captains of business and industry and film personalities at his residence – all without holding any position of power.

In the Thick of Politics

In September 1970, the Shiv Sena tasted its first significant victory, riding on support from the RSS. Krishna Desai, a communist MLA from Parel, Mumbai (then Bombay), had been murdered, necessitating a by-election. The Sena fielded Vaman Mahadik in the by-election while the communists had Desai's widow Sarojini in the fray. Nine parties, including the Congress, supported Sarojini. Comrade S.A. Dange and senior Congress leaders Mohan Dharia and Shankarrao Chavan campaigned for Sarojini, while RSS leader Moropant Pingale publicly appealed for votes for the Sena. Mahadik won the seat.

Neither Thackeray nor his party had any formal ties with the Nagpur-headquartered RSS. In fact, the Sena founder had nothing to do with the RSS, the Jana Sangh, the Hindu Mahasabha or the Vishwa Hindu Parishad.

In the 1980 Assembly elections in Maharashtra, the Sena did not field any candidates against the Congress. The Congress won the election and Abdul Rahman Antulay, a personal friend of Thackeray, became chief minister. Antulay was, however, forced to resign about a year and a half into his rule, following a controversy over granting cement quotas.

Later, too, Thackeray would support the Congress's presidential nominees in 2007 and 2012. He backed Pratibha Patil on grounds of her being a 'Marathi *Manoos*' (fellow Marathi). In 2012, when Pranab Mukherjee was Congress-UPA's presidential nominee, Shiv Sena was with the NDA, but Thackeray went public supporting Mukherjee saying, 'It was but natural for the "Maratha tiger to support the Royal Bengal tiger."'[481] In the third volume of his autobiography *The Coalition Years: 1996–2012*, Mukherjee mentioned that Sonia

Gandhi was upset with him for meeting Thackeray. Mukherjee said NCP Chief Sharad Pawar, a coalition partner of the then UPA-II government, had insisted that he should meet Thackeray. When Mukherjee met Thackeray at *Matosree* at Bandra, he realized that Thackeray had made elaborate arrangements to welcome him. Mukherjee saw wisdom in Pawar's advice that Thackeray would have considered it a personal insult if he had not met him during his visit to Mumbai.[482]

Thackeray's biggest moment in politics came when he struck an alliance with the BJP in 1995 and formed a government in Maharashtra for the first time, tempering his strident pro-Marathi ideology and embracing a broader Hindu nationalist agenda. Much of the credit for bringing the Sena and the BJP close went to BJP's Pramod Mahajan, a Maharashtrian, who enjoyed Thackeray's trust. Mahajan, an astute politician, had realized that a Hindutva agenda and a strong alliance with the Shiv Sena was the only way to rule Maharashtra.

The Sena–BJP combine owed its political success to the March 1993 Mumbai serial blasts, which further polarized voters to their advantage. The riots that had broken out two months before leaving nearly a thousand people dead had paved the way for this successful combine. The Justice B.N. Srikrishna Commission, which probed the December 1992–January 1993 riots, had squarely accused Thackeray of sparking anti-Muslim violence in Mumbai. The judge, himself a devout Hindu, had described Thackeray as a 'veteran general who commanded his loyal Shiv Sainiks to retaliate by organised attacks against Muslims' during the riots.[483] Thackeray not only rubbished the commission's findings, he had also cast aspersions on the integrity of the judge.

Within days of the Sena-led Manohar Joshi government assuming charge, Thackeray decided to make clear who the real boss was – the 'remote control', as he often described himself. A bash had been organized for a select few in Mumbai to celebrate the victory. When

Thackeray walked in, he was dismayed to note that liquor was not being served. On being told that liquor was not supposed to flow in the presence of the chief minister, Thackeray lost his cool and immediately ordered champagne. A sheepish Joshi had moved to a corner to avoid getting photographed amid champagne bubbles. Thackeray also pressured Joshi to reject the findings of the Srikrishna Commission on the floor of the Assembly.

For the next four years, Joshi sought to project the Sena as a responsible party of governance. But Thackeray had him removed just before the March 2000 polls. Joshi was in Pune on 30 January 1999, meeting Marathi literary figures at a writers' conference. When he returned to Mumbai late in the afternoon, he got a fax message from Thackeray asking him to step down. Joshi called Thackeray to assure him that his demand would be honoured.

Joshi's successor was Narayan Tatu Rane, who pushed for an aggressive, communal mobilization, which however ultimately failed the Sena–BJP. The Congress and the newly formed Nationalist Congress Party, led by former Congressman Sharad Pawar, rode to power in 2000. Rane subsequently joined the Congress and then, in 2017, switched over to the BJP.

Politics of Hate

Thackeray thrived on the politics of hate, regardless of whether he was targeting south Indians, Gujaratis or Muslims; he once likened the minority Muslim community to 'cancer', while calling for suicide bombers to counter what he would call 'Islamist terrorism'.[484] Towards the later part of his life, his vitriolic attack shifted from Muslims to Pakistan.

He favoured strong-arm tactics, often forcing the central and state governments to call off cricket matches with Pakistan and performances by Pakistani artistes. In October 1991, Shiv Sainiks had dug up the Wankhede Stadium's pitch to prevent the Pakistan cricket team from playing in Mumbai. The P.V. Narasimha Rao government and the Board of Control for Cricket in India (BCCI) had been forced to call off the entire series. Seven years later, the Sena–BJP regime would again get the January 1999 Test match in Mumbai cancelled. When the seniors weren't playing spoilsport, the cubs were at it. In April 2005, the Bharatiya Vidyarthi Sena, the Shiv Sena's student wing, tried to prevent an India–Pakistan One-Day International in New Delhi.

The Sena–BJP alliance would eventually come unstuck in November 2019, when Thackeray's son, Uddhav, turned the tables on his party's long-time ally to create history by becoming the first Thackeray to be the chief minister of Maharashtra, aligning with state rival Pawar's NCP and the Congress. Thackeray was not around to see that day.

The Congress decision to support the Sena was not an easy one. Insiders point out that several senior leaders – including Sonia Gandhi, Rahul Gandhi, Manmohan Singh and A.K. Antony – were 'instinctively' against the alliance. But Kamal Nath, Ahmed Patel, Kapil Sibal and the party's Maharashtra unit had passionately argued for it, recalling how in 1979–80, when the Congress was out of power, it had adopted a 'pragmatic' approach to seek Thackeray's friendship who, incidentally, had supported the Emergency. It was also argued that while the Sena, since its inception, was a chauvinistic party, it was not affiliated to the RSS.

This line of pragmatism had been gaining momentum within the Congress since March 1995, when the party lost its last big citadel, handing over the reins of Maharashtra to the Shiv Sena–BJP combine. This was a big blow to the Congress as it had already lost Uttar Pradesh, Bihar, Tamil Nadu and Bengal.

Thackeray loved taking positions to provoke the elite. When former prime minister Morarji Desai died, Thackeray's acerbic remark was that Desai's only achievement was that he had lived a hundred years. He also enjoyed targeting Pawar and actor Dilip Kumar – both long-time friends of the Sena boss.

Thackeray went berserk when the government of Pakistan conferred the Nishan-e-Imtiaz, their highest civilian award, on Dilip Kumar. He objected to the actor going to Pakistan to receive it. His objection kicked off a massive political row. What upset Dilip Kumar the most was that his cartoonist-turned-politician friend of three decades had cast doubts on his patriotism.

Journalist Sujata Anandan remembers Thackeray attacking Pawar too sometime in 1989–90 at a rally in the Konkan region, recounting the chief minister's 'bad habits' to those who had gathered in large numbers. Thackeray thundered that Pawar was a 'boozer', adding that he sat with his 'capitalist cronies' every evening and guzzled imported Scotch through the night, while he (Thackeray) was a nationalist who drank only Indian beer. Two bottles of warm beer were good for his stomach problems but Pawar, he claimed, could only end up with a liver problem.[485]

Minutes after Thackeray's rally had ended, Anandan said, she spotted two village teens at the local pharmacy demanding warm beer. Outraged at being directed to the liquor store instead, they demanded beer for their stomach problems. The pharmacist tried to explain that they could not get beer at a pharmacy, but they cited Thackeray's speech as evidence. The pharmacist prescribed something better than beer for a stomach ache but they left unhappy, Anandan would later recall.[486] The incident only underscored how deep and wide Thackeray's influence went, an indisputable legacy of the man who never held a formal public office but knew how to control the levers of the mind.

However, his legacy was dubious in more than one way. The politics of hate apart, he also ended up getting himself disenfranchised. Congress politician Prabhakar Kunte had filed a case in the Bombay High Court, alleging that the Sena was guilty of corrupt electoral practices. Kunte had lost an Assembly by-election in 1986 from Vile Parle, in Bombay North-West, to Ramesh Prabhoo of the Shiv Sena.

The case had later reached the Supreme Court, which convicted Thackeray of corrupt electoral practices and advised the President of India to debar him from contesting or voting in elections for six years. The Election Commission thus implemented this from 1995 to 2001, while Maharashtra's chief electoral officer, D.K. Sankaran, ordered that Thackeray's name be struck off the voters' list altogether. It was a humiliating rap for the Sena boss, though Thackeray always made light of the punishment.

The Twilight Years

By late 2012, Thackeray's health had begun to fail. At the Sena's Dussehra rally held on 24 October 2012, the Tiger's roar was missing. In a pre-recorded video address, Thackeray, then 86, announced his retirement from public life and urged his followers to stand by his son Uddhav and grandson Aditya, setting out the succession plan in the Sena. Following a feud with his cousin Uddhav, Thackeray's nephew Raj had earlier parted ways in 2006 to form a more hawkish party, the Maharashtra Navnirman Sena (MNS).

Thackeray died on 17 November 2012 after a prolonged illness. He was admitted at Mumbai's Lilavati Hospital for breathlessness and constipation. His body was kept at the Shivaji Park ground in central Mumbai for everyone to pay their last respects. Movie theatres, shops and commercial establishments throughout Mumbai remained closed for two days.

The leader's passing on a Saturday spared Congress chief minister Prithviraj Chavan the tricky decision of whether to declare a public holiday. But Chavan would not be dissuaded from ordering a state funeral, which entails carrying the body on a gun-carriage, the coffin draped in the tricolour and a 21-gun salute ahead of the funeral – an honour normally reserved only for those who have held constitutional posts. Chavan disregarded murmurs from within the Congress and stuck to his decision, saying he would go by 'public sentiments'.

It would be Thackeray's apotheosis, albeit posthumous; it would be an exit memorable enough to blur the stain of his former disenfranchisement.

MOTILAL VORA
(1928–2020)

MOTILAL VORA WAS IN THE LEAGUE OF A SELECT BAND OF CONGRESS leaders who wouldn't share party secrets with even their spouses or children. For him, loyalty towards the Nehru–Gandhi family was absolute and non-negotiable. A quintessential Congressman, he was the AICC treasurer for eighteen years – the longest among his party peers. Another measure of his political longevity and the esteem he enjoyed was that since 1980, he had an uninterrupted run either as a key post-holding party member or as a government minister.

But holding high offices, such as those of chief minister, Union minister, governor, Madhya Pradesh Congress chief, or AICC treasurer never produced an iota of arrogance in Vora. He would always pick up the phone himself, even when landlines were the key mode of communication, and see off guests as a matter of routine.

Vora would often chastise anyone who left a half-consumed cup of tea. 'It costs money. *Aath rupaye ki chai aati hai* (A cup of tea costs ₹8),' he would say smiling, driving home the point that nothing should be wasted.

When a rather overwhelmed Vijay Bahuguna sat at his feet as a mark of his gratitude moments after becoming the chief minister of Uttarakhand, Vora had told the much younger man, '*Bahugunaji, ab aap mukhya mantri hain. Neeche baithna achchha nahi lagta hai.* (Bahugunaji, you are now a chief minister. It does not seem proper for you to sit on the floor.)'[487] Vora had played a key role in propping up Bahugana, considered a rank outsider in Uttrakhand politics until then.

An Illustrious Career

Bahuguna wasn't alone in his gratitude. During the UPA years, many ministers felt that they owed their offices to him. When Charan Das Mahant became a minister of state in July 2011, he was seen prostrating himself before Vora. The AICC treasurer nudged him gently, saying, 'Thank God, thank Soniaji. I am inconsequential.'[488]

He was being characteristically modest. Vora was anything but inconsequential. Congress folklore has it that once Dr Manmohan Singh, who was the prime minister then, had approached Dasari Narayana Rao, the minister of state for coal, gently suggesting a person's name – perhaps someone he knew personally – as having the perfect credentials for the allocation of a coal block. The prime minister was told to route the suggestion through Vora.

In fact, throughout the ten years from 2004, when the Congress-led UPA was in power at the Centre, telephone calls and oral messages from Vora and fellow party veteran Ahmed Patel carried more weight in the corridors of power than those of cabinet ministers and the Prime Minister's Office.

At 15 Gurudwara Rakabgunj Marg, which worked as the Congress's war room, Vora had a room to himself. In the mini conference room, a chair was earmarked for him. Even when party stalwarts P. Chidambaram, Pranab Mukherjee, A.K. Antony and Sushil Kumar Shinde attended a meeting, the chair meant for 'babuji' was not to be occupied. Invariably, after every meeting,

Vora and Patel, who too passed away recently, would stay back for a 'review'. The two leaders – who until October–November 2020 had the joint authority to sign cheques at the party's 24 Akbar Road headquarters – enjoyed an excellent rapport and seldom disagreed even in private conversations.

Vora had almost become the President of India in 2007 when Bahujan Samaj Party supremo Mayawati pitched for him. Mayawati, then chief minister of Uttar Pradesh and supporting the UPA from outside, had reasons to back a Brahmin although her party represents the historically underprivileged sections of society. She believed that Vora was the man who had saved her life in 1995 when out-of-control workers of Mulayam Singh Yadav's Samajwadi Party had reportedly launched a murderous attack and tried to break into a Lucknow guest house while she was inside. Vora was then governor of Uttar Pradesh and had moved swiftly to throw a protective ring around her. The reason for the attack was BSP's decision to pull out of a coalition government with the Samajwadi Party. Vora had recommended President's Rule in the heartland state.

Mayawati was not alone among non-Congress leaders who held Vora in high esteem. In 2015, Prime Minister Narendra Modi, while speaking in the Rajya Sabha, showered lavish praise on Vora for the 'superlative' work in his Saansad Adarsh Gram Yojana, a scheme where MPs take the lead in adopting and developing villages.

On another occasion, Vice President M. Venkaiah Naidu had urged Congress MPs in the House to 'learn' parliamentary decorum and propriety from Vora.

A couple of years ago, a photograph of Union Minister Smriti Irani chatting happily with Vora had gone viral on social media. Apparently, Irani was recommending an orthopaedic doctor for the Congress veteran. Indeed, Vora enjoyed a degree of acceptability even across the political divide and counted Atal Bihari Vajpayee, Rajnath Singh and Arun Jaitley among his many 'friends' in the BJP.

A Right to Information query in August 2014 (three months after Modi had taken over as the Prime minister) revealed that Vora occupied nine government accommodations in Lutyens' Delhi. As a Rajya Sabha member and AICC treasurer, Vora had been allotted 33 Lodhi Estate. But he had also been given six more bungalows and two government flats where Congress leaders from Maharashtra and Chhattisgarh stayed as his 'guests'.

Within his party, Vora enjoyed the respect of the Nehru–Gandhis too. Not only Sonia Gandhi, but also her children Rahul Gandhi and Priyanka Gandhi Vadra held Vora in high esteem despite the generational tensions in the party. An incident in October 2020 showed the veteran's importance to the Gandhis. Vora had tested positive for Covid-19 in October 2020 when rumours announcing the nonagenarian leader's death started doing the rounds. The Gandhis got so upset that a Congress MP, who had tweeted a condolence message 'in memory of Voraji', was spoken to by personal aides of the Gandhis, prompting the beleaguered MP to apologize and delete the tweet.

Vora finally died on 21 December 2020 from Covid-related complications. In his death, Sonia Gandhi lost a faithful ally who, like Ahmed Patel, knew the most fiercely guarded secrets of the Grand Old Party – especially details of how money came into the party's coffers and how it was spent. Vora also knew the identity of every faceless donor the Congress had.

The timing of his exit may have put the Congress in a spot of bother. Vora, who served as AICC treasurer for nearly eighteen years, would have been a reassuring presence for Pawan Kumar Bansal, who succeeded Ahmed Patel as treasurer. Patel had replaced Vora in 2018 but the duo continued to manage party's finances together and Vora was a joint signatory of all cheque books of the AICC accounts.

In fact, one of the last full telephonic conversations Ahmed Patel is said to have had before he slipped into a coma was with Vora. Most of the discussion reportedly revolved around matters related to money.

An Eventful Career

Vora's career was as eventful as it was illustrious. He remained a run-of-the-mill kind of politician until 1977, when he defied the Janata Party wave that had swept across the country to retain his Durg Assembly seat. His big moment came in 1985, when he headed the Madhya Pradesh Congress Committee and Arjun Singh had just been sworn in as chief minister of the state. After the swearing-in, Singh had come to Delhi to get Rajiv Gandhi's seal of approval for his cabinet when the then prime minister asked him to become the governor of Punjab.

There are many stories relating to the appointment of Arjun Singh's successor Vora. Vora beat Madhavrao Scindia, the Shukla brothers Shyama Charan and Vidya Charan, P.C. Sethi and others to the chief minister's post. According to those hostile to Vora then, when Rajiv Gandhi asked Singh about his possible successor, the chief minister had tried to involve Vora in the discussion who was standing at a distance from them. Somehow it later dawned upon Singh, it is believed, that his call saying, 'woh raha' was misconstrued as 'Vora'.[489]

Another account says that Rajiv Gandhi wanted Madhavrao Scindia to replace Arjun Singh. When Scindia and Vora left together in a chartered plane, the titular maharaja of Gwalior began asking about life and Bhopal and the work schedule of a chief minister. When the aircraft landed at Bhopal, Scindia had rushed to a public telephone to call up Rajiv Gandhi asking him to consider Vora for the chief minister's post. As for himself, Scindia said, he would prefer to be a Union minister with a hectic social life in Delhi. Whatever be the reason, Vora remained grateful to Scindia. In fact, the 'Madhav–Moti' jodi would be a talking point throughout Vora's tenure as chief minister.

Vora had a knack for striking up friendships and operating in small groups. During the UPA years (2004–2014), he teamed up with Ahmed Patel and Janardan Dwivedi to run the AICC secretariat.

The trio were informally nicknamed the party's 'Brahma Vishnu Mahesh' and Vora's hand in the induction of some ministers of state in Manmohan Singh's council of ministers is a well-documented fact.

Vora was a man of ready wit. Old-timers recall one instance of how Vora had silenced pessimists without sounding dismissive. A big tree had fallen inside the party's 24 Akbar Road compound. This was when Atal Bihari Vajpayee was the prime minister and Congress fortunes were dwindling. Someone had likened the tree to the Congress, implying that the party's roots were decaying. Vora made no attempt to get into an argument. Instead, pointing at the vacant space the tree had left, he said in a loud voice, 'Dekho, kitni khali jagah nikal aayi (Look, how much vacant space as now become available!).'[490]

At night, Vora would often be seen strolling in the compound of 24 Akbar Road. He would say it was a routine, after-dinner walk. A closer look revealed something more. Vora would politely ask bystanders and party workers to leave the office premises. Minutes later, invariably, a vehicle would arrive, carrying 'goods' that required safe, urgent and discreet parking.[491]

When Sitaram Kesri demitted the office of AICC treasurer, Vora discovered a false ceiling in a room in the party office. He was unusually wary of inspecting it. When asked, Vora had said nonchalantly, 'Do you expect him to leave anything unattended?'[492]

He was, famously, unfailingly courteous and there are anecdotes about this too. Every visitor would be treated to a hot cup of tea. At times, this practice made his appointment schedule go haywire. So Vora had an AICC canteen boy stationed at his office with a thermos, cups and saucers. The boy's duty was to rush in with tea each time a visitor sat down. The appointment would often be over by the time the tea had been gulped down.

Strange as it might sound, Vora would meet everyone outside his door. Once, sometime in the 1990s, a man – apparently mentally unbalanced – had made his way in, introducing himself as Priyanka's husband. Vora waited for him to finish his tea and said *namaste* instead of summoning the security guard.

Vora's long, eventful and illustrious career could only be brought to an end in one. Unlike Jyoti Basu, who retired when occupying the office of the chief minister, Indian politicians are not known to say goodbye to public life. Motilal Vora was not an exception.

NOTES

1. Leftist historian Tariq Ali has claimed that Abdullah was Jehan's second husband and that she had earlier married T.E. Lawrence, Lawrence of Arabia, in 1928 when the British intelligence officer was on a visit to Kashmir. It took decades for Abdullah's granddaughter, Nyla Ali Khan, a US-based Kashmiri academic, to debunk the myth that Jehan married Abdullah after her divorce from Lawrence. Nyla Ali Khan has said that Jehan herself had told her that 'this tall tale was just another fabrication, the purpose of which was to denigrate her and to belittle her work'. Nyla mentions Stephen E. Tabachnick, a Lawrence scholar, to make her point: 'Tabachnick unequivocally pointed out the story of that betrothal or marriage is completely false. If it had happened, it would have been impossible to keep it a secret, considering Lawrence's world-wide fame.' Naseer Ganai, 'Revealed: Sheikh Abdullah's grand-daughter says her grandmother never wed "Lawrence of Arabia"', *Mail Online*. U.S., 8 February 2015.

2. Lok Sabha Secretariat. *Sheikh Mohammad Abdullah: Eminent Parliamentarians Monograph Series.* New Delhi: Lok Sabha Secretariat, 1990.

3. Constituent Assembly Debates, 2 November 1947. Also cited by S.S. Gill, *The Dynasty: A Political Biography of the Premier Ruling Family of Modern India.* HarperCollins India, 1 January 1997.

4. Telegram 402 Primin-2227 dated 27 October 1947 to the PM of Pakistan, repeating telegram addressed to PM of UK.

5. M.L. Kotru, 'Book review: *Aatish-E-Chinar* by Sheikh Mohammed Abdullah', *India Today*, 28 January 2014.

6. Gowhar Geelani, 'Why Kashmir's Lal Chowk is an eyewitness to wretched political history since 1947', *Daily O*, 13 August 2015.

7. South Asia Terrorism Portal. 'Excerpts of Sheikh Abdullah's February 5, 1948, speech in the UN Security Council'. Accessed on 10 June 2021.

8–9. Ibid.

10. Lok Sabha Secretariat. *Sheikh Mohammad Abdullah: Eminent Parliamentarians Monograph Series*. New Delhi: Lok Sabha Secretariat, 1990.

11. When Abdullah began toying with the idea of autonomy/independence, Nehru was in a dilemma. The growing chasm between him and Abdullah can be noticed in a letter that Nehru wrote to Maulana Abul Kalam Azad in March 1953. 'I fear that Sheikh Saheb's mind is utterly confused... All kinds of pressures are being brought to bear upon him and he is getting more and more into a tangle. There is nobody with him who can help him very much, because he does not trust anyone fully, and yet everyone influences him. My fear is that Sheikh Saheb, in his present state of mind, is likely to do something or take some step, which might make things worse,' Nehru had written in the letter.

A.G. Noorani, 'Roots of the Kashmir dispute', *Frontline* magazine, 27 May 2016.

12. Adlai Ewing Stevenson and Walter Johnson, *The Papers of Adlai E. Stevenson*. Little, Brown & Company, 31 December 1972.

13. Moosa Raza, *Kashmir: Land of Regrets*. Context, 31 August 2019.

14. E.S. Reddy and A.K. Damodaran, (eds), *Krishna Menon on Kashmir: Speeches at United Nations*. Sanchar, in association with Krishna Menon National Memorial Committee, 1 January 1992.

15. S.S. Gill, *The Dynasty*. HarperCollins India, 1 January 1997.

16. Sisir Gupta, *Kashmir: Study in India and Pakistan Relations*. Asia Publishing House, 1 March 1967.

17. Rajendra Sareen, *Pakistan, The India Factor*. Generic, 1 January 1984.

18. Ibid, pp. 432.

19. V.P. Menon, *The Story of the Integration of the Indian States*. Arno Press, 1 January 1972, pp. 394.

20. V. Shankar, *My Reminiscences of Sardar Patel (Vol. 1)*. Macmillan, 1 January 1974, pp. 127.

21. Sarvepalli Gopal, *Jawaharlal Nehru: A Biography*. Oxford University Press, 14 December 2011.

22. In his memoir, *Aatish-e-Chinar*, Abdullah has written a moving account of his last meeting with Nehru, who he said had been his friend as well as

his 'persecutor'. 'From the (Delhi) airport I drove straight to Teen Murti House with Indiraji, and Panditji received me with great warmth. But he was not the same person. I was meeting him after 11 years. When I had met him 11 years ago, he was as fresh as a rose and now he looked like a withered flower. His back was bent, his face was wrinkled and the effects of the stroke he had suffered were all too evident. And he seemed to say: *"Koi dam ka mahman hoon, ai ahle mehfil, chiragh-ee sehar hoon bujah chahta hoon."* ("I am a guest here for a few moments, and like a candle I am about to burn myself as the morning approaches.")' Abdullah has said he regarded Nehru as his brother and that what the Indian prime minister did to him was part of politics.

Masood Hussain, 'Those 4 days', *KashmirLife*, 1 June 2015.

23. *Reuters*, 'Mohammad Abdullah dies; led India's state of Kashmir', *The New York Times*, 9 September 1982.

24. Kotru believes that Abdullah felt betrayed by some of his closest friends, be it Nehru, Bakshi Ghulam Mohammad, Ghulam Mohammad Sadiq (chief ministers of J&K) or his 'inquisitors' Maulana Abul Kalam Azad and Rafi Ahmed Kidwai (both union ministers in the Nehru cabinet), who resented his mass appeal among Muslims.

M.L. Kotru, 'Book review: *Aatish-E-Chinar* by Sheikh Mohammed Abdullah', *India Today*, 28 January 2014.

25. Sheikh Mohammed Abdullah, *Aatish-e-Chinar*. Ali Mohammed & Sons.

26. Ibid.

27. Muzaffar Raina, 'Sheikh Abdullah's sad inheritance', *Telegraph*, 14 August 2019.

28. Dev Anand, *Romancing with Life: An Autobiography*. Penguin Books India, 14 December 2011.

29–33. Ibid.

34. Rasheed Kidwai, *Neta Abhineta: Bollywood Star Power in Indian Politics*. Hachette India, 5 September 2018.

35. Rajkumar Keshwani, 'One reel for politics', *Outlook*, 5 February 2022.

36. Ibid.

37. Dev Anand, *Romancing with Life*. Penguin Books India, 14 December 2011.

38. Rajkumar Keshwani, 'One reel for politics', *Outlook*, 5 February 2022.

39. Coomi Kapoor, 'I do not believe in exploiting religion: A.R. Antulay', *India Today*, 11 April 2014.

40. Rasheed Kidwai, *24 Akbar Road: A Short History of the People Behind the Fall and Rise of the Congress*. Hachette India, 15 July 2011.

41. 'First victim of "scam" passes away', *The Telegraph Online*, 3 December 2014.

42. Ibid.

43. Radhika Ramaseshan and Rasheed Kidwai, 'Amit's loss is Sonia's too', *The Telegraph Online*, 22 December 2007.

44. Ibid.

45. Rasheed Kidwai, *Neta Abhineta*. Hachette India, 5 September 2018.

46. Ibid.

47. Sumant Mishra, *Main Amitabh Bol Raha Hoon*. Egmont, 1 January 1993.

48. Rasheed Kidwai, *Neta Abhineta*. Hachette India, 5 September 2018.

49. Ibid.

50. Arnab Goswami, 'Amitabh Bachchan on Frankly Speaking with Arnab Goswami', *Times Now*, 15 October 2012.

51. Rasheed Kidwai, *Neta Abhineta*. Hachette India, 5 September 2018.

52. Harivanshrai Bachchan, *Dashdwar Se Sopan Tak*. Rajpal Publishing, 1 April 1997.

53. Divya Goyal, 'Amitabh Bachchan: After *Deewar* my mother wept like a child', *NDTV*, 12 August 2014.

54. Ibid.

55. Promilla Kalhan, *Black Wednesday: Power Politics, Emergency and Elections*. Sterling, 1 July 1977.

56. 'Arjun Singh never forgave me to for decision on Jyoti Basu: Yechury', *Firstpost*, 11 April 2016.

57. Amit Roy, 'The second home: London, the land that turned Basu into a Marxist, was also his favourite holiday destination', *The Telegraph Online*, 18 January 2010.

58. Gopalkrishna Gandhi, 'A patriarch remembered', *The Telegraph Online*, 18 January 2010.

59. Shekhar Gupta, 'Walk the talk with Jyoti Basu', *The Indian Express*, 3 May 2004.

60. Anindya Sengupta, 'Blunder becomes Basu "refusal" in stamp plea', *The Telegraph Online*, 19 June 2013.

61. Sumit Mitra, 'The red star: Jyoti Basu shaped modern India, but history has not been kind to him', *India Today*, 15 September 2017.

62. Pranab Mukherjee, *The Coalition Years: 1996–2012*. Rupa Publications, 13 October 2017.

63. Ramdas Menon, 'The legacy of Jyoti "candlelight" Basu', *The New Indian Express*, 16 May 2012.

64. Ibid.

65. Sundeep Dougal, 'Jyoti Basu: A summing up'. *Outlook*, 18 January 2010.

66. Ibid.

67. Ibid.

68. Monobina Gupta, 'Remembering Jyoti Basu', *Kafila*, 17 January 2010.

69. Barun Ghosh, 'How Basu saved my job in *Telegraph*', *The Telegraph Online*, 18 January 2010.

70–72. Ibid.

73. 'Lord Paul says Basu was a great PM India never had', *Deccan Herald*, 17 January 2010.

74. 'Basu's death, immense loss for Bangladesh: Hasina', *The Hindu*, 15 December 2016.

75. Ananya Sengupta, 'Bangla to fulfil Basu wish: Barudi house to be turned into library and museum', *The Telegraph Online*, 19 August 2010.

76. Ibid.

77. Rakeeb Hossain, 'In death, Basu fulfils pledge, donates body and eyes', *Hindustan Times*, 18 January 2010.

78. K. Natwar Singh, 'Thatcher, Chandraswami and I', *The Hindu*, 4 December 2021.

79. Bhavdeep Kang, *Gurus: Stories of India's Leading Babas*. Westland, 7 June 2016.

80–84. Ibid.

85. K. Natwar Singh, *Walking with Lions: Tales from a Diplomatic Past*. HarperCollins India, 16 January 2013.

86–93. Ibid.

94. Anusha Chaitanya, 'Celebrating Dalit history: The power of Phoolan Devi!', *Medium*, 4 April 2018.

95. John Arquilla, *Insurgents, Raiders and Bandits: How Masters of Irregular Warfare Have Shaped Our World*. Ivan R Dee Inc., 16 August 2011.

96. Anusha Chaitanya, 'Celebrating Dalit history: The power of Phoolan Devi!', *Medium*, 4 April 2018.

97. Phoolan Devi, Marie-Thérèse Cuny and Paul Rambali, *The Bandit Queen of India: An Indian Woman's Amazing Journey from Peasant to International Legend*. Globe Pequot Press, 1 August 2006.

98. Ibid.

99. Tarun Kumar Bhaduri, *Off the Record*. Vikas Publishing, 1 January 1989.

100. Luke Harding, 'The queen is dead', *The Guardian*, 26 July 2001.

101. Treena Orchard, 'A painful power: Coming of age, sexuality and relationships, social reform, and HIV/AIDS among devadasi sex workers in rural Karnataka, India', PhD diss., University of Manitoba, 2004.

102. Jalna Hanmer and Mary Maynard, eds, *Women, Violence and Social Control*. Humanities Press International, 1987.

103. Mary Anne Weaver, 'Tracking India's Bandit Queen', *The Atlantic*, November 1996.

104. Tarun Kumar Bhaduri, *Off the Record*. Vikas Publishing, 1 January 1989.

105. Ibid.

106. Ambereen Ali Shah, 'Phoolan's purse and chilling poster', *The Telegraph Online*, 30 July 2001.

107. Ibid.

108. Sunil Sethi, 'AICC session turns Gauhati flat land into miniature township', *India Today*, 17 November 2011.

109. Vijay Kranti, 'Evenings in Paris with Phoolan', *Sunday Guardian Live*, 4 January 2020.

110–15. Ibid.

116. Sachin Ketkar, 'A Language of Heterogeneity: The Poetry of Namdeo Dhasal', *Sahapedia*, 21 June 2016.

117. J.V. Pawar, *Dalit Panthers: An Authoritative History*. Forward Press Books, 1 January 2018.

118. Subodh More, 'History headline: The rise, dissolution of Panthers', *The Indian Express*, 21 July 2019.

119. Yogesh Maitreya, 'Namdeo Dhasal's poetry, and how it gave form to the Dalit experience in Maharashtra', *Firstpost*, 28 October 2017.

120. Namdeo Dhasal and Dilip Chitre (trans.), *Namdeo Dhasal: Poet of the Underworld*. Navayana Publishers, 1 August 2000.

121. Sachin Ketkar, 'A Language of Heterogeneity: The Poetry of Namdeo Dhasal', *Sahapedia*, 21 June 2016.

122. Sachin Ketkar, 'In the Organized Harem of the Octopus: Poetics and Politics of Namdeo Dhasal', *ResearchGate*, June 2016.

123. Satish Kalsekar, 'Everyone's rebel poet', *Sahapedia*, 21 June 2016.

124. Ibid.

125. Sachin Ketkar, 'In the Organized Harem of the Octopus: Poetics and Politics of Namdeo Dhasal', *ResearchGate*, June 2016.

126. Sachin Ketkar, 'A Language of Heterogeneity: The Poetry of Namdeo Dhasal', *Sahapedia*, 21 June 2016.

127. Ibid.

128. Unnati Sharma, 'Poet & Dalit panther Dhasal's poetry embraced those discarded by society', *The Print*, 15 January 2021.

129. Ibid.

130. Namdeo Dhasal, 'So that my mother may be convinced...', 'Bulletin of Concerned Asian Scholars', 10:3, 8-11, DOI: 10.1080/14672715.1978.10 409094.

131. Ibid.

132. Malik Amar Sheikh, *I Want to Destroy Myself*. Speaking Tiger, 12 September 2016.

133–34. Ibid.

135. Dipti Nagpaul, 'The heart is a lonely woman', *The Indian Express*, 26 November 2016.

136. Rasheed Kidwai, 'R.K. Dhawan stood by Sonia Gandhi when no one else did', *The Print*, 7 August 2018.

137. Ritu Sarin, 'Want to write tell-all book on Indira and Rajiv, says Dhawan', *The Indian Express*, 31 October 2014.

138. Coomi Kapoor, *The Emergency: A Personal History*. Penguin Books India, 18 June 2015.

139. Ibid.

140. Rasheed Kidwai, 'The stenotypist who got Indira to offer namaaz', *Mumbai Mirror*, 9 August 2018.

141. Rasheed Kidwai, *Sonia: A Biography*. Penguin Books India, 6 May 2011.

142. Sharad Pawar, 'When PA Sangma questioned Sonia Gandhi's foreign origin', *Scroll.in*, 4 March 2016.

143. Ibid.

144. Ritu Sarin, 'Soulmates: The love story of Mr and Mrs R.K. Dhawan', *The Indian Express*, 22 July 2012.

145. Janardan Thakur, *All the Prime Minister's Men*. Vikas Publishing, 1 January 1977.

146. Rasheed Kidwai, 'When Sheila Dikshit gave up the chance to be India's Home Minister for a role in Delhi', *Daily O*, 20 July 2019.

147. Ibid.

148. M.L. Fotedar, *The Chinar Leaves: A Political Memoir*. HarperCollins India, 2 November 2015.

149. Ibid.

150. Rasheed Kidwai, 'Indira loyalist who spilled the beans on Rajiv and Amitabh', *The Telegraph Online*, 29 September 2017.

151. M.L. Fotedar, *The Chinar Leaves*. HarperCollins India, 2 November 2015.

152–58. Ibid.

159. Katherine Frank, *Indira: The Life of Indira Nehru Gandhi*. HarperCollins India, 5 March 2007.

160. William E. Smith, 'Indira Gandhi: Death in the garden', *Time*, 12 November 1984.

161. P.C. Alexander, *My Years with Indira Gandhi*. Vision Books, 15 February 2007.

162. Justice M.P. Thakkar, et al, *Report of Justice Thakkar Commission of Inquiry on the Assassination of the Late Prime Minister Smt. Indira Gandhi: final report*; Ramindar Singh, 'There are weighty reasons to suspect the complicity or involvement of Dhawan in the crime', *India Today*, 15 April 1989.

163. Rasheed Kidwai, 'Kiss for grandkids, prep for dinner with a princess: Indira Gandhi's final moments before 36 gunshots', *News18*, 31 October 2019.

164. Ibid.

165. A.G. Noorani, 'Indira Gandhi and Indian Muslims', *Economic and Political Weekly* (Vol. 25, No. 44), 3 November 1990, pp. 2417–20.

166. S.S. Gill, *The Dynasty*. HarperCollins India, 1 January 1997.

167. Ibid.

168. Nana Deshmukh, 'Moments of Soul Searching', *Pratipaksh*, 8 November 1984.

169. Mark Tully and Satish Jacob, *Amritsar: Mrs Gandhi's Last Battle*. Rupa Publications, 1 May 2006.

170. Ibid.

171. Katherine Frank, *Indira*. HarperCollins India, 8 July 2010.

172. Pupul Jayakar, *Indira Gandhi: A Biography*. Penguin Books India, 14 October 2000.

173. Inder Malhotra, *Indira Gandhi: A Personal and Political Biography*. Hay House India, 1 February 2014.

174. Ibid.

175. M.O. Mathai, *My Days with Nehru*. Vikas Publishing, 1 January 1980.

176. Rasheed Kidwai, *24 Akbar Road*. Hachette India, 15 July 2011.

177. Zareer Masani, *Indira Gandhi: A Biography*. Hamish Hamilton, 12 June 1975.

178. V. Krishna Ananth, 'Why 1967 general election was a watershed in Indian politics and the lessons it left behind', *DNA*, 28 February 2017.

179. Premkumar Mani, 'Who are the Bahujans really worshipping?', *Forward Press*, 1 October 2011.

180. Pupul Jayakar, *Indira Gandhi*. Penguin Books India, 14 October 2000.

181. K.A. Abbas, *20th March 1977: A Day Like Any Other*. Vikas Publishing, 1 January 1978.

182. Ibid.

183. Arvind Rajagopal, *Politics after Television: Hindu Nationalism and the Reshaping of the Public in India*. Cambridge University Press, 2001.

184. Swraj Paul, *Indira Gandhi*. Robert Royce, 1 November 1985.

185. Neena Gopal, *The Assassination of Rajiv Gandhi*. Penguin Random House India, 18 July 2016.

186–87. Ibid.

188. Kumkum Chadha, *The Marigold Story: Indira Gandhi & Others*. Tranquebar, 30 January 2019.

189. 'Mixture of hard work and aggressive campaigning made Rajiv Gandhi a winner', *India Today*, 21 February 2014.

190. Rasheed Kidwai, *Ballot: Ten Episodes that have Shaped India's Democracy*. Hachette India, 20 January 2022.

191. Rasheed Kidwai, 'Political naivety overshadowed much of Rajiv Gandhi's positive work', *The Week*, 20 May 2021.

192. Ibid.

193. Sheela Bhatt, 'The misunderstood Nehru', Rediff.com, 26 July 2013.

194. Wajahat Habibullah, *My Years with Rajiv Gandhi: Triumph and Tragedy*. Westland, 26 October 2020.

195. S.S. Gill, *The Dynasty*. HarperCollins India, 1 January 1997.

196. Rasheed Kidwai, 'Babulal Gaur: Politician who loved courting controversies', *ABP Live*, 22 August 2019.

197–208. Ibid.

209. Siddharth Ranjan Das, 'Drinking is a fundamental right, says Madhya Pradesh minister Babulal Gaur', *NDTV*, 30 June 2015.

210. 'Gaur in row after invoking caste', *The Indian Express*, 8 November 2011.

211. Tarun Gogoi, *Turnaround: Leading Assam from the Front*. HarperCollins India, 20 April 2016.

212. 'Gogoi's Autobiography *Turnaround: Leading Assam from the Front*', *Business Standard*, 14 May 2016.

213–14. Ibid.

215. Sunil Sethi, 'AICC session turns Guahati flat land into miniature township', *India Today*, 27 November 2006.

216. Samudra Gupta Kashyap, 'I am real Hindu, they are fake, says Assam CM Tarun Gogoi', *The Indian Express*, 26 March 2016.

217. Ibid.

218. 'BJP exploiting Ram's name for "politics games", claims Tarun Gogoi', *The Sentinel*, 6 August 2020.

219. Priyanka Dubey, 'How Bhopal and I betrayed our own', *Yahoo! News*, 1 December 2014.

220. Ibid.

221. Rasheed Kidwai, 'Bhopal gas tragedy activist awarded the Padma Shri posthumously', *The Quint*, 26 January 2020.

222–24. Ibid.

225. Rasheed Kidwai, 'Blood feud: From NTR to Chirag Paswan, the saga of family coup in Indian politics', *India Today*, 15 June 2021.

226. Karuna Madan, 'Lesser-known facts about Jayalalitha', *Gulf News*, 11 May 2015.

227. Vaasanthi, *Amma: Jayalalithaa's Journey from Movie Star to Political Queen*. Juggernaut, 29 August 2016.

228. 'How Jayalalithaa lived up to the promise she made to MGR', ScoopWhoop, 6 July 2017. Also see, Jafar Sadik, *Ammu to Amma: The Life and Times of Jayalalithaa*. Educreation Publishing, 15 January 2018.

229. Robert L. Hardgrave, Jr, 'Politics and the film in Tamilnadu: The stars and the DMK', *Asian Survey*, Vol. 13, No. 3 (March 1973), pp. 288-305, University of California Press.

230. G.C. Shekhar, 'Jayalalitha's foster son married off amid extravagance and controversy', *India Today*, 26 June 2013.

231. Vaasanthi, *Amma*. Juggernaut, 29 August 2016.

232. Ibid.

233. Ramya Kannan, 'Why Jayalalithaa was given a burial', *The Hindu*, 17 November 2021.

234. 'Why was Jayalalithaa buried, and not cremated?', *The News Minute*, 6 December 2016.

235. Ibid.

236. Vijayakanth had teamed up with the BJP in the 2014 general elections and is often referred to as 'Captain' – a sobriquet inspired by a character he had played in one of his films. Such titles and aliases are conspicuously used for both film actors and politicians in Tamil Nadu. The state's tradition and its fascination for the world of cinema is thus well and thriving in its politics.

237. Rasheed Kidwai, 'Ajit Jogi played in Congress' big-boy league, convinced each camp he was their "utility" man', *The Print*, 29 May 2020.

238–41. Ibid.

242. Santwana Bhattacharya, 'India's dirtiest elections ever', *The New Indian Express*, 1 December 2013.

243. Rasheed Kidwai, 'Missile Man's moonlight dream', *The Telegraph Online*, 11 June 2002.

244. A.P.J. Abdul Kalam and Y.S. Rajan, *India 2020: A Vision for the New Millennium*. Penguin Books India, August 2014.

245–47. Ibid.

248. A.P.J. Abdul Kalam, *Turning Points: A Journey through Challenges*. HarperCollins India, 24 November 2014.

249–61. Ibid.

262. Robert L. Hardgrave, Jr, 'Politics and the film in Tamilnadu: The stars and the DMK', *Asian Survey*, Vol. 13, No. 3 (March 1973), pp. 288-305, University of California Press.

263. Ibid.

264. L.V. Kuchi, 'M. Karunanidhi (1924–2018): A Legacy of National Relevance', *The Hindu Centre*, 11 August 2018.

265. Ibid.

266. Rasheed Kidwai, *Sonia*. Penguin Books India, 6 May 2011.

267–68. Ibid.

269. Rasheed Kidwai, *24 Akbar Road*. Hachette India, 15 July 2011.

270–71. Ibid.

272. Rasheed Kidwai, 'Vinod Khanna: From films to politics via Osho ashram', *ABP Live*, 28 April 2017.

273. Rasheed Kidwai, *Neta Abhineta*. Hachette India, 5 September 2018.

274–75. Ibid.

276. 'Khanna promises Gurdaspur Paris, Congress says he will cut and run', Rediff.com, 9 February 1998.

277. Dilip Kumar, *The Substance and the Shadow: An Autobiography*. Hay House India, 8 June 2014.

278. Pankaj Vohra, 'The Interview: Dilip Kumar', *Hindustan Times*, 26 April 1996.

279. Lord Meghnad Desai, a well-known economist in his own right, would highlight this in his biography of the actor. Lord Meghnad Desai, *Nehru's Hero: Dilip Kumar in the Life of India*. Lotus Collection, 31 December 2004.

280. Vaibhav Purandare, *Bal Thackeray and the Rise of the Shiv Sena*. Lotus Collection, 1 December 2012.

281. Dilip Kumar, *The Substance and the Shadow*. Hay House India, 8 June 2014.

282. Vir Sanghvi, 'When Dilip Kumar met Vajpayee...', Rediff.com, 8 July 2021.

283. Dilip Kumar, *The Substance and the Shadow*. Hay House India, 8 June 2014.

284–88. Ibid.

289. Anupama Chandra, 'Interview with Dilip Kumar', *Sunday*, Issue of 28 February–6 March 1993.

290. Ibid.

291. Tim McGirk, 'Indian actors join real world: Communal strife is intruding on the world's largest film industry', *Independent*, 2 February 1993.

292. Khurshid Mahmud Kasuri, *Neither a Hawk nor a Dove: An Insider's Account of Pakistan's Foreign Policy*. Viking, 12 October 2015.

293. Naseeruddin Shah, 'Did Dilip Kumar, the holy grail of acting in Hindi cinema, facilitate the star-centricity of the industry today?', *The Indian Express*, 10 July 2021.

294–95. Ibid.

296. Mohammad Asim Siddiqui, 'Why Naseeruddin Shah is WRONG about Dilip Kumar', Rediff.com, 28 July 2021.

297–99. Ibid.

300. Indranil Banerjie, 'Mizoram accord between Indian govt and rebel leader Laldenga promises to bring peace', *India Today*, 6 February 2014.

301. Nandini Sundar, 'Interning Insurgent Populations: The Buried Histories of Indian Democracy', *Economic and Political Weekly*, Vol. 46, 5–11 February 2011.

302. Avirook Sen, 'Mizoram produces largest number of literates in India, but most suffer for want of jobs', *India Today*, 8 February 2013.

303. John Zothansanga, '28 years on, Laldenga is still Mizoram's tallest leader', *The Indian Express*, 14 July 2018.

304. Rasheed Kidwai, 'Why we miss scholars like Maulana Madani today', Observer Research Foundation, 21 September 2018.

305. Peter Hardy, *The Muslims of British India*. Cambridge University Press, 10 January 2002.

306. Rizwan Malik, 'Mawlana Husâyn Ahmad Madani and Jami'yat 'Ulama'-i Hind, 1920–1957: Status of Islam and Muslims in India', PhD diss., University of Toronto, 1995.

307. Barbara D. Metcalf, *Husāin Ahmad Madani: The Jihad for Islam and Indīa's Freedom*. Oneworld Academic, 2009.

308. Rasheed Kidwai, 'Why we miss scholars like Maulana Madani today', Observer Research Foundation, 21 September 2018.

309. Barbara D. Metcalf, *Husain Ahmad Madani*. Oneworld Academic, 2009.

310. Dr Mohd Hashim Qidwani, *Jadeed Hindustan ke Siyasi aur Samaji Afkar*. NCPUL Publication, 1 January 2004.

311. Barbara D. Metcalf, *Husain Ahmad Madani*. Oneworld Academic, 2009.

312. 'No Hindi, no PM says Pranab', *India Today*, 15 May 2009.

313. Among his innumerable traits and attributes, Mukherjee was known to keep pace with changing times and observe propriety in the best possible way. It was a hallmark of his personality. Old-timers recall Mukherjee as someone who was a stickler for rules. In the early 1980s, he was finance minister and the number two in the Indira Gandhi cabinet. Mukherjee used to stay in a private accommodation at S-22 Greater Kailash, New Delhi. Each time his official car would cross Savitri Cinema, he would ask the driver not to sound the car's siren as it would disturb the neighbours.

314. Rasheed Kidwai, 'Pranab Mukherjee (1935–2020): The finest Prime Minister India never had', *Mumbai Mirror*, 1 September 2020.

315. Ibid.

316. Minhaz Merchant, *Rajiv Gandhi: The End of a Dream*. Viking, 26 September 1991.

317. Rasheed Kidwai, 'Pranab Mukherjee (1935–2020): The finest Prime Minister India never had', *Mumbai Mirror*, 1 September 2020.

318. Inderjit Badhwar, 'I do not know what I have done to be classified as a dissident: Pranab Mukherjee', *India Today*, 31 January 2014.

319. Pranab Mukherjee, *The Turbulent Years: 1980–1996*. Rupa Publications, 1 February 2016.

320–28. Ibid.

329. Utpal Kumar, 'Pranab Mukherjee: The man who knew "too much"', *The Daily Guardian*, 1 September 2020.

330. Aditi Phadnis, *Business Standard: Political Profiles of Cabals and Kings*. Business Standard Books, 1 January 2009.

331. Pranab Mukherjee, *The Coalition Years: 1996–2012*. Rupa Publications, 13 October 2017.

332. Ibid.

333. 'I have overstayed my wicket, says Pranab Mukherjee', *India Today*, 15 October 2010.

334. For a while, Mukherjee lived at Lutyens' Delhi at 2 Jantar Mantar Lane, sharing a boundary wall with 6 Raisina Road, where Atal Bihari Vajpayee lived. Despite sharp ideological differences, Mukherjee would often join Vajpayee for a post-dinner stroll. Many times, Vajpayee's foster daughter, Namrata, would rush in asking Pranab Mukherjee's wife, Surva, for some 'Bengali achaar' (pickle). After her marriage Namrata became a Bhattacharya. With a new Bengali connection, Vajpayee's bond with the Mukherjees strengthened and continued till his death.

335. Rasheed Kidwai, *24 Akbar Road*. Hachette India, 15 July 2011.

336. Rasheed Kidwai, 'Death bridges a bitter family divide', *The Telegraph Online*, 27 July 2013.

337. Ibid.

338. Pranay Gupte, *Mother India: A Political Biography of Indira Gandhi*. Penguin Books India, 20 June 2011.

339. Rasheed Kidwai, 'Death bridges a bitter family divide', *The Telegraph Online*, 27 July 2013.

340. Pupul Jayakar, *Indira Gandhi*. Penguin Books India, 14 October 2000.

341. Premkumar Mani, 'Who are the Bahujans really worshipping?', *Forward Press*, 1 October 2011.

342. Ibid.

343. Rasheed Kidwai, 'Atal doffs hat to nuke father, Rao?', *The Telegraph Online*, 26 December 2004.

344. Ibid.

345. Ullekh N.P., *The Untold Vajpayee: Politician and Paradox*. Penguin Books India, 1 January 2018.

346. Rasheed Kidwai, *Sonia*. Penguin Books India, 6 May 2011.

347. Ibid.

348. Ibid, pp. 94–95.

349. Rasheed Kidwai, 'Need major CVE programme to engage with Muslim community', Observer Research Foundation, 20 June 2018.

350. AIMIM, '1948 – AIMIM ceases to exist'.

351. Rahul Sampal, 'The Ayodhya connection to Asaduddin Owaisi's Delhi home', *The Print*, 15 October 2019.

352. Mohammed Siddique, 'Lakhs bid tearful adieu to Owaisi', Rediff.com, 30 September 2008.

353. Ibid.

354. Sobhana K. Nair, 'Ram Vilas Paswan obituary: Dalit leader who wore many a hat', *The Hindu*, 8 October 2020.

355. Ibid.

356. Abdul Khaliq, 'Ram Vilas Paswan used his capital to speak for the most vulnerable', *The Indian Express*, 10 October 2020.

357. Sobhana K. Nair, 'Ram Vilas Paswan obituary: Dalit leader who wore many a hat', *The Hindu*, 8 October 2020.

358. This was not the only time Paswan took such a stance in support of minorities. Back in February 2005, when Assembly elections were held in Bihar, Paswan's LJP had allied with the Congress. The results had thrown up a hung Assembly, the LJP winning 29 seats, its highest tally ever in the state, but Paswan had refused to support either Janata Dal (United) leader, Nitish Kumar, or Rashtriya Janta Dal (RJD) boss, Lalu Prasad. Instead, he had insisted that a Muslim be made the chief minister. The state went to the polls again later that year and Nitish Kumar won.

359. Rasheed Kidwai, 'How "irreplaceable comrade" Ahmed Patel became the 4th most powerful man in UPA after Sonia', *News18*, 25 November 2020.

360. Rasheed Kidwai, 'Rajesh Pilot dies in car crash', *The Telegraph Online*, 11 June 2000.

361. Rajesh Pilot, *Flight to Parliament*. Gaurav Publishing House, 1 April 1985.

362. Rasheed Kidwai, 'Rajesh Pilot dies in car crash', *The Telegraph Online*, 11 June 2000.

363. Rasheed Kidwai, *Sonia*. Penguin Books India, 6 May 2011.

364. Rasheed Kidwai, 'Man who knew the truth about Bofors', *The Telegraph Online*, 14 July 2013.

365. Ibid.

366. Indian Kanoon, 'Lok Sabha Debates: Regarding the Defreezing of Accounts'.

367. Rasheed Kidwai, 'A mouche to impress Mush – Walrus whiskers convey wisdom, says proud owner', *The Telegraph Online*, 1 April 2007.

368–71. Ibid.

372. Rasheed Kidwai, 'Praised by Musharraf but unable to impress son: This Cong leader's life is an ode to walrus moustache', *News 18*, 10 April 2020.

373. Badri Narayan, *Kanshiram: Leader of the Dalits*. Penguin Books India, 21 April 2014.

374. Kanshi Ram, *The Chamcha Age: An Era of the Stooge*. Samyak Prakashan, 1 January 2018.

375. Vivek Kaul, 'How Cong "chamchagiri" made Sonia India's No 1 politician', *Firstpost*, 27 November 2012.

376. Ramchandra Guha, *Patriots and Partisans*. Penguin Books India, 1 October 2013.

377. Ibid.

378. Badri Narayan, 'Ambedkar and Kanshi Ram – so alike, yet so different', *The Hindu*, 11 July 2016.

379. Bhaskar Roy, 'Mahendra Singh Tikait, Syed Shahabuddin, Kanshi Ram, represent powerful electoral triumvirate', *India Today*, 31 October 1989.

380. Vivek Kumar and Uday Sinha, *Dalit Assertion and Bahujan Samaj Party: A Perspective from Below*. Bahujan Sahitya Sansthan, Lucknow, 2001.

381. 'Mayawati claims Kanshi Ram's legacy', Rediff.com, 16 October 2006.

382. P.V. Narasimha Rao, *Ayodhya: 6 December 1992*. Penguin Books India, 14 November 2019.

383–93. Ibid.

394. M.L. Fotedar, *The Chinar Leaves*. HarperCollins India, 2 November 2015.

395. Rasheed Kidwai, 'Will Manmohan Singh once again succeed in making a comeback to politics?', Observer Research Foundation, 20 June 2019.

396. Ibid.

397. 'Sonia, Rahul Gandhi praise "bold" PV Narasimha Rao, neglected for years', *Hindustan Times*, 24 July 2020.

398. Radhika Ramaseshan. 'Time Cong, BJP had policy on appointing CM', *The Tribune*, 20 December 2018.

399. S. Venkat Narayan, *NTR: A Biography*. Vikas Publishing, 1 January 1983.

400–01. Ibid.

402. Rasheed Kidwai, *Ballot*. Hachette India, 20 January 2022.

403. Ibid.

404. S. Venkat Narayan, *NTR*. Vikas Publishing, 1 January 1983.

405. Dr Daggubati Venkateswara Rao, *The Other Side of Truth: A Journey into the Past*. Nivedita Publications, 2009.

406–10. Ibid.

411. '"Revolt" done to save party: Chandrababu on TDP Split', *Outlook*, 29 May 2011; 'Chandrababu Naidu: "CEO" CM who superseded his famous father-in-law', *The Economic Times*, 11 February 2019.

412. Film Heritage Foundation, 'Nandamuri Taraka Rama Rao (NTR)', Facebook, 13 August 2019.

413. Rasheed Kidwai, 'Pragmatism was at the core of his politics', *The Tribune*, 29 July 2019.

414. Bhavdeep Kang, *Gurus: Stories of India's Leading Babas*. Westland, 7 June 2016.

415. Rasheed Kidwai, 'Pragmatism was at the core of his politics', *The Tribune*, 29 July 2019.

416. Ibid.

417. Shekhar Gupta, 'How Rajiv Gandhi, "such a nice man", won and ruined India's biggest mandate', *The Print*, 21 May 2018.

418. Rasheed Kidwai, 'Pragmatism was at the core of his politics', *The Tribune*, 29 July 2019.

419. Ibid.

420. Rasheed Kidwai, *Sonia*. Penguin Books India, 6 May 2011.

421. Bilal Handoo, 'Indira's Man in Kashmir', *Kashmir Life*, 12 January 2016.

422. Shekhar Gupta, 'N.D. Tiwari searches for right niche and time', *India Today*, 14 August 1993.

423. 'ND Tiwari, man who disgraced Raj Bhavan, dies at 93', *Deccan Chronicle*, 20 October 2018.

424. Naziya Alvi, 'Child has the right to know his father', *India Today*, 24 December 2010.

425. Shashi Sunny, 'Ban the word bastard', *The Economic Times*, 23 May 2014.

426. Ibid.

427. Rasheed Kidwai, 'The Tiwaris and a paternity suit to remember', *Mumbai Mirror*, 19 April 2019.

428. Ibid.

429. '"Madhavrao Scindia would have been Prime Minister", says former foreign Minister Natwar Singh after Jyotiraditya resigns', *The Free Press Journal*, 10 March 2020.

430. Rasheed Kidwai, *The House of Scindias: A Saga of Power, Politics and Intrigue*. Roli Books, 5 June 2021.

431–32. Ibid.

433. Rasheed Kidwai, 'Two sons, two different stories as verdict 2019 changes face of Lutyens' Delhi', *News 18*, 16 June 2019.

434. Rasheed Kidwai, 'Remembering Jaffer Sharief, Indira Gandhi's point man', *The Wire*, 26 November 2018.

435. Inderjit Badhwar and Prabhu Chawla, 'Satish Sharma, Rajiv Gandhi land in midst of heavy weather they never experienced before', *India Today*, 7 January 2014.

436. Ibid.

437. Rasheed Kidwai, 'High-flyer in politics: In Capt Satish's demise, Sonia lost precious link with life & times of Rajiv, Indira', *Network 18*, 18 February 2021.

438–41. Ibid.

442. Rasheed Kidwai, *Sonia*. Penguin Books India, 6 May 2011.

443–44. Ibid.

445. Nayantara Sahgal, *A Voice for Freedom*. Hind Pocket Books, 1977.

446. Ibid.

447. M.V. Kamath, *Gandhi's Coolie: Life and Times of Ramkrishna Bajaj*. Allied Publishers, 1 June 1988.

448. Ibid.

449. Rasheed Kidwai, *Sonia*. Penguin Books India, 6 May 2011.

450. Aditi Phadnis, 'The second coming of Amar Singh', *Business Standard*, 18 May 2016.

451. Priya Sahgal, 'Cover Story by Priya Sahgal: Amar Singh Exclusive', *NewsX*, 4 June 2016.

452. Rasheed Kidwai, 'Amar and Amitabh: Story of 2 brothers', *Mumbai Mirror*, 3 August 2020.

453. Rasheed Kidwai, *Neta Abhineta*. Hachette India, 5 September 2018.

454. Ibid.

455. Incidentally, Aradhya, Aishwarya Rai and Abhishek Bachchan's daughter, called Singh 'Dada Chacha', which is usually a title that a child

would use to address her grandfather's brother – in this case Amitabh Bachchan.

456. Rasheed Kidwai, *Neta Abhineta*. Hachette India, 5 September 2018.

457–58. Ibid.

459. In fact, Amitabh and a newly engaged Abhishek and Aishwarya were said to have stayed there once.

460. Ananya Sengupta, 'Amar's parting kick: Good actor need not be a good human being', *The Telegraph Online*, 21 May 2015.

461. Ibid.

462. Arjun Singh and Ashok Chopra, *A Grain of Sand in the Hourglass of Time: An Autobiography*. Hay House India, 5 July 2012.

463–71. Ibid.

472. Rasheed Kidwai, 'When the gas leaked, Arjun flew away to pray', *The Telegraph Online*, 4 July 2012.

473. Ibid.

474. Arjun Singh and Ashok Chopra, *A Grain of Sand in the Hourglass of Time*. Hay House India, 5 July 2012.

475. Pankaj Pachauri and Prabhu Chawla, 'Buta Singh emerges one-man demolition squad in Rajiv Gandhi's cabinet', *India Today*, 15 March 1988.

476. Ibid.

477. Vir Sanghvi, 'The only language Thackeray understands is strength', 6 February 2010.

478. Sujata Anandan, *Samrat Balasaheb Thackeray*. HarperCollins India, 25 March 2019.

479. Kumar Ketkar, 'Bal Thackeray's fractured legacy', *Forbes*, 23 November 2012.

480. Sujata Anandan, *Hindu Hriday Samrat: How the Shiv Sena Changed Mumbai Forever*. HarperCollins India, 3 July 2014

481. Pranab Mukherjee, *The Coalition Years: 1996–2012*. Rupa Publications, 13 October 2017.

482. Ibid.

483. V. Shankar Aiyar and Smruti Koppikar, 'Srikrishna panel report indicts Shiv Sena chief Bal Thackeray for role in 1993 Mumbai riots', *India Today*, 23 March 2013.

484. Coomi Kapoor, 'Fury of communal violence burns 80 km stretch from tip of south Bombay to Bhiwandi town', *India Today*, 21 April 2014.

485. Sujata Anandan, *Samrat Balasaheb Thackeray*. HarperCollins India, 25 March 2019.

486. Ibid.

487. Rasheed Kidwai, 'Motilal Vora: Congressman whose words once weighed more than those of PMO', *India Today*, 22 December 2020.

488. Ibid.

489. Rasheed Kidwai, 'Guarding deep Cong secrets, Motilal Vohra & Ahmed Patel until last month were signing cheques at party HQ', *News18*, 21 December 2020.

490–92. Ibid.

NETA ABHINETA: BOLLYWOOD STAR POWER IN INDIAN POLITICS

Rs 599

'Abundant in precious anecdotes about iconic films and political personalities.' – *Deccan Herald*

'The rare anecdotes and popular gossip make it an excellent book. Those weaned on Bollywood, its actors and their capers, will find this book worth lapping [up].' – *Free Press Journal*

What draws the larger-than-life personalities who entertain us on-screen to the world of governance and politics off-screen?

Neta Abhineta: Bollywood Star Power in Indian Politics traces this phenomenon through intimate and compelling portrayals of some of the most popular actors in Hindi cinema who have, from the years leading up to India's independence in 1947, entered Indian politics for reasons ranging from a sense of social commitment to a desperate quest for a second chance at fame when their star power dimmed. Dilip Kumar, Nargis and Sunil Dutt, Rajesh Khanna, Jaya and Amitabh Bachchan, Shatrughan Sinha, Hema Malini, Mithun Chakraborty, Jaya Prada, Vinod Khanna, Govinda, Raj Babbar and Paresh Rawal are some of the more prominent names that feature in this engaging account involving film veterans, superstars and also-rans.

Blending history with hard facts and entertaining anecdotes about personal and professional rivalries, clandestine romantic liaisons and cruel betrayals, Rasheed Kidwai presents a potent cocktail. With its clear-eyed perspective on the peculiar nature of Indian politics, this book reveals what ensues when the two worlds – as intensely alluring as they are dangerously fickle – merge.

24 AKBAR ROAD

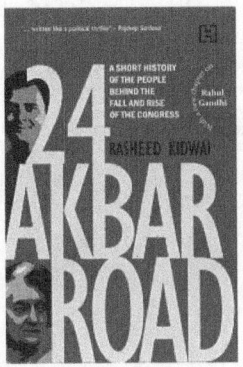

Rs 399

'An absorbing tale rather than a scholarly history, written in a racy style... [A]n enjoyable read.' – *Outlook*

'Here is the stuff of fiction, found in real men and women who matter – from manipulation and intrigue to assertions of power, from the humdrum details of life to the pinnacles of tragedy.' – *Telegraph*

'It is a book that will be a talking point in Congress circles – and beyond – for a long time to come.' – *Hindustan Times*

In his bestselling book, *24 Akbar Road*, seasoned journalist and veteran Congress-watcher Rasheed Kidwai puts together an incisive and engaging account of the Congress's shape-shifting nature and its tenuous hold at the Centre, providing a dispassionate observer's glance at affairs within the party. Kidwai brilliantly tracks the story of the contemporary Congress in the years after the Emergency, using the party's seat of power at 24 Akbar Road as his vantage to draw a compelling account of its leadership from Indira, Sanjay and Rajiv Gandhi to Narasimha Rao and Sitaram Kesri, to the trinity of Sonia Gandhi, Manmohan Singh and Rahul Gandhi.

BALLOT

Rs 399

'Kidwai's style is breezy, anecdotal and full of interesting bon mots.' – *The Hindu*

'A fascinating kaleidoscope of India's democratic experience and experiment over the past seven decades... A must-read for all those who are interested in discerning how this chaotic, anarchic land of a million mutinies is also a democratic continuum ever since its liberation from British imperialism.' – *Asian Age*

'For both the initiated and the uninitiated, the apolitical and the overly political, the book has something.' – *Deccan Herald*

543 Lok Sabha seats. More than 4,000 state constituencies. Over 800 million voters. The world's largest democracy.

From the time of its inception, democracy in India has been dubbed 'miraculous' by the world's media, and its elections as a spectacular exercise in human management.

In *Ballot*, Rasheed Kidwai takes us through his pick of seminal elections that have shaped Indian democracy both at the centre and in select states. Highlighting the unique challenges faced by a country that adopted universal adult franchise at the very outset, profiling personalities who have triggered ground-shifts, and analysing the causes and consequences of key electoral episodes, he traces the very evolution of India's democratic process.

Combining insightful commentary and colourful anecdotes, *Ballot* provides a brief, incisive examination of India's most momentous elections.